DIVIDED ALLIES

DIVIDED ALLIES

STRATEGIC COOPERATION
AGAINST THE COMMUNIST
THREAT IN THE ASIA-PACIFIC
DURING THE EARLY COLD WAR

THOMAS K. ROBB AND DAVID JAMES GILL

CORNELL UNIVERSITY PRESS

Ithaca and London

First published 2019 by Cornell University Press

Library of Congress Cataloging-in-Publication Data

Names: Robb, Thomas, author. | Gill, David James, 1982– author.
Title: Divided allies : security cooperation in the Asia-Pacific, 1945–55 / Thomas K. Robb and David James Gill.
Description: Ithaca : Cornell University Press, [2019] | Includes bibliographical references and index.
Identifiers: LCCN 2019020279 (print) | LCCN 2019021559 (ebook) | ISBN 9781501741845 (cloth)
Subjects: LCSH: United States—Foreign relations—Asia. | Asia—Foreign relations—United States. | United States—Foreign relations—Pacific Area. | Pacific Area—Foreign relations—United States. | United States—Foreign relations—1945–1953. | English-speaking countries—Foreign relations. | Cold War. | Security, International—History—20th century. | Asian cooperation. | Pacific Area cooperation.
Classification: LCC DS518.8 .R63 2019 (print) | LCC DS518.8 (ebook) | DDC 950.4/24—dc23
LC record available at https://lccn.loc.gov/2019020279
LC ebook record available at https://lccn.loc.gov/2019021559

ISBN 978-1-5017-4185-2 (epub/mobi ebook)
ISBN 978-1-5017-4186-9 (pdf ebook)

For Donna, Gemma, Matthew, and Thomas

CONTENTS

Acknowledgments   *ix*

Abbreviations   *xi*

Introduction   1

1. National Interests   10

2. Crisis and Cooperation   40

3. A Negotiated Alliance   65

4. Selective Membership   87

5. An Unwelcome Ally   110

6. Divided Action   134

7. The Costs of Compromise   156

Conclusion   180

Notes   *183*

Bibliography   *219*

Index   *267*

ACKNOWLEDGMENTS

Portions of the text have appeared in the following article: Thomas K. Robb and David James Gill, "The ANZUS Treaty during the Cold War: A Reinterpretation of U.S. Diplomacy in the Southwest Pacific," *Journal of Cold War Studies* 17.4 (Fall 2015): 109–57, © 2015 by the President and Fellows of Harvard College and the Massachusetts Institute of Technology, reprinted by permission of the MIT Press. We are thankful to MIT Press for allowing us to reproduce elements of our research in this book.

We are grateful to everyone who helped us produce *Divided Allies*. We thank Nicholas Clayton for his research assistance and the numerous archivists who have helped us locate material for this book. We benefited from interactions with knowledgeable and supportive staff in person and online at the Australian National Archive, Australian National Library, Birmingham University, British National Archives, Cambridge University, Eisenhower Presidential Library, Oxford University, U.S. National Archives II, New Zealand National Archives, Princeton University, Roosevelt Presidential Library, and Truman Presidential Library. Without such dedicated staff, the process of writing history would be significantly more challenging.

We are grateful to James Curran, Charles Giovanni Vanzan Coutinho, Michael Gill, Wen-Qing Ngoei, Paul McGarr, Luke Nichter, Bevan Sewell, and two anonymous reviewers for advice and feedback on earlier drafts of the manuscript. Their suggestions made the book considerably better. We would also like to thank Christopher and Alison Curran for their hospitality in Australia. Special thanks to Cornell University Press. Meagan Dermody, Carmen Adriana Torrado Gonzalez, Ange Romeo-Hall, and Marie Flaherty-Jones have all been very helpful during the publication process. We are particularly grateful to Michael McGandy for his advice and support in successfully guiding the book from proposal to publication. Our friends and colleagues in Cambridge, London, Nottingham, and Oxford deserve considerable thanks for their kindness throughout the many years of researching and writing the book. Most important, thank you to our families for their support and patience. We dedicate this book to them.

TKR and DJG

ABBREVIATIONS

The following abbreviations appear in the main text:

ANZAM	Australia, New Zealand, Malaya Agreement
ANZUS	Australia, New Zealand, United States Security Treaty
DEA	Department of External Affairs (New Zealand)
FO	Foreign Office
HMNZS	Her Majesty's New Zealand Ship
JCS	Joint Chiefs of Staff (United States)
MEA	Ministry of External Affairs (Australia)
MP	Member of Parliament (United Kingdom)
NATO	North Atlantic Treaty Organization
NSC	National Security Council (United States)
NZ	New Zealand
PRC	People's Republic of China
RAAF	Royal Australian Air Force
ROC	Republic of China
SEACDT	Southeast Asia Collective Defense Treaty
SEATO	Southeast Asia Treaty Organization
UK	United Kingdom
UN	United Nations
USA	United States of America
USSR	Union of Soviet Socialist Republics

DIVIDED ALLIES

Introduction

States united by the most serious of threats can struggle to cooperate. In contrast to the broad strategic cooperation that emerged in Europe after World War II, no formal alliances between Western powers existed throughout the Asia-Pacific until the 1950s.[1] Even when established, these security agreements remained limited in terms of military planning and scope of membership, despite the rising threat posed by the Soviet Union and the People's Republic of China. To be sure, the Western powers that exerted most influence on security pacts in the region—the United States, United Kingdom, Australia, and New Zealand—continued to enjoy close relations in many quarters and each held serious concerns about the Communist threat. All four states shared the ties of ancestry, language, and democratic institutions and maintained close economic and security relationships around the world. Yet, however close these four powers might have been to one another, they remained separate, sovereign states with their own interests. Although the pressures created by the Cold War could unite Western powers on an ad hoc basis, long-term strategic cooperation in the Asia-Pacific remained curiously limited.

The purpose of this book is to examine why strategic cooperation among these four powers was so challenging in the Asia-Pacific during the early Cold War. We pay particular attention to relations surrounding two international strategic agreements—namely, the Australia, New Zealand, United States

Security Treaty (ANZUS) and the Manila Treaty or Southeast Asia Collective Defense Treaty (SEACDT) that led to the formation of Southeast Asia Treaty Organization (SEATO)—which represent the most important examples of formalized cooperation among Western powers in the region.[2] The book concludes in 1955 following the creation of SEATO, which resulted in a formal organization for the collective defense of Southeast Asia. The creation of this Asian-Pacific security alliance allowed the United States and its allies to construct a geostrategic great wall around both the Soviet Union and People's Republic of China.[3] After almost a decade since the conclusion of World War II, a formal defense pact for the Asia-Pacific involving the United States, United Kingdom, Australia, and New Zealand had finally materialized.[4]

To explain why strategic disunity among these four powers persisted for so long, we offer an analysis of quadrilateral cooperation in the Asia-Pacific that extends from the postwar period until the mid-1950s. By treating U.S., British, Australian, and New Zealand security policies as interwoven, rather than separate, we stress the complex and interconnected nature of international relations. All four countries share responsibility for the limitations and achievements of cooperation in the Asia-Pacific. This book draws on archival materials from the United States, Britain, Australia, and New Zealand to explain the problems of strategic cooperation in the region. In doing so, we provide six insights into a pivotal episode of Cold War history.

Our first argument considers states' use of rhetoric on race and imperialism as a tool of diplomacy. Perceptions about foreign peoples and practices informed U.S., British, Australian, and New Zealand actions on the global stage. Many Western policymakers' decisions were influenced by, or were responses to, racist, prejudiced, or stereotypical viewpoints of nonwhite peoples and states. Nevertheless, U.S., and to a lesser extent Australian, policymakers also used ideas about race or imperialism to legitimize or obscure the pursuit of other interests. Both states made claims that British membership in ANZUS, for instance, would create an alliance that could project an image of a "white man's club" to international observers. This impression would damage relations with other nonwhite countries in the Asia-Pacific and legitimize Soviet propaganda about Western racism. Yet such rhetoric also helped to avoid problematic demands for the creation of a broader and more expensive alliance system. Indeed, onlookers would struggle to see how the addition of the United Kingdom would somehow make ANZUS a "white man's club" given that this was effectively already the case, especially when considering the "white Australia" and "white New Zealand" immigration policies that existed at this time. British policymakers nevertheless proved unable to overcome these objections. Claims about race and imperialism therefore helped sustain the treaty on terms preferable to U.S. and Australian interests.

U.S. representatives also stressed the importance of racial inclusivity throughout the Manila Treaty negotiations. Yet they increasingly focused their attention on Western powers as the security situation deteriorated in Indochina. The United States ultimately accepted only a limited membership of SEATO—thereby excluding Japan, Nationalist China, and the Republic of Korea—following pressure from Western allies who could exert more material power in the region. The United States was not unique in prioritizing its security interests over racial or imperial concerns. The British Commonwealth powers were all willing to forgo racial equality in strategic planning. Australian officials, with the support of their New Zealand counterparts, even proposed that ANZUS could "serve as a cover for what would in effect be SEATO strategic planning—its true purpose not being known—and that 'make believe' planning be undertaken bilaterally by the U.S. with each of the other four countries."[5]

Our second insight highlights the importance of trade policies and financial considerations in slowing progress toward formalized strategic cooperation. Tensions between all four powers concerning the costs of collective security are well-known. Nevertheless, such burdens represent merely one strand of each state's economic motivations. Disagreements about trade practices, international borrowing, and foreign investment slowed progress toward cooperation and complicated security debates. The pursuit of these economic interests is therefore integral to understanding the course of strategic planning among Western powers in the Asia-Pacific.

This wider set of economic influences on foreign policy clearly illustrates that the difficulty of cooperation in the early Cold War was not only predicated on strategic concerns. Tensions between the United States and the British Commonwealth states concerning the revival of Japan, for instance, were more than merely the result of strategic disagreement about opposing Communism in the Asia-Pacific or a reflection of their respective experiences of World War II. Disagreements also reflected competing ideas about economic practices in the wider region, most notably the persistence of the imperial preference trade system between members of the British Commonwealth. The United States was concerned about the exclusive nature of economic cooperation between the United Kingdom and the two antipodean powers that threatened to undermine the structure of international trade and impede Japanese revival. The ANZUS Treaty, however, allowed the United States to encourage Australia and New Zealand's trade relations with Japan and provided an opportunity to question the imperial preference of their commercial policies. Before the treaty was agreed, the U.S. State Department produced an internal position paper that stressed the need to "continue to point out to Australian officials the economic objections to such [trade] arrangements." ANZUS, the note continued, provided a useful platform to encourage both Canberra and Wellington to "gradually counteract the narrow trade concepts of the past," thereby strengthening international trade in general and Japanese recovery.[6]

Economic divisions also help explain the motivations for, and difficulties surrounding, the creation of SEATO. The British repeatedly stressed the need for an economic alliance, whereas the U.S. desired a military solution. Such disagreements came to a head following the conclusion of the Geneva conference in July 1954, in which representatives from the East and West discussed outstanding issues concerning the Korean peninsula, the situation in Vietnam, and the possibility of restoring peace to Indochina. British support for establishing a new organization for Asian-Pacific security had grown considerably by now. Senior officials in London would go on to suggest that a treaty could "provide an umbrella beneath which we can persuade the Americans to spend money" in the region, both in terms of military and economic investment.[7]

Although SEATO's military shortcomings are well documented, its socio-economic ambitions also fell short of initial expectations.[8] Australia and New Zealand believed that the organization should concentrate on the economic aspects of regional security. Nevertheless, the United States largely ignored antipodean preferences. Although all signatories to the Manila Treaty sought to improve levels of investment and trade more broadly in the region, budgetary limitations and domestic pressures made SEATO an inappropriate framework with which to assist economic development in the wider region. Differences concerning threat assessment are therefore only one facet of strategic disunity in the Asia-Pacific. Economic interests repeatedly complicated and slowed international security cooperation.

Our third insight concerns the competitive nature of relations between these four states in the Asia-Pacific. Popular notions of cooperative and cordial diplomacy between English-speaking democracies, which respected the sanctity of strategic cohesion in the Cold War, are sometimes misleading. Relations were often compromised or hindered by the different strategic agendas and priorities pursued by all four states. The intensity of these disagreements and their risks to wider cooperation deserve more attention. Defection was never contemplated, but all four states sometimes attempted to secure policy outcomes by threatening military withdrawal.[9] Such behavior contributes to an important debate among historians concerning the troubled nature of diplomacy among democracies in the Cold War.[10]

The course of alliance diplomacy was often far rougher than commonly assumed by historians or scholars of international relations. The United States certainly intimated that it was willing to withdraw support from its allies if they pursued policies that ran counter to U.S. interests. As a case in point, Washington had repeatedly informed Canberra and Wellington that it wanted ANZUS to remain as an exclusive tripartite alliance and was unwilling to include the United Kingdom for fear of costly and expanded regional commitments. In a frank exchange in 1953, the Australians informed the British that the U.S. secretary of state John Foster Dulles had "at one stage professed readiness, if Australia and New Zealand really wished it, to let the United Kingdom into Anzus. But he made it clear that if that happened, it would therefore be the end of Anzus as a treaty having any value to the three parties."[11] Dulles's implication was clear: if the antipodean powers refused to cooperate, the United States was willing to abandon its security agreement. Similarly, the United States was clear in 1954 that if the United Kingdom failed to support its efforts in Indochina, there would be consequences for British interests in the Asia-Pacific. As President Dwight D. Eisenhower informed one his aides, "My argument to the British has been that if we all went in together into Indochina at the same time, that would be fine but if they don't go in with us, they don't expect us to help them defend Hong Kong."[12]

The United Kingdom also employed similar threats to Australia and New Zealand in pursuit of its regional interests. Throughout 1951 and 1952, London persistently pressured Canberra and Wellington to support its membership of ANZUS. British policymakers believed that inclusion would allow Britain to exert more influence over U.S. strategy in the region and to retain good strategic relations with Australia and New Zealand. By 1953, London put Canberra and Wellington under significant pressure to support British entry into this regional security pact. During a meeting with the prime ministers Robert Menzies and Sidney Holland, Prime Minister Winston Churchill took the opportunity to press his case. Stressing that "very intimate relations . . . might be impaired in future if a solution were not found to the problem of planning Pacific strategy," he concluded that "in view of the difficulty of associating the United Kingdom with ANZUS, some wider form of Pacific pact should be considered."[13]

The threat of strategic abandonment was not unique to Britain and the United States. Australia and New Zealand sometimes used similar threats. In 1951, the antipodean powers made it clear to the United States that if

ANZUS failed to provide some form of security guarantee they would have to reassess their Cold War commitments outside the region. The Australian foreign minister Percy Spender, with the support of his New Zealand counterpart Frederick Doidge, stressed that in the absence of such agreement, "Australia's capacity to discharge her obligations in the event of war in Malaya as well as outside the Pacific area would be gravely impaired."[14] All four states evidently engaged in rough diplomacy to advance their own interests despite the significant and growing Communist threats that existed in the Asia-Pacific region.

Our fourth finding illuminates the influence of domestic politics on security planning within all four governments. Although external threats drove policymaking in the main, internal concerns informed the timing and intensity of Western states' strategies in the Asia-Pacific and help explain how policymakers interpreted and responded to the rising Communist threat in the postwar period. Leaders in all four democratic states needed to generate support from within their own political systems to conduct foreign policy and to court popular opinion to survive in office. Domestic as well as international interests therefore shaped the course of strategic planning in Washington, London, Canberra, and Wellington.

Unilateral U.S. military action in Indochina proved difficult to achieve in 1954, for instance, largely due to political resistance in Congress. As Eisenhower told his national security team with "great emphasis," there was "no possibility whatever of U.S. unilateral intervention in Indochina, and we had best face that fact. Even if we tried such a course, we would have to take it to Congress and fight for it like dogs, and with very little hope of success."[15] Congressional leaders made clear to the White House that their support for any military intervention was contingent on being able to "internationalize" the conflict. As Dulles admitted during one conversation, there was little chance of Congress endorsing the United States "going it alone" in Southeast Asia.[16] These domestic pressures therefore not only inhibited military action but encouraged alliance-building efforts.

Domestic-political considerations also help explain the curious absence of Japan in SEATO. Japan was a growing economic power in the Asia-Pacific that could have provided valuable support for the security of the region. Nevertheless, the Australian government informed the United States in 1954 that it would view Japanese membership as "deeply provocative" given the horrors of World War II that still lingered in the popular imagination. As such, Canberra stressed to Washington that domestic opposition would make it politically impossible for it to enter any formal security alliance that included its former adversary.[17] New Zealand shared Australia's sentiment. Officials in the Menzies and Holland governments were clear that Japanese membership in SEATO would be an "impossible" condition for them to accept.[18] Domestic-political concerns therefore explain why Australia and New Zealand were both willing to jeopardize a more comprehensive security alliance with the United States despite the significant strategic interests at stake.

Our fifth insight is that planning in all four states was informed by early but sometimes competing notions of what would later be known as the "domino theory"—namely, the belief that if Communism took control over one state in a region, neighboring countries would likely succumb as well. The concept would receive widespread attention after April 1954, when Eisenhower suggested in a public address, concerning U.S. involvement in Vietnam, that allowing one Communist success would precipitate a "domino effect" throughout Indochina.[19] Washington's fears were shared in London, Canberra, and Wellington, but each could sometimes interpret the threat posed by falling dominoes differently. British strategic planners, for instance, accepted the validity of the domino theory but looked beyond Indochina. As the British Joint Intelligence Committee concluded, "The risk of a Communist invasion of Siam, should the Viet Minh secure part or whole of the Indo-Chinese frontier, would be slight." Instead, the real danger would be that Communist forces could infiltrate other states in the region with the objective of "fomenting trouble" among the preexisting dissident groups. Such "trouble" was seen as likely to spread to Malaya, where the British were continuing to fight a Communist-backed insurgency.[20]

Looking at policymaking in London, Canberra, and Wellington also reveals that concerns about falling dominoes informed strategic planning in the Asia-Pacific before Eisenhower's public espousal of such perceived dangers.[21] By the late 1940s, for instance, London feared that Mao Zedong's revolutionary ambitions would extend beyond mainland China and into other parts of the Asia-Pacific. The British Joint Intelligence Committee concluded that without preventative action and substantial material support, the countries of Southeast Asia might fall under Communist control by the mid-1950s. "Should Siam fall," one report concluded, "a land threat to Singapore will develop. Should Burma fall it is likely that India would be so re-occupied."[22] Similar assumptions informed antipodean strategic thinking. At the ANZUS council meeting of November 1952, Australian, New Zealand, and U.S. staff planners reached a conclusion that was clearly motivated by concerns about falling dominoes: "The loss to the Communists of the Tonkin Delta in Indochina, which is presently the area most directly threatened, would greatly simplify continued Communist expansion in Southeast Asia while compounding the difficulties of friendly forces. It would probably lead to the collapse of Burma and Thailand, and to a dangerous weakening of internal security in Malaya, Indonesia and the Philippines."[23] The fear of falling dominoes evidently informed strategic planning in Western capitals around the world before the specter of Communist success in Vietnam.

Our sixth claim highlights the significant influence of smaller powers in alliance structures. The United States and the United Kingdom were materially much more powerful than either Australia or New Zealand. Consequently, they exerted more influence over the course of the Cold War in the Asia-Pacific region. Nevertheless, the antipodean powers occupied an important role in the Asia-Pacific and successfully utilized quadrilateral diplomacy to advance their own ambitions, sometimes at the expense of British and U.S. interests. The diplomatic influence they wielded was sometimes disproportionate to their military and economic power. The ability of these comparatively smaller powers to shape security cooperation in the region demonstrates that the behavior of alliances reflects more than just the wishes of their most powerful members.

As a case in point, Australia and New Zealand exploited U.S. interest in a Japanese peace treaty to secure a tripartite security pact from a reluctant Truman administration in 1951. The United States desired a lenient Japanese peace treaty to help rebuild the country and consequently contain Communist influence in the Asia-Pacific. Australia and New Zealand were far more reticent about cooperation with Japan, fearing that reindustrialization would lead to a return to militaristic foreign policies. Security guarantees from Washington became the necessary quid pro quo for gaining approval in Canberra and Wellington. In talks with antipodean representatives, Dulles directly questioned the necessity of such a security arrangement given the negligible threat of a direct Communist attack on either Australia or New Zealand. Spender responded skillfully, arguing that because the risk of a Communist attack was negligible, the U.S. could provide a security guarantee without fear of it ever being called upon. Dulles failed to contest this argument and negotiations proceeded smoothly. The influence of the antipodean powers during these talks helped forge a tripartite security alliance despite the United States' initial hesitation.

Australia and New Zealand also helped stymie U.S. efforts to create a regional alliance that would undertake military action inside Indochina to prevent France's collapse in 1954. Despite considerable diplomatic pressure, Wellington and Canberra informed Washington that they were unwilling to support U.S. proposals for "United Action." Antipodean resistance added an important voice to the growing chorus of opposition to action both inside and outside of Washington, which halted military action and led to the creation of SEATO later that year.

These six insights help us understand a crucial period in the early Cold War. Competing national interests repeatedly slowed the pursuit of regional security. Different strategic priorities, economic limitations, ideas about race, and domestic political influences complicated relations between all four states. Alliances did eventually emerge over time in response to a growing Communist threat. Yet ANZUS failed to guarantee the antipodean powers joint staff talks, integrated military planning, or a greater voice in international security arrangements. These were concessions that would have turned the idea of a pact into a functioning security alliance. SEATO fared even less well. After failing to prevent the Communist takeover of Indochina, and ongoing divisions within the alliance, it formally dissolved in 1977.

ANZUS and SEATO nevertheless played an important role in the course of the Cold War. The ANZUS Treaty helped the United States by removing obstacles to a Japanese peace treaty and created a platform from which to advance its trade and commercial objectives in the region, largely at the expense of British interests. The same treaty provided Australia and New Zealand with a U.S. security guarantee, presenting an alternative to the one supplied by the United Kingdom, which afforded them greater flexibility in the pursuit of national security. The Manila Treaty would establish a viable forum for strategic cooperation, but one that failed to address ongoing security concerns adequately. Doubts about military commitments to the region encouraged the antipodean powers to refocus their attention away from the Middle East and on events closer to home. In conjunction with growing concerns about the security of Southeast Asia and growing economic pressures, the treaties catalyzed and cemented a fundamental shift in antipodean strategy, namely Australia and New Zealand's subsequent transition toward regional security concerns in the 1950s. Paying closer attention to ANZUS and SEATO helps us understand the difficult course of security planning and the complicated nature of international cooperation in the Cold War. It is tempting to assume that such treaties would have emerged naturally and efficiently in the face of clear and significant challenges. Our account of these international strategic agreements instead reveals why democratic states sometimes struggle to cooperate against mutual threats.

CHAPTER 1

National Interests

During the course of World War II, the United States, United Kingdom, Australia, and New Zealand established unprecedented levels of strategic cooperation. Such cooperation, however, should not obscure the existence of significant and persistent differences during and after the conflict. All four states held different views about the future of security and economic cooperation in the Asia-Pacific. This chapter provides a broad survey of events from the end of World War II through to the early years of the Cold War. It contrasts U.S., British, Australian, and New Zealand national interests as well as regional objectives in the Asia-Pacific to show that postwar relations between all four states were not always conducive to future cooperation.[1] Differences in national interests, military capabilities, economic preferences, domestic-political contexts, and security concerns repeatedly undermined cooperation in the Asia-Pacific.

The United States of America

Following the Japanese attack at Pearl Harbor in December 1941, the United States formally entered World War II. U.S. involvement was vital if the United Kingdom was to defeat Nazi Germany and withstand a Japanese assault on the British Empire. On learning of the Japanese attack, the British prime minister Winston Churchill wrote in his diary, "I knew the United States was in the War now up to the neck, so we had won after all."[2] Hitler's decision to declare war against the United States after the events at Pearl Harbor even saved President Franklin Roosevelt the trouble of legitimizing war against Germany.[3]

The history of World War II is widely viewed as a global conflagration between the Allied and Axis powers. Recognizing the existence of a series of regional conflicts within a broader global struggle, however, provides a more nuanced account of events.[4] The United Kingdom and the United States adopted a "Germany first" strategy, prioritizing the defense of the British homeland alongside Middle Eastern and Mediterranean assets. The Allies would consequently follow a holding approach in the Asia-Pacific, which would contain Japanese power until they had vanquished Germany. Nevertheless, the U.S. continued to invest considerable military resources in the region. Under General Douglas MacArthur, U.S. forces in the Pacific would soon go on the offensive and wrest back control of areas occupied by the Japanese Imperial Army. Many in the British government found U.S. efforts troubling and believed that their U.S. ally should have focused on prosecuting the war in Europe, North Africa, and the Middle East.[5]

To promote wartime efficiency, the two powers eventually agreed to a division of labor. The United Kingdom assumed responsibility for British India and Southeast Asia and took strategic leadership in the Mediterranean. The United States took leadership in the broader Pacific region, with China also coming under its purview. As the war continued, the United States came to have a greater say in operations throughout the Mediterranean and Western European theaters. The United States would eventually insist on the opening of a second front in northern France and ensured that an American, Dwight D. Eisenhower, would act as the supreme allied commander for Allied forces invading France in June 1944. Such decisions largely reflected the United States' growing power. On multiple military and economic indexes, from military production to spending, the U.S. dwarfed the United Kingdom.[6] In addition, the United States alone in 1945 possessed atomic weaponry.

The shifting balance of power between the United States and its Western allies allowed the U.S. to extend its influence around the world.[7] As David Reynolds notes, this included the Pacific, East Asia, and the Middle East, areas where the United Kingdom had tended to lead: "World War II, then, marked a decisive moment in the shift of world power, and each government often formulated policy with one eye on the Axis and the other on its rival ally."[8] Determining strategic priorities in the Asia-Pacific was often fraught with difficulty. Following the launch of an offensive strategy in the South Pacific in 1943, tensions between the Allies mounted as they approached

Japan. The refusal of U.S. commanders to give the United Kingdom much of a say in how to manage Japan's final defeat angered many senior officials in London. As the British field marshal Lord Alanbrooke complained in his diary, "We want a greater share in the control of the strategy in the Pacific and [the United States] are apparently reluctant to provide this share."[9] U.S. reluctance reflected reasonable concerns that the United Kingdom would prioritize reclaiming its lost Asian territories over actually defeating Japan.[10] In such circumstances, British self-interest risked considerable amounts of U.S. blood and treasure.

A fundamental tension underlay disagreements concerning strategic decision making in the Asia-Pacific. Many Americans at the highest levels of office felt the British remained unable to accept that the struggle to attain and retain imperial holdings had heavily contributed to the current war. Roosevelt and Churchill repeatedly clashed on the issue of whether the United Kingdom should reclaim its fallen Asian empire after the conflict. As far as Roosevelt viewed matters, it was preferable that the peoples of the Asia-Pacific be afforded political autonomy from their European rulers. U.S. policymakers held racist views, to be sure, heightened by the barbarism of the war in the Pacific.[11] Roosevelt nevertheless believed that postwar stability would be better guaranteed by promoting sovereignty and self-determination. The president subsequently proposed that European colonial territories throughout the Asia-Pacific be placed under an international trusteeship, which would eventually allow former European colonies to be granted full sovereignty. Such a solution mirrored the United States' handling of the Philippines' approach to full independence. This proposal met fierce resistance. Churchill believed that questions about sovereignty were a decision for the British Empire, not the United States. When Roosevelt broached the subject of turning British colonies into trusteeships at the Yalta Conference in February 1945, Churchill was furious about "fumbling fingers" that were "prying into British heritage."[12]

The president quietly dropped his proposal for fear of creating a fundamental break within the wartime alliance that could hinder progress toward the strategic priority of defeating the Axis powers. More pressing concerns therefore concealed these difficulties for the time being. Nevertheless, U.S.-UK differences concerning the future of the British Empire were acute and, as the Allies appeared to be moving closer to victory, ongoing tensions intensified in the minds of Allied policymakers.[13] Consequently, as W. M. Roger Louis explains, "the wartime archives amply reveal that the sense of historic antagonism between Britain and the United States continued to exist along with the spirit of co-operation generated by the war."[14] Churchill nevertheless downplayed such U.S.-UK tensions thereafter, even softening such differences of opinion in his published account of the history of World War II.[15]

The wartime meetings held at Yalta are crucial to understanding the future of the postwar world. Agreements about the partition of Germany, the future of Eastern Europe, and the nature of reparations were vigorously debated by the Allied powers. The decisions reached at Yalta were also important to the future security of the Asia-Pacific. Secret agreements reached between Joseph Stalin, Churchill, and Roosevelt would see the Soviet Union occupy the Japanese-held Sakhalin and Kuril islands. Agreement was reached to also allow the Soviet Union access to Port Arthur, which China then controlled.[16] Stalin immediately grasped the longer-term strategic ramifications of the secret Far East agreements. Ownership of these islands would provide the Soviet Union with control over the Sea of Okhotsk and gave the Soviet navy access to warm-water ports in the east.[17] Possession of these ports would allow the Soviet Union to exercise naval influence in the Pacific Ocean. Stalin was not the only one to notice the strategic benefits that possession of these islands provided to the Soviet Union. As the Australian Chiefs of Staff Committee reported in March 1946, if the Soviet Union developed its naval power, its influence could now extend to the South Pacific, where it could pose "[a] major threat" to Western interests.[18] U.S. concessions to the Soviet Union largely reflect the context of wartime cooperation and ambitions for the postwar world. Roosevelt sought continued Soviet cooperation against Germany and Stalin's agreement to declare war against Japan thereafter. In addition, the president wanted Soviet support for the World Organization concept, later known as the United Nations, to which he was passionately committed. In order to achieve these ambitions, Roosevelt provided the Soviet leader with certain incentives.[19]

U.S.-Soviet discussions about ceding parts of the Asia-Pacific to Soviet authority occurred bilaterally. Roosevelt and Stalin had negotiated the agreement on the Sakhalin and Kuril islands without informing Churchill. Bilateral diplomacy at Yalta reflected a clear disparity in comparative military capability and economic power between the members of the Grand Alliance, which was especially pronounced in the Asia-Pacific. U.S.-Soviet discussions about placing Korea under some sort of trusteeship, which also occurred without Churchill's knowledge, further demonstrated the comparative decline of British influence.[20] U.S.-Soviet bilateralism so concerned the prime minister that he subsequently insisted he sign this secret Far East agreement on hearing reports of its existence. The prime minister believed his signature would help convey the impression that the United Kingdom remained on par as a great power with the United States and Soviet Union.[21]

By the time of the Potsdam conference, held later that year in July and August, Harry Truman had assumed the presidency following Roosevelt's sudden death. A change of personalities was matched by a change in strategic realities as Germany was defeated and occupied by the members of the Grand Alliance. The Allies' focus now shifted to a European peace settlement and the conclusion of the war in the Pacific. In Truman's estimation, the defeat of Germany alongside the United States' possession of the atomic bomb meant that the U.S. would not have to be as accommodating to Soviet or British demands.[22] There was a clear hardening in U.S. diplomacy vis-à-vis the Soviet Union. Potsdam thus became a "divorce settlement" between the members of the Grand Alliance. As Marc Trachtenberg explains, the agreements at Potsdam essentially meant that the United States and Soviet Union would "pull apart" from one another and divide the continent of Europe into two spheres of influence.[23] Such divisions were mirrored throughout the Asia-Pacific. The U.S. vigorously exerted its authority by steadfastly refusing to allow Soviet influence over the strategic direction of the Allied war effort against Japan. Plans for the invasion of the main home islands of Japan assumed an effort predominately led by U.S. forces, which limited the United Kingdom's role. The use of the atomic bomb on Hiroshima and Nagasaki, in conjunction with the Soviet Union's entry into the Pacific war, brought about the hasty surrender of Japan.[24] The United States subsequently assumed control of Japan and its accompanying islands before the arrival of any Soviet troops.

World War II marked a watershed in U.S. foreign policy.[25] U.S. politicians became far more engaged in shaping international events to maintain U.S. security. Truman was certainly determined to play a central role in international affairs. The president carried out a veritable revolution in the field of foreign and national security policy. Under his orders, the government grew to include a Central Intelligence Agency, an integrated war planning bureaucracy, and a central signals interception agency. Truman effectively established the national security state. By the time he left office, foreign policy issues had become a central part of U.S. politics.[26]

Throughout the summer of 1945, Truman made a concerted effort to implement his predecessor's vision for the international system. The United States would stand at the center of world politics. It would become a founding member of the United Nations, hold the chair of the World Bank, and establish the dollar as the world's premier reserve currency. In contrast to its allies, the United States had experienced an economic boom during World

War II, which created enormous growth in industrial production. The global order subsequently became increasingly reliant on U.S. economic and military power.[27]

The restoration of a flourishing European economy became central to U.S. conceptions of a stable postwar world. One of the lessons taken from the origins of World War II was that economic imperialism and inequality had fueled the fires of nationalism and revisionist ambitions. A stable economic order, which provided opportunities for all states, would reduce the likelihood of another global war. Alongside economic prosperity, Roosevelt had hoped that international cooperation among the great powers—namely, the United States, Soviet Union, United Kingdom, and China—would maintain global security. Deteriorating U.S.-Soviet relations soon undermined visions of a new international order. Uncertainty about U.S. intentions did little to calm Stalin's anxiety about aggression from the West.[28] Truman's actions therefore brought about a clear hardening in U.S. policy toward the Soviet Union. Yet there was no conscious decision taken by the president or his chief adviser and secretary of state, James Byrnes, to expel Soviet influence from the Asia-Pacific. Truman chose not to reverse the decisions reached at Yalta, explaining to the Soviet minister of foreign affairs Vyacheslav Molotov that if all parties honored their agreements there would be no quarrel.[29]

Such hopes proved illusory as the state of U.S.-Soviet relations continued to deteriorate in the postwar period. Truman and his national security team soon came to believe that the Soviet Union posed an existential security challenge to the United States. In order to meet such a threat the Truman administration concluded that it was imperative for the United States to "contain" Soviet power and influence.[30] The secretary of the navy James Forrestal spoke for many in Washington when he noted that there was no point in dealing with Stalin with "understanding and sympathy" as he only understood the currency of power: "We tried that once with Hitler. There are no returns on appeasement."[31]

Such forceful diplomacy required considerable military strength.[32] Washington remained deeply concerned that its nuclear arsenal alone would be insufficient to win any future war against the Soviet Union. Following the end of World War II, the United States had rapidly demobilized its forces. By 1947, the Soviet Union had such a material advantage in military power in Europe that some U.S. policymakers demanded the return of military conscription.[33] Cooperation with other powers in Europe therefore became essential to provide the military strength necessary to withstand any potential Soviet challenge. The United Kingdom assumed special importance due to its military, economic, and political position in Europe. In a detailed State

Department memorandum, the situation was set out clearly: "If Soviet Russia is to be denied hegemony of Europe, the United Kingdom must continue in existence as the principal power in Western Europe economically and militarily."[34] The United States also sought to preserve Western influence throughout the Middle East because of its significant petroleum reserves and strategic importance to U.S. national security interests.[35]

The U.S. thus prioritized Europe and the Middle East in its efforts to contain Soviet influence but did not neglect the Asia-Pacific. World War II had encouraged the United States to take a more rigorous approach toward securing the region, especially maintaining military rights to utilize a number of Pacific islands. During the war, the United States had lacked sufficient permanent bases to station its naval and aerial forces with which to project its power against Japan.[36] U.S. assets had instead been stationed and deployed from islands that were captured from Japanese control or leased islands from allies including those from New Zealand, Australia, and the United Kingdom.[37]

Following the end of the war, the United Nations placed the formerly Japanese-controlled islands under an international trusteeship. Leases to exercise military rights on the Allied-controlled Pacific islands were also set to expire within six months of Japan's surrender. This presented a strategic dilemma for the U.S., which wished to support the UN but also to maintain its military rights in the region into the postwar world. U.S. policymakers understood that Pacific bases would provide the United States with the necessary outposts for projecting military might throughout the region if ever required. As the Joint Chiefs of Staff argued, the United States should never be caught strategically unaware again as it had been in 1941.[38] Bases throughout the Pacific were, as the JCS reasoned in July 1945, "an inescapable requirement for United States security in the event of a failure of the United Nations Organization to preserve world peace, but that the provision of this system of bases will contribute materially to the effectiveness of that organization in maintaining peace throughout the world."[39] Similar arguments were advanced the following year.[40] Following bureaucratic battles in Washington, Truman ultimately supported a compromise, creating trusteeships for former enemy-controlled islands but with the specific condition that the United States would maintain its existing military rights.[41]

The United States was prepared to be as forceful as necessary with its wartime allies to acquire the rights to island bases in the Pacific Ocean. U.S. diplomats brushed aside antipodean efforts to discuss the issue, arguing that it was imperative for the U.S. to retain its military rights on these islands. When Francis Forde, deputy prime minister of Australia, brought up the matter with Truman in June 1945, the president dismissed it.[42] Efforts by Carl Berendsen, New Zealand's minister to the United States, to discreetly settle the matter failed to lead to any positive results for antipodean interests.[43] Australia's minister for external affairs, H. V. Evatt, had attempted to achieve some sort of U.S. regional security guarantee in exchange for British Commonwealth cooperation over Pacific island bases, but these attempts also proved ineffective.[44] As one Australian official noted, the United States was "not discussing" the matter. The U.S. was instead demanding that the British Commonwealth simply rubber-stamp its approval for U.S. military bases throughout the Asia-Pacific.[45] Efforts by Australian and New Zealand officials to extract some sort of post-war U.S. security guarantee as a quid pro quo for allowing U.S. control over certain Pacific islands proved unsuccessful.[46]

Truman gave clarity to U.S. ambitions when he publicly declared at the beginning of 1946 that the United States would continue to control the Pacific islands it had utilized in the war. By the summer of 1947, the United States administered some ninety-eight islands and island clusters under a United Nations trusteeship and secured approval for military bases on Allied-controlled territories. The trusteeship was essentially a facade; the islands were to function as U.S. military bases. As the then U.S. secretary of state George Marshall made clear in his testimony before the U.S. Senate, "We have provisions in the agreement which allow us almost complete liberty of action."[47] This episode demonstrated that the United States was preparing to take a much more assertive approach to securing its international interests throughout the Asia-Pacific. Such rigorous diplomacy may have disgruntled officials in Canberra and Wellington, but Washington had been extremely successful at promoting its strategic interests in the region.[48]

More tensions would emerge between erstwhile allies. The Truman administration promoted the ideals of free trade and sought to strengthen its economic position in the region, which brought U.S. interests into direct conflict with the United Kingdom, Australia, and New Zealand. Complicating relations was the issue of the imperial preference system as practiced throughout the British Empire.[49] The U.S. State Department remained especially unhappy about exclusive Australian–New Zealand–British economic cooperation and special tariffs, which came at the expense of U.S. interests. Imperial preference could impede wider economic revival in the region, especially postwar trade with Japan, and therefore posed a threat to U.S. security ambitions. Of special concern for U.S. policymakers was Australia's practice of entering into long-term bulk purchase agreements. Such agreements, by channeling trade and fixing prices, threatened to undermine the structure of international trade, particularly if replicated throughout the rest of the British Empire. Difficult negotiations between Britain and the United States had occurred on this issue in late 1945. London ultimately pledged to promote multilateral trade and end the system of imperial preference in the future.[50] In the meantime, the U.S. would encourage relevant states to question their support for the imperial preference system.[51]

One of the key questions for the U.S. in the Asia-Pacific, and an issue that would continually divide the Western powers, was the future of Japan. U.S. policymakers were clear that the answer would be largely determined in Washington. Dean Acheson, the U.S. secretary of state from 1949 to 1953, noted in his memoirs, "We had no intention of denying the participation that our allies, especially the Commonwealth allies who had fought the Far Eastern battles from the beginning, were entitled to. But we were determined that it should be advisory."[52] MacArthur, citing his ability to understand the "Asian mind," consequently assumed de facto leadership of Japan as the supreme allied commander for the Allied powers and implemented sweeping changes to Japanese society soon after the war ended.[53]

Mirroring concerns about the future of Germany, Truman's advisers concluded that if Japan fell into the possession of the Soviet Union, the Communist bloc would harness its economic and industrial might and threaten U.S. interests throughout the region.[54] The primary threat posed to Japan by the Soviet Union was internal subversion, whereby an indigenous Communist party controlled by Moscow would take power, as most policymakers viewed an outright invasion as improbable. Many believed that MacArthur's control of Japan risked internal subversion because his leadership had not brought about the economic improvements necessary to dissuade the population from being swayed into supporting Communism.[55] Assuring Japan's economic recovery therefore became a central component of U.S. strategy for Asia-Pacific security. Following the signature of the Japanese instruments of surrender, the issue of a formal peace treaty was left unresolved. In the U.S. estimation, such a treaty was essential to end occupation and facilitate economic recovery. The peace treaty would ideally be nonpunitive and allow for Japan's industrial revival. As such, the U.S. had adopted a pragmatic line to rehabilitate Japan in preparation for a potential Cold War confrontation in the region.[56]

The United States' commitment to the Asia-Pacific was complicated by interdepartmental rivalries, especially between the JCS, the State Department, and the White House, who disagreed about the importance of the region.[57] The Truman administration was nevertheless committed to securing a number of Pacific islands to maintain U.S. aerial and naval bases. In doing so, the United States would be suitably positioned to project its military power throughout the region if necessary.[58] Yet such efforts pale in comparison to U.S. efforts throughout Europe and the Middle East where U.S. diplomats were at the forefront of establishing united economic, industrial, and, eventually, military responses to the perceived threat posed by the Soviet Union.[59] The Truman administration had prioritized other concerns and had not yet established a clear foreign policy for the Asia-Pacific.[60]

The United Kingdom

British policymakers had long debated whether the United Kingdom should pursue an imperial defense policy or one that focused on homeland defense. One of the perennial fears about taking a more rigorous approach to the German threat in the interwar period had been that Italy and Japan would take the opportunity of a European war to expand their own imperial ambitions. World War II proved such predictions correct. Once the United Kingdom became engaged in a fight for its survival inside Europe, Italy and Japan moved to seize Britain's imperial possessions. The war highlighted the delicacy of the United Kingdom's hold on its empire. By the start of 1942, the Japanese had overrun Britain's numerous Asian assets, while Italian and German forces fought to secure possession of British interests in the Middle East and North Africa. Even maintaining a hold over India, the "jewel in the British crown," looked far from certain following the surrender at Singapore in February 1942.[61]

With the adoption of the "Germany first" strategy, the United Kingdom prioritized the defense of the homeland and its interests in Africa and the Middle East over that of its Asian empire.[62] To be sure, the United Kingdom, drawing on enormous contributions from its empire, remained engaged in heavy fighting throughout the Pacific during the war.[63] Sustained interest in this region was understandable. The Japanese Imperial Army had conquered large swaths of Asian territory. It had also brought about the surrender of the British army at Singapore.[64] Yet much of the burden came to fall on U.S. shoulders. When Churchill dispatched a naval taskforce to Sydney in 1944 to prepare for a planned invasion of Japan in the following year, the British fleet paled in comparison to the U.S. contribution. It is with good reason that historians refer to the British fleet in the Pacific as "attached" to the U.S. fleet.[65]

Shifting geostrategic realities did not mean that the United Kingdom would suddenly relinquish its imperial holdings throughout the region. Agreement at Yalta to pursue the unconditional surrender of Japan meant that there could be no negotiated settlement of the war, which in turn committed the United Kingdom to long-term military operations in the Asia-Pacific.[66] The

British government was determined to reclaim all of its imperial possessions throughout the region, for matters relating to both prestige and strategy.[67] Churchill had insisted that British forces personally reclaim Singapore and Hong Kong and oversee the surrender of Japanese forces in the Dutch East Indies and Indochina.[68] By the end of the war, and in spite of the enormous cost involved and international criticism generated, the United Kingdom had reclaimed its Asian empire. As Churchill boasted in private in late 1944, "'Hands off the British Empire' is our maxim and it must not be weakened or smirched to please sob-stuff merchants at home or foreigners of any hue."[69]

Whether the United Kingdom could retain its Asian empire in the longer term was questionable. Churchill may have hoped that the inhabitants of these territories would see the British as liberators, but the disasters of 1941–42 were difficult to erase from popular memory. The United Kingdom's failure to provide the necessary security to these territories coupled with the brutality of the Japanese occupation in the war encouraged the growth of opinion that independence from the empire was preferable to continued British rule. The events of the war had encouraged nationalist movements throughout Asia to resist European colonial control. The British Empire, for many observers, appeared to be on borrowed time.[70]

The economic consequences of World War II also presented a series of challenges to Britain's continued hold on its Asian empire.[71] The British government had become reliant on the continued assistance of the lend-lease program to support the UK economy in wartime. The Truman administration nevertheless abruptly canceled lend-lease following the surrender of Germany.[72] As Truman would retrospectively admit, the cancellation of lend-lease had unintentionally hit the British the "hardest."[73] At the end of the war, the British government owed approximately £31 billion to the U.S. Treasury, reflecting initial "cash and carry" lending and lend-lease debt.[74] Such agreements "left bills to be paid later."[75] Following negotiations between London and Washington, the United Kingdom would agree to repay $650 million of the total $31 billion borrowed, and would receive additional loans in the postwar period, but the British economy remained in a perilous position owing to its weakened trade position and significant levels of external debt.[76] The British government could simply not afford to maintain a significant military presence all over the world.

Given the weakened state of British power, policymakers realized that they would struggle to afford another major military conflict in the near future. They believed that the likelihood of such an occurrence, however, remained low. The Grand Alliance now occupied Germany, which lay in ruins. A vanquished Italy also no longer posed a challenge to British interests in the Mediterranean. Japan, having been defeated and now occupied, posed no immediate threat to Britain's Asian empire. The only viable challengers were now the United States and the Soviet Union. The British government never considered the United States a serious military threat, despite the U.S. taking decisions that undermined Britain's position in Asia-Pacific, most notably its insistence on equal commercial access. Averell Harriman, who would become the U.S. ambassador to the United Kingdom in April 1946, accurately portrayed British thinking when he informed Washington that the British government has a "passionate desire for military and diplomatic co-operation with the U.S. coupled with the fear of [U.S.] economic power."[77]

The Soviet Union presented a greater concern. Roosevelt's decision at Yalta to allow the Soviet Union direct access into the Pacific enabled Stalin to threaten Britain's Asian interests. Occupation of the northern half of Korea provided the Soviet Union with a strong foothold in mainland Asia. As Churchill reasoned, Stalin had achieved what his imperial ancestors had been unable to secure, namely access to the Pacific. With warm-water ports in Asia, the Soviet Union could now extend its influence into the Pacific if it chose to do so.[78] Many in the British government had seen the Grand Alliance as merely a means to an end. Cooperation entailed forgetting about the "bad blood" accrued in Anglo-Soviet relations since 1917 and focusing on the objective of defeating Nazi Germany.[79] This was manageable while Nazi Germany represented a common and supreme danger but would be difficult to maintain in the long term.[80] During the later stages of the war, Anthony Eden, Britain's foreign secretary, confessed to a "growing apprehension that Russia has vast aims, and that these may include the domination of Eastern Europe and even the Mediterranean and the 'communizing' of much that remains."[81] The British military chiefs were especially alarmed about the growing power of the Soviet Union and the inability of the United States to recognize the menace posed by Stalin.[82] Membership in the Grand Alliance can therefore be viewed as a hiatus in the Anglo-Soviet "Cold War," which began with the Bolshevik Revolution in 1917.[83]

In his memoirs, Churchill portrayed himself as the wise prophet that warned of the future menace posed by Stalin. His writing of history deliberately emphasized the growing likelihood of a Cold War. Churchill certainly did warn his peers of future trouble with the Soviet Union, and he was concerned that both Roosevelt and Truman remained hopelessly naive about Stalin's real intentions.[84] The prime minister even ordered Britain's military chiefs to devise a plan advocating that the Western Allies should not stop their advance across Europe until they had pushed the Soviet Union back to its pre-1939 borders. This was a fantastic policy; planning for such an operation was entitled "Operation Unthinkable."[85] Yet Churchill had also talked about how he believed he could "trust" Stalin and that Anglo-Soviet differences in the postwar world could be managed. The prime minister remained confident that he could maintain a workable partnership with Stalin into the postwar world. As Churchill put it, "Poor Neville Chamberlain believed he could trust Hitler. He was wrong. But I don't think I'm wrong about Stalin."[86] Many key officials within the British Foreign Office shared such sentiments. For the likes of Eden, the central issue in international politics had to be resolving the "German question." If a solution could emerge that adequately protected the interests of the Soviet Union, then there was no need for any geopolitical confrontation. All told, Churchill, along with senior policymakers inside the British Foreign Office, remained committed to working with Stalin in the postwar world.[87]

British foreign policy would evolve following a change of political leadership. Prime Minister Clement Attlee came to office on July 26, 1945, following a decisive electoral victory for his Labour Party.[88] The Labour government now faced the myriad of foreign policy challenges that World War II had generated and exacerbated. The advent of nuclear weapons particularly concerned the prime minister, who noted in communication with Truman that these new weapons had the ability to "suddenly and without warning utterly destroy the nerve centre of a great nation."[89] Fears of nuclear annihilation aside, Attlee and his foreign secretary, Ernest Bevin, understood that they would have to make hard choices about Britain's geopolitical position during their time in office. Policymakers and large swaths of the general public nevertheless clung to the belief that Britain remained a global power. Such a conclusion was reasonable given commercial interests spanning the globe, British forces stationed in over forty countries globally, and victory in World War II. Britain's troubling financial status, however, made it more difficult to maintain such a global position. The rise of nationalist movements and increasing calls for independence throughout the British Empire presented further serious challenges to the maintenance of the status quo.[90]

There were also growing challenges to the British Empire from external forces. When the Potsdam Conference ended in early August 1945, Attlee's government found itself increasingly unwilling to continue the "appeasement" of the Soviet Union. As far as British policymakers were concerned, they had to oppose the Soviet Union resolutely.[91] Even prior to the defeat of the Axis powers, British security planners had already begun to prepare for future threats around the globe. Eden, for example, had admitted that the British government held little confidence that the end of the war would

usher in a system of international relations predicated on justice and negotiation rather than power.[92] Bevin, Eden's successor, largely agreed with
such sentiments. Attlee, while less convinced about the danger posed by
the Soviet Union, did conclude that the Soviet Union's "ambitions were
imperialistic" and it was essential for the United Kingdom to "balance Soviet
influence."[93]

Limited financial resources coupled with war weariness restricted the
options available to British strategists with which to address this perceived
Soviet threat.[94] British policymakers had to maintain a global empire with
fewer economic resources in a world increasingly dominated by two superpowers. One British official spoke for many when he informed Bevin,
"Unless appearances are deceptive, the United States is also now groping
towards a new order of things in which Great Britain, whilst occupying a
highly important position as a bastion of Western European security and as
the focal point of a far-flung oceanic system, will nevertheless be expected
to take her place as junior partner in an orbit of power predominantly under
American aegis."[95] The United Kingdom's role in the world was changing.
The British government would now have to consider its position in a new
global order.

When the British government sought to enforce their favorable prewar
trade and commercial practices in China, for instance, they immediately
came into conflict with the United States, which wanted the country committed to free trade.[96] British officials believed such policies would conve-
niently promote U.S. business and commercial interests that had secured
Chinese markets when the United Kingdom's influence had collapsed during World War II. U.S.-UK differences over the future of China would persist, but the Moscow Conference of December 1945 clearly demonstrated
that Washington would have its way much to the chagrin of British policymakers. The U.S. largely ignored British complaints about commercial
rights inside China and pressed ahead with its plans for fairer access for U.S.
commerce in the country, overturning long-standing British trade treaties
in the region.[97]

Attlee and Bevin soon came to appreciate that the United Kingdom was
no longer in a position from which it could face either the Soviet Union or
the United States as an equal. In order to survive in this new postwar world,
strategic prioritization was now essential. Such a solution would entail an
uncomfortable scaling back of Britain's global obligations. Even Churchill,
who had talked on a number of occasions about his determination not to
preside over the liquidation of the British Empire, had come to recognize
this problem.[98] His premiership recognized that while Britain retained global

interests, the priority for strategic defense was now Europe and the Middle East. Europe remained an essential security and economic concern for the British government, not least because of its geographic proximity and valuable trade flows.[99] Under Attlee, British policymakers also acknowledged the importance of the Middle East. The United Kingdom retained strategically important military bases throughout the region, most notably in Aden and the Suez Canal area. In addition, as Bevin put it, the Middle East was a "lake of oil" that had to remain in British hands.[100]

Because of these factors, the British government scaled down the number of existing military bases throughout the Pacific with naval and aerial assets focused in Aden, Cyprus, Malta, and homeports.[101] In the immediate postwar period, British Dominions, such as Australia and New Zealand, were encouraged to take a much greater share of the burden in British Commonwealth defense throughout the Asia-Pacific.[102] As London informed Canberra, British planning in a global war was predicated on five key factors: securing the integrity of Commonwealth countries, mounting a strategic air offensive against the Soviet Union, holding the Soviet Union as far East as possible in Western Europe, maintaining a firm hold on the Middle East, and retaining essential sea communications.[103] It was clear in such planning that the defense of the Asia-Pacific in any global war was lower on the list of British priorities. As Attlee had earlier suggested, the United Kingdom should look at ways of directly limiting its imperial obligations by ceding ownership of certain portions of the British Empire.[104]

As the British government prioritized its global commitments, it also sought to enhance the U.S.-UK "special relationship." Sustaining and enhancing close relations between London and Washington now became a cornerstone of British security policy, which would aid British ambitions of containing the Soviet Union and allow greater influence over the United States to promote policies along lines more amenable to British interests.[105] By the end of 1946, Bevin had managed to establish an official intelligence-sharing agreement and staff talks with the United States. As Ritchie Ovendale has noted, Bevin's efforts led to the creation of "an informal military alliance" between the two states.[106] Security cooperation nevertheless remained limited in the Asia-Pacific region. The U.S. rebuffed British suggestions about stationing a liaison officer in Singapore and refused to open talks concerning Asia-Pacific security. Cooperation in either matter failed to serve U.S. interests.[107] As U.S. intelligence assessments rightly appreciated, the United Kingdom was a weakened global power and sensible British strategists would recognize that strategic priorities should lie much closer to the British Isles.[108]

The granting of independence to India in 1947 and the partition of Palestine in 1948 highlighted the decline of the United Kingdom's role as a great
power. Attlee decided against costly and potentially embarrassing military
efforts to retain control of either state. He instead concentrated resources
on Western Europe and the Middle East. Indian independence represented
a particularly damaging blow for British strategic influence, undermining its
capacity to maintain the armed forces necessary for the projection of international power.[109]

The gradual decline of the British Empire, the rise of U.S. power, and the
strengthening of Asian self-determination movements represent an important mix of elements in explaining the events that unfolded throughout the
region following World War II. Withdrawal from India increased the attention that British policymakers placed on their other assets throughout the
Asia-Pacific, with a special focus on the Communist insurgencies developing
in Malaya. British military bases remained in Singapore and Hong Kong,
while commercial interests spread throughout the wider region.[110] The
maintenance of imperial preference trading practices throughout the Commonwealth also ensured that significant international markets remained
open to British commerce on a preferential basis.[111] The British government
consequently retained a keen interest in events throughout the Asia-Pacific.

Australia

The Australian experience of World War II in the Pacific was traumatic. The
disasters of 1941–42, when the British army collapsed in Singapore and the
United States retreated from the Philippines, had a major impact on policymakers in Canberra and the broader public. Australia had been left strategically exposed to Japan, an expansionist rival with greater militarily strength,
yet most of its own forces were committed to fighting in northern Africa
against German and Italian forces because of long-standing agreements
with the United Kingdom. Japan had subsequently been able to strike the
Australian mainland in 1941 and 1942, bombing Darwin and sinking naval
vessels in Sydney harbor with midget submarines. The brutality of the Japanese army, and their treatment of Australian prisoners of war, compounded
such trauma.[112] During the conflict, the United Kingdom failed to provide
adequate defense in the Asia-Pacific region, which sparked an ongoing controversy about whether the United Kingdom "betrayed" Australia in 1942.[113]
Churchill's private but ill-tempered reaction to the Australian prime minister
John Curtin's appeals for assistance are revealing: "London had not made a
fuss when it was bombed. Why should Australia?"[114]

The British government was unwilling to refocus its resources to help defend the Australian mainland at that time. Churchill's insistence that the U.S. should dispatch forces for Australian mainland protection so that the Australian and New Zealand Army Corps (ANZAC) forces could remain stationed in North Africa only exacerbated tensions between London and Canberra.[115] The agreement between the United States and United Kingdom in 1942 to make the defense of the Asia-Pacific region the primary responsibility of the U.S. government represents a turning point in defense policy; Australia could no longer rely solely on its defensive alliance with the United Kingdom. During World War II, it was U.S. rather than British soldiers that had flooded the cities of Sydney, Melbourne, and Brisbane. Well over 1 million GIs would pass through Australia during the course of the war. As Prime Minister Curtin declared to the Australian people, "Without any inhibitions of any kind, I made it quite clear that Australia looks to America [for security], free of any pangs as to our traditional links or kinship with the United Kingdom."[116]

Such rhetoric should not obscure the fact that the U.S.-Australian alliance was a "marriage of necessity" for both parties.[117] It would also be a mistake to assume harmonious relations followed thereafter.[118] As the war progressed, Australia sought a greater say in Allied strategy concerning the defeat of Japan. During British Commonwealth discussions, for instance, Curtin stressed that the other powers could not automatically assume Australian support for any Allied strategy.[119] The United Kingdom and the United States would instead have to discuss the contours of strategy and reach agreement via consultation. Curtin expected Australia to receive a greater say in alliance decision making and to be treated as an equal rather than as a Dominion within an empire.[120]

Australian diplomacy was even more forthright when it came to the terms of Japanese surrender in 1945. At the request of the United States, the British government was initially invited to sign the instruments of surrender on behalf of the Dominions of the British Commonwealth. Herbert Evatt, Australia's minister for external affairs, reacted to Australian exclusion negatively, blaming the United Kingdom for the United States' decision.[121] Tensions within the British Commonwealth soon became public. British newspapers reported that Evatt had complained about the arrogance of the Foreign Office and claimed that the Dominion minister Lord Addison lied about how the Allies would handle the Japanese surrender. Ben Chifley, who succeeded Francis Forde's brief period as prime minister following Curtin's death in July 1945, followed suit by dispatching a scathing letter to London that accused the British government of acting in a fashion that had relegated

Australia to a "subordinate status" and had treated Australia "not on a footing of equality."[122] The prime minister's claim had some merit, considering the limited involvement of Australia in the Yalta and Potsdam conferences despite discussions concerning the Asia-Pacific.

Evatt's actions sparked a public relations row between Australia and the United Kingdom.[123] While some solace was taken in the fact that New Zealand's prime minister Peter Fraser had "deprecated" in "round terms" the behavior of Evatt, the British government was increasingly concerned about the implications of such divisions. After further discussion, the U.S., largely as a gesture of goodwill, acquiesced to Australian demands that Canberra could sign the Japanese surrender instruments as a separate signatory. This concession was unpopular in London. Greater Australian independence and new foreign policy objectives were unwelcome developments. British officials feared this would set a precedent among other members of the empire to seek more independent foreign policies and thus contribute to the retreat of British global influence.[124]

Australian confidence continued to grow on the international stage. The end of World War II had left the Australian economy in a comparatively favorable position. From the beginning of the war and in the decades that followed, the Australian economy performed ably on many indicators.[125] The Australian government made concerted efforts to address ongoing economic instabilities, strengthen national defense, and promote long-term development.[126] This latent power would also increasingly translate into military might. By the end of the 1940s, Australian defense expenditure was significant for a country of only 8 million inhabitants.[127]

Chifley also prioritized economic development. He concentrated on the need to maintain full employment in face of deteriorating economic conditions abroad and the need to toe the sterling area line, especially in the light of chronic dollar shortages and doubts about U.S. support.[128] Thus, despite lingering diplomatic tensions, Australia remained largely committed to the United Kingdom in the economic realm during the immediate postwar period. Australia had vigorously opposed any efforts by the United States to dismantle the sterling bloc, which comprised the United Kingdom, its colonies, and the major Dominions with the exception of Canada, and maintained the system of imperial preference. The convertibility crisis of 1947 led Australia to tighten trading and financial connections with Britain and the rest of the sterling area. The Australian government agreed to devalue its currency in 1949 to remain a member of the sterling bloc despite increasing the price of domestic consumer items. Loyalty and self-interest explained this decision, especially as Australia generally benefited from imperial preference.[129]

Postwar economic cooperation with the United Kingdom contrasted with growing doubts about national security. The Australian government had been nominally independent in the conduct of foreign policy since 1931 as the Statute of Westminster provided Australia with the right to conduct foreign policy independently of the United Kingdom. The effect was delayed, however, as Canberra did not pass it into law until 1942. World War II served as the necessary catalyst for Australian policymakers to assume a more independent approach to national security.[130] The British Empire, as demonstrated early on in the war, was unable to ensure Australian security in the Asia-Pacific. As the Australian Chiefs of Staff concluded in one report, "The recent war has reduced the military and economic strength of the United Kingdom considerably, with the result that Australia can no longer rely, to the same extent, on the assistance previously provided by the United Kingdom in both these aspects."[131] Chifley and Evatt were certainly concerned with Britain's future ability to uphold Australia's security. The "United Kingdom has not the capacity and strength she formerly possessed," Chifley informed his cabinet colleagues. Australia would have to assume a greater burden for its own security in the region.[132]

Australian security planners attempted to diversify security cooperation with the creation of the ANZAC Pact in 1944, which sought to maintain and strengthen the close relations already shared with New Zealand. The Australian government also pressed its antipodean neighbor to establish joint planning forums so that regional security matters could be discussed in depth between them.[133] The 1945–46 Australia, New Zealand, and Malaya (ANZAM) understanding with the United Kingdom further demonstrates the growing independence of Australia in the postwar period.[134] Although never a formal defense treaty, there followed staff talks between the three British Commonwealth states, informal interchanges of global security assessments, and defense preparations and planning for the Asia-Pacific.[135]

Australian officials were keenly aware that ANZAM planning was of limited value given that, without U.S. assistance in the event of a global war against the Soviet Union, there was little chance of success for the British Commonwealth powers.[136] In addition, the ANZAM understanding did not commit any of the countries to take action.[137] Nevertheless, from the perspective of Canberra, ANZAM ensured Australian leadership in conducting regional defense in the event of a war.[138] The ANZAM understanding therefore accepted that Australia had a "special role" in the region and Canberra would now take the lead in formulating and providing for its own regional security, which the British government largely welcomed.[139]

Canberra also led a concerted and ultimately successful effort to place Australia at the head of British Commonwealth defense planning for the West Pacific. Although the British were reluctant to surrender any control within the Commonwealth, there was little choice given the strategic and economic challenges facing the United Kingdom. As Evatt argued in discussion with the British, only by allowing Australia to take the lead in securing its own regional security could a repetition of the "embarrassments" of 1939 and 1942 be avoided.[140] Accordingly, Australian diplomats managed to convince their British counterparts that they, and not British planners, should take the lead in formulating the plans for Asia-Pacific defense.[141]

Australian efforts at securing formalized postwar military cooperation with the U.S. would prove less successful. The government looked to exploit the fact that the United States sought permission from Australia to build military bases on a number of Pacific islands. Canberra's thinking was premised on the idea that they could use this U.S. ambition as political leverage to convince Washington to provide formalized military cooperation. As Evatt outlined to the prime minister, they should "see that if United States gets the use of facilities they will be required in return to give us definite and tangible benefits of a Defence character."[142] The Truman administration was determined to secure military base rights throughout the Asia-Pacific but was unprepared to offer defense commitments to interested parties as a quid pro quo. When Chifley visited Truman in May 1946 he did briefly raise the subject of creating a formal security pact for the Asia-Pacific, but he found little U.S. enthusiasm. Efforts by Evatt in the following year would prove equally unsuccessful.[143]

The absence of any formalized security cooperation between the United States and Australia in the Asia-Pacific did little to help growing differences about the necessity of regional security planning and the nature of the threat posed by the Soviet Union. The British and U.S. governments concluded that the Soviet Union presented the fundamental challenge to global security and undertook defense planning in response to this presumed threat. Accordingly, their efforts would focus on the defense of Western Europe, the Mediterranean, and the Middle East. The Chifley government, however, remained focused primarily on regional security. When the British suggested that Australia should assume strategic defense responsibilities for British Commonwealth interests throughout the rest of the Asia-Pacific, the Chifley government refused.[144] Canberra did not accept that the Soviet Union posed the geopolitical threat that London and Washington claimed.[145] Such different

interpretations about the nature of the Soviet threat resulted in uncooperative policies. In response to the Washington Conference of February 1946,
Chifley made it clear that "if the United Kingdom and New Zealand Governments feel they are committed to going ahead with the Washington conference, the Australian Government must reserve all rights in regard to conclusions which may be reached."[146]

Indeed, Chifley's position back in Canberra was one of increasing skepti-
cism about the hardening attitudes of Washington and London vis-à-vis the
Soviet Union. The Australian prime minister was determined to maintain a
neutral position in what was turning into a global Cold War. Some Australian
policymakers believed that international cooperation with the Soviet Union
was possible and rejected U.S. and British assumptions about the emerging
threat. Many in the Australian government deemed such attitudes overly
aggressive, risking disaster for both Australia and the interests of the British Commonwealth.[147] Chifley and Evatt believed that the United Nations
should assume a far greater role in the conduct of international affairs.[148]
Under their leadership, Australian foreign policy sought to emphasize ideas
of justice in the settling of international disagreements.[149]

The Australian government consequently assumed an uncooperative
attitude when it came to alliance building inside Europe. Chifley publicly
and privately suggested that any European security alliance would justly be
viewed as a provocation in Moscow and would actually destabilize the security situation in Europe. Such criticism from Canberra was clearly unwelcome in London. Officials inside the Dominions and Commonwealth office
believed criticism of recent British alliance-building efforts within Europe to
be "destructive," "unpleasant," and "inaccurate." Chifley's position certainly
contrasted with the more positive attitudes of other Commonwealth states,
including the governments of Mackenzie King of Canada and Peter Fraser
of New Zealand.[150]

When London sought public support for the Western European Union
(WEU) concept, which would bring about a military alliance between the
United Kingdom, France, Belgium, Luxembourg, and the Netherlands,
Chifley's government refused to oblige. Not only did the Australian leadership believe that the WEU was unlikely to prove helpful, but noted that the
United Kingdom and United States had conducted their negotiations about
European and Middle East security planning without any type of consultation with Australia. As Chifley complained, "We are very concerned to
see developments in United Kingdom government policy . . . undertaken
and practically crystallized before we were even informed."[151] The plans of
the Truman administration to turn former colonies into "trusteeships," as

opposed to according them full independence, also attracted the opposition of the Chifley government. As Evatt informed Washington, he had predicated Australia's rejection on "reasons of justice."[152]

The Australian leadership rejected British Cold War strategies, accusing the Attlee government of forgetting its spiritual basis in foreign policy and of pursuing a foreign policy based solely on material and strategic concerns.[153] Canberra's criticism of both British and U.S. Cold War strategy did not sit well in either London or Washington. Evatt was seen as an irritation in both capitals. One U.S. analyst speculated whether Evatt's vocal opposition to U.S.-UK Cold War policies was genuinely driven by his appreciation of the threats posed by the Soviet Union or rather by his egotism, which meant he desired the publicity that such opposition generated to advance his own political agenda inside Australia.[154] Ultimately, Evatt's criticism was of little consequence as both London and Washington pushed ahead with their alliance-building efforts in Europe.

Chifley's position on other matters did have a far more direct effect on British interests, however, not least when it came to the security of the Middle East. British security planners desired commitments from British Commonwealth countries to either station forces in the Middle East or to dispatch them to the region in the event of a war with the Soviet Union. The Chifley government refused to commit, station, or dispatch Australian forces in the Middle East in the event of a war with the Soviet Union. It believed that such efforts would be a misdirection of resources and an unnecessary provocation of the Soviet Union.[155]

Anglo-Australian relations failed to improve when the British government pressed ahead with its support for the Marshall Plan and the creation of the North Atlantic Treaty Organization. Evatt suggested that U.S. ambitions were motivated by "mercenary greed." The United States, he argued, was becoming a global hegemon to which the British Commonwealth was becoming increasingly subservient. Evatt explained to the British that he had recently refused a loan from the United States in order to prevent Australia becoming a "slave to U.S. financers." Instead of pursuing the alliance with the United States, the Australian foreign minister suggested that the three socialist governments of the Commonwealth—namely the United Kingdom, Australia, and Canada—should seek to pursue a "third way" in the Cold War between Soviet Communism and U.S. capitalism. The Australian prime minister agreed with this "third way" approach to international affairs and encouraged Evatt to push his ideas in discussion with the British.[156]

The Chifley government had also rejected the familiar method of acquiescing to British policy decisions in order to influence strategy from within.

As a case in point, Evatt's response to the issue of who should have veto rights in the Far East Commission, which governed Japan, is illuminating: "My Government desires to point out that the implication of the veto provision is that in relation to the Pacific and South East Asia, Australia's status is to be regarded as in some way inferior to that of other powers." The foreign minister explained, "Australia is not only a member of the Security Council but its sustained and decisive contribution to victory against Japan—fully recognized by your Government—entitles it to be regarded as a party principal in all Pacific affairs."[157] When the United States sought to move ahead with a Japanese peace treaty in the Asia-Pacific in 1949, it again brought a strong rebuke from Canberra concerning Washington's apparent unilateralism.[158] The Australian government was determined not to be ignored in the postwar world.[159]

The governments of John Curtin and Ben Chifley ushered in an increasingly independent foreign policy based on an assessment of Australian rather than British Commonwealth interests. Nevertheless, Australia remained party to a number of agreements with the United Kingdom that tied the two countries together.[160] There were also no viable alternatives to continued reliance on the United Kingdom. As Australian policymakers well understood, the United States would not yet provide the type of security guarantees that Australia desired. Only the United Kingdom and New Zealand appeared willing to help uphold the existing interests of the British Commonwealth and, in turn, contribute toward Australian security.[161]

The Chifley government looked to sustain or enhance existing ties with Britain. For example, MI5 and its Australian counterpart, the Australian Security Intelligence Organisation (ASIO), regularly exchanged intelligence. Work was also undertaken to establish an Australian version of the Joint Intelligence Bureau so that it could coordinate strategy for defending Southeast Asia with its British counterpart.[162] Australia also undertook elements of cooperation that supported U.S.-UK strategic ambitions. The prime minister committed to missile testing inside Australia, for instance, and approved the building of new facilities. He did so without reaching agreement with London as to whether these tests or buildings were required or how they would be funded.[163] In addition, the Chifley government was determined to create formal and permanent security cooperation institutions between the United Kingdom and the Dominion powers. Between 1946 and 1949, Australian officials and the wider defense bureaucracy repeatedly pushed for such cooperation.[164]

The Chifley government, which had been the most charitable in its assessments of Soviet intentions, had become increasingly alarmed about the threat posed by Stalin's Soviet Union, not least following the Soviet-sponsored coup in Czechoslovakia in 1948. By now, Australian intelligence assessments stressed that the Communist threat to Australian security had become more pronounced because the Soviet Union was focusing its attention on Southeast Asia. As the Australian Joint Intelligence Committee argued, "A threat to the zone will be as a consequence of hostile moves in the Far East by the U.S.S.R. with the collaboration of communist controlled China and the pro-Soviet factions in French Indochina, Malaya and Burma."[165] Australian appreciation of the Soviet threat now aligned with the assessments of the U.S. and British intelligence communities. Indeed, there was growing cooperation between all three states.[166] Preventing Communist domination of Southeast Asia was now emerging as a major strategic ambition of Australian foreign policy.

Given the relative power differences between Australia and the Soviet Union, it was only natural that Canberra would look for multilateral solutions to its strategic dilemma. One solution was to establish some sort of Asia-Pacific security pact with which to bring both the United Kingdom and United States together in defense of the region. Australian diplomacy consequently centered on creating this new organization with Chifley pressing both his British and U.S. counterparts to formulate a comprehensive strategy for maintaining Asia-Pacific security. Such calls, however, fell on deaf ears. Both the Attlee and Truman administrations argued that they did not have the resources to enter such an Asia-Pacific security alliance. More to the point, as London and Washington stressed, they had accorded strategic prioritization to Europe and the Middle East. Such insights provide a subtle challenge to the existing interpretations concerning the nature of Chifley's foreign policy. While often skeptical about the dangers posed by Communism, and often assuming positions that London and Washington deemed unhelpful, his actions nevertheless drew Australia into the Cold War. Thus, the coming to power of the Menzies government does not signify the beginning of Australia's Cold War as often suggested.[167]

New Zealand

New Zealand's experience of World War II was in many ways unique among the Western powers.[168] The country never endured attacks on its home islands, and its air and ground forces were overwhelmingly committed to the European and Mediterranean theaters respectively; only the Royal New Zealand Navy committed the bulk of its strength to operations in the Pacific. Postwar calculations indicated that the ratio of killed per million of population was the highest of any country in the British Commonwealth.[169]

Japan's invasion of Southeast Asia and the subsequent collapse of British forces in Singapore in 1942 sent a shockwave throughout the country, which would go on to experience an invasion scare later that same year. New Zealand's worries were understandable, but Japan had never seriously considered an invasion at that stage of the war. Still, New Zealand warmly welcomed support from the United States against the Japanese. Some 100,000 U.S. troops would arrive between 1942 and 1944, and New Zealand became a base of operations for U.S. forces fighting in the Solomon Islands campaign of 1942–43. These experiences demonstrated the importance for New Zealand of securing a military alliance with the United States in the postwar period.

New Zealand's postwar economic fortunes also represented somewhat of a contrast to Australian growth and British relative decline. Growth rates remained consistent with those of the prewar period, although the country faced ongoing balance of payments difficulties.[170] New Zealand remained a relatively wealthy country. The war actually helped stave off a potential default to external creditors in 1939 and ultimately reduced national debt ratios dramatically.[171] The government had funded its war effort via a mix of taxation, spending controls, and rationing. The consequence, however, was a fall in the terms of trade during the war years. Import costs rose but there was limited adjustment in the prices of goods sold to Britain. The country still depended on export industries to supply equipment and materials needed for an increasing population with high living standards. As such, New Zealand remained committed to existing trade practices established with the United Kingdom and the British Commonwealth. Cooperation was also motivated by concerns regarding the growing economic importance of the United States and its influence over international finance.[172]

Despite this strategic and economic context, New Zealand demonstrated increasing independence in foreign and security policy. In contrast to its entry into World War I, for instance, New Zealand independently declared war on Germany on September 3, 1939. Australia instead accepted that the king's declaration of war applied to all of the Dominions. The decision between the United Kingdom and the United States to seek the unconditional surrender of Japan and the eventual public articulation of this in the form of the Cairo Declaration in December 1943 was a further case in point. Throughout 1942 and 1943, Wellington, as well as Canberra, demanded that London consult them on how to best wage the war against Japan.[173]

New Zealand increasingly enjoyed strategic independence in the postwar world.[174] The ratification of the Statute of Westminster into law in 1947 allowed the self-governing Dominions of the British Commonwealth to exercise their foreign policies independently of the United Kingdom. New Zealand soon exercised its independence over the question of a Japanese peace treaty. Although the eventual defeat of Japan allayed many immediate security concerns in Wellington, the onset of the Cold War and U.S. efforts to reindustrialize Japan stirred anxieties about a resurgent rival in the region. New Zealand, as an independent signatory to the Japanese instruments of surrender, resisted the idea of a lenient Japanese peace settlement.[175]

Given the inadequate security commitments to the Asia-Pacific region provided by the United States or the United Kingdom, New Zealand policymakers believed that the continued occupation of Japan was essential for regional security so as to prevent a repetition of the military disasters of 1941–42. The brutality with which the Japanese military conducted itself toward Allied troops operating in the Pacific theater, especially toward prisoners of war, only magnified these concerns. Policymakers and the public in New Zealand were strongly opposed to the reindustrialization of Japan without adequate economic and security safeguards in place.[176] Strategic concerns coupled with domestic pressure help explain why successive New Zealand governments placed the future of Japan at the forefront of their thinking.

The New Zealand Department of External Affairs (DEA) summarized its position clearly: "The history of Japanese preparations for aggression, the evidence that militarist projects won almost unanimous support of Japanese politicians, businessmen and workers, and the record of Japanese atrocities upon uniformed soldiers and defenseless civilians, makes it imperative that our primary aim should be to impose the most rigorous security control upon Japan."[177] The DEA held little hope for cooperation between these two different countries: "The lesson that we must draw from our experience is that no action we might take is in itself likely to make the Japanese feel goodwill for us, and any trust we put in Japanese promises or good faith or peaceful intentions is likely to prove misplaced."[178] Yet recent events provide only a partial explanation for anxiety about a resurgent Japan. Underlying New Zealand's attitude to Japan and the wider Asia-Pacific, and much in keeping with Australia, Britain, and the United States, was a sense of cultural superiority, deeply embedded in the national consciousness through more than a century of imperialism, comparative prosperity, and racial exclusiveness.[179]

The concept of a broad Asian security pact remained unappealing to New Zealand.[180] In July 1948, London had informed Wellington of its intention to establish under the United Nations Charter a series of regional pacts that would provide a global system of collective security.[181] New Zealand's prime minister Peter Fraser was clear that he did not envisage how this would act as a solution to New Zealand's security concerns. In the same month he said, "Any regional association intended to include New Zealand should consist of countries having full confidence in one another, as is happily the case with those northern powers. . . . There are countries in Asia with which our relations, though we hope they will always be friendly, cannot be expected to have the intimate character necessary for a genuine security grouping."[182] Fraser's clear preference was for an alliance with the Western powers in the region. "In order that a regional association might effectively contribute to our security," he concluded, "it should in our view comprise the United Kingdom, the United States, Australia, ourselves and only such other countries having interests in the Pacific area as may seem to us (and we to them) deserving of full confidence."[183] Attlee informed Fraser that a Pacific pact would "develop" but, crucially, only if the "need arose," which the British prime minister suggested it would not for the time being.[184]

In addition to disagreements about security planning between New Zealand and the United Kingdom in the Asia-Pacific, there were also subtle but important strategic tensions between Australia and New Zealand. Fraser and his foreign minister, Alister McIntosh, shared concerns that Australia's growing power would force New Zealand into assuming strategic policies that did not support its best interests. As the New Zealand high commissioner in London warned: "Australia [has] just come of age and throwing her weight about and likely to get us into more trouble than she gets us out of."[185] Fraser also took great personal delight in pursing opposite policies to Australia at times, so that Wellington could "embarrass" Canberra.[186] The antipodean powers were evidently not always united on security issues.

It would nevertheless be a mistake to exaggerate Wellington's differences with Canberra, London, or Washington. Maintaining close cooperation with these Western powers remained the central objective of New Zealand security policy. New Zealand policymakers, often in contrast to their antipodean neighbors, were largely in agreement with U.S. and British interpretations of the dangers posed to Western interests by the Soviet Union. New Zealand's relative economic and military weakness meant that it remained reliant on existing security arrangements with both the United Kingdom and Australia if it was to assure its security vis-à-vis the revival of Japanese or Asian militarism, the latter in the guise of Soviet-sponsored Communist threats.[187] In addition, New Zealand's policymakers were aware that the country's economic vitality relied on continued access to British Commonwealth markets. Good relations with the United Kingdom were thus crucial for New Zealand's economic prosperity and future security.[188] As one New Zealand official noted, New Zealand was "tied to the coat-tails of Britain and

Australia."[189] New Zealand policymakers were also increasingly concerned about the superpowers' growing influence on the global stage. The British Commonwealth needed to be strengthened so that it could stand on par with both the United States and Soviet Union and thus safeguard New Zealand's long-term security and economic interests.

As New Zealand's Joint Planning Committee observed in May 1947: "The strategic interests of New Zealand in the Pacific area cannot be disassociated from those of the British Commonwealth since N[ew] Z[ealand] is not an independent entity in affairs of world security. She could not, if standing alone, defend herself against a major invasion, nor unaided keep open those sea communications upon which her vital export trade depends."[190] New Zealand policymakers believed that the antipodean powers would have to accept a greater burden of providing for regional security in the postwar world. As noted in discussion with Australian security planners, "Both Australia and New Zealand were in agreement that the Dominions would have to afford more assistance for Commonwealth defence than in the past."[191]

New Zealand sought the centralization of foreign policy and strategic planning alongside the pooling of resources to ensure its long-term security, but other members of the Commonwealth opposed increased levels of coordination and cooperation.[192] Given the lack of common British Commonwealth strategy, New Zealand remained reliant on the United Kingdom's security guarantee despite reservations about its effectiveness.[193] Wellington was keen to retain close ties with London and there were few viable alternatives, especially as the framework of a truly global organization that could arbitrate international disputes failed to materialize due to the escalation of the Cold War. Ultimately, the Fraser government concluded that "until the United Nations could be made effective, the Commonwealth would have to seek self-defence through traditional means."[194]

Ongoing cooperation came at a cost. The United Kingdom requested that New Zealand continue to commit military forces to the defense of the Middle East. The United Kingdom, the traditional protector of Australia and New Zealand, saw the "front line" in any global war involving the Soviet Union as existing in the Middle East and Europe.[195] The British Chiefs of Staff accepted that New Zealand should ensure its own defense first, but in the absence of any serious threats, the bulk of the army and air force should be sent to the Middle East in war, while the navy would guard the sea routes. British requests exceeded the size of New Zealand forces at the time. The Labour government of Peter Fraser, as well as the successor national government of Sidney Holland that took office in December 1949, were nevertheless willing to meet these requirements. Both of New Zealand's major political parties stressed the importance of good relations with Britain and the Commonwealth throughout the early Cold War.[196]

New Zealand was eager to retain close ties with the United Kingdom but also identified most imperial interests as its own. Much of the country was suspicious of perceived attempts by Australia, Canada, and South Africa to weaken the bonds of empire.[197] New Zealand committed significant resources to the defense of the Middle East, which included the introduction of compulsory peace-term military service following a referendum in early 1949 and an agreement to dispatch forces within seventy days.[198] As Ian McGibbon has noted, "The attention of all three [military] services was inevitably focused on the Middle East."[199] Policymakers in New Zealand believed that Australia's focus on the ANZAM region did not necessarily better promote their interests than committing to the Middle East.[200] As noted by senior New Zealand officials, the vital theater of operations would be in the Middle East, Mediterranean, and Western Europe in the event of a global war. In essence, New Zealand policy planners agreed with British assumptions about the strategic importance of the Middle East and were prepared to provide the necessary assistance for helping to maintain British Commonwealth interests in these areas.[201]

New Zealand's security relationship with the United States was patchy in the absence of any formal mechanisms for the exchange of military information, joint planning, or staff talks.[202] As Fraser candidly admitted, onlookers could hardly expect his country to compel the United States to enter a security alliance with New Zealand. Australian efforts to convince the Truman administration to do just that had proven unsuccessful. If Canberra could not extract improved security cooperation with Washington, then Wellington was unlikely to fare any better.[203] The United States was simply uninterested in entering either a bilateral or a trilateral security pact at that time. Consequently, New Zealand was fully committed to maintaining its existing security cooperation with the United Kingdom via expensive commitments to the Middle East and Mediterranean.[204]

Nevertheless, New Zealand remained interested in forging a security relationship with the United States. A U.S. State Department assessment of antipodean defense policy ably captures this shift. "The impact of the war," the document stressed, "has brought an awareness of the strategic dependence of New Zealand and Australia upon the U.S. for defense in the Pacific and of the importance of maintaining close and friendly relations with the U.S. and furthering cooperation between the two countries in matters connected with the Pacific area."[205] A Pacific security pact thus became a pressing concern. New Zealand's position on the matter was clear by August 1949:

"Our main objective in considering a Pacific Pact is to strengthen United States interest and commitments in the Pacific and to obtain American aid for New Zealand and also (since we are so closely bound together) for Australia. The only moves we should make in the direction of a pact should therefore be with this end in view."[206]

The end of World War II revealed, and in some cases intensified, tensions and misunderstandings between the United States, United Kingdom, Australia, and New Zealand. America now occupied Japan, one of its main prewar rivals to strategic hegemony of the Pacific, and the United Kingdom no longer had the resources to contest strategic leadership of the region. These powers had contested strategic leadership of the Pacific for the past five decades, but the competition was now over.[207] Washington and London's prioritization of the European and Middle Eastern theaters, however, meant that such geostrategic shifts remained secondary concerns at that time. In turn, Canberra and Wellington had to adjust to these new strategic realities. In the immediate postwar period, the United States, United Kingdom, Australia, and New Zealand held different ambitions throughout the wider region. Competing national interests would come to weaken and confuse their response to the rising Communist challenge in the Asia-Pacific.

CHAPTER 2

Crisis and Cooperation

The United States, United Kingdom, Australia, and New Zealand slowly developed elements of strategic cooperation in the Asia-Pacific region following crises in Malaya and Korea between 1948 and 1951. The extent of cooperation varied between states and rarely reflected purely strategic concerns. Whereas New Zealand supported the United Kingdom in the Malayan Emergency, the U.S. and Australia were initially far more cautious in offering assistance. Although the United Kingdom, Australia, and New Zealand did support the United States in the Korean War, their efforts also reflected attempts to build closer strategic relations, generate diplomatic capital, and restrain their superpower ally from escalating the conflict. In both instances, all four states held different assumptions about the causes and management of conflict. Divergent national interests therefore weakened a coherent and united response to the Communist challenge from the Western powers.

In this period, Australia and New Zealand grew increasingly concerned by the absence of a security pact with the United States to safeguard their interest against the spread of Communism in the Asia-Pacific. The rapidly changing international situation would slowly help lessen resistance within Washington to the idea of a Pacific security pact. Alongside growing East-West tensions, including crises in Berlin and the surprise emergence of Soviet atomic power, U.S. concerns about the future of the Asia-Pacific also began to grow. The United States' "loss" of China, which took place between events in Malaya and Korea and resulted in more than 500 million people being firmly placed in the Communist camp, fueled fears that Communism was on the march.[1] When viewed together, events in Malaya, China, and Korea help explain progress toward closer cooperation throughout the Asia-Pacific.

These concerns, however, proved insufficient to secure formal strategic cooperation between the Western powers. Despite these challenges in the region, and in contrast to the creation of NATO in 1949, the British and U.S. governments remained reluctant to enter into any formal Asia-Pacific security pact despite ongoing requests from Australia and New Zealand. Economic concerns about the ongoing costs of the Cold War, alongside doubts about the comparative strategic importance of the region, repeatedly undermined such ambitions throughout this period.

Malaya

British policymakers had afforded strategic priority to their interests in the Middle East and Europe following the end of World War II. Nevertheless, the potential Communist threat in the Asia-Pacific helped refocus their attention on the region. Although London assumed that the economic weakness of the Soviet Union would delay an attack on Western Europe until at least the mid-1950s, security planners believed that Soviet interference globally would persist and continue to damage their national interests. Moscow would likely view the Asia-Pacific region as a "soft" target given its relative unpreparedness in relation to, say, Western Europe. Of particular concern was Indochina, where French forces were engaged in a desperate struggle to retain political authority against the indigenous nationalist revolutionary group, the Viet Minh. The success of Communist-nationalist groups could encourage similar uprisings in other colonial territories thereby threatening British strategic and commercial interests. Moreover, according to the British Joint Intelligence Committee (JIC), the Viet Minh's success in Indochina could spread across into Siam, Malaya, and Singapore. British security planners evidently subscribed to elements of what later became known as domino theory, a concept that would dominate U.S. strategic planning.[2] Given the United Kingdom's vast territorial holdings throughout Asia and Africa, such nationalist uprisings were most unwelcome. Thus, the British had initially supported French efforts to quell the Viet Minh in 1946 by providing much of the necessary logistical and political support.[3]

A combination of strategic and commercial concerns led the United Kingdom to become involved in fighting the Communist-backed insurgency inside Malaya. The Malayan Emergency of 1948, which developed into a lengthy guerrilla war fought between British Commonwealth armed forces and the military arm of the Malayan Communist Party, stoked suspicions about the Soviet Union's global intentions. London believed that the Malayan National Liberation Army was a puppet of Moscow.[4] A decision to put down the rebellion inside Malaya therefore held broader strategic consequences as the British government would now have to commit its entire military reserve stationed in the Far East theater as well as an additional brigade from the United Kingdom itself to manage this emergency. Fighting an insurgency inside Malaya with such resources would leave areas such as Hong Kong and Borneo lightly defended as well as reducing its European resources.[5] As the JIC warned, "The Communist attack in Malaya is thus of far more than local importance."[6]

The British government did not initially request assistance from the United States, Australia, New Zealand, or its other Commonwealth allies.[7] Unilateral action in 1948 is curious on first inspection. Although Washington did not appear to have taken a direct interest in Malaya, believing it was the British Commonwealth's responsibility, the insurgency assumed a high priority inside the halls of powers in Canberra and Wellington. Both remained committed to defending the British Commonwealth, and the Australia, New Zealand, and Malaya (ANZAM) understanding with the United Kingdom underlined antipodean interest in cooperation. The level of importance attached to Malaya by Australian security planners was especially high given its strategic significance during World War II. Japanese forces had struck the Malayan port of Kota Baharu several hours before the attack on Pearl Harbor in 1941. When Malaya eventually fell, the Japanese air force was able to launch attacks against the Australian mainland. For Australia, keeping Malaya out of enemy hands was a top priority.[8] Security planners were concerned that if the Communists took power inside Malaya it would produce a domino-like effect southward. In addition, as the Australian Chiefs of Staff reasoned, "By virtue of her geographical position, Australia should assume increased responsibilities in British Commonwealth matters in the Indian Ocean, South East Asia and the Pacific."[9]

The United Kingdom's decision not to seek immediate assistance from Australia and New Zealand is nevertheless understandable. The explanation rests on a mixture of British confidence in being able to defeat the insurgency alone and wider geostrategic considerations. If the United Kingdom requested significant support for operations inside Malaya, it could damage the chances of convincing Australia to follow New Zealand's lead and commit to the defense of the Middle East in the event of a global war. The United

Kingdom therefore had to demonstrate to Australia that it could provide the type of local security assurances with which Australian policymakers were now increasingly concerned.[10]

By early 1949, events in Malaya encouraged a change of opinion in London. The situation steadily worsened as Communist attacks against areas of economic significance increased in scale and frequency. British policymakers now deemed the benefits of support from Australia and New Zealand to outweigh any negative ramifications.[11] British officials thus made discreet overtures to determine whether Australia and New Zealand would dispatch forces to Malaya. The response from Canberra and Wellington was markedly different. Fraser responded positively to the British request due to his government's commitment to check Communist expansion in the region. New Zealand would go on to support and serve in emergency operations from 1949 onward, just as it would be a founding contributor of troops, aircraft, and ships to the British Commonwealth Far East Strategic Reserve based in Singapore a few years later.[12]

The Australian government was less supportive. As Chifley quietly informed London, if forces were requested to fight in Malaya, his government would "feel obliged to decline." The British government therefore issued no request for Australian assistance.[13] Despite the clear strategic case for intervention, Chifley faced increasing pressure from the left wing of his Labour Party to pursue a foreign policy that focused on the promotion of international justice rather than the challenge of international Communism. He was consequently reluctant to engage in military action that others could construe as directed not at the forces of international Communism but at an indigenous people that had a legitimate right to self-government. This was how the left wing of the ruling Labour government depicted British action, and Chifley, given his growing problems managing the party, had no desire to fuel such criticisms.[14]

In contrast to Australia's subdued response, the U.S. met British requests for assistance rather more positively. While U.S. security planners remained reluctant to become directly involved in events inside Malaya, and had been initially unwilling to provide arms for the British, they soon recognized that the United Kingdom was resisting forces that also opposed U.S. interests.[15] If the British were to lose control of Malaya they would subsequently lose its dollar earnings, which the United States believed would hurt Britain's capacity to maintain its existing defense commitments for Europe and the Middle East. In addition, the consequent impact to strategic materials and balance of payment positions of the NATO countries could result in a serious setback for any rearmament program inside Europe.[16] It was because of these broader strategic considerations that the Truman administration would eventually approve additional arms supplies to British forces and made available logistical support for British operations inside Malaya during the summer of 1949. U.S. assistance for British efforts in Malaya would steadily grow throughout the remaining years of Truman's presidency.[17]

The election of Robert Menzies and his Liberal Party in December 1949 brought about a clear shift in Australian policy, reflecting the values of the conservative center Right that sympathized with U.S. foreign policy. Menzies had talked openly about wishing to defeat Communism inside Australia during the general election. Soon after taking office, the Australian prime minister honored his electoral promises by seeking to pass legislation that would ban the Communist Party from Australian politics. Menzies also stated publicly that it was imperative for Australia to improve the strength of the British Commonwealth so that it could adequately face the threat posed by the Soviet Union. This was welcome news in London, not least because the British government could potentially exploit the Australian prime minister's rhetoric for assistance in Malaya and in underpinning its security interests in the Middle East.[18] Although Menzies was keen to improve defense preparation and fit into U.S. and UK strategic planning, his economic policies were less complementary to British interests. The Australian prime minister sought to forge a new economic relationship with the United States, which he believed would facilitate rapid economic development and thereby allow greater defense preparations.[19]

In April 1950, appreciating the changing political climate in Canberra, London sent a formal request to the Australian government to provide military assistance for their ongoing campaign inside Malaya. The request was limited to the provision of a small number of aircraft. Although a modest appeal, the United Kingdom was critically short of the relevant aircraft needed to execute its campaign inside Malaya and felt that Canberra could provide such support without diverting Australian attention and resources away from areas of greater strategic importance, namely the Middle East. After deliberating on the request, the Menzies government approved the deployment of Royal Australian Air Force (RAAF) transport aircraft and Lincoln bombers to Singapore in June 1950 to begin immediate operations.[20] In addition to highlighting Menzies's commitment to resisting Communism, helping in Malaya also deflected criticism away from Australia's decision to withdraw from the British Commonwealth force stationed in Japan.[21] Having received this positive reaction from Canberra, British officials hoped that they could soon secure a broader commitment from the Menzies government to commit forces to the defense of the Middle East in the event of a war with the Soviet Union.[22]

Political changes had also taken place in New Zealand. The narrow victory of Sidney Holland in the election of November 1949 brought the National Party to power by the end of the year.[23] The new government saw no reason to change the orientation of its predecessor's efforts in Malaya or the Middle East, which had fashioned a defense policy that incorporated its forces into a collective Commonwealth defense system.[24] Nevertheless, New Zealand's already significant commitments continued to grow. Wellington had agreed to commit a division and five air squadrons to the Middle East in event of a war with the Soviet Union despite the costs involved.[25] London, as well as Washington, believed that New Zealand's commitment to deploying forces to the Middle East was vital if the British were to maintain their position there in the event of war.[26] This commitment was significant from New Zealand's perspective as it would involve the deployment of the vast majority of the country's armed forces, leaving little for home defense.[27] Although Holland sought to restore stability and sound finance by reducing government expenditure and borrowing, the country's relatively healthy financial position allowed for extra spending on defense.[28] Nevertheless, the government could only make the promised military commitments by greatly increasing its manpower and material resources. Such commitments were expensive. By financial year 1952–53, the country spent some £107 million on defense, which accounted for the same amount it spent on state housing, education, and major energy infrastructure projects.[29]

By the middle of 1950, all four Western powers were cooperating on military operations inside Southeast Asia. Such cooperation represents a subtle challenge to the extant Cold War historiography, which tends to assume that Mao's ascension to power in China was the catalyst for all four powers to take Asia-Pacific security more seriously.[30] The Malayan Emergency nevertheless highlighted the difficulty of cooperation in the early Cold War period. Convergent perceptions of threat and overlapping national interests did lead to eventual cooperation but it was often limited and contingent.

Menzies and his cabinet were still concerned that a British failure in Malaya would precipitate a domino-like effect throughout the Asia-Pacific, bringing the Communist menace closer to Australian shores. Some in the Australian cabinet believed that the insurgency inside Malaya heralded the PRC's intention to expand throughout the rest of Southeast Asia. A Communist-sponsored success in Malaya seemed to parallel how Japan had taken over Manchuria in 1931. A forward defense was therefore preferable to waiting until the problem intensified. The Australian government also calculated that if it refused this formal request for military assistance then it would hardly encourage the British to accept the Australian case for establishing a broader Pacific defense pact. If Australia wanted to argue that it could commit to a broader security arrangement, it would have to demonstrate that it could effectively deal with localized security problems. Australia's commitment to Malaya was therefore an important element in its broader strategic ambitions in the region and not merely a response to the Communist threat.[31]

Racial considerations also informed the decision-making process for both antipodean powers in Malaya. David Lowe suggests that the long-held fear of the "yellow peril" clearly influenced Australian ministers. The recent Communist incarnation was but the latest threat posed by this perceived "Asian expansion."[32] Ideas about race were even more pronounced inside New Zealand policy-making circles. Ian McGibbon has noted that "underlying New Zealand's attitude to Asia and Asians was a sense of racial superiority, deeply embedded in the national consciousness through more than a century of perceiving that part of the world throughout imperialist lenses."[33] The archives help substantiate these claims. In a long and detailed memorandum, the New Zealand Ministry of External Affairs (MEA) explained that one of its "primary and vital objectives of our Pacific policy," was "to protect ourselves from the threat of Asian racial expansion."[34] Fears about expansionism, especially from Asian states no longer under European rule, were never the determining forces behind Australian or New Zealand foreign or security policy. Ideas about Asian states, race, and colonialism informed but rarely drove the development of foreign policy.[35] The aforementioned memorandum noted that cooperation with Asian countries should not undermine the country's security interests, especially strengthening U.S. commitments throughout the Asia-Pacific or helping to obtain U.S. aid for New Zealand and Australia. Any agreements, however, should be "as vague and harmless as possible."[36]

The Malayan Emergency, which would continue until 1960, highlighted the limitations of British postwar power. The United Kingdom had been unable to quell the rising challenge to its position inside Malaya and had to seek the assistance of its British Commonwealth allies. Australia and New Zealand came to recognize that Britain's diminished power in the region had serious implications for their own security interests. Both the Menzies and Holland governments would thus redouble their efforts at obtaining a pact with the United States to buttress their own security. As one report for the New Zealand prime minister noted, "Our main objective in considering a Pacific Pact is to strengthen United States interest and commitments in the Pacific and to obtain American aid for New Zealand and also (since we are so closely bound together) for Australia. The only moves we should make in the direction of a pact should therefore be with this end in view."[37] Antipodean appeals would gradually find a more receptive audience as the threat of Communist expansion throughout the Asia-Pacific appeared to grow.

China

Between the onset of crises in Malaya and Korea was the emergence of Communist China in 1949. This geopolitical shift would encourage the United States, Britain, Australia, and New Zealand to cooperate more closely to check the expansion of the Communist threat. Nevertheless, cooperation between all four powers remained limited. With the ejection of Japan from China in 1945, the problems facing the Chinese government escalated as an increasingly violent civil war between the Nationalist government's forces, led by Chiang Kai-shek's Kuomintang (KMT), and the Communist Party of China (CPC), led by Mao Ze-dong, raged on. Most observers had not deemed Mao the likely victor in the Chinese Civil War. Even Stalin had not thought much of his fellow Communist's chances and provided limited assistance to the CPC's cause. By early 1948, however, the CPC seized control of the northeast portion of the country, which resulted in the surrender of the New First Army of the Kuomintang.[38]

The U.S. government had experienced a difficult relationship with China during World War II and its immediate aftermath. Officials viewed Chiang Kai-shek as a problematic associate given his authoritarian and often repressive rule.[39] Strategic calculations nevertheless overcame such concerns as the alternative was a Communist China that U.S. policymakers believed had the potential to "tip the balance" in favor of the Soviet Union in the Cold War.[40] A Sino-Soviet alliance was, according to Julian Zelizer, the "worst nightmare" for policymakers in Washington.[41] As an interdepartmentally agreed intelligence assessment noted, the strategic importance of China was manifold and considerable because the "spread of Soviet influence and power would be inimical to United States strategic interests. A non-friendly China would allow the Soviet Union to place air bases in a region which would allow it to conduct neutralizing attacks against U.S. forces in Japan, the Ryukyus, and the Philippines."[42]

In the minds of Washington's policymakers, this nightmare was now turning into a reality. Sources in China warned the Truman administration in September 1947 that "the Soviet Union is proceeding, slowly and circumspectly, towards eventual domination of China."[43] Reports supplied to Washington in the following year were just as gloomy, predicting a defeat for the

Nationalist forces inside China.[44] The Truman administration assigned Secretary of State Marshall the task of negotiating a ceasefire to the Chinese Civil War. Under Marshall's leadership, the United States opted not to engage militarily and accepted that saving the Nationalist government was no longer possible.[45] Yet the Truman administration still sought a "friendly China" that would not be utilized as "an instrument of Soviet policy."[46]

After sustained fighting between April and September 1948, the KMT endured further heavy losses, and the CPC gained control of the majority of central China. With Chiang's forces broken, Nationalist defeat was now all but assured. The Pingjin Campaign, which ran between November 21, 1948, and January 31, 1949, removed any doubts about the future of China. The campaign proved catastrophic for the KMT as the remaining backbone of its fighting forces were killed, wounded, or captured during the fighting. A series of tactical retreats served only to delay inevitable defeat, and the KMT eventually took refuge on the island of Formosa (modern-day Taiwan) as Mao assumed control of mainland China.[47]

U.S. hopes of sustaining "friendly relations" with China were disappointed as Mao swiftly emerged as a committed Communist revolutionary. In December 1949, Mao visited Stalin in Moscow. Despite their difficult relationship, there followed the signature of the Sino-Soviet Treaty on February 14, 1950.[48] Domestic criticism of the Truman administration quickly followed as Republican opponents demanded an answer to the question "Who lost China?"[49] Truman's political opponents certainly looked to exploit what they believed was a U.S. foreign policy failure. As John Foster Dulles, a leading Republican spokesperson on foreign policy as well as a consultant to the secretary of state, wrote in 1950, "China with its population of about 450,000,000 has already come almost wholly under a rule which takes its guidance from Moscow. In Asia and the Pacific there are about 600,000,000 more people whom Soviet Communism does not yet dominate, but whom it has a good chance of dominating. If it should win this further area, or any substantial part of it, Soviet Communism would control considerably more than half of the total population of the world."[50] Senator Joseph McCarthy alleged that the explanation for U.S. diplomatic failure lay in the fact that Communist spies and subversive elements had infiltrated the U.S. government. McCarthy ratcheted up both his rhetoric and his investigations into subversives and Communist penetration of the U.S. government, even going as far as to suggest that George Marshall had designed his arbitration efforts in China to fail because he was in fact a Communist agent.[51] After meeting with two senior Republican senators, William Knowland and Alexander Smith, Dean Acheson was left in no doubt that the Republican Party blamed the Truman administration's "spirit of defeatism" for the "loss" of China.[52]

There was also growing alarm in Washington about the threat posed to the United States throughout the Asia-Pacific by Communist-backed forces, especially given U.S. weakness in the region. As Charles B. Deane, a Democrat in the House of Representatives, wrote to the president, "The United States is not prepared to meet a serious emergency in the Far East and the Pacific."[53] Deane had a point. After World War II, the United States had rapidly demobilized and cut back its defense expenditure, and was consequently ill-equipped to deal with such challenges.[54] Following Communist success in China, the takeover of Czechoslovakia in 1948, and the crises in Berlin of 1948–49, Washington saw Soviet-backed Communism as on the march. Assessments in Washington suggested that the "USSR has an overwhelming preponderance of immediately available military power on the Eurasian continent and a consequent ability to resort to war at any time as a means of imposing its will in that area."[55] In the eyes of Washington's policymakers, coupled with the revelation that the Soviet Union had exploded its first atomic bomb in August 1949, Communism was not only growing more powerful but was now spreading rapidly around the globe.[56]

A mixture of domestic-political and strategic concerns therefore encouraged the Truman administration to respond to Mao's victory in China in a strong fashion. The United States' refusal to recognize the PRC was the first indication of this hardening in U.S. policy.[57] The rhetoric emanating from the Truman administration reflected the decision to pursue a firmer line vis-à-vis the Communist powers and to be seen publicly pursuing such a course. Acheson, for example, gave a series of speeches throughout the first half of 1950, in which he lambasted both Soviet and Chinese global policies. During one such speech, Acheson noted that "we are faced with a system which denies the basis to our modern civilization, the belief in freedom, and that those who hold to the Soviet doctrine have picked out this country as their chief target. . . . [They seek] to change the balance of productive power in the world in their favor."[58] Policymakers in Washington now sought to devise firmer policies to respond to these altered international circumstances. The president's advisers provided him with a solution in the form of NSC-68.[59] This placed a much greater emphasis on the United States' military prowess. Public opinion and congressional pressure had encouraged the president to take a bolder approach to the perceived Communist threat.[60]

Across the Atlantic, Mao's rise to power also deeply concerned British policymakers. The UK's relationship with China was complex, but many British officials believed that U.S. support for the KMT had been ill-judged.[61] While they had limited enthusiasm for Chiang, there was far less respect for his successor. Early evidence that Mao would create considerable problems for British interests surfaced during the Amethyst crisis when Chinese Communist forces fired on a Royal Navy warship as it protected the British Embassy in Nanking in 1949. A rescue effort by HMS *London* saw it too come under fire, resulting in 125 casualties. Although subsequently blocked from sailing away, HMS *Amethyst* eventually managed to break out from port under Communist fire.[62] Direct military provocation aside, London feared that Mao's revolutionary ambitions would not be limited to mainland China and that he would seek to export his revolution throughout the rest of the Asia-Pacific. The British JIC, for instance, concluded that without preventative action and substantial material support, the countries of Southeast Asia might fall under Communist control by the mid-1950s. "Should Siam fall," the report concluded, "a land threat to Singapore will develop. Should Burma fall it is likely that India would be so re-occupied."[63] Senior elements within the British government shared these concerns and were early advocates of the domino theory that would become a motif of U.S. grand strategy later in the decade.

The British government nevertheless decided to recognize Mao's Communist China on January 6, 1950, and applied pressure on Australia and New Zealand to do likewise, even in the face of considerable criticism from the United States.[64] This decision partially reflected growing concerns about the future of Hong Kong, which Bevin informed Acheson had assumed a position of "vital" importance, akin to that of Berlin for U.S. strategists.[65] Although Hong Kong was not of strategic significance per se, its loss would signal to Britain's adversaries that the United Kingdom was not capable of maintaining its global interests, which could subsequently encourage further aggression. Hong Kong also represented an important link to China and an emerging center for regional and global trade.[66]

In the months preceding the decision to recognize China, it gradually dawned on British policymakers that with the limited military resources now at their disposal it would be impossible to safeguard Hong Kong in the face of a Chinese Communist invasion.[67] London consequently concluded that its garrison required reinforcements.[68] The British government made tentative approaches about reinforcing the Hong Kong garrison to several Commonwealth powers, but all met with limited enthusiasm. Representative of such feeling was Chifley's warning to Attlee that reinforcing the Hong Kong garrison would needlessly antagonize Communist China and actually increase the likelihood of confrontation. Evatt informed the British government that it would do better by reaching an accommodation with Mao that respected the sovereignty of Hong Kong.[69] After months of deliberation, and an absence of viable alternatives, London decided that some sort of accommodation with Mao's China was essential if they were to retain Hong Kong. The British would officially recognize Mao's rule and, in return, Mao would agree to leave Hong Kong in British hands. In order for this policy to work, a degree of mutual toleration with Communist China became essential.[70]

Australia and New Zealand looked at developments inside China and their ramifications for national security closely. Mao's success only reinforced earlier antipodean assessments about the necessity of securing a formal security pact with the United States, as no other power was capable of resisting Communist expansion into the Asia-Pacific. The form of any such alliance remained unclear. An alliance with Washington could function on a tripartite basis or include British membership in the form of some sort of Pacific security pact. This latter option was preferable because it would create an alliance with two stronger powers thereby complementing existing security arrangements between London, Canberra, and Wellington and providing greater material support in defense of the Asia-Pacific region. Regardless of its final formation, Australian and New Zealand policymakers were clear that they wanted a formal security alliance with the United States.[71]

Early efforts by Australia and New Zealand to convince the U.S. to create such a Pacific security pact proved unsuccessful. The Truman administration had fought tremendously hard to pass the necessary legislation to ensure the creation of the NATO alliance and the National Security Act. Such legislation challenged the United States' historical aversion to binding alliances and generated considerable concerns about the power of the federal government.[72] Critics alleged that NATO would be the first of many "entangling alliances" into which the president would enter. Truman, already under considerable domestic pressure for his alleged foreign policy failures, wished to avoid stoking further criticism by entering into any new security pact for the Asia-Pacific.[73] As Acheson informed the press, "I have taken pains to make clear on several occasions, the United States is not currently considering participation in any further special collective defense arrangements other than the North Atlantic Treaty."[74]

U.S. plans focused on resisting Soviet influence in Western Europe and ensuring a functioning and credible security alliance inside Europe. As the Joint Chiefs of Staff argued, peripheral issues should not distract the United States from its central objectives. Forming a European security pact and equipping it with substantial military resources was presently the top priority of U.S. national security policy.[75] Given the economic weakness of Europe, the U.S. would have to help finance the enormous additional costs of this newly emerging security alliance via deficit spending and tax increases. As was estimated at the time, the United States would have to spend close to $40 billion to create a force still heavily outnumbered by Soviet forces brandishing superior equipment.[76]

Assistance programs for Europe took their toll as the U.S. economy lurched into recession in fiscal year 1948–49.[77] The president was aware that there were limited funds with which the United States could uphold international security. The U.S. therefore prioritized the economic and military rebuilding of Western Europe and upholding Western influence throughout the Mediterranean and Middle East. While the Truman administration was committed to furnishing support "to help to strengthen the free nations of the non-Soviet world in their effort to resist Soviet-Communist aggression," such commitments required careful targeting.[78] The Asia-Pacific remained a secondary priority for the Truman administration. The "loss" of China was insufficient motivation to establish more formalized security cooperation with interested parties throughout the region. Tellingly, both Australia and New Zealand had been classed as an area "without priority" in late 1948.[79]

Although domestic-political and strategic-economic concerns explain most of the United States' reluctance to commit to a new Pacific security pact, broader ideological concerns also played a role. Communist propagandists claimed that the U.S. was a neo-imperialist power that supported European colonialism against the people of Asia, who strove for nationhood. Such accusations did not just emanate from the Kremlin. The prime minister of India, Jawaharlal Nehru, admonished the United States for its supposed neo-imperialism. U.S. policymakers were sensitive to such charges and sought a foreign policy that would retain support among the nonaligned states in the Cold War.[80] George Kennan warned that the Asia-Pacific was vulnerable to Communist expansion not least because the peoples of Asia were generally more sympathetic to the Communist ideology. As Kennan wrote, "Most peoples of area [Asia-Pacific] dangerously vulnerable to communist penetration by virtue of: (1) Political immaturity (2) General present state of flux and instability (3) Stubborn misconceptions about [W]estern nations, including ourselves arising out of past experiences with colonialism and imperialism."[81] Such stereotypes of the region ably demonstrate how racial and cultural assumptions influenced U.S. foreign policymaking and increased anxiety about any actions that might encourage Communist sympathies.[82]

U.S. reluctance to provide additional security commitments to Australia and New Zealand despite the "loss" of China encouraged both the Menzies and Holland governments to look at ways in which the United Kingdom could improve security cooperation throughout the entirety of the British Commonwealth. Of the two antipodean leaders, Menzies was the more enthusiastic about improving security provision in the region because he believed that London had prioritized the defense of the Middle East and Europe to the point that it was dangerously neglecting security in the Asia-Pacific. The United Kingdom retained military bases in Hong Kong and Singapore and was engaged in fighting a Communist insurgency inside Malaya. British troops still formed a part, though dwindling, of the Occupation Force stationed in Japan. In the opinion of Menzies, the Western powers in the Asia-Pacific should replicate the collective security efforts undertaken in Europe, such as the WEU and NATO, throughout the region. Many in the Australian government also viewed collective security defense arrangements in Europe as having the potential to undermine national security as the antipodeans states' principal allies focused their attentions elsewhere.[83]

Initial efforts by Canberra and Wellington to improve levels of security cooperation with London in the Asia-Pacific region soon encountered stiff opposition. In British estimations, antipodean security demands were both excessive and strategically misplaced. The British government was concerned that a Pacific security pact, especially one that could expand to include other Asian states, would divert valuable resources from European and Middle Eastern defense. Such thinking was clear in British planning for a global war as articulated in Plan SPEEDWAY, which served as the basis for joint U.S.-UK defense plans in the event of a war with the Soviet Union. The plan worked on the assumption that the Soviets would launch two major offensives into Western Europe and the Middle East, which would immediately throw the Western powers onto the defensive. The priority, then, was to deter Soviet aggression by improving the position of the Western powers in Europe and the Middle East. British efforts thus focused on securing British Commonwealth commitments to the defense of these regions. Antipodean ideas about creating a Pacific security pact were consequently discouraged.[84]

The United Kingdom, Australia, and New Zealand evidently held competing ideas about global security planning. These differing conceptions would clash at the Colombo Conference of Commonwealth ministers, held in Ceylon, modern-day Sri Lanka, in January 1950.[85] The conference was set to discuss a series of economic proposals tabled by the Indian ambassador to China, Kavalam Madhava Panikkar. Panikkar had argued for the creation of a multilateral fund to provide support for the economic development of countries throughout Asia. Events in Malaya and China only underlined the need for serious efforts to promote economic prosperity and thus fend off Communist expansion. During the conference, the attendees established a framework for encouraging such efforts. Canberra largely welcomed the idea because Percy Spender, the Australian minister for external affairs who was present at the conference, accepted the logic that development throughout Southeast Asia was essential to stop the region gravitating toward Communism and its promises of economic security.[86] British and New Zealand officials were far more cautious. London and Wellington feared that they would have to provide the majority of the money for such a fund at a time of serious financial strain.[87]

As the conference continued, British, Australian, and New Zealand concerns about global war planning came to a head. Given that New Zealand had already committed to the Middle East, Australia now became the focus of British diplomacy. Australia remained keen to avoid such commitments due to the risks of excessive military expenditure and limited resources for security needs closer to the mainland.[88] Spender argued forcefully that the United Kingdom's prioritization of the defense of Europe and the Middle East left the Asia-Pacific region vulnerable to Communist attack. Because the NATO alliance and cooperative economic forums ensured European security, the Soviet Union would be encouraged to look toward the Asia-Pacific for its global advances. Spender stressed that the British Commonwealth powers had to improve strategic cooperation for the defense of the region and needed to encourage the United States to establish a Pacific security pact of some kind if he was to consider the possibility of making any commitments to Middle Eastern security. Spender even went so far as to outline possible membership of this new organization, which would have to include the United States, New Zealand, Canada, and India.[89]

Ernest Bevin, the British foreign secretary, deflected such demands by arguing, albeit disingenuously, that it had been economic cooperation inside Europe that had thwarted a Communist takeover of power. The Organisation of European Economic Co-operation, rather than NATO, was the organization that they should thus seek to replicate throughout the Asia-Pacific.[90] Bevin was evidently prepared to downplay the severity of the challenge posed by the mixture of Communism, nationalism, anticolonialism, and Chinese militarism throughout the region. He instead wanted the British Commonwealth to focus its attention on the Middle Eastern and European theaters. Agreeing to support calls for a Pacific security pact would have potentially undermined security networks in Europe and the Middle East by diverting limited British Commonwealth resources. Australian and New Zealand interests in securing a Pacific security pact therefore remained a secondary concern for the British government.[91] In the absence of agreement, Australia would have to reconsider whether its commitments to the Middle East now served its own security interests better than concentrating on Southeast Asia.

Although the United States had not been directly involved in the negotiations in Colombo, U.S. assistance was of fundamental importance for any of the proposals to succeed. As a sign of the shifting power away from the United Kingdom in the region, Spender argued that whatever agreements they reached during the conference, all would require the full support of the United States.[92] The realities of the postwar world meant that the United Kingdom and the wider British Commonwealth no longer possessed the necessary material power to undertake such bold political-economic initiatives alone.

The Korean War

Events in Malaya and China had encouraged a greater degree of strategic collaboration between the United States, United Kingdom, Australia, and New Zealand, but formal security agreements were still absent. Events in Korea would help enhance cooperation.[93] On the morning of June 25, 1950, North Korean artillery covered a combined force of tank and infantry columns crossing the thirty-eighth parallel into South Korea. The North Korean invasion caught Western intelligence services by surprise. Acheson only first learned of the invasion by listening to a United Press news bulletin.[94] For Washington, such surprises invoked the memory of the Japanese attack at Pearl Harbor and reinforced preconceived ideas about the futility of appeasing dictatorships. Truman subsequently delivered a speech to the American people, damning North Korean actions: "I recalled some earlier instances: Manchuria, Ethiopia, Austria. I remembered how each time that the democracies failed to act, it had encouraged the aggressors to keep going ahead. Communism was acting in Korea just as Hitler, Mussolini and the Japanese had acted ten, fifteen and twenty years earlier."[95] Washington's policymakers largely agreed as to the ambition of the invaders: "The north Koreans are engaged in an all-out offensive to subjugate South Korea."[96]

Washington was nevertheless unclear as to whether local factors or the Soviet Union's desire to expand its interests throughout Asia drove the northern invasion. Some analysts even feared that the invasion was a diversion to disguise a Soviet attack on Western Europe. The conclusion reached by U.S. analysts, accurately, as the archives would reveal, was that the Soviet Union and PRC had sanctioned the North Korean invasion, which probably reflected a broader effort by Stalin to press Soviet influence into Asia. The Soviet Union was betting on the United States allowing Korea to become a "neutral" zone but was not seeking to engage the United States in a full-scale war.[97]

On the evening of June 25, Truman hurried back from a vacation in his home state of Missouri to meet with his national security team at Blair House in Washington. It was here that his gathered advisers decided on their response to events in Korea.[98] All present recommended a military reaction to the Northern invasion. Truman had already adopted the strategy of "symmetrical containment," whereby the United States would oppose Soviet threats with equal and opposite reactions wherever they were encountered. The overall objective was to "restrict communism within its existing borders, then let it destroy itself through internal corrosion and decay."[99] Reacting in a like-for-like fashion in Korea therefore accorded with the overarching strategic vision of the administration. The president's advisers all believed that a nonmilitary response would only encourage future Communist aggression, which would increase the likelihood of a global war. As General Omar Bradley, the chairmen of the JCS put it, "We must draw the line somewhere." The president concurred.[100]

Strategic competition provides only a partial explanation of the United States' decision to exercise military force in the defense of South Korea. Domestic-political pressure meant that a nonmilitary response would have been politically poisonous for a president that was already facing congressional and popular criticism about how he had "lost" China. On learning of the northern assault, Knowland told the Senate that "Korea today stands in the same position as did Manchuria, Ethiopia, Austria and Czechoslovakia of an earlier date. In each of those instances a firm stand by the law-abiding nations of the world might have saved the peace."[101] As Truman believed, the best way to refute allegations of appeasement was to take decisive action against transgressors of international law. The opinion of leading newspapers further encouraged the president to do something, with public opinion generally stressing the need to take a stand against this latest Communist threat.[102] Religious groups even weighed in on the debate. Billy Graham, the evangelical leader who had achieved celebrity status in 1949, chided the Truman administration for being "too soft" on Communism, which only invited further Communist aggression.[103] As the president had apparently informed Acheson on learning of the invasion, "We've got to stop the sons of bitches no matter what."[104] Truman subsequently authorized General Douglas MacArthur, the supreme commander for the Allied Powers in Japan, to immediately utilize available airpower against North Korean forces hindering the evacuation of civilians from the war zone and to support the resupply of ammunition to South Korean forces.[105]

Truman sought to obtain wider international support to legitimize a military response as well as to share the potentially heavy burden of war.

The U.S. government therefore looked toward the United Nations Security Council to authorize a UN effort to expel the northern forces from South Korea. International support was duly forthcoming. The Soviet Union, the one country that could have prevented the passing of a UN resolution by exercising its right of veto, happened to be boycotting the United Nations Security Council following differences concerning China's role in the organization. The United Nations Security Council authorized a "police action" inside Korea, which equated to the removal of North Korean forces from the south of the country.[106]

The British ambassador to the United Nations Sir Gladwyn Jebb had roundly condemned the invasion and voted in favor of the UN resolution.[107] In London, however, there was considerable disagreement within the cabinet about whether to support Western military action. For the British chancellor the exchequer, Stafford Cripps, the North's invasion of the south could not have come at a more inopportune time. Cripps had been determined to limit Britain's defense expenditure to safeguard the building of the welfare state and the recovery of the British economy. He consequently argued that remaining neutral would best serve the United Kingdom's interests. If a military response proved unavoidable, then the United Kingdom's contribution should be limited to utilizing its existing naval vessels already stationed in the region.[108]

Strategic imperatives, however, undermined economic caution. Anxiety about the Soviet threat and a fear that the United States might refocus its attentions away from Europe ultimately encouraged Cripps to authorize substantial increases in Britain's defense expenditure.[109] Despite the recent devaluation of the pound and accompanying deflationary measures that followed, Cripps proposed an increase in defense expenditure from £2,590 million over the next three years to £3,400 million. Attlee accepted the need for such a marked increase and the consequent restrictions on social spending this commitment would entail.[110]

Yet the British government's contributions to the war effort proved inadequate. Over the coming months, U.S. representatives expressed dissatisfaction with the level of British military assistance. On December 18, Attlee asked the cabinet for authorization to further increase defense expenditure, stressing the need to support their allies and protect the U.S.-UK partnership.[111] Following extensive discussions, the British cabinet concluded that "it was the clear duty of the United Kingdom Government to do everything in their power, in concert with other members of the United Nations, to help the South Koreans to resist this aggression."[112] The defense budget subsequently increased to £4,700 million in January 1951.

Attlee's decision would prove unpalatable for some within the cabinet as well as the wider Labour Party and led to the resignation of several ministers. Yet Attlee risked his own political fortunes for what he believed to be in the best national security interests of the United Kingdom. For both Attlee and Bevin, the northern invasion of South Korea had similar parallels to how Hitler had challenged the rule of international law in the 1930s. In their opinion, if the United Kingdom was to "appease" this blatant aggression of the North, then it would only encourage aggression from the Communist bloc in the future. Security concerns consequently swept aside political and economic considerations.[113]

Alliance considerations also influenced the prime minister's judgment. Attlee was convinced that without Britain there to "guide" the United States, overzealous U.S. actions could precipitate a global war against the Soviet Union. The British government was evidently determined to exercise "power by proxy," which had been a cornerstone of British grand strategy ever since the creation of the U.S.-UK "special relationship."[114] In addition, as Oliver Franks, the British ambassador to Washington, reasoned, the United Kingdom had to commit military resources to the conflict so that the United Kingdom could demonstrate "to the Americans that we were one of the two world powers outside Russia." Matters of prestige were evidently of some concern for British policymakers. As such, if the United States was committed to repelling the North Korean invasion of the south, then the British prime minister believed it was necessary for the United Kingdom to do likewise. The secretary of state for defence Manny Shinwell's comment during the cabinet discussions that British intervention was not "militarily desirable" but was "politically inevitable" summed up the predicament facing Attlee's government succinctly.[115]

Australia and New Zealand would also come to play an important role in the Korean War. Though aware of the potential costs, both antipodean economies were in a position to commit resources to the conflict.[116] More important, Canberra and Wellington concurred with the assessments of Washington and London that the North Korean invasion of its neighbor was an act of blatant Communist expansion. A response was therefore required, not least because a nonreaction could precipitate further acts of Communist aggression. Menzies was clear on this point in discussion with the British high commissioner in Canberra, E. J. Williams, arguing that if the United Nations did not resist Communist aggression in Korea, the "next stab" would be against Hong Kong, followed by further aggression against Malaya.[117] Holland and his policy advisers all drew parallels with how appeasing Hitler in the lead-up to World War II had actually encouraged, rather than deterred, further aggression.[118] While the diagnosis of revisionist Communist ambitions and the risk of falling dominoes was clear, the remedy remained up for debate.

Canberra and Wellington approached the situation in markedly different manners. Menzies pursued a cautious line of action, whereas Holland offered to commit whatever resources were required. The New Zealand government was one of the first states to announce its intention to meet the call from the UN Security Council and dispatch forces to Korea. The initial idea of a contribution to the Korea campaign caused concern in New Zealand, to be sure, which was presently readying forces for the Middle East. Policymakers worried about how to meet its strategic obligations in both regions.[119] Nevertheless, the urgency of the situation and the potential rewards of cooperation encouraged swift action. As McGibbon has noted, "The traditional approach of supporting Britain in war was reinforced by aspirations to secure some form of long-term security commitment from the United States. The Korean situation offered an opportunity to advance this latter cause."[120] Holland announced his commitment prior to any declaration from the British or Australian government.[121] Consequently, HMNZS *Tutira* and HMNZS *Pukaki* left their port in Auckland on July 3, 1950, to join with other UN forces at Sasebo, Japan. The New Zealand government also supplied land forces, with recruiting stations overrun by volunteers seeking to join a British Commonwealth force. These were considerable commitments from the New Zealand government given that it provided, pro rata, the third-largest contribution to the UN police action behind only that of South Korea and the United States.[122]

New Zealand's commitment stood in stark contrast to the uncertainty demonstrated by Australia. Although such delays appear curious, given Australia's newfound commitment to stemming Communist expansion under the Menzies government and its desire to secure a long-term security guarantee from the United States, such behavior is understandable. As the first foreign policy crisis to confront the new Menzies government, there followed a degree of indecision and procrastination from Canberra. While resolute in his denunciation of the North Korean invasion, and swift in his provision of naval and air assets to the UN police action, the Australian prime minister remained undecided about whether to commit further resources.[123] Menzies had arranged to visit London and Washington prior to the onset of the crisis. These meetings would now provide him with a forum in which to understand the direction of U.S. and British military action inside Korea, and thus the issue of escalation, as well as an opportunity to discuss other Australian interests.[124]

Menzies arrived in England on July 13 and held a series of discussions with British officials throughout the week.[125] Financial matters dominated the agenda, but the Australian prime minister eventually offered increased Australian support for the United Nations mission and committed two warships and a fighter squadron for immediate operations inside Korea.[126] At that time, neither the British nor Australian governments had yet reached a final decision on the subject of committing further resources to Korea but both agreed to keep each other fully informed. On July 22, Menzies departed for Washington aboard the *Queen Mary*, and it was during this five-day voyage that the British government decided to commit ground forces to the conflict in Korea following requests from the United States.

In Washington, Secretary of State Acheson and Secretary of Defense Louis Johnson discussed how much pressure the U.S. should apply to the United Kingdom and other allied states to ensure that they committed additional resources to the war in Korea.[127] Canberra, in an effort to avoid being upstaged, decided to announce its own ground force commitment prior to London's public announcement. The Australian cabinet did not want to harm Menzies's negotiations in Washington by delaying a response, and consequently issued its commitment without first seeking formal approval from the prime minister, who remained out of reach aboard the *Queen Mary*.[128]

Military cooperation between the four powers inside Korea evidently reflected a range of motives beyond merely opposing Communist aggression. All four states shared concerns about Communist expansion, but it is important to recognize the other motivations at play and not to exaggerate the scope of cooperation. The Korean War produced only an ad-hoc agreement between the Western powers. Despite a growing recognition of the importance of security in the Asia-Pacific and the increasing military commitments to the region, the four countries were still unable to find firm agreement for a Pacific security pact.

By the end of August 1950, the United States had led a united response to the North's invasion of South Korea. The international coalition under MacArthur's leadership managed to prevent South Korea's collapse. The situation nevertheless remained hazardous. South Korean forces faced an enemy equipped with superior firepower and an apparent greater willingness to fight. The capital, Seoul, had already fallen to the North. Following further fighting the remnants of the South Korean army, along with the reinforced UN contingent, became penned into the Pusan perimeter, the southeastern corner of the peninsula, surrounded by Northern forces. Defeat and the fall of the Korean peninsula now seemed probable.[129]

Given this predicament, Truman endorsed MacArthur's plan for a counterattack against North Korean forces via an amphibious landing at Inchon. On September 15, UN forces landed ashore and caught the North Korean forces by surprise. Following brutal fighting, UN forces successfully managed to establish their position on the beachhead. MacArthur seized Kimpo two days later, allowing the UN to utilize tactical air support against North Korean forces, cutting enemy supply routes, and harassing enemy forces. The general's decision to land at Inchon proved spectacularly successful as North Korean forces, now attacked from the rear and from reinforced UN units inside the Pusan perimeter, began to retreat northward. While the fighting was extremely bloody, the UN managed to liberate Seoul by the end of September 1950.[130]

The decision now confronting policymakers was whether to continue with the war. MacArthur's position was unequivocal; U.S.-led forces should seek to reunite Korea. Opinion inside Washington was rather less decisive. In an effort to force policymakers to make a decision, MacArthur ordered his forces to begin the pursuit of North Korean forces across the thirty-eighth parallel. In Washington, there was considerable debate about the best course of action. The president and his national security team ultimately agreed with MacArthur's ambitions in Korea and, as the military position looked favorable, authorized the general to press ahead with uniting Korea.[131]

The task of U.S. diplomacy was now to carry its allies in support of this new objective. The British government's agreement that the war should now expand into North Korea swiftly put to rest any concerns that foreign support might not be forthcoming. Indeed, it was a British resolution carried by the UN General Assembly on October 7 that called on international forces to cross the thirty-eighth parallel, restore stability throughout Korea, and hold national elections in the country. Attlee and Bevin embarked on this path in the belief that it was Britain's responsibility, in common with the United States, to safeguard democracy against the global threat from Moscow. The sending of troops to Korea would also enhance British influence over U.S. policy in the conduct of the war. Uppermost in British thinking was the idea that they alone could temper the more hawkish attitudes of certain policymakers in Washington that might try to utilize this war as a good excuse to precipitate a war against Communist China. Just as the British decision to enter the war in June reflected in part concerns with their ally, so too did the decision to escalate military efforts in October.[132]

Australia and New Zealand followed the U.S.-UK lead in committing to the unification of Korea and agreed to support the escalation of the United Nation's war aims. Senior policymakers in Canberra and Wellington were anxious that the new objective of reunifying Korea could evolve into a broader war against China and the Soviet Union. Yet, as antipodean policymakers realized, their opposition would never prevent the United States and United Kingdom from expanding the war. The Australian and New Zealand governments therefore made the decision to support U.S.-UK efforts.[133] Support was preferable because it potentially provided political capital with Washington and London that they could exploit to promote their own interests. It was not a coincidence that when Spender discussed Australian support for U.S. actions in Korea, he continually raised the twin issues of the Japanese peace treaty and the possibility of some form of a Pacific security pact.[134] Both antipodean states accepted the need for military involvement in Korea but retained a keen eye on exploiting this commitment for the furtherance of their broader objective of establishing a fuller security commitment from the United States.

Under MacArthur's leadership the UN continued to push the North Korean forces farther north and rapidly advanced toward the Yalu River in late October. By now, Chinese "volunteers" had engaged in fighting against UN forces.[135] The PRC leadership was evidently unwilling to tolerate the outright defeat of its North Korean ally or allow UN forces so close to its own border. MacArthur nevertheless downplayed the likelihood of Chinese intervention in a number of dispatches to Washington. Even if Chinese forces did intervene, the general believed that U.S. airpower would be sufficient to deal with them. On November 25, the PRC launched a full-scale counteroffensive against UN forces. U.S. airpower proved unable to stop the Chinese advance. MacArthur now declared that the United States faced "an entirely new war." Overwhelmed by Chinese forces in November and December, UN forces swiftly retreated, allowing Seoul to fall once again.[136]

The situation looked bleak. MacArthur publicly suggested that it was now necessary to utilize nuclear weapons to help reverse the course of the war. He also claimed that nuclear strikes against the PRC would help destroy the war capacity of the enemy. MacArthur's detractors would suggest that he had underestimated the likelihood of Chinese intervention and was now looking to rectify his mistake by any means.[137] MacArthur did believe that nuclear weapons were the best option for helping to reverse the military situation, however, and reasoned that by not utilizing nuclear weapons the United States was prolonging the war and effectively appeasing both Communist China and the Soviet Union.[138]

Public discussion concerning the use of nuclear weapons inside Korea or against the PRC unsettled opinion in London, Canberra, and Wellington. Attlee was so concerned that he flew to Washington to speak with Truman directly about the escalating situation. Following a long discussion, the president promised the prime minister that the United States would not utilize nuclear weapons without first consulting with the British government but bluntly refused to provide Attlee with any written assurance.[139] Moreover, Acheson had rejected British suggestions about brokering a possible peace agreement with the North Koreans and the PRC, noting existing cooperation in Europe. As Acheson reported: "[I] informed the British that we could not separate our foreign policy into two compartments—the Far East and the European. The Secretary went on to say that Americans would not accept a surrender in the Far East in accord with the desire of some of our Allies and then cooperate in Europe with the same Allies who have urged us to be conciliatory in the Far East."[140]

London informed Canberra and Wellington of the unofficial agreements that Attlee had reached with Truman but made no mention of the strong resistance he had encountered from Acheson. Nor did it make mention of the quite alarmist rhetoric that the president and his key national security advisers had used on numerous occasions during their talks. Such information could have proven problematic because opinion in Australia and New Zealand remained highly apprehensive about the possible course of U.S. actions in Korea.[141] The seriousness of recent events had an almost paralyzing effect on policymaking in Wellington. The first secretary of foreign affairs Alister McIntosh informed New Zealand's minister to the United States Carl Berendsen in Washington that there was an almost "unreal" attitude displayed in the cabinet and a clear lack of leadership shown by either Holland or the minister of external affairs Frederick Doidge.[142]

More worrying, a major military disaster, which could precipitate the utilization of nuclear weapons, seemed ever more likely. By the end of December, it appeared as if Communist forces would drive the UN from the Korean peninsula as the U.S. Eighth Army began to make a disorganized retreat toward the Pusan perimeter.[143] As the military historian Thomas Fleming noted, an "American Dunkirk loomed."[144] Such was the turnaround in the military position of the United Nations inside Korea that Truman requested an additional $16.8 billion for Defense appropriations and approved significant increases to the size of the U.S. military.[145] On December 16, he declared a "national emergency" that "require[d] that the military, naval, air, and civilian defenses of this country be strengthened as speedily as possible to the end that we may be able to repel any and all threats against our national security."[146] Acheson would justifiably term events as "December Despondency" within his memoirs.[147] Many in U.S., British, Australian, and New Zealand policy-making circles shared the opinion that the future looked bleak. As the former British diplomat Harold Nicholson wrote in his diary, "The year closes in a mist of anxiety. We shall be lucky if we get through 1951 without a war."[148] Before a meeting of influential congressmen, Acheson, perhaps engaging in hyperbole to help win the needed congressional funding for sustaining U.S. presence in Korea, explained that the Soviet Union was engaging in an "all-out attack" against the "power position of the United States."[149]

By the end of February 1951, a semblance of stability had returned to the war. Under General Matthew Ridgeway, who replaced MacArthur as overall commander later that year following his dismissal for insubordination, the Eighth Army fought tenaciously to slow down the advance of Communist forces. Aerial support and much-needed infantry had reinforced UN forces, which helped stop the Communist advance. From here, UN forces were able to force their Communist opponents back to around the thirty-eighth parallel and stabilize the frontier. While nearly three further years of bloody fighting were yet to come, the broad front on which this war would continue was now set.[150]

The global situation remained tense. Policymakers in Western states had grown concerned that they were finding themselves in an increasingly unfavorable position in the Cold War.[151] It is telling that the likes of George Kennan, who, at the beginning of 1950, had argued that "we are holding our own," left office in favor of more hawkish advisers such as Paul Nitze.[152] The Joint Chiefs of Staff in Washington were encouraging the president to approve further, radical increases in U.S. defense expenditure to account for the fact that U.S. planning had to justify a "long and difficult undertaking" in the Asia-Pacific theater whereas previously U.S. commitments were to be "comparatively short-term."[153]

Successive crises in Malaya, China, and Korea had encouraged closer cooperation between the four powers. Cooperation was nevertheless motivated by much more than merely shared perceptions of a common threat. Moreover, these ad-hoc efforts contrasted with the formal security alliance that existed for Europe in the form of NATO. These crises had proved insufficient to motivate formal security arrangements. As Acheson at the time noted, there had been no "organized effort . . . to pool information, skills and techniques among the friendly nations who have a common interest in defeating [Communist] activity" throughout the Asia-Pacific.[154] The president remained unwilling to authorize extended global security commitments throughout the region for fear of overstretching and misappropriating the United States' finite resources.[155]

CHAPTER 3

A Negotiated Alliance

The Korean War had served to emphasize the strategic importance of the Asia-Pacific region to the Truman administration. Developments in Southeast Asia were becoming increasingly significant. Paul Nitze, the U.S. State Department's director of policy, suggested that this would be a "primary area of Soviet-Communist action."[1] "It is recognized that the threat of communist aggression against Indochina," one National Security Council report concluded, "is only one phase of anticipated communist plans to seize all of Southeast Asia."[2] Accordingly, U.S. policymakers began to reconsider the types of support that the United States could provide to France in its war inside Indochina. France was no longer viewed as fighting to save a colonial possession but was instead resisting the forces of international Communism.[3]

Nevertheless, Truman remained reluctant to enter into formal security pacts in the wider region due to the prioritization of other strategic interests and domestic-political restraints, most pressingly growing concerns about the affordability of fighting the Cold War. Entangling alliances in the Asia-Pacific would be expensive and risked open-ended commitments. Rebuilding Japan, considered by strategic planners in Washington to be the most suitable bulwark against the rising Communist tide throughout Asia-Pacific, instead became the focal point of efforts to resist Communism. The Truman administration concluded that the recovery of Japan was strategically and economically essential for the security of the region. Imperative to achieving such ambitions was ending formal occupation by Allied forces and providing a Japanese peace treaty that would allow for its full economic and industrial recovery.

U.S. plans encountered considerable opposition. The United Kingdom, Australia, and New Zealand resented a new commercial challenger in the region and feared a Japanese military revival. As all were signatories to the Japanese instruments of surrender, their support was essential to secure the two-thirds majority required to end formal occupation. The United States' desire for a Japanese peace treaty provided Australia and New Zealand with the opportunity to push for their longtime goal of a security treaty with the United States. Following negotiations, the Australia, New Zealand, and United States Security Treaty (ANZUS) emerged in February 1951. The United States, however, excluded the United Kingdom from this newly formed security pact. Washington also brushed aside London's efforts at drafting its own Japanese peace treaty, instead pushing forward a more lenient agreement that largely reflected U.S. wishes.[4]

Although Australia and New Zealand initially welcomed British inclusion, the need for a security pact meant that they would follow the United States' lead on the issue of tripartite membership. The United States explained British omission from ANZUS by citing concerns about appearing as a racist or imperial power and the consequent fear of provoking criticism from Asian states. The decision to exclude the United Kingdom, however, reflected a mixture of influences downplayed in the history of the origins of the ANZUS Treaty. U.S. concerns about racism or imperialism were significant but they also helped legitimize exclusion and obscure more self-interested strategic and economic motivations that Britain would have been better placed to resist.

Seeking Security

Throughout 1950, Australia and New Zealand continued to discuss the possibility of a Pacific security pact. Both antipodean powers welcomed a security arrangement that involved the United Kingdom and the United States, but New Zealand remained skeptical of securing U.S. involvement.[5] Robert Menzies's planned visit to the United Kingdom and United States over the summer gave the Australian prime minister the chance to advance his cause. These trips presented a valuable opportunity for the Australian government to make its voice heard in the key Western capitals and duly influence the course of both UK and U.S. international policy, not least regarding the proposed Japanese peace treaty. Prior to his departure, Menzies gave a long public speech emphasizing the need for increased cooperation across the British Commonwealth, which would streamline strategic planning in preparation for a global war.[6] He likely used calls for Commonwealth solidarity to temper British concerns that Canberra sought closer relations with Washington at the expense of London. The British increasingly believed that Australia's ultimate objective was to obtain a security guarantee from the United States.[7]

Menzies certainly wanted a security pact with the United States. The Australian prime minister, however, remained flexible as to what this security pact would involve. Cooperation could come in the form of a bilateral or trilateral (including New Zealand) agreement, or the security pact with the United States could come within the broader makeup of a Pacific security pact that included the United Kingdom. As the Australian minister for external affairs Percy Spender had made clear in discussion with his New Zealand counterparts, it was preferable to have a security pact that included both the United Kingdom and United States.[8] Yet Menzies simply desired a security guarantee from the United States; its final design was open to discussion.

On Menzies's arrival in London in July 1950, talks began in earnest. There was clear agreement about the undesirability of U.S. proposals for the Japanese peace treaty. As Menzies and Bevin agreed, the current plans for Japan would hurt the economic interests of the Commonwealth. More troubling, U.S. plans did not adequately safeguard against a repetition of Japanese militarism. British and Australian interests converged on this point, which threatened a united front against U.S. proposals by potentially drawing in the support of France and the Netherlands, who were believed to share such sympathies. Such a coalition would represent the one-third majority of the original signatories to the Japanese instruments of surrender that was necessary to block the U.S. draft of the treaty.

Menzies also demonstrated his commitment to a more assertive Cold War foreign policy by confirming that he would dispatch Australian forces into the Middle East if a general global war broke out.[9] An Australian commitment to the Middle East had long been an ambition of British and U.S. foreign policy, which the Chifley government had previously resisted. Menzies's decision marked a clear divergence to the strategic and foreign policy of the preceding Australian government.[10] Menzies also renewed his commitment to fighting in Korea and Malaya. Yet the Australian prime minister made no clear pitch for a Pacific security pact, which Attlee had already prepared to reject in a delicate fashion.[11]

The British appeared to have been the main beneficiaries of the decisions reached during the London talks. The results of the discussions, however, were not as one-sided as they might seem. Menzies believed that Australian forces should be engaged in a region of fundamental importance in any global war.[12] The Australian prime minster remained committed to resisting Communism and believed that in a global war, Australian forces should be actively engaged in fighting. His decision to commit forces to the Middle East was therefore not simply a concession to the British. Moreover, all such contributions were limited. Australia remained as a junior partner in the relationship, and the British only desired that a "token" force be dispatched to the Middle East in peacetime for political reasons. Nor was such a commitment binding. The Australian prime minister had been careful to note that the final decision for dispatching forces into the Middle East would be a "political one." In effect, the Australian cabinet would need to agree, in a formal capacity, to send Australian forces if war broke out. In the absence of antipodean support, the United Kingdom's ability to uphold its wider Commonwealth security interests would become more challenging.

It is important to appreciate that the majority of the discussions in London focused on Menzies's upcoming talks in Washington, where he would raise the possibility of Australia receiving a dollar loan to help with capital purchases for major infrastructure programs.[13] This loan, as Chancellor of the Exchequer Stafford Cripps had made known during his discussion with Menzies, could hurt Britain's financial interests. The United Kingdom had accumulated major debts in sterling to other countries, including the antipodean powers, during the Second World War, and this proposed development program risked inflation that could force Australia to draw heavily on these sterling balances.[14] In addition, Australia would incur new liabilities despite already running a dollar trade deficit.[15] Menzies nevertheless received the blessing of Cripps to negotiate this loan with the United States as he saw fit and without any British interference. The relationship between Australian forces in the Middle East and British approval of a U.S. loan is therefore suggestive of an informal quid pro quo.

Menzies certainly proved more cooperative in terms of Commonwealth strategy than Chifley, as evidenced by events in Malaya and the recent Middle East agreement, but the demise of the Australian Labour government encouraged a reversal of international economic policy. In the immediate postwar period, Australia had increased financial and trading links with Britain and the rest of the sterling area. In return, the United Kingdom expanded its exports to Australia and also provided a major source of labor and capital. By now, however, the limitations of British industrial capacity were beginning to prove insufficient to meet Australian needs, which encouraged Australia to turn to the dollar area to secure additional resources for economic development. Undercurrents of "economic disengagement" with the United Kingdom therefore help explain why Australia would go on to commit more fully to economic relations with the United States.[16]

Following his discussions in London, Menzies departed for Washington to liaise with both Truman and Acheson. The Australian prime minister played his hand skillfully in Washington. Menzies chose not to push the case for any sort of U.S.-Australian security pact, much to the surprise of U.S. policymakers.[17] Aware of the growing disquiet in the United States that he had not yet detailed Australia's commitment to the war in Korea, Menzies declared in front of the U.S. House of Representatives that he would ensure the dispatch of a first-class combat group to the war effort.[18] Menzies subsequently pushed for his economic and commercial objectives in private discussions with Acheson. By dampening down possible criticism of Australian policy toward the war in Korea, he had gained political leverage with which to secure his economic objectives. Menzies's efforts proved fruitful as the U.S. government approved a $100 million loan.[19] With agreement reached, future discussions could now focus more heavily on security arrangements.

Menzies nevertheless chose not to press his opposition to U.S. plans for Japan thereafter and made little effort to try to convince either Washington or London to provide more formalized security cooperation for the Asia-Pacific. Menzies claimed in one correspondence that "we do not need a pact with America. They are already overwhelmingly friendly to us."[20] Such claims were disingenuous and reflected Menzies's desire to show his domestic audience that his diplomatic tours of the United Kingdom and United States had been successful. The prime minister remained convinced that Australia had to prepare for the possibility of a global war and his actions thereafter signaled his intention to take a far more robust approach to enhancing Australia's regional security. He led the overhaul of Australia's armed forces, which saw the defense budget increase significantly, and oversaw a change to enlistment policies whereby Australian personnel could serve anywhere in the world and not just for local area defense. The prime minister also continued to press for the successful implementation of the Communist Party Dissolution Act through the Australian legislature. Although the Australian Supreme Court rejected the proposal, his efforts to ban the Communist Party and remove its influence on Australian life are reflective of his commitment to fight Communism.[21]

Whereas Menzies had been careful not to appear too assertive in his dealings with U.S. and British leaders, Spender felt no such inhibitions. In a strongly worded message to Attlee in September 1950, the minister of external affairs asserted that Britain was simply ignoring Australian opinion on a whole host of matters concerning the future of Asia-Pacific security.[22] Washington would receive similar warnings. Meeting with Acheson, Spender argued that the terms of any peace treaty with Japan had to take adequately into account the legitimate security concerns of the Australian government. He explained that he would only countenance Australian support for a lenient peace treaty if the United States could provide adequate security guarantees, preferably in the guise of a bilateral or trilateral security agreement.[23]

New Zealand was keen to support such efforts even if they felt them unlikely to succeed. Lending support to Spender was Sir Carl Berendsen, New Zealand's minister to Washington. Mirroring the substance if not the style of Spender's complaints, Berendsen outlined Wellington's disgruntlement with how the United States was pushing forward with the Japanese peace treaty. As he suggested, if the United States could adequately safeguard both Australian and New Zealand security against any resurgence in Japanese militarism, antipodean support for a lenient Japanese peace treaty would be forthcoming.[24] The antipodean powers were evidently working in tandem to strengthen their efforts in negotiations with the United States concerning both a Japanese peace treaty and a future security pact.

A Japanese Peace Treaty

U.S. policymakers increasingly recognized the importance of Japan in the Cold War. The Truman administration nevertheless remained divided on how best to utilize Japanese power in the struggle against Communism.[25] The Joint Chiefs of Staff argued that it was essential for the United States to secure Japanese approval for U.S. military bases, especially naval ports, on the two main home islands. According to the Joint Chiefs, such bases would help the United States challenge the Soviet navy in the northern Pacific as well as assist in maintaining an "Asian offshore island chain" to provide a "cordon" around China and help "constitute in effect a system of strong outposts for our strategic position."[26] As one assessment concluded: "Our control over the strategically located Japanese home islands are essential, not only to resist the spread of Communism in the Far East, but also, if need be, to implement our present war concepts."[27]

Following Mao's ascension to power, the JCS became even more convinced of the importance of retaining U.S. bases on Japan.[28] U.S. bases on Japan had certainly proved their worth in the Korean War by allowing for the efficient supply of ground forces. In sum, Japan represented an "unsinkable aircraft carrier" that was located in a strategically desirable position for aiding U.S. ambitions to contain the Soviet Union and Communist China. Furthermore, the JCS deemed it imperative to start harnessing Japan's economic potential in order to prevent the Soviet Union seizing control of the country and using it to their advantage: "Under USSR control, Japan would provide both the arsenal personnel and the manpower for aggressive military campaigns in the Pacific and to the southwest. If United States influence predominates, Japan can be expected, with planned initial United States assistance, at least to protect herself and, provided logistic necessities can be made available to her, to contribute importantly to military operations against the Soviets in Asia, thus forcing the USSR to fight on the Asiatic front as well as elsewhere."[29] For the JCS, securing Japan, and thus bolstering the United States' strategic position, was of considerable importance.[30]

The U.S. State Department was rather less concerned with securing military bases in Japan. It instead believed, as Secretary of State Acheson made clear, that the United States should push for the speedy resolution of a Japanese peace treaty on lenient terms. In particular, Japan should pay no reparations for its conduct in World War II. Acheson's proposals were not an act of altruism. Leniency would allow the U.S. to bring Japan firmly into the fold of the Western alliance, mitigate any risk of an internal Communist takeover of power, and ensure a peace agreement without Soviet or Communist Chinese influence.[31] In contrast, Louis Johnson, Truman's secretary of defense, was concerned that a peace treaty would involve U.S. forces having to leave Japan. Such a situation would prove deleterious for the United States' fighting of the Korean War and hurt the nation's ability to maintain the close cordon containment of both the Soviet Union and Communist China in the Pacific. For Johnson, any peace settlement had to ensure U.S. military bases remained in Japan.[32]

The supreme commander for the Allied Powers in Japan, Douglas MacArthur, added yet another perspective to these debates. He had been determined to "rehabilitate" Japan by convincing the population of the merits of freedom, liberty, and Christianity. Under his stewardship, MacArthur introduced a new constitution that brought into being for the first time a democratic government. Such was MacArthur's confidence in his changes to Japanese society that he urged Washington throughout 1947–50 to end the occupation of Japan and call for a conference to settle the final terms of a peace agreement. As MacArthur claimed, "The Japanese have earned the right to a treaty of peace, and our failure to proceed cannot but cause loss of faith in our moral integrity and leadership, not only in Japan but throughout

Asia."[33] MacArthur was nevertheless initially opposed to remilitarization because he believed such a course was unnecessary for containing Communist influence in the region. The United States, he argued, should instead build any necessary military bases on Okinawa and ensure U.S. access to the Ryukyu and Bonin Islands. These locations would provide the outlet for defending the northern Pacific against potential Soviet aggression.[34] Washington evidently remained divided on the issue of how best to serve U.S. interests in relation to Japan and its regional security interests more broadly. Domestic pressures emanating from the Japan lobby in Washington, which pushed for a lenient peace treaty, further complicated the thinking of the Truman administration.[35]

External factors throughout Asia helped sweep away initial opposition to providing a peace treaty, which would reindustrialize Japan and ensure the continuation of a U.S. military presence in the region. Mao's ascension to power in China and the outbreak of the Korean War convinced MacArthur that Japan was now central to the strategic containment of both the Soviet Union and Communist China. Johnson also now concluded that the United States had to bring Japan fully into the Western alliance and accepted that a peace treaty was necessary to achieve this objective. The Truman administration's priority now became the establishment of a peace treaty on nonpunitive terms. Illustrative of the leniency of this proposed peace treaty was Washington's suggestion that Japan needed to pay no reparations to the victims of its aggression throughout 1931–45.[36] The envisaged peace treaty would therefore end the occupation of Japan, where close to 100,000 U.S. service personnel remained, and begin to harness its economic and industrial potential in the containment of Communism.[37]

Finalizing the terms of a Japanese peace treaty remained a complex task. The Japanese instruments of surrender contained the signatures of nine powers, including the United Kingdom, Australia, and New Zealand as well as the Soviet Union. The creation of the Far East Commission, established to administer Japan and decide the terms of its peace settlement, comprised eleven members.[38] The preliminary peace conference established in 1947 mandated that any final peace treaty would require the approval of a two-thirds majority. Given the Cold War context, the United States was prepared to press ahead with a peace treaty that excluded the Soviet Union.[39] Finding diplomatic support for a nonpunitive agreement from the likes of the United Kingdom, Australia, and New Zealand was now essential. The Truman administration could not simply ignore these three states because it needed to secure the necessary two-thirds majority.

While the British government had previously pressed the Truman administration to create a Japanese peace treaty, it was unhappy with the current U.S. proposals for a mixture of strategic and economic reasons.[40] U.S. plans seemed to suggest that Japan would enjoy unsupervised economic redevelopment, which risked aggression in the future. Cultural and historical concerns also informed British thinking. In their assessment, the Japanese population had largely followed the militaristic wishes of the armed forces during the war and appeared to be unfazed by their imperial forces' often-brutal conduct. British policymakers believed that it was essential to "reeducate" the Japanese population and were concerned that MacArthur's efforts had not been as successful as Washington believed. They feared that the United States was going to engage in some "half-baked" idea of rehabilitation without providing adequate safeguards against a repetition of Japanese militarism.[41] In the British estimation, the necessary cultural and political transformations would take a long time and security guarantees were required in the interim. Until adequate political and military safeguards were in place, the British government was reluctant to remove any occupying forces from Japan.[42]

In addition, U.S. proposals suggesting that Japan should pay no reparations to the victims of its actions were controversial. The United Kingdom's own experience as well as the close links with numerous British Commonwealth states that had been the direct victims of Japanese behavior encouraged stiff resistance to this suggestion. Rather, a suitable level of reparations in British assessments was for Japan to surrender its gold stocks.[43] Furthermore, the British government resented the fact that the United States continued to insist that Japan could not recognize the PRC as it removed the possibility of trade between either state. British officials concluded that this situation would force the Japanese to look for markets elsewhere. Japan had been a major prewar competitor for British commerce and enterprise throughout Asia, and Japan's defeat in 1945 had seen the United Kingdom quickly fill the void left by the collapse of the Japanese Empire throughout Southeast Asia. If, as the United States insisted, Japan could not trade with the PRC, it would look toward Southeast Asia for commercial opportunities and markets presently dominated by the United Kingdom.[44] British concerns proved well founded; the United States would encourage Japan to look for markets in Southeast Asia in the 1950s as an alternative to trading with the PRC.[45]

Both the Australian and New Zealand governments argued that any peace treaty had to prevent a resurgence of Japanese militarism. In the judgment of Australian officials, U.S. proposals would allow Japan complete freedom over its economic and industrial development without providing adequate safeguards against this economic power being utilized for military purposes. As Spender had stressed in January 1950, "there could be no doubt that it would be many years before the Australians would forget the barbarism shown by the Japanese during the war. Nor did they believe that the Japanese character was likely to change rapidly."[46] New Zealand officials remained "aghast" at U.S. proposals.[47] During a British Commonwealth conference held in Canberra in August 1947, Fraser had continually emphasized that his primary interest in a Japanese settlement was ensuring New Zealand's security. Providing this security would mean the implementation of limitations on Japan's industrial, economic, and military development.[48]

Both Canberra and Wellington remained anxious as to whether a "few major Powers," would be able to railroad through a Japanese peace settlement and sought security provisions if this outcome proved unavoidable.[49] As the New Zealand Department of External Affairs noted, "Since the security threat from Japan will arise especially if some power or groups of powers encourage her resurgence, New Zealand will be interested in obtaining international agreement on the military and industrial disarmament of Japan as much for the purpose of security restrictions on the activities of world powers competing for Japan's favour as for the purpose of restricting the unaided activities of Japan herself."[50]

Australian and New Zealand resistance toward the peace treaty was therefore not a cynical ploy designed to win a U.S. security agreement but reflected sincere fears about Japan. In addition, antipodean policymakers had concluded that the Truman administration would reject the idea of a trilateral security pact out of hand. New Zealand officials agreed that the subject of a formal security pact was unlikely to receive U.S. support and was thus not worth pursuing too forcefully at this point.[51] Such pessimism was well founded. By the winter of 1950, an opportunity to discuss a Pacific security pact emerged when Dulles, who had been appointed by Acheson to negotiate a Japanese peace treaty, met with New Zealand representatives. As noted by those in attendance, Dulles reasoned that there were compelling reasons why such a security pact was unwise: "First of all, that it gave rise to great embarrassment as to those who wish to be included. [Dulles] felt, moreover, that, as compared with Europe, there was lack of common civilization of real community of interest and trust among the diverse countries of the Pacific area."[52]

Ultimately, the two antipodean powers concluded that they needed to work closely with one another and the United Kingdom to safeguard their interests. Exploiting the concerns of Canberra and Wellington, London began to draft its own Japanese peace treaty that emphasized far harsher terms than those proposed by Washington. British proposals, for instance, suggested that Japan pay reparations to the victims of their wartime aggression. London also put forward ideas on how to limit Japanese commercial access to specific global markets, a proposal likely designed to generate sympathy in Canberra and Wellington and secure British interests in the region.[53] By the end of the year, it was clear that if the United States was to acquire its Japanese peace treaty it would require serious concessions.

The United Kingdom, Australia, and New Zealand's position as signatories to the Japanese surrender instruments meant that their opinion carried considerable weight. In addition, there existed wider international resistance. The president of the Philippines Elpidio Quirino had made similar complaints about a revanchist Japan and the need for a security guarantee. More worrying yet from Washington's perspective were utterances from the likes of Quirino that if security guarantees were not provided then he would seek to create an Asian Union which would exclude Japan, and perhaps even Australia and New Zealand.[54] If ideas such as an Asian Union gained traction, they would have at least three detrimental consequences. First, any such union would likely be anti-Japanese in its design, which would harm collective security and economic growth in the region. Second, it would establish an alliance in Asia outside of Western control, complicating resistance to the Communist powers. Third, it would clearly segregate Asia according to racial boundaries, which would empower Communist accusations that U.S. foreign policy was racially discriminative.

By late 1950, opinion within Washington was shifting in favor of a limited security agreement between the United States and the antipodean powers. As Acheson explained, it was "politically necessary" to accommodate antipodean demands concerning security cooperation, in part for the purposes of economic revival in the region and in part to garner a more cooperative position concerning the drafting of the Japanese peace treaty.[55] In the minds of U.S. policymakers, economic and security concerns were clearly interwoven.[56] Without Australian support for a peace treaty, the U.S. believed Menzies would pursue economic policies that could inhibit Japan's economic revival. Where Australia led, the United States believed New Zealand would follow, all of which would embolden British policies in the region.[57] Such policies would undermine Japanese economic revival and risked the country's internal stability. Replicating arguments about European economic recovery from the likes of Dean Acheson and George Marshall, Dulles argued that if Japan failed to improve its economy, then it would be "futile to expect the Japanese to keep away from communism."[58]

It is difficult to exaggerate the United States' concern over foreign economic stability. The European Recovery Program, or Marshall Plan as it is more commonly referred to, was largely motivated by the belief that without economic recovery European living standards would not improve. Without improvement, the promises of the Communist model would assure a Soviet victory. In spite of the enormous resources pumped into Europe, however, the economic situation remained precarious. During a meeting between Truman and president-elect Eisenhower in 1952, for instance, both men agreed the economic underpinning of the Western alliance was "too flimsy for safety. The slightest diminution of American aid or American defense spending might produce economic consequences which might seriously weaken the countries most closely associated with [the] U.S."[59] Eisenhower would echo such thinking once in office. Japan was simply too important from an economic standpoint to ignore.[60]

Antipodean diplomats sought to exploit these shifting perceptions in pursuit of their long sought-after security pact with the United States. An opportunity to advance the cause came in January 1951 during the visit of Senator Theodore F. Green and Senator Homer Ferguson, who were undertaking a bipartisan foreign policy tour of several Asian-Pacific states. During discussions in Canberra, New Zealand representatives championed the cause of a Pacific security pact most loudly. They argued that a broad Pacific security pact—that would include membership for the United States, United Kingdom, Canada, Australia, and New Zealand—should emerge as swiftly as possible to better prepare these states to confront the shared threat posed by Communist forces throughout the Asia-Pacific region.[61]

Such a comprehensive security pact again encountered opposition in Washington. Nevertheless, recent events in the region had encouraged a subtle shift in U.S. thinking toward finding limited agreements with regional powers to help uphold U.S. security interests.[62] As Washington well understood, both Australia and New Zealand would continue to oppose a nonpunitive Japanese peace treaty, which would block successful implementation.[63] It was evident that a Pacific security pact was required to win their approval for the proposed Japanese peace treaty.[64] In order to gain Australian and New Zealand approval for a lenient agreement, and thus ensure the necessary two-thirds support from the allied occupying powers, the United States would have to guarantee that the revitalization of Japan's economy would not lead to future military aggression.

For the U.S. government, the diplomatic impasse was clear. To undermine suggestions that a nonpunitive Japanese peace treaty would facilitate the unhindered economic redevelopment of Japan, which could lead to the return of militaristic policies, the U.S. would need to provide firmer security guarantees for all concerned parties. As the Truman administration came to realize, U.S. security guarantees would be the necessary quid pro quo for gaining Australian and New Zealand approval for its version of the Japanese peace treaty. These powers now needed to negotiate the form of such a security guarantee.[65] Progress therefore rested on the United States' ability to provide the Australian and New Zealand governments with a suitable agreement.

In private discussions in January 1951, senior U.S. officials hinted to their New Zealand counterparts that they would consider entering some type of security pact.[66] A possible U.S.-antipodean pact had now become a serious possibility by the time of Sidney Holland's visit to Washington in early February. During subsequent meetings, Truman and Acheson hinted that the United States would countenance a U.S. commitment to defend New Zealand if this would guarantee continued commitments to the Middle East.[67] Holland had also suggested a similar arrangement. The New Zealand prime minister accepted that the likelihood of a direct attack on his country "was remote," and thus military forces "could best be utilized in some other theatre," but "New Zealand would have to know, in the event the unlikely occurred and they were attacked, that someone, preferably the United States, would 'give them a hand.'"[68] As New Zealand would be sending approximately 35,000 men to the Middle East in wartime, effectively stripping away much of its defenses, a U.S. security arrangement was essential.[69]

The United States, Australia, and New Zealand all held divergent views as to how a security arrangement would work. Holland remained wedded to the idea that a security pact should include membership for the United Kingdom, a point he emphasized during his talks with Truman and Acheson. As Holland told Acheson, "The security of New Zealand is largely dependent on the United States," but "New Zealand is British, 90 to 95 per cent of the population being of British extraction, and proud of it."[70] As such, a security pact that brought together the United States, Australia, and New Zealand should include membership for the United Kingdom.[71]

For both Australia and the United States, however, membership for the United Kingdom was a lesser concern. The Menzies government shared Holland's opinion that a security pact that included British membership would be a stronger one but the priority had to be attaining U.S. agreement.[72] The United States certainly preferred a limited agreement focused on the Pacific states, and even then, only if they agreed to accept Washington's general outlines for a Japanese peace treaty.[73] In early 1951, the Truman administration had set the stage for some type of security agreement with Australia and New Zealand.

The Canberra Talks

U.S., Australian, and New Zealand delegations met in Canberra in February 1951 to commence negotiations about the nature of a Japanese peace settlement and a security pact. Both Spender and his New Zealand counterpart, Frederick Doidge, made good use of their respective countries' commitments to the Middle East in persuading Dulles of the merits of a tripartite security guarantee. Spender stressed that a lenient Japanese peace settlement, which did not in turn provide some type of security guarantee, would ultimately lead Australia to reassess its Cold War commitments. In such a situation, "Australia's capacity to discharge her obligations in the event of war in Malaya as well as outside the Pacific area would be gravely impaired."[74] Spender went on to suggest that a tripartite security organization between the United States, Australia, and New Zealand would provide the necessary security guarantees for both antipodean powers to support a lenient Japanese peace treaty.[75] Over the next two days, Doidge continually supported Spender's fundamental points. Antipodean endorsement for a lenient Japanese peace settlement would require a security guarantee from the United States.[76]

Dulles questioned the necessity of such an arrangement given the negligible threat of a direct Communist attack on either Australia or New Zealand. Spender responded skillfully, arguing that because the risk of a Communist attack was negligible, the U.S. could provide a security guarantee without fear of it ever being called on.[77] In return, Dulles stressed that if the United States agreed to the tripartite security arrangement, any security pact would contain no formal pledge in the fashion of the NATO alliance.[78] Following further discussions about the nature of the alliance, and possible expansion of the security pact to include the Philippines, the representatives reached agreement concerning the general contours of the ANZUS Treaty on February 17. There emerged a tripartite agreement without binding security commitments.[79]

In assessing the terms of the treaty, no single power achieved all of its objectives.[80] Nevertheless, the resultant agreement benefited all of the participants. From an Australian and New Zealand perspective, the agreement provided a security guarantee that offered assurances against resurgent Japanese militarism and against any attack from an outside power. Given that the New Zealand government believed that the best that they could hope for from the Canberra talks was some type of informal U.S. defense commitment, the final agreement was therefore somewhat of a coup.[81] The best way to prepare for the risk that Japan would again utilize its economic power in the pursuit of military aggrandizement was to obtain a direct security guarantee from the United States. At the end of the Canberra talks, the antipodean powers had certainly achieved this objective.

Furthermore, Australian and New Zealand policymakers never seriously countenanced neutrality in the Cold War. The Soviet Union was a clear and present security threat that both states wished to help contain.[82] A security pact with the United States, which Doidge referred to as "the richest prize in New Zealand diplomacy," would defend both antipodean powers from Communist threats and allow them to maintain their broader Cold War commitments.[83] It is no surprise, then, that Berendsen concluded that the United States had "offered on a platter the greatest gift that the most powerful country in the world can offer to a small comparatively helpless group of people."[84] Wellington believed that a security guarantee from the United States would defend against the Soviet Union and its Communist satellites in the short term and potential Asian expansionism in the long term.[85]

Nevertheless, the agreement was limited in several regards. No mechanism emerged with which to secure access to other areas of U.S. strategic thinking. Specifically, the Australian government had sought to link the ANZUS agreement with the regular exchanges of information and staff officers with the U.S. defense establishment.[86] The New Zealand government had also desired a greater voice in international security arrangements.[87] The JCS, however, were unwilling to allow more service chiefs in Washington than necessary. As a general point, the JCS were "lukewarm" about ANZUS, which they allegedly viewed as "of no great importance."[88] Thus, the United States swiftly rejected Spender's effort in the Canberra talks to "establish a framework of formal consultation and . . . provide a link with the North Atlantic Treaty Organization."[89] Efforts by antipodean policymakers to utilize their newfound security relationship later in the year to establish broader strategic cooperation between the United States, Australia, and New Zealand would prove equally fruitless.[90]

The United States certainly benefited from the agreement. It achieved the ambition of securing antipodean cooperation toward the U.S.-inspired peace settlement with Japan, which policymakers believed to be of even greater importance throughout 1951. Dulles had also ensured that the treaty was limited in nature and scope, disappointing Australian and New Zealand efforts to establish integrated military planning. At no point did the treaty guarantee joint staff talks or strategic planning, concessions that would turn the idea of a pact into a functioning security alliance. In addition, by agreeing to the ANZUS Treaty, the United States received a guarantee from both Australia and New Zealand to maintain their commitment to the defense of the Middle East, which had come to assume greater importance within U.S. strategic thinking, and to remain active in the Cold War more broadly.[91]

This outcome is not to suggest that Australian or New Zealand diplomats had been blindsided, only that American efforts had catalyzed cooperation. Since coming to office, Menzies had made it known that he wanted Australia to take a more active role in the Cold War, and refrain from the "busybody" approach adopted by the preceding Chifley government. In the wake of events in Korea, he wanted Australian forces to be committed to a region where they would actually have an impact on the outcome of any future global war. For Menzies, committing Australian forces to the defense of the Middle East made strategic sense at this time.[92] Holland's election to office in December 1949 had likewise brought to power a prime minister that believed much more seriously in the threat posed by the forces of international Communism. New Zealand officials concluded that a third world war instigated by the Soviet Union was increasingly likely. One appraisal of the world situation composed by Berendsen mirrors the more damning indictments of Soviet intentions that are traditionally associated with the likes of John Foster Dulles. Berendsen believed that "international gangsters" led the Soviet Union, which sought "domination of the world." The world situation was, he concluded, "a struggle between two totally incompatible and irreconcilable theories of human relations and human government."[93]

The New Zealand Joint Planning Committee was equally clear when it claimed that the "only possible enemy in the foreseeable future is the Soviet Union acting with the assistance of her European and Asiatic satellites."[94] Prior to the commencement of the talks with Dulles in Canberra of February 1951, the New Zealand Military Committee, which planned New Zealand's strategic policies, suggested that it was a "fundamental aim" of New Zealand policy to "obtain an undertaking from the United States to underwrite the security of New Zealand against any threat which might arise in the Pacific."[95] Both antipodean states were committed to fighting the Cold War and the ANZUS arrangement complemented this ambition.

Beyond ensuring broader security interests, the U.S. enjoyed several economic benefits from the successful conclusion of negotiations. ANZUS complemented a broader attempt by the Truman administration to strengthen its economic position throughout the Asia-Pacific region. The U.S. State Department was already concerned about the exclusive nature of economic cooperation between the United Kingdom and the two antipodean powers.

The Dominions' temporary wartime bulk purchase agreements, aspects of which continued for several years after hostilities had ended, were especially troubling. Such agreements threatened to undermine the structure of international trade and impede Japanese revival. While the United States would not break these historic trade connections, the treaty provided confidence to improve Australia and New Zealand's trade relations with Japan and thus an opportunity to question the imperial preference of their commercial policies, which the United States had actively sought to end since World War II.[96]

Before the treaty was agreed, the State Department stressed the need to "continue to point out to Australian officials the economic objections to such [trade] arrangements."[97] ANZUS provided a useful platform to encourage both Canberra and Wellington to "gradually counteract the narrow trade concepts of the past," thereby strengthening international trade in general and Japanese recovery in particular.[98] As Clifton Webb, the New Zealand minister of justice and close confident of the prime minister, noted in cabinet discussion, the creation of ANZUS meant that New Zealand could no longer "pound the table on the matter of imperial preference."[99] In this way, ANZUS respected the Truman administration's belief that the United States could pursue economic and security objectives in tandem.[100]

Yet even the United States could not obtain all that it wanted. Prior to the Canberra talks, Acheson instructed Dulles to negotiate a wider security pact. Dulles followed his instructions and called for ANZUS to include membership for at least the Philippines. Spender and Doidge successfully resisted Dulles's efforts, supported by ongoing British opposition to a larger pact, although both had in fact left the negotiations believing that the Philippines was likely to be included as a founding member of ANZUS.[101] Australia and New Zealand were determined that the United States should treat them as "Western" powers. A security pact that included the Philippines would signal that both were in fact Southwest Pacific powers that would limit antipodean ambitions of influencing U.S. strategy beyond the region.[102] Furthermore, a pact involving any Asian powers could also potentially drag both states into the defense of areas that had no direct bearing on their own interests.[103]

As the Truman administration privately recognized, the limited membership of ANZUS reflected a strong Australian and New Zealand preference for a "white" Pacific pact.[104] U.S. acquiescence to excluding the Philippines from the ANZUS arrangement was therefore met with great satisfaction in Australia and New Zealand.[105] Racial issues permeated antipodean thinking. As Alan Watt, the secretary to the Department of External Affairs in Australia, candidly admitted in private discussions with his New Zealand colleagues, there were three overarching reasons why Australia desired a security guarantee from the United States. These were to counter against a rearmed Japan, against Communist imperialism in Asia, and "against Asian expansionism generally." As the record of this conversation noted, "The third reason, which [Watt] agreed was the strongest, could not, however, be made public."[106]

Excluding the United Kingdom

The completion of the ANZUS Treaty brought with it both Australian and New Zealand support for the U.S. version of the Japanese peace treaty. A majority of signatories followed thereafter, and the British government grudgingly cooperated.[107] The United Kingdom could now no longer effectively check the signature of the peace treaty, which allowed Japan to become a fully integrated member of the global economic system and a serious challenger to British commercial interests.[108]

Throughout this period of negotiation, the United Kingdom was excluded from formal proceedings concerning ANZUS. It nevertheless played a subtle role in the formation of the treaty. Interference from the British government certainly helps explain the exclusive tripartite nature of the ANZUS Treaty. As London made clear to Washington at the time, the United Kingdom could tolerate its own omission, albeit only for the time being, from a strictly tripartite alliance. If a broader Asian security alliance emerged, however, British policymakers would have demanded membership of such a pact given their interests in the region.[109]

London informed both Canberra and Wellington that the British government would be "welcoming of a three-party pact" but had "great concern at the American suggestion that the Philippines should be invited to join."[110] The diplomatic language did not cloak the severity of the British government's opposition to a broader Pacific security pact that excluded them. As one New Zealand observer noted, the British government was looking to "torpedo" the creation of a wider security pact that excluded their participation, which in turn could have jeopardized ANZUS itself.[111] "Torpedo" overstates the degree of British influence, but as Dean Rusk admitted, it had encouraged Washington to agree to settle on a tripartite ANZUS arrangement.[112] The limited nature of the ANZUS Treaty therefore reflects the influence of four, rather than three, states in negotiations.[113] The United States agreed to forgo Philippine membership in ANZUS and instead concluded a bilateral agreement, titled the U.S.-Philippine Mutual Assistance Treaty, in August 1951. British opposition to a broader and more inclusive Pacific security pact helps explain the exclusion of other regional powers from ANZUS.[114]

In addition to limiting the membership of this new security alliance, the ANZUS agreement was also a vicarious success for the British government. ANZUS guaranteed ongoing Australian commitments to the war in Korea and to the insurgency inside Malaya. The agreement also provided the regional security guarantees that in turn allowed both Canberra and Wellington to commit their forces to the Middle East in the event of a war with the Soviet Union.[115] It was not a coincidence that following the signing of the agreement, the U.S. applied further pressure on Australia to commit to the defense of the Middle East in a formal capacity, utilizing the ANZUS guarantee as the reason why such security commitments could now be undertaken.[116]

The British government nevertheless remained uneasy about the treaty. British exclusion touched on deep-rooted U.S.-UK disagreements about how to coordinate Western strategy against Soviet Communism and concerns about the future of the British Commonwealth. The growing influence of the United States in the region was increasingly concerning. As the British secretary of state for Commonwealth relations Patrick Gordon Walker noted, "We cannot ignore the danger that Australia will be drawn into the American orbit of civilisation."[117] Throughout the creation of the ANZUS Treaty, the United Kingdom was omitted from the negotiation process and largely ignorant of the details. British officials had made it known to their antipodean counterparts that they would not "favor the idea of a Pacific defense organization which excluded the United Kingdom," but this proved to be the eventual result of the Canberra talks.[118] As A. W. Martin has noted, British policymakers did not deem Australia or New Zealand to be a "foreign country," yet they had largely acted as such during the creation of ANZUS.[119]

Security concerns largely explain this shift in behavior. As Spender reminded his colleagues, "It is above all becoming clear that the United Kingdom, with added commitments in the Middle East over and above its responsibilities to the North Atlantic Treaty Organization, will have few resources to spare for active participation in the defence of the Australasian region." British objections, as Menzies noted, would not prevent him from seeking a security pact with the United States.[120] Although both antipodean governments would have preferred British inclusion, they were unwilling to see their designs for a security treaty scuppered by British grievances.[121] As officials in Wellington privately noted, "We should have welcomed [the] inclusion of [the] U.K but [it] did not seem possible without jeopardizing [the] whole arrangement."[122] "Loyalty and affection" was how Doidge described

New Zealand's sentiment toward the United Kingdom, but this clearly had limitations in how it affected New Zealand's foreign policy.[123]

Britain's financial weakness since the end of World War II, along with the prioritization of interests in the Middle East, Mediterranean, and Western Europe, hardly encouraged confidence in Australia and New Zealand. Few antipodean policymakers believed that the British would be able to prevent any southern strike in Southeast Asia from Japan, China, or the Soviet Union. The British had also given their approval to Australia to finalize its leadership of ANZAM planning, which again suggested that Australia would need to play a larger role in the Asia-Pacific region. That Canberra and Wellington increasingly sought other avenues for securing its own regional security should not have come as a surprise to policymakers in London.

The fashion in which ANZUS had emerged demonstrated the evolving nature of the U.S.-UK alliance and a clear shift in the distribution of power within the British Commonwealth. While the United States recognized that the United Kingdom was its "strongest and most reliable ally," this did not prevent the U.S. from pursuing its own interests in the Asia-Pacific.[124] During cabinet discussions in London, Attlee had suggested in the face of opposition that ANZUS aligned with the overarching British policy to encourage allies to take a lead in the defense of their own regions.[125] As the British prime minister saw it, the fact that his government had prioritized the Middle East and Europe in the event of a global war meant that members of the British Commonwealth in the Asia-Pacific had to look at other ways of promoting their own security. In Attlee's estimation events in the region were of secondary importance, and the prime minister and his officials emphasized this point in conversation with U.S. policymakers.[126]

Competing accounts and the subsequent actions of British diplomats betray Attlee's calm. Foreign Office officials had sought to obtain membership of any new U.S. security pact for the Pacific prior to Dulles's negotiations in Canberra.[127] After the talks, British concern was obvious. The Foreign Secretary Herbert Morrison complained to Dulles that U.S. public announcements about the ANZUS Treaty negotiations undermined the impression that London had been fully consulted over the treaty.[128] All Gordon Walker could do was request that both Canberra and Wellington inform London about when the formal ANZUS Treaty would be signed and publicly announced.[129] There were also concerns about potential tensions between ANZUS and ANZAM, whereby overlapping areas of interest were now answerable to different authorities. Furthermore, the United Kingdom's exclusion from a defense treaty with two of its Dominions hardly supported British ambitions of retaining the image, or reality, of being a world power.[130]

Nor did it correlate with the idea of a "special relationship" whereby the British and Americans cooperated closely.

Exclusion also revealed the limits of the United Kingdom's influence on the world stage. British lobbying of officials from New Zealand, Australia, and the United States in the lead-up to the Canberra talks to ensure their inclusion in any security pact proved ultimately unsuccessful.[131] The British Chiefs of Staff, officials within the Foreign Office, members of the opposition Conservative Party, including Winston Churchill and Anthony Eden, elements of the British press, and members of the Joint Intelligence Committee would go on to criticize the treaty once it had been agreed in Canberra.[132] Such criticism evoked little sympathy in the Southern Hemisphere. Despite preferring British inclusion, Australian and New Zealand policymakers were unwilling to see their designs for a security treaty undermined by British complaints.[133] Holland conceded that "New Zealand was moving towards closer solidarity with the United States of America," even though he was keen to stress that this "was not incompatible with [the] Dominion's devotion to the Mother Country."[134]

The timing of the ANZUS Treaty also complemented important economic shifts away from British interests. As Australia's goals for diversifying its industrial structure developed, the United Kingdom struggled to provide the necessary capital. Australia subsequently renegotiated its trade relations in the 1950s and placed greater emphasis on relations with the United States. The economic recovery in the Asia-Pacific region, along with the liberalization of trading practices, weakened Britain's privilege within the imperial trading system and encouraged rival markets for potential Australian goods and services. By the late 1960s, Japan would become a more important market for Australian products than the United Kingdom.[135] Taken together, then, exclusion from the ANZUS Treaty was a costly and embarrassing failure for the British government despite Australian forces remaining committed to the Middle East. Events clearly had broader implications than simply a blow to British self-esteem.[136]

By the end of 1951, the United States, Australia, and New Zealand had all benefited from the agreement reached during the Canberra talks. The U.S. could now progress with rebuilding Japan, which represented a crucial part of its emerging Cold War strategy in the Asia-Pacific that sought to support regional powers in the containment of the Soviet Union. ANZUS therefore complemented U.S. grand strategy in the Cold War. Antipodean policymakers used their position as a signatory of the Japanese instruments of surrender and their limited Cold War security commitments to extract the U.S. security guarantee that they deemed essential for upholding their long-term security interests. Exclusion from ANZUS, however, meant that the British government lost a significant degree of influence in the Asia-Pacific. Major discussions about the future of the region would now take place without the involvement of the United Kingdom. For the British government, however, the matter remained far from settled.

CHAPTER 4

Selective Membership

Exclusion from ANZUS embarrassed British policymakers and undermined many of the United Kingdom's interests in the Asia-Pacific region. Clement Attlee had initially accepted exclusion, but Winston Churchill's election to office in October 1951 resulted in a concerted effort to gain membership. Although Australia and New Zealand remained sympathetic to an expanded treaty, both feared that pushing British membership too forcefully risked the United States dissolving the ANZUS Treaty. Despite enjoying a degree of recovery, economic limitations and ongoing commitments to Europe and the Middle East meant that the United Kingdom was unable to offer the antipodean states a credible alternative to existing arrangements.[1] Australia and New Zealand consequently attempted to secure membership for Britain but prioritized ongoing cooperation with the United States.

The major obstacle to British membership in ANZUS remained the United States. Despite concerted diplomatic efforts, U.S. concerns about incorporating the United Kingdom and broader British Commonwealth commitments into ANZUS proved irresolvable. As far as U.S. policymakers interpreted matters, British inclusion provided few benefits and considerable economic and strategic drawbacks. Yet U.S. officials preferred to use arguments about race and imperialism to justify British omission from the treaty. The United States remained committed to maintaining ANZUS in its existing form and rebuffed efforts by the antipodean powers to secure British inclusion.

Explaining Exclusion

All the members of ANZUS had agreed to exclude the United Kingdom from membership in early 1951. London accurately perceived Washington to be the driving force behind this decision. Explanations for exclusion, however, differed on either side of the Atlantic. Senior elements within the Labour government and the Conservative opposition believed that British exclusion reflected Attlee's decision to recognize Mao's China in January 1950. London's choice was certainly distasteful to U.S. policymakers given that the president himself believed that the British had not played "very squarely with us on this matter."[2] Yet, as the British ambassador to Washington reported to London, the U.S. reaction was "less violent than we feared."[3] Moreover, little mention of the United Kingdom's China policy surfaces in U.S. documentation concerning British exclusion from ANZUS. To be sure, both countries would increasingly divide in their strategic approach toward China in the early 1950s, a schism in which Australia and New Zealand were reluctant to be drawn.[4] Nevertheless, Britain's decision to recognize Mao's China was at best only a marginal factor behind U.S. decision making concerning ANZUS.

The United States' public explanations for maintaining the existing agreement instead centered on perceptions of race and inequality in the Asia-Pacific region. U.S. officials explained that British exclusion from ANZUS reflected anxieties about creating an "Anglo-Saxon" or "white man's club" in Asia rather than citing strategic or economic concerns. British membership would apparently create such a club, whereas a limited agreement would help win the propaganda battle against the Soviet Union, pacify complaints emanating from the Indian government about U.S. racism, and avoid antagonizing the United States' Asian allies such as the Philippines.[5]

U.S. justifications for excluding the United Kingdom from ANZUS were not insincere rhetoric. Ideas about race were important to many key U.S. policymakers. John Foster Dulles, for example, had long been concerned that the United States' domestic racial inequality would undermine its international position and hurt what he saw as the country's mission to promote international justice.[6] Dulles had grown increasingly anxious throughout the Japanese peace treaty negotiations that Asia-Pacific countries would construe the U.S.'s dictating of terms as an example of imperialism. The Soviet Union certainly stressed the domination of the negotiations by the

United States with its allies in such terms. Such rhetoric was important not only because of the ongoing propaganda battle between East and West but also because accusations of racism and imperialism would make the task of agreeing and implementing the terms of a sustainable and legitimate Japanese peace treaty much more difficult. U.S. policymakers therefore made a concerted effort to downplay such allegations and sought to convince the international community that they were committed to the fair and equal treatment of all peoples regardless of race. Dulles informed his British counterparts in 1951 that the U.S. had to ensure that Western immigration laws did not continue to treat the Japanese as an "inferior people," and that the "policies of the United States, Australia, and New Zealand present a problem" in this regard.[7]

Dean Acheson, in conversation with his Filipino counterpart, Carlos Romulo, agreed that the creation of any new Pacific security pact should not have a "racial foundation" and could not exclusively comprise "white" countries.[8] Acheson was also concerned that the international community would construe U.S. actions in the Asia-Pacific as acting in a "colonialist fashion." As the U.S. secretary of state learned following the recent decision by Washington to provide support to France for its war inside Indochina, U.S. foreign policy gave the "impression that we were helping maintain a vestige of French, British or Dutch control." As such, Washington had unintentionally bolstered "the remnants of hated colonial regimes in this area."[9] As the *Washington Post* opined in its op-ed, the United Kingdom had to be excluded from ANZUS to ensure that the United States was not supporting "colonialism" in the region.[10] Other leaders also expressed similar concerns. South Korea's foreign minister Ben Limb, for instance, wrote in *Foreign Affairs* that ANZUS could be viewed by Asian states as a "white man's pact" that would hurt the United States' alliances in the region.[11]

These issues mattered over the longer term because Communism had become more attractive to the nationalist movements across Southeast Asia that were assuming greater prominence in the region.[12] The United States' domestic actions were just as important as senior policymakers throughout the Truman administration were similarly concerned that domestic racial problems in the U.S. would infringe on the nation's ability to fight the Cold War. Communist propagandists certainly targeted such issues and U.S. diplomats were sensitive to such charges and their Cold War implications.[13] Accusations of acting in a racist and colonist fashion in both the domestic and international realm therefore mattered to policymakers in Washington. Nevertheless, explaining the U.S. motivation to exclude the United Kingdom from ANZUS on grounds of racial equality is only partially convincing.

As many U.S. policymakers understood, the creation of ANZUS had already established a "white man's pact" in the region. The creation of the trilateral alliance would soon give the impression to some Asian countries that the United States was "appearing to join with other Western powers behind the backs of the Asians in organizations for the defense of the Far East or parts of the Far East."[14] As one Australian memorandum from March 1951 notes, "There was a danger that a security pact limited to the three white Pacific nations would raise serious political problems for the United States in the Philippines."[15] Dulles was understandably concerned about an exclusively "white" security pact, and in part this explains why he pushed for Philippine membership of ANZUS during the Canberra talks. Washington also privately recognized that both Australia and New Zealand had wanted to exclude the Philippines from membership largely because they desired a "white" Pacific security pact.[16]

Conceivably, British inclusion could have signaled an unwelcome revival of "Western imperialism," given the country's still vast empire, or could have intensified claims of racism. Yet onlookers would surely struggle to see how the addition of the United Kingdom would somehow make ANZUS dramatically more "Western" or a "white man's club" given that each was effectively already the case, especially considering the "white Australia" and "white New Zealand" immigration policies that existed at this time. While the antipodean governments were slowly dismantling such policies, strict immigration controls against nonwhites persisted in both countries until the 1960s. The creation of ANZUS therefore clearly associated the United States, which itself was afflicted with enormous racial injustice, with two countries that practiced racial discrimination.[17] Washington was willing to accept such an association, however, if it complemented its broader strategic and economic ambitions.

References to race, specifically the dangers of creating a "white man's club," helped defend British exclusion from ANZUS and obscured more self-interested motivations behind U.S. policy. Two other factors help explain why the United States preferred to exclude the United Kingdom from the ANZUS arrangement. The first revolved around a continued fear within the U.S. policymaking establishment that British membership in ANZUS would inevitably lead to problematic calls from other states, including France, the Netherlands, Portugal, Japan, Singapore, Indonesia, and Thailand, to be included in a U.S. security umbrella for the entire Asia-Pacific. Such a broad-based security alliance was something that U.S. policymakers believed was simply unaffordable.[18] Truman's rearmament program had already produced a considerable strain on the U.S. economy.[19] U.S. strategic planners feared the misallocation of scarce resources. They were concerned that British membership in a new Pacific security pact would misdirect both Washington's and London's limited military and economic power away from strategic priorities, namely Western Europe, the Mediterranean, and the Middle East. From Washington's perspective, the British economy remained in a perilous state and was afflicted with "underlying difficulties" that stemmed from the "British failure to shake out the rigidities in their economy and become competitive."[20] Given this economic weakness, the Truman administration concluded that U.S. interests were best served by encouraging the United Kingdom to become a much more regionalized power and integrate itself into the emerging political-economic union in Western Europe.[21]

The second factor, which emanated from the JCS and the Department of Defense in Washington, concerned the risk of European powers manipulating the United States into defending their colonial possessions under the guise of fighting against Communism. Such fears had merit given the fact that Britain was already fighting an insurgency inside Malaya. Membership of ANZUS would allow London to pressure Washington to provide greater assistance for such wars, despite being largely a British responsibility.[22] Such a network could allow the United Kingdom to exercise more influence over strategic planning for the region, which the United States now currently dominated. During their discussions with the United Kingdom on other highly sensitive matters, the U.S. made a point of refusing to discuss their strategic plans for the Asia-Pacific. If membership extended to the British, then the French would likely seek inclusion. ANZUS would then assume the character of a Southeast Asian security pact, which France could consequently utilize as a means to encourage greater assistance for French forces inside Indochina. The JCS were unwilling to expand membership of ANZUS and risk either the British or French using it to save their colonial positions.[23]

Seeking Inclusion

The Attlee government had sought to downplay the United Kingdom's exclusion from ANZUS throughout 1951. Some British policymakers nevertheless found claims of creating a "white man's pact" unconvincing given current ANZUS membership and the United States' close association with the United Kingdom in many other parts of the globe. They protested in private that U.S. domestic policies toward nonwhite Americans hardly placed the United States in a position to lecture others about racial equality. The British government also feared that other states might construe U.S. comments about a "white man's pact" as carrying negative racial undertones thereby undermining British efforts to maintain possessions throughout the Asia-Pacific and hampering efforts to improve security ties with countries across the region.[24]

Both the British Foreign Office and the Colonial Office continued with their efforts to convince the prime minister to push the case for membership in ANZUS more forcefully with the United States. The British ambassador to Washington, Sir Oliver Franks, raised the subject with Acheson but could not convince the U.S. secretary of state to change his mind.[25] Such failures were disappointing for London. Yet the British prime minister steadfastly refused to allow the topic to divert from his central tasks of maintaining close U.S.-UK relations and prioritizing the defense of Europe and the Middle East.[26] Exclusion from ANZUS was irritating, but rectifying this situation would not become a central ambition of British foreign policy while Attlee remained in office.

Electoral defeat for Attlee in the 1951 general election brought with it a swift reversal in policy. On October 26, Winston Churchill returned to office with a small parliamentary majority. He had returned to Downing Street for his final premiership at the age of almost seventy-seven. Out of office, Churchill had publicly lamented how the Labour government followed policies that weakened the British Empire. Britain's handling of India, coupled with retreat from Palestine, was strategic folly, which, in Churchill's mind, cast serious doubt about the strength of Britain's global position. As Churchill announced to the House of Commons, "The British Empire seems to be running off. . . . The haste is appalling. 'Scuttle' is the word, and the only word, that can be applied."[27] Exclusion from the ANZUS Treaty in Churchill's assessment was indicative of the Labour government's mishandling of Britain's position as a great power. Shortly after taking office, therefore, the prime minister demanded membership in ANZUS.

Churchill's attitude to British exclusion from ANZUS reflected a mixture of belief and strategy.[28] The prime minister genuinely believed in the connection between the "mother country" and the "Dominions." Churchill was committed to the maintenance of the British Empire and Commonwealth and understood it to be a force for good in the world. Churchill's doctor, Lord Moran, noted that his patient's attachment to the defense of the British Empire was not simply "bravado" exercised in front of various audiences. Instead, Churchill "was affirming a faith for which he was prepared to give his life."[29] Others including the Canadian prime minister Mackenzie King observed that "the British Empire and Commonwealth is a religion" to Churchill.[30] It is fair to suggest that the British Empire held a lifelong emotional pull over the prime minister.[31] Exclusion from ANZUS therefore represented a direct challenge to the maintenance of what Churchill still referred to as the British Empire. If Australia and New Zealand, seen by many in London as the most loyal of all the Dominions, were "going off" with the United States, then the future looked bleak for the British Commonwealth. Churchill was determined to ensure that Britain secured membership in ANZUS or, if this objective proved impossible, to make the organization irrelevant by creating something better.

These factors explain only part of Churchill's interest in the ANZUS Treaty. Although Churchill's attachment to the British Empire may have been strong, it had never prevented him from prioritizing the defense of the mother country over Britain's possessions throughout the Asia-Pacific as evidenced during World War II. As events throughout the region grew steadily more important to the developing global Cold War, inclusion in ANZUS became ever more significant as it would allow Britain to exert more influence over U.S. strategy throughout the region. Churchill understood that if both Australia and New Zealand shared an exclusive arrangement with the United States, then it was likely that both powers would prioritize their own strategic defense rather than that of the British Commonwealth. In essence, both Canberra and Wellington would look to defend the "near north" to the detriment of the Middle East, Mediterranean, and Western Europe, which Churchill believed should remain the core focus of British Commonwealth security efforts.[32]

Churchill had also grown increasingly concerned about the course of international relations. Washington's Cold War policies were, in the private estimations of the prime minister, nearly as dangerous to global peace as the policies pursued by the Kremlin.[33] The advent of the atomic age convinced the prime minister that it was imperative to avoid escalating political disagreement with the Communist world into a global war. Unnecessary provocation of the Soviet Union risked the very survival of the British Commonwealth. Churchill was clear that continual confrontation between the West and the Communist powers had to be tempered and negotiations about fundamental political differences needed to resume. Preventing an escalation of hostilities inside Korea became a key element of Churchill's diplomacy with Washington.[34] Inside Europe, the British government had played a key role as a partner to the United States within NATO and as one of the four occupying powers inside Germany. Throughout Asia and the Pacific, however, no such position existed. This was an omission that Churchill sought to rectify.[35]

Churchill's ideas ranged from the grandiose—namely, a large Pacific security pact that would bring together numerous states to combat the rising influence of Communism throughout the region—to the mundane, such as Britain securing "observer status" within ANZUS. As the term suggests, a British observer would be present during private meetings of the ANZUS Council and would thus be able to make a full record of the discussions.[36] All such efforts reflected the desire of the British government to exert a greater degree of influence over Western strategy for the Pacific. This would ensure Australian and New Zealand commitments to British priorities, soothe unnecessarily belligerent U.S. policies toward Communist China, and in turn promote superpower détente. As such, gaining entry into ANZUS was a priority for Churchill.[37]

Committing resources to ANZUS or creating a new Pacific security pact would cost money, however, which the British government lacked. On taking office, Chancellor of the Exchequer Richard Austin "Rab" Butler was horrified to learn of the magnitude of national borrowing and public expenditure of the Attlee government. As Butler informed the cabinet, the United Kingdom was simply doing "too much" for Western defense. Butler subsequently advised Churchill that it was imperative for the United Kingdom to reduce defense expenditure and let others spend more on their own security needs.[38] Economic concerns had assumed greater prominence as the Korean War stabilized. The Conservative government consequently pursued further defense cutbacks in order to improve the state of the British economy.[39] Financial weakness restricted the type of security guarantees the British government could offer to Australian and New Zealand policymakers. Indeed, the limitations of the United Kingdom's supply capacity encouraged Australia to turn toward the United States for additional resources for accelerated economic development.[40]

Churchill would have to utilize his personal charisma and exploit the emotional ties with antipodean policymakers to achieve his objective of ANZUS membership or a wider security pact in the region. To be sure, other areas of alliance cooperation existed between the three states, which helped in a broader sense. Both Australia and New Zealand had gained access to U.S. signals intelligence and a trickle of gossip via the British relationship with the United States.[41] Yet there appears to be no mention of coercive diplomacy, where threats to repeal existing commitments could be used to British advantage. The absence of such an approach likely reflects doubts about what such efforts might accomplish, or simply fear that the U.S. would provide any intelligence assessments to Canberra and Wellington bilaterally. London instead adopted a two-pronged diplomatic strategy, making clear appeals to Washington while pursuing assertive efforts with Canberra and Wellington.

The diplomatic approach first involved directly lobbying Washington for British membership in ANZUS followed by efforts to grant Britain at least observer status. Churchill's personal standing and celebrity offered some diplomatic advantage. According to Acheson, Truman "often spoke of Churchill as the greatest public figure of our age," a point that Acheson himself believed to be an "understatement."[42] Furthermore, the United Kingdom remained, as one internal U.S. policy-planning document termed it, "of critical importance" to promoting U.S. strategic interests, not least in being able to counter likely Soviet moves in a general war.[43] As such, London's voice would have to be heard. British insistence on raising ANZUS membership therefore forced U.S. policymakers to confront the issue of the United Kingdom's exclusion head on.

Churchill took the opportunity to raise the subject during his visit to Washington during December 1951. The prime minister's hosts gently deflected his suggestions and sought to downplay all his concerns. Truman and his key advisers believed that Churchill's best days were behind him and had not been keen on the prime minister's visit, contrary to what the president suggested in his memoirs.[44] Moreover, U.S. planning material for the visit was more concerned with the declining fortunes of the British economy. Economic malaise could hurt U.S. efforts to galvanize the Western alliance in containing Soviet power.[45] The visit nevertheless went without major incident, and the Truman administration politely listened to the prime minister's complaints and suggestions.[46] Such delicacy should not obscure Washington's decision to ignore Churchill's appeals on ANZUS. Furthermore, when Truman and Acheson suggested to Churchill that they would seek British views on "creating some real power in the Far East," they had both deliberately separated this topic from the question of British membership in ANZUS. The question of British membership was a subject on which the president and his staff refused to be drawn.[47] Many British policymakers perceived growing U.S. power as an increasing challenge to Britain's global interests. Harold Macmillan, rising star of the Conservative Party and future prime minister, later lamented in his diary about how the United States treated Britain: "They treat us worse than they do any country in Europe. They undermine our political and commercial influence all over the world. Yet all this they do (so ambivalent is their policy) with only one half of their mind and purpose. The other half is just as friendly and loyal as in the days of the war."[48]

Facing resistance from Washington, Churchill focused on Canberra and Wellington. He now asked for both Menzies and Holland to lobby the United States to expand the membership of ANZUS. Canberra and Wellington were sympathetic, not least because antipodean officials recognized that expanding ANZUS might provide them with additional benefits. British membership could encourage the United States to commit to more extensive security planning and cooperation and would avoid repeating strategic defense planning within the framework of ANZAM planning.[49] Such potential benefits, however, had to balance against the likely risks. The United States had always made clear its objections to British membership in ANZUS, and both antipodean powers feared that by pushing for such a change they might jeopardize the treaty itself.

To help persuade Canberra and Wellington to support British efforts toward obtaining ANZUS membership, Churchill sought to improve existing British Commonwealth security cooperation in the Asia-Pacific. Despite repeated warnings from the Treasury about the precious state of national finances, the British prime minister had few qualms about offering additional resources.[50] Churchill offered detailed staff talks about how to uphold security throughout the ANZAM region in the longer term and suggestions about what the British would provide militarily to the region to make such planning credible. Churchill also mentioned the creation of a broader Pacific security framework, which would establish a central political body that could dictate interalliance strategy throughout the region and would have a special focus on Southeast Asia. The offer also included the alluring concession that Australia would take the leading role in such an organization.[51] Most of Churchill's Pacific security proposals in this period remained abstract and largely undeveloped, which raises questions about their credibility, especially given the weakened state of British finances. Nevertheless, he had designed such efforts to show that the United Kingdom was still capable of exercising material influence over events in the Asia-Pacific and would therefore be a positive addition to ANZUS.

Both Canberra and Wellington gave Churchill's ideas considerable thought. In April 1952, Holland confirmed that "the United Kingdom must be brought in" to ANZUS.[52] Of the three members of ANZUS, New Zealand had always been the most favorable to British membership. Holland sought the inclusion of the United Kingdom at least partially as a means of ensuring broader and more comprehensive security cooperation in the region that would benefit his country's security.[53] These strategic calculations also helped spark Menzies's interest in Churchill's ideas. He concluded that they provided an opportunity to turn ANZUS into a functioning security alliance, which would include detailed strategic planning and allocating the requisite military resources. As the Australian prime minister suggested to his closest security advisers, British membership would increase the level of importance attached to the defense of the Asia-Pacific by the United Kingdom and United States.[54] There was considerable support for Menzies's thinking in the Australian Defence Department. As strategic planning between Australia, New Zealand, and the United Kingdom already existed within the context of ANZAM, it was illogical to replicate this within the framework of some future ANZUS planning that omitted the British entirely. In addition, in the event of a global war, Britain's military contribution would be imperative to ensuring that Australian sea-lanes remained open. Finding a solution to British omission from ANZUS was therefore important.[55]

Churchill's plans clearly placed far greater importance on the Asia-Pacific as a strategic area of concern and could potentially improve U.S. security commitments to the region. Australian officials remained keenly aware that ANZAM planning was of limited value without U.S. assistance in the event of a global war. As the Australian Defence Committee had privately concluded, "Defence arrangements for the ANZAM region must be related to Allied global strategy."[56] The ideas emanating from London could also perhaps convince Washington to take a keener interest in ANZUS. In the assessment of Australian and New Zealand officials, the U.S. had shown a disappointing lack of interest in ANZUS.[57] Obtaining a formal association with NATO or establishing something similar in the Pacific motivated antipodean enthusiasm for Churchill's plans. Canberra agreed with Wellington that they would both support London's ambition to join ANZUS. Alternatively, at the very least, they should grant the United Kingdom observer status within ANZUS with a view to a more formal association in the future. U.S. resistance, however, would once again undermine the pursuit of an extended security pact in the Asia-Pacific region.

Debating Membership

Throughout 1952, the antipodean powers continued discussions concerning the nature of the ANZUS alliance.[58] New Zealand remained more committed to British inclusion than Australia, but both countries agreed that they would benefit from such an expanded membership. Menzies's return visit to Washington over the summer of 1952 provided an opportunity to assess the United States' position on this matter. Yet when the Australian prime minister ventured abroad in May, contrary to the expectations of the Truman administration, he focused not on ANZUS but on discussing the terms of a possible economic development package for Australia. Menzies had again emphasized to Acheson the need for further economic assistance for Australia because it did not possess the necessary dollars to purchase vital military equipment that was required to uphold its existing security commitments. A loan from the United States was required because other viable sources, such as the United Kingdom, did not have sufficient quantities of dollars. The World Bank, which did have the resources, could not offer loans to countries to purchase military equipment.[59]

In subsequent discussions with Acheson in June, Menzies never really advanced the cause for British membership in ANZUS. Acheson would only go as far to suggest that he was willing to grant Britain observer status, but he was concerned that such a move would lead to similar requests from the likes of the Philippines and Indonesia. Menzies agreed with Acheson that they should put to one side the subject of ANZUS expansion for the time being.[60] Menzies once again avoided direct confrontation on the matter, preferring to leave the issue until the outcome looked more favorable.

In his talks in Washington, Menzies instead focused on three other major international issues. First, he sought to convince the president of the need for much fuller cooperation between the ANZUS powers. Second, he sought a deeper U.S. commitment to the Southeast Asian region. U.S. planning for Southeast Asia could also include the participation of the United Kingdom, thereby distributing these additional responsibilities throughout the Western alliance. Third, Menzies tried to persuade the president that Australia needed formal access to NATO planning so that it could improve its support for broader U.S. designs in the Cold War.[61]

Menzies understood geographical factors meant that Australia could not be a member of NATO and so did not request membership. He did say, however, that he felt decisions taken by NATO "had a direct effect on Australia and that therefore Australia had a very real interest in the activity of NATO." Menzies was clear that Australia "really wanted two things: (a) some access to the thinking and doing of NATO and (b) some right to offer views to NATO on matters directly affecting Australian interests."[62] Percy Spender, now serving as the Australian ambassador to Washington, suggested that Australia should have the right to be heard not only with respect to general strategic considerations but especially on matters directly affecting Australia. The ambassador said that Australia was not content to be "the hair on the tail of the dog." They felt they, at least, should be part of "the hide of the dog itself."[63]

Menzies was unable to convince the administration to shift current U.S. policies and grant Australia formal access to NATO planning. Nor was he able to secure a major loan, principally due to the difficulty of allocating U.S. resources to less pressing concerns. The best that Menzies could obtain was a vague assurance that the United States remained "open minded" on "working out some method [of] dealing with countries outside [the] NATO area."[64] The Australian prime minister therefore reluctantly conceded defeat on this issue but maintained hopes of progress in future negotiations.

The Australian prime minister subsequently visited the United Kingdom in June 1952. Menzies had been concerned that a serious argument with Churchill would develop so had instructed his officials to provide him with detailed briefing material that would contain a wide array of data to prove that Australia was more than pulling its weight in providing for British Commonwealth defense.[65] Discussions remained cordial, but obvious tensions between the two prime ministers concerning British exclusion from ANZUS were never far from the surface.[66] Churchill once again pushed for membership, but the issue proved to be less contentious than Australian officials had initially feared. Menzies helped matters by explaining, albeit disingenuously, that he had discussed British membership in ANZUS in his recent talks with Truman. By raising the subject briefly in Washington, Menzies could plausibly claim to have acted in good faith. But by doing so in such a limited manner, he avoided risking the United States' commitment to the ANZUS Treaty. The Australian prime minister sensibly claimed that he personally wanted Britain to be a member of ANZUS, but the major obstacle remained the United States. Menzies thus redirected British complaints toward the U.S., which was in a better position than either Australia or New Zealand to absorb such criticism. By focusing London's ire against Washington, the United Kingdom could in turn perhaps convince the United States to provide a more comprehensive security alliance for the Asia-Pacific. Menzies's diplomacy therefore sought to safeguard and promote Australian interests regardless of the outcome of U.S.-UK diplomacy.

London once again directed its attention to Washington but patience across the Atlantic was wearing thin.[67] The Truman administration had repeatedly explained to the British that ANZUS was a limited security pact. Moreover, the treaty supported British interests by providing the security guarantee that would allow Australia and New Zealand to uphold their crucial military contributions to British Commonwealth commitments in the Middle East and Mediterranean. As strategic planners in Washington believed, if the United Kingdom was to uphold its strategic responsibilities in the defense of the general area of the Middle East, then "substantial armed forces from Australia and New Zealand as well as other commonwealth nations will, in all probability, have to be provided."[68] At a British Commonwealth Defence Ministers meeting in June 1951, Australian and New Zealand representatives emphasized how the U.S. guarantee in the Asia-Pacific would allow both Canberra and Wellington to fulfill their British Commonwealth obligations in the Middle East and Mediterranean.[69] Australia later demonstrated its commitment with the eventual dispatch of two fighter squadrons to Malta in July 1952.[70]

The Truman administration further reasoned that U.S.-UK discussions about Asia-Pacific security already occurred during existing bilateral discussions and had included the participation of Spender. Accordingly, the U.S. government did not accept that complaints about omission from ANZUS had markedly negative consequences for British interests.[71] U.S. officials were keen to stress that British demands were unreasonable given that the Conservative government was embarking on a round of defense cuts, which called into question London's ability to maintain its existing global security commitments. The foreign secretary Anthony Eden had certainly articulated to the British cabinet that the United Kingdom could not extend its global responsibilities any further. Churchill reluctantly accepted this point but still believed that he should seek membership in any new security organizations in the Asia-Pacific. Existing resources would simply have to stretch a little further.[72]

London had managed to place considerable pressure on Washington, Canberra, and Wellington by continually raising the issue of British exclusion in bilateral forums.[73] Because of this pressure, the first meeting of the ANZUS Council, held in Honolulu, Hawaii, on 4–6 August 1952, surrendered a considerable amount of time discussing the United Kingdom's relationship to the treaty. During discussions, Australia's minister for external affairs, Richard Casey, suggested that they needed to do something to appease British sensibilities. Failure to do so, he warned, risked ANZUS expanding into a larger and more dangerous political issue. Casey proposed that if membership was impossible, then the United Kingdom should secure observer status. The New Zealand representative, Clifton Webb, supported Casey's claims. As Casey emphasized, the latter proposal would allow the United Kingdom to send an official to observe but not participate in ANZUS discussions. Such a compromise would help undermine British complaints that decisions of strategic importance were taking place without their knowledge. Casey's efforts, however, failed to convince Acheson. As the New Zealand minute of the meeting noted, the question of British participation in ANZUS proved to be one of "considerable difficulty."[74] Hinting at broader strategic priorities, Acheson argued that allowing the British observer status would cause "acute embarrassment" for other countries not given similar privileges. If the United Kingdom secured either observer status or membership in ANZUS, then similar concessions would have to be offered to the likes of France and the Philippines.[75]

Casey took Acheson's reluctance as an indicator to move the discussion forward. "Putting the flesh" onto the bones of ANZUS remained the primary task for both Casey and Webb. Evolving security developments in the Asia-Pacific increasingly concerned the antipodean powers. Recent French setbacks in Indochina, for instance, so alarmed the New Zealand policymaking bureaucracy that Leslie Munro, the New Zealand minister to Washington, met with Acheson to press the case that additional U.S. support should be provided to France to prevent Communist success in Indochina. This action from Wellington mirrored that by Canberra as Menzies had also personally urged Truman and Acheson to increase U.S. assistance for France in Indochina.[76] When the matter was again raised at the ANZUS Council meeting in August 1952, Acheson explained that "the Americans were convinced that the French forces could hold Indochina, and that there was no need to send more troops there at the moment."[77]

British membership in ANZUS was an important subject, but the priority for both Australia and New Zealand was to establish real military cooperation between the existing three members. Antipodean ambitions thus focused on reaching agreement with the United States on implementing joint military planning within the framework of ANZUS as well as trying to pry information out of the Americans concerning their broader strategic plans for regional security. Casey was especially forthright in trying to press the Americans to accept the establishment of a formal link between ANZUS planning and U.S. global strategic planning. This proposal would involve basing military representatives from Canberra in Washington so that they could liaise with the U.S. Joint Chiefs of Staff. In response, Acheson made clear to Casey that the JCS were extremely reluctant to accommodate any additional staff officers in Washington. The JCS and Department of Defense had continued to express their disinclination to provide any "military organization" in connection to ANZUS.[78] Furthermore, as Acheson argued, all discussion on Asia-Pacific strategy actually took place in Honolulu so it made better sense to base antipodean representatives there.[79] Acheson's statement revealed that the U.S. saw ANZUS as a strictly regional security pact. By insisting that Australian and New Zealand representatives be based in Honolulu and not Washington, Acheson had clearly demarcated where he believed the antipodean powers should direct their efforts in the Cold War.

Subsequent discussion failed to shift Acheson's initial position. The U.S. secretary of state repeatedly rebuffed Australian and New Zealand suggestions for the creation of joint military planning or for antipodean representatives to be based in Washington.[80] Though it was reported that the "Americans were very frank in discussing . . . their military thinking over a wide range of South East Asian problems," the U.S. government preferred not to formalize military planning within ANZUS and wanted all military discussions between the three countries to function principally in an advisory fashion.[81] Efforts to link ANZUS to broader U.S. plans for global strategy proved equally futile. As Webb outlined to his cabinet colleagues on returning to Wellington, Acheson simply would not agree to undertake increased military planning at this stage.[82]

Yet it would be a mistake to conclude that the recent ANZUS Council meeting was a complete failure for Australian and New Zealand strategic ambitions. Webb, for instance, told his colleagues that he believed the meeting to have been a success.[83] To justify this claim, he explained that "we were very lucky" to have ANZUS.[84] Indeed, Acheson had mentioned that the burgeoning military cooperation between the countries could improve in the future and that existing military machinery was "provisional" and "subject to change in the light of experience."[85] In addition, during Acheson's closing conference speech, he announced that he hoped the work of the ANZUS Council would lead to an "even closer relationship" with Australia and New Zealand. Such rhetoric gained substance as Acheson announced that Admiral Radford, commander of the U.S. Pacific Fleet, would now begin to liaise with Australian and New Zealand representatives in Honolulu about future security cooperation.[86]

Antipodean ambitions for closer military cooperation with Washington had evidently made some progress by the end of the first ANZUS Council meeting, even if it had not gone as far as Canberra or Wellington had desired. As such, at the conclusion of the ANZUS conference in August 1952, the participants issued a joint communiqué, which, while not strictly forbidding British membership, made it clear that none of the member states were looking to expand the agreement in the immediate future.[87] Both the Menzies and Holland governments might have preferred British membership in ANZUS, but they were unwilling to push the point for fear it could endanger the nascent treaty.[88]

Maintaining Exclusion

British officials had watched the ANZUS discussions closely to learn whether the United Kingdom would secure membership in the organization. The public communiqué issued at the end of the conference made clear that Britain's exclusion would continue. London nevertheless sought confirmation from the ANZUS members that this was in fact the whole story.[89] The response, which confirmed British suspicions of continued exclusion, left senior policymakers seething.[90] They were especially angered by the United States' claim that British inclusion was unacceptable because it would necessitate membership for other European states. "What impudence to suggest that France and I suppose Portugal (who have interests in these waters)," Churchill wrote to Eden, "are on the same terms with Australia and New Zealand as Britain. If this point became public in either of these countries, I am sure that would be a violent re-action. This is not a thing to let slip. We should bite hard."[91]

Churchill exhibited his anger in conversation with both the high commissioners from Australia and New Zealand. As the New Zealand high commissioner reported, he was "trying to calm [Churchill] down" but he was "worked up" because "he was led to believe that Australia and New Zealand desired British participation but submitted to American pressure and even more, because the American reply put Britain and the Philippines on the same level."[92] There was growing frustration in British policymaking circles regarding the seemingly illogical exclusion of the United Kingdom from ANZUS. According to the New Zealand high commissioner in London: "[Churchill] argues that it would be militarily impossible to plan defence of Australia and New Zealand against Russia, China or Japan without considering the whole potential threat from Asia and of course concentrating primarily on South East Asia. . . . If the ANZUS partners are to plan for the defence of areas which include British territories and large British commitments he claims Britain has at least right to an observer."[93] Lord Salisbury, the secretary of state for the Dominions, was equally as frustrated, grumbling that the attitude of the Dominions was "deplorable" and "tiresome."[94] Admiral McGrigor, the first sea lord, was, as reported in Australian circles, "rampaging" about Australia's attitude.[95] The United States' recent treaties with Japan and the Philippines only highlighted how it intended to exclude the United Kingdom from serious discussion as it pertained to the future of security in the Asia-Pacific region. As one British diplomat noted, "It is disquieting that while the Americans seem ready to fall over backward to avoid hurting Philippine or Japanese feelings, they do not seem to have a similar regard for British susceptibilities."[96]

British policymakers saw their omission from ANZUS as more than merely a political embarrassment, but rather as a challenge to their broader international interests. The British had managed to obtain agreement that Australia and New Zealand would station fighter planes on Malta and Cyprus.[97] Australia was nevertheless becoming more assertive in its requests for clarity on what Britain would in turn provide concerning ANZAM defense planning and resources.[98] This confidence reflected in part the existence of ANZUS and its associated security guarantee from the United States. Burgeoning levels of discussion between the ANZUS powers also encouraged new ideas about where to station forces globally. While still officially U.S. policy to support the dispatch of antipodean forces into the Middle East and Mediterranean in the event of a global war, discussions between U.S. service personnel and their antipodean counterparts revealed that elements within the U.S. military were keen to explore how Australia and New Zealand could increase their own commitments to Asia-Pacific security.[99]

It had been a longer-term objective of the Joint Chiefs of Staff in Washington to encourage both Australia and New Zealand to commit additional resources to the defense of the "near north," which included Indochina, Burma, Thailand, and Malaya.[100] In particular, France's ongoing struggle to maintain its position in Indochina in the face of a Communist-led national liberation movement led some U.S. policymakers and military officials to rethink security provision in the region.[101] Acheson's decision to allow Australian and New Zealand representatives to discuss military matters with U.S. commanders in Honolulu helped encourage Canberra to consider more actively the prioritization of its own regional security throughout the Asia-Pacific over that of British Commonwealth responsibilities in the Middle East or Mediterranean.[102]

The Australian cabinet had decided in December of the previous year to accept a definite commitment to deploy to the Middle East the first army and air force contingents raised in Australia. It nevertheless postponed informing the British government of its decision, largely due to interdepartmental wrangling concerning the terms of the commitment and the deteriorating strategic situation in Southeast Asia. Menzies believed that if French forces withdrew from the region, Thailand would soon fall to Communism. In turn, he was worried that the United Kingdom would not be able to reinforce Malaya, which would come under further Communist pressure in the event of French withdrawal from Indochina. Menzies believed that the Australian people would not permit the dispatch of Australian forces to the Middle East following the loss of Indochina, which would bring the Communist threat closer to the mainland. Statements by the United States stressing that there would be no U.S. ground forces made available in the event of a Chinese attack of Indochina only heightened Australian concerns. On a visit to Washington in May 1952, Acheson confirmed Menzies's fears when he informed him that the U.S. would not prioritize the defense of Southeast Asia in the event of general war.[103]

Australia's ever-growing interest in Southeast Asia was a troubling element for both London and Wellington. British policymakers had always been concerned that exclusion from ANZUS would mean strategic decisions pertaining to broader Asia-Pacific security questions would occur without their participation. Prioritizing this region could undermine the United Kingdom's position in the Middle East and Mediterranean by limiting Australia's military contributions to the British Commonwealth. From Wellington's perspective, they too believed that Canberra was overly concerned with Southeast Asia to the detriment of their more vital global commitments. As Webb reported to the New Zealand cabinet following the ANZUS Council meeting of August 1952, and after recent French military successes in Indochina, "The Australians were in some difficulty concerning their emphasis on the importance of South East Asia as a reason for not committing themselves in the Middle East."[104] If the above analysis was correct, namely that the danger from Southeast Asia had receded, there was less reason for Australia withholding support for the Middle East.

In response to these developments, the British government decided to intensify its lobbying of Washington, Canberra, and Wellington for membership in ANZUS from late 1952 onward. The press baron Lord Beaverbrook, with Churchill's approval, oversaw a public relations strategy designed to win popular approval inside Australia and New Zealand for the British cause. Britain's exclusion from ANZUS deeply upset Beaverbrook. He believed that Menzies had behaved "shamefully" in agreeing to such an exclusive security alliance with the United States. Beaverbrook's newspapers attacked Britain's exclusion from ANZUS and targeted Canberra's political elite for criticism. In one broadside, Beaverbrook personally accused Casey of being "anti-British."[105] Such commentary stoked criticism of the Menzies government in his own parliament as critical questions about British exclusion from ANZUS grew in number.[106] The Holland government endured similar attacks, which would continue for over a year, and which exacerbated tensions within the New Zealand government concerning disloyalty toward the United Kingdom.[107]

London's actions proved irritating to both the Menzies and Holland governments and encouraged a direct response from Canberra. Casey wrote to Eden that the personal attacks directed at him by the British press were ill-informed and unfair. As Casey reasoned, the United Kingdom's exclusion from ANZUS was not because of an effort by the Menzies government to distance itself from the British Commonwealth. Instead, it reflected the consensus opinion of the members of ANZUS that British membership would inevitably lead to calls from France for membership, which in turn could see the ANZUS powers drawn directly into France's imbroglio in Indochina.[108]

British pressure was more effective against the Holland government as it forced the New Zealand prime minister to justify again to his entire cabinet why the United Kingdom had been excluded from ANZUS. During a cabinet session in September 1952, Holland, in an effort to play down suggestions that the United States had railroaded Australia and New Zealand into excluding the United Kingdom from ANZUS, emphasized that all three members of the treaty had reached this decision together.[109] For the New Zealand prime minister, the entire episode was one he would have rather avoided. As Holland suggested to a close adviser, he had cause to "regret" that British exclusion from ANZUS had become a matter of "public controversy."[110]

At this time, Canberra also tried to convince London that British membership in ANZUS was in fact unnecessary. Rather disingenuously, Casey argued that the existing ANZAM arrangements provided comprehensive avenues for Commonwealth security cooperation.[111] Yet ANZAM only involved serviceled cooperation rather than political agreement to engage in action in time of war.[112] Casey received a terse response that noted, "We could not regard ANZAM as an alternative to United Kingdom association with ANZUS."[113] It was also around this time, in late September 1952, that Australian officials began to invoke racial arguments in favor of British exclusion from ANZUS. Following the U.S. lead, Casey wrote to Eden stressing that British membership in ANZUS would create the impression in some Asian states that this was a "white man's pact" being established.[114] The importance of such concerns to Australia was questionable, especially given its own internal racial policies and the limited attention such issues had previously generated. Such explanations failed to deter London.

In bilateral discussion with both Australian and New Zealand officials, the British continued to press the case for ANZUS membership.[115] Canberra and Wellington's patience was now being sorely tested. While Australian policymakers accepted that the British government had a legitimate basis to be disgruntled about its exclusion from ANZUS, they did not believe this to be a good enough reason to push the case with Washington. More to the point, Menzies and Casey claimed that the British government's irritation was better explained by virtue of harm to its prestige rather than its material interests.[116] Similar opinion had emerged in New Zealand policymaking circles.[117]

ANZUS remained extremely important for the antipodean powers. From the very origins of the treaty, the Truman administration made it clear that the treaty was to be a regional security pact only with a very specific remit and limited membership. Antipodean policymakers may not have seen ANZUS in the same terms, but the dynamics of power meant that they had to accept U.S. wishes. If Canberra and Wellington desired ANZUS to morph into a fully comprehensive security pact, then policymakers would have to pursue this ambition very carefully. British membership in ANZUS would not come before the establishment of more comprehensive strategic cooperation between New Zealand, Australia, and the U.S. Therefore, when London again requested that Canberra and Wellington reopen the issue of British observer status to ANZUS at the next ANZUS military council, scheduled for November 1952, both the Menzies and Holland governments rejected the suggestion.[118]

It was apparent that if the British government wanted to obtain ANZUS membership then it would have to convince the United States to change its existing policy. When British officials once again pressed their U.S. counterparts, they received further resistance. During conversations with the British government, the Truman administration continually made it known that it would not establish any permanent military machinery for wider regional defense planning, nor would it countenance dispatching military forces.[119]

As the JCS noted, however, events in the Asia-Pacific were becoming increasingly important to U.S. security: "The immediately pressing problem of the West in Asia is the containment of Soviet-dominated communism to prevent its spread into Indochina and Southeast Asia. United States assistance to Indochina will be necessary, particularly since the conquest of that area by Soviet-dominated Communists would have serious consequences throughout southeast and southern Asia and Japan."[120]

The United States would continue to support the French in their efforts in Indochina and the British in Malaya. Senior U.S. policymakers now made the connection between their own efforts in Korea, French efforts in Indochina, and British Commonwealth efforts in Malaya as part of the same struggle against Communist insurrection and perfidy throughout the Asia-Pacific.[121] Important limitations on U.S. efforts in the Asia-Pacific, however, still existed. Doubts about the efficacy of intervention, alongside ongoing concerns about the costs of checking Communist expansion, served to limit military commitments to the region. In addition, under no circumstances would the United States assume responsibility for upholding wider European colonial interests in the region.[122]

Ongoing differences between the U.S. State Department and the Joint Chiefs concerning how to fight a war in Southeast Asia, assuming that the PRC invaded Indochina, also helps explain Washington's reluctance to make a firm commitment to a wider regional security pact. The State Department argued for a "holding type" action whereby U.S. forces would target only the approaches into Indochina. The JCS argued that the United States should target the "source" of the attack—namely, Communist

China—via air assault and a full-scale naval blockade.[123] The president was unable to resolve this dispute, and he appeared more concerned about the impending 1952 elections, especially the result's impact on the United States' long-term security.

Questions surrounding the expansion of ANZUS or the creation of a wider Pacific security pact held limited interest to the president at this time. As such, Acheson relied on existing excuses and explained that ANZUS could not be expanded as it would appear as a "White Man's Pact" that was "cloaking some new form of Imperialism."[124] Such an explanation was a much more convenient excuse than explaining U.S. concerns that the United Kingdom would manipulate the United States into defending British Commonwealth assets throughout the Asia-Pacific. Arguments predicated on racial justice were a fair representation of U.S. concerns and helped challenge Soviet propaganda about Western imperialism, to be sure, but they also served as a convenient tool for obscuring more pressing strategic and economic concerns.

Senior policymakers in London never believed Washington's concerns about racial equality alone drove their decision. The British Chiefs of Staff, for instance, assumed that far less altruistic reasons governed U.S. policy: "The United States desire to keep control of Far East planning in their own hands, and their own attitude towards ANZUS is governed by that desire."[125] Likewise, British officials complained that the U.S. argument lacked substance. Onlookers could hardly deem the addition of Britain to ANZUS, given its existing alliances with all three members, as unnatural. The United States was instead motivated by a desire to exclude Britain from Asia-Pacific security planning to ensure its own strategic and commercial interests were advanced.[126] In a perverse fashion, U.S. excuses about racial equality allowed the British government to save face. Fairness, not weakness, appeared to explain British exclusion to international onlookers, which perhaps explains why this diplomatic tool was rarely challenged publicly.

Rhetoric nevertheless had its limits, and the U.S. engaged in some subtle diplomacy to make it clear that Britain would not secure membership in ANZUS. In a further demonstration of Washington's rigid position, U.S. officials outlined clearly that if Britain continued to press its claims for ANZUS membership, then the United States would have to reconsider its commitments to the security pact. Washington had therefore threatened to create a crisis between London, Canberra, and Wellington. The antipodean powers were aggrieved that this latest U.S.-UK spat was directly affecting their security interests. Washington immediately denied this story, but was prepared to push for its interests in an extremely stern manner with London if necessary.[127]

The major obstacle to British membership in ANZUS was always the United States. Despite concerted diplomatic efforts, the rivalry between the U.S. and the UK in the region, coupled with U.S. concerns about incorporating Commonwealth commitments into ANZUS, proved irresolvable. As British officials concluded in the fall of 1952, if they were going to join ANZUS, then they would have to wait for a new administration to take over in Washington.[128] Dwight D. Eisenhower's electoral victory in November 1952 raised such hopes. Expectations that a new administration would bring with it a changed attitude to the subject of British membership in ANZUS would soon prove to be mistaken.

CHAPTER 5

An Unwelcome Ally

Following the arrival of a new U.S. administration in 1953, the British government resumed its efforts to improve its position in the Asia-Pacific. The need for greater influence in the region would only become more pressing as there began a serious shift of strategic focus by Australia away from the Middle East and toward Southeast Asia, which the United Kingdom and to a lesser extent New Zealand were keen to arrest. France's military difficulties in Indochina had encouraged Australia's decision to shift strategic emphasis, which also increased the risk of New Zealand mirroring such behavior. This potential redirection of antipodean interests presented a major challenge to the United Kingdom's defense plans for prioritizing security in Western Europe, the Mediterranean, and the Middle East by diverting the resources of the wider British Commonwealth.

The United Kingdom again sought membership in ANZUS but also offered an alternative in the form of a Pacific security pact. This larger alliance would provide a more comprehensive global defense umbrella that would allow the British government to continue to prioritize the defense of its preferred regions. The United States rejected such proposals, fearing that any Pacific security pact would inevitably involve greater contributions to the region and risked drawing it into the defense of other territories. U.S. policymakers and diplomats again used the concept of race to defend British exclusion, however, rather than stressing strategic or economic concerns. In contrast to the events of the preceding year, the United States reacted more forcefully against British efforts and adopted rougher diplomacy with Australia and New Zealand. Formal cooperation between all four powers in the Asia-Pacific looked unlikely by the close of 1953.

Redoubled Efforts

From early 1953 onward, Churchill redoubled his efforts to join ANZUS or, if this proved impossible, to undermine the treaty and encourage the creation of an alternative that would include British membership. In the estimation of British policymakers, ANZUS had resulted in a contradictory situation whereby existing arrangements within the ANZAM understanding produced overlapping areas of interests, but the organizations were answerable to different authorities.[1] The British government proposed to Australia and New Zealand that all three states should seriously reexamine their existing ANZAM security commitments. London sought to give clear evidence to both Canberra and Wellington that it was far more concerned with the Asia-Pacific than had hitherto been the case. While Churchill was not placing the region on par with the Middle East or Europe, he was providing a clear sign that the region's security was important. The prime minister believed that further consultative measures would improve ANZAM, which would consequently dwarf ANZUS, and could encourage Australia and New Zealand to insist that ANZUS incorporate ANZAM defense planning. Such developments would in turn provide the United Kingdom with a greater influence over strategic decision making in the Asia-Pacific region.[2]

The gradual recovery of the British economy and the development of an indigenous nuclear weapons program afforded Churchill's suggestions of a more active foreign policy a greater degree of credibility.[3] His designs were somewhat ambiguous, however, as he was proposing both the creation of a Five Power Staff Agency, comprising the United States, Australia, New Zealand, UK, and France as well as a broader Pacific Defense Pact, which would bring together these five powers with the Philippines, Singapore, Malaya, India, and Pakistan. In a sign that Churchill understood the necessity to placate U.S. racial arguments previously used against him, the inclusion of these "nonwhite" states helped undermine the arguments against a broader security alliance that included the United Kingdom.[4] Although it seems unlikely that British policymakers fully accepted U.S. arguments about race, they nevertheless conceded the need to engage with them.

Churchill had his first opportunity to see whether he could gain support for his new plans when he met with Menzies and Holland in December

1952 during the London Economic Conference. The British prime minister made, as the Australian delegation noted, "the usual arguments" for British inclusion in ANZUS. Menzies attempted to justify the continued exclusion of Britain. To push the United States too quickly on this subject, he reasoned, could bring an "end of effective planning and a grave danger to security of information."[5] Moreover, the Australian prime minister stressed that ANZUS was not designed to push the United Kingdom's influence out of the Asia-Pacific. Rather, as he explained, it served to contain future Japanese or Chinese power throughout the region and to free up resources for use in the wider Cold War. Menzies also challenged accusations of disloyalty from the British press and sections of the Conservative Party. Australia had always served the British Empire and would continue to do so.[6] The New Zealand prime minister went further in trying to address British concerns. Holland suggested that he supported Churchill's proposal and "was convinced that satisfactory machinery leading to a 'marriage of ANZUS and ANZAM' could be achieved" along the lines advocated by Churchill, potentially as a prelude to "joint machinery" or detailed international planning for control of the Asia-Pacific, including Southeast Asia. Moreover, "admission of [the] United Kingdom as an observer in ANZUS would be quite insufficient," given the lack of influence that such status provided.[7]

Menzies and Holland agreed to issue a communiqué at the end of the discussions, which stated that Australia would approach the United States for a "friendly discussion" about the future security provisions of the Asia-Pacific.[8] Menzies had also given his support to Churchill's idea of a Pacific security agreement and consequently avoided descent into a broader political confrontation. As one contemporary report noted, the meeting between the prime ministers managed to "sooth" relations between the three countries.[9] Yet Menzies and Holland had not done so at the expense of relations with the United States. By agreeing to have a "friendly discussion" with Washington about ANZUS, the Australian prime minister provided only vague assurances to London and did not commit to a definite course of action. Holland had gone further in suggesting a "marriage of ANZUS and ANZAM," but this remained a vague solution. Nor did Holland propose anything to which Menzies had not already indicated he was supportive, stating only that it was necessary to "arrange liaison on high military level between ANZUS and ANZAM."[10] Given that a new administration was now in power in Washington, a "friendly discussion" on a matter of supreme importance to Australian interests was a natural undertaking. Thus, by the exercise of astute diplomacy, Menzies had placed any responsibility for altering ANZUS squarely with the United States.

President Eisenhower came to office in January 1953. Eisenhower had secured an overwhelming electoral victory, aided in large part by rising fears of the Communist threat and the United States' impasse in the Korean War.[11] Churchill believed that this changed situation provided him with a valuable opportunity for advancing Britain's ambitions concerning ANZUS. During World War II, both men had worked closely together as Eisenhower rose up the ranks to assume the position of supreme allied commander and led the liberation of occupied Europe. The prime minister believed that he would be able to exploit his personal relationship with the president to help guide U.S. foreign policy along a course more amenable for British interests. As Churchill viewed matters, Eisenhower's election to office was an opportunity to bolster his chances of exercising influence over policymaking in the United States.[12]

Many U.S. political commentators seemed to suggest that Churchill's ideas for expanding ANZUS would meet with a receptive audience in the new Eisenhower administration.[13] Such hopes soon proved illusory. While always respectful of Churchill, Eisenhower believed that given his age he was no longer suitable for public office in the changed circumstances of the Cold War. As the president suggested, perhaps regrettably given his successor's eventual performance during the Suez Crisis, the prime minister should have moved over for younger men.[14] Churchill would never enjoy the degree of influence over Eisenhower that he initially believed possible, especially given the economic and strategic risks his proposals posed to the United States.

Eisenhower's decision to appoint John Foster Dulles as his secretary of state dealt a blow to British ambitions. Dulles had demonstrated during the ANZUS and Japanese peace treaty negotiations, as well as in the question of recognizing the People's Republic of China, that he was willing to challenge British interests in the Asia-Pacific.[15] Churchill and Eden also disliked Dulles for what they believed was his overly moralistic and legalistic approach to foreign affairs. Dulles had a long history of advocating Christian principles in U.S. foreign policy. During his tenure as the chairman of the Federal Council of Churches' Commission in the 1930s, for example, he openly criticized the legitimacy of European colonialism. Dulles had become even more vehemently committed to such principles in the decade before he took office for a mixture of idealistic reasons and political expediency.[16] British statesmen feared that Dulles's Christianity would encourage him to engage the United States in some sort of neo-crusade against the godless Communist powers. The secretary of state's public claims attacking the Truman administration's policy of "containment," engaging in the "rollback" of Soviet Communism, and public musings about nuclear weapons did little to quell London's fears about Dulles.[17] His sanctimonious demeanor only exacerbated tensions. Eden's frustration with Dulles was clear in his statement that he had found Nazi foreign minister Joachim Von Ribbentrop easier to handle.[18] Churchill's first meeting with Dulles as secretary of state went so poorly that in a fit of pique, he declared he would have nothing further to do with him.[19]

Dulles had originally negotiated the terms of ANZUS, and so his appointment suggested no change in U.S. policy toward Britain's membership in the treaty. Achieving a greater say in Asia-Pacific strategy was also unlikely given Dulles's lack of sensitivity to British opinion throughout the negotiations for the Japanese peace treaty. For the secretary of state, only the United States, the Soviet Union, China, and Japan could act as great powers throughout the region; the British were only of importance to the Middle East and Europe. As Dulles noted to MacArthur, "The United States and Japan are the only significant sources of Western power in the Pacific, we actual, they potential."[20] Eisenhower had also signaled his belief that the British should concentrate their efforts on areas much closer to home. Churchill chose to ignore these signals and remained determined that the United Kingdom should retain influence in the Asia-Pacific region.[21]

Eisenhower's major priorities were U.S. relations with the Soviet Union, checking the rise of Communist China, balancing the federal budget, and limiting the growth of federal power inside the United States. When it came to U.S.-UK relations, the president was far more concerned with intelligence and nuclear cooperation alongside developments in the Middle East.[22] British grievances about ANZUS were therefore of limited concern. The president had been careful not to commit to any specific policies in relation to the treaty.[23] As Dulles noted about the Churchill-Eisenhower meeting in January 1953, "Mr. Churchill made it very plain that he was much put out by the exclusion of Great Britain from the ANZUS Council and went through the familiar arguments as to why Great Britain should be included. General Eisenhower was apparently non-committal."[24]

During these discussions, Churchill requested full membership in ANZUS or, at the very least, for Britain to secure observer status in the organization.[25] Once again, however, U.S. officials demurred and suggested that British membership was not at this point possible.[26] In an effort to overcome arguments that British membership in ANZUS would establish a "white man's pact," London proposed that the treaty could be turned into a broader Pacific security pact that included "nonwhite" countries. The United States rejected these proposals. As private discussions in Washington reveal, racial inclusion failed to convince policymakers of the merits of a broader Pacific security pact. The proposal instead only stoked fears of additional and unwanted economic and military contributions to the region.[27]

New Zealand and Australia were aware that Churchill had made a "tremendous plug" to Eisenhower for British membership in ANZUS and that he had suggested the merging of ANZAM and ANZUS planning.[28] In February 1953, Churchill put forward a more detailed proposal for the creation of a Five Power Staff Agency—which would bring together the United States, Britain, France, Australia, New Zealand to discuss and plan logistical, intelligence and "operational planning to counter Chinese aggression." He also proposed the establishment of a "central machinery" to govern allied strategy in the Asia-Pacific.[29] Such proposals were deeply concerning for the Menzies government. As Percy Spender warned Canberra from Washington: "I know the grand old man [Churchill] does not like ANZUS and will do his best to reduce it to bare bones—perhaps by putting forward the Five Power Staff Agency, and by seeking agreement to broad political directives—which can always be interpreted as one is disposed to interpret them—directed to the Staff agency. But we have achieved a special place in the Pacific through ANZUS and I know you will forgive me when I say, we must hang on to it."[30] Spender's advice reflected the strategic and political rewards that ANZUS afforded Australia. If London could attain some sort of separate agreement with Washington, it could potentially marginalize Canberra's interests. Although keen to protect the treaty, Wellington was less apprehensive, believing that Churchill's intervention would not necessarily lead to disastrous results for the future of ANZUS.[31]

To Canberra, London was simply unable to accept the realities of the postwar world where Menzies, and not Churchill, would agree to alterations in Australia's security policies. The Five Power Staff Agency or the creation of some "central machinery" to coordinate allied strategic policy was especially concerning as Australian officials perceived it as a potential downgrade to Australia's status vis-à-vis the United States. The Australian government currently enjoyed direct access to Admiral Radford in Honolulu whereby it could discuss Asia-Pacific planning. The establishment of the Radford-Collins Agreement allowed for the coordination of ANZAM and United States' plans for a maritime war in the Asia-Pacific.[32] As the Joint Chiefs in Washington noted, the "exchange of intelligence" and "plans with Australia" was ongoing through the Radford channel.[33] Agreeing to some new organization risked future access to U.S. strategic planning. Furthermore, reexamining the entire ANZAM concept was a concern for Australian diplomats, who feared the British idea was a ploy designed to destroy ANZUS because of their continued exclusion from the organization.[34]

The fashion in which the British had put their proposals forward for reexamining the ANZAM concept, which they pushed via military and not diplomatic channels, also raised concerns for Australian and New Zealand policymakers. While the British Joint Chiefs of Staff routinely entered into discussions with their antipodean partners, it was evident that these talks did not focus on purely military matters. Instead, the latest proposals put forward by the British clearly had a number of political and diplomatic matters on the agenda, which included the relationship of the United Kingdom to ANZUS, the future of ANZAM planning, and the Australian attitude to the British-inspired plan for a broader Pacific security pact. Canberra was therefore concerned that London would pressure Australia and New Zealand into undertaking major alterations to each state's security commitments through the back door, thereby antagonizing the United States.[35]

As Australian concern grew, British efforts began to encounter greater opposition in Canberra. Alan Watt, the secretary of the Department of External Affairs, remarked that the British proposals were all designed to "submerge ANZAM and ANZUS in a wider arrangement and to put Australia on the fringe."[36] Other influential policymaking figures inside the Menzies government were similarly skeptical about British motivations concerning a reexamination of ANZAM. Churchill's style of diplomacy was also increasingly unpopular. Menzies, for instance, described one letter from Churchill on this subject as a "stinker."[37] The Australian government decided that it would defer making any firm decisions. As Watt informed the United States, it was unwise at this stage to allow British membership in ANZUS.[38] In a further blow to British ambitions, Canberra informed London that military talks about ANZAM could be undertaken but this would be the only matter for discussion. Under no circumstance would talks about ANZAM be allowed to develop into a discussion about Britain's relationship to ANZUS.[39]

Canberra nevertheless recognized that British proposals could offer some potentially valuable political leverage in their dealings with Washington. Churchill's proposed Pacific security pact was especially useful because it could encourage a major U.S. military commitment to the Asia-Pacific region, which had been a long-term ambition of Australian foreign policy. Canberra perceived such a security commitment to be increasingly important as intelligence assessments suggested that the region would be an area of growing strategic competition in the Cold War.[40] Such developments, however, could not come at the expense of existing agreements. One memorandum by the Australian minister for external affairs and defense clearly articulated such thinking: "It is an essential Australian interest that there should be effective defence arrangements in the

Pacific and South East Asia . . . it must be ensured that any new arrangement preserves both the status and advantages now enjoyed by Australia throughout membership of ANZAM and ANZUS. It will also be desirable to devise means by which the sensitivity of some Asian states at exclusion from such arrangements can be kept to a minimum."[41] Australian policymakers remained conscious that ANZAM and ANZUS held overlapping interests despite being answerable to different authorities.[42] The Menzies government was therefore in agreement with its British counterparts that the outstanding questions related to the relationship between ANZAM and ANZUS had to be resolved. New Zealand military officials shared this opinion. Air Commodore Cyril Kay had pushed for this discussion to take place during a meeting with his British and Australian counterparts in London in February 1953.[43] Nevertheless, while all three powers sought greater clarity on the ANZUS-ANZAM issue, Canberra clearly differed from Wellington and London on the preferred answer to such questions.

Following the advice of his defense and foreign ministers, Menzies concluded that in any reexamination of ANZAM, the United Kingdom would have to accept that Australia had a "special position" in the region.[44] Only then would Menzies consider whether military planning could be directly coordinated with ANZUS. Menzies appeared to be opening the door for the British government to achieve membership of ANZUS. By bringing together ANZAM with ANZUS, the Australian prime minister hoped that strategic planning in the region would come to reflect "reality" by making "the Americans realize the significance of ANZAM," which would lead to a "system of liaison on high military level between ANZUS and ANZAM."[45] If Menzies could successfully reinterpret the ANZAM arrangement, he could potentially obtain an improved position for Australia vis-à-vis the United States and United Kingdom. ANZAM would benefit from greater attention from the United Kingdom and cement Australian leadership in the strategic planning for the area. Marrying ANZAM to ANZUS could also potentially create an effective security alliance in the Asia-Pacific. U.S. policymakers consequently faced British and Australian pressure to reassess their existing Pacific security commitments. Reexamining U.S. commitments to the region and to the entire ANZUS concept would become a subject for serious discussion throughout the summer and winter of 1953.

The reaction of the New Zealand government to Churchill's proposals for a Five Power Staff Agency was rather more relaxed than that of the Menzies government. Wellington took a detached position whereby it monitored the evolving diplomacy between Canberra and London before assuming any firm policies itself. As New Zealand officials accurately noted, "Australia is particularly apprehensive lest the Five Power Agency resolve itself into a NATO type Standing Group of France, United States and the United Kingdom with Australia and New Zealand out in the cold."[46] Wellington had not yet adopted a position on the proposal but soon came under pressure from London and Canberra to support their respective approaches to the creation of the five-power agency. Canberra was especially keen to shore up support. Menzies wrote to Holland requesting that Wellington back Canberra's stance toward London, namely that Churchill had to clarify what he meant by a five-power agency before either country could endorse its creation.[47] Wellington eventually agreed to follow Canberra's lead. Both antipodean powers agreed that prudence was required at this stage. With the details still unclear, there was little advantage in pressing ahead too quickly.[48]

Debating Inclusion

British, Australian, and New Zealand suggestions that the United States needed to reassess its Asia-Pacific security commitments met with considerable opposition in the U.S. Economic considerations help explain much of the resistance. To be sure, existing security arrangements provided a measure of economic reward for the United States. ANZUS, for instance, provided a forum in which the United States could ask the antipodean powers to make trade concessions and support the restoration of Japan.[49] Nevertheless, U.S. Treasury Secretary George Humphrey warned Eisenhower soon after the president took office that existing levels of U.S. public expenditure were unsustainable. Cost savings were essential, which would include significant reductions in the defense budget. The president had complained at length before entering the White House about the Truman administration's profligacy. For Eisenhower, economic imperatives meant that the United States would have to devise a different strategy for fighting the Cold War. This would come about in the form of the "New Look" national security strategy, which attempted to better balance military commitments with financial resources.[50]

In one cabinet session held soon after Eisenhower entered office, Humphrey talked at length about the dangers inherent in the United States' economic position if it continued to run current account deficits, which partially reflected substantial rises in defense expenditure. In 1948, for example, the United States spent just under $11 billion on defense. When Truman left office, this figure had grown to approximately $50 billion.[51] Humphrey argued that substantial cutbacks in U.S. defense expenditure were now required. Eisenhower's cabinet were divided in their support of this recommendation. Dulles was especially keen to point out that defense cut-backs had broader strategic ramifications. Nevertheless, there was general acceptance that existing levels of public expenditure required substantial reduction. A new strategic posture was required that would reflect Eisenhower's wish to reduce the size of government spending.[52]

Implementing this new strategic course involved difficult choices. An end to the war in Korea would achieve savings somewhere in the region of $5 billion per annum. Long-term savings would nevertheless have to come from the United States' existing arsenal and changes to the makeup of its national force posture. After a summer of indecision and bureaucratic infighting, Washington agreed that the United States would reduce its reliance on conventional forces and rely more heavily on nuclear armaments. As Eisenhower argued, the Soviet Union would never challenge the core interests of the United States because of the risks of nuclear retaliation. Providing a similar deterrent in conventional terms was simply unaffordable.[53] Eisenhower also altered the premise of overall U.S. grand strategy. Under Truman, symmetrical containment had essentially been the basis of U.S. Cold War policy. Such a strategy meant that the United States met every action made by the Soviet Union with an equal and opposite reaction.[54] Eisenhower instead adopted an asymmetrical approach to containing the Soviet Union. The United States should identify its core interests and ensure they were not lost to the Soviet Union or its proxies. Areas such as Western Europe and the Middle East thus remained the highest priority, but the U.S. would now not necessarily meet Communist challenges in areas of lesser significance.

This alteration in U.S. strategy meant that the president had no intention of placing additional conventional forces into areas where considerable commitments already existed or expanding obligations elsewhere, which included the Asia-Pacific region. Eisenhower would therefore continue to reject suggestions that the United Kingdom gain membership in ANZUS for any such agreement could potentially obligate the United States to defend British interests in the region, such as Hong Kong and Malaya.[55] Churchill's plan for a broader Pacific security pact was equally unwelcome, as it would require additional expenditure and resources to establish and maintain, as well as potentially drawing the United States into France's open conflict in Indochina. Expanding ANZUS membership could also lead to the dilution of British commitments inside Europe or the Middle East if the United Kingdom was to move additional armed forces into the area. Furthermore, Australia and New Zealand could perhaps utilize British membership as leverage in convincing the United States to provide additional resources to the defense of the wider Asia-Pacific.

Concerns with appearing to act in a racist or in an imperial fashion also informed broader U.S. strategic considerations. The creation of ANZUS had already unsettled a number of Asian countries that claimed the United States had excluded them in favor of working with other Western powers in the defense of the region.[56] As one U.S. official warned Dulles in January 1953, expanding ANZUS to include the United Kingdom would only "intensify that impression" and undermine U.S. relations with a number of key Asian states.[57] Senior U.S. officials suggested that British membership in ANZUS could also encourage "the implication that ANZUS represented either a revival of 'western imperialism' or an instrument of 'white supremacy'" in the Pacific.[58] Racial sensitivities remained secondary to more pressing strategic concerns, however, which explains why this pact continued to exist with only "white powers." Indeed, ANZUS was already fundamentally "Western" or a "white man's club" without the United Kingdom, so the propaganda rewards of continued exclusion were relatively limited.

Yet the United States could not simply dismiss Churchill's proposals concerning the Asia-Pacific given Britain's global importance. The United States required the United Kingdom's cooperation in upholding the Western financial system as well as containing the Soviet Union in Europe and throughout the Middle East. British military officers were also involved in the Five Power talks conducted in Honolulu to discuss Southeast Asia and Pacific security more broadly.[59] Yet in the Eisenhower administration's assessment, the question of British participation in ANZUS, or a future Pacific security pact, was a peripheral issue that should not undermine U.S.-UK cooperation in other areas of vital significance. Eisenhower therefore sought to compartmentalize points of difference in order to push ahead with cooperation in Europe and the Middle East.

Dulles consequently looked at ways in which the United States could provide some type of a "gesture" that would placate British criticisms. Churchill's persistence, despite opposition from Australian and U.S. officials, had eventually yielded the potential for some rewards. What this gesture would involve was unspecified but its limits were clear. In February, Dulles informed his Australian counterpart that he would prefer the United Kingdom to assume an "informal" association with ANZUS; he explicitly ruled out membership.[60] The British nevertheless sought membership in ANZUS—which they believed was the only way to influence events in the region significantly—or a new Pacific security pact. Dulles's vague offer therefore proved unsatisfactory.

With Washington clearly opposed to British membership in ANZUS and critical of any new Pacific security pact, Canberra and Wellington had to reconsider their approach to the issue. Assessments about international threats in the Southern Hemisphere encouraged the Australian prime minister in his belief that it was essential to improve security provisions for the Asia-Pacific. The death of Stalin in March 1953 did little to change this position. A DEA briefing paper for Menzies remained skeptical of future cooperation or the possibility of a "peace opportunity" between East and West: "the phrase 'change of heart' is meaningless in this context: it implies a subjective approach to history which a communist by definition cannot accept. . . . The fundamental objective of Soviet and world-communist policy must remain the establishment of a communist world."[61] For the Australian government, Communist objectives in Asia remained ambitious and deeply threatening. Australian fears included the unification of Korea on Communist terms, the absorption of Formosa into the PRC, and the establishment of Communist rule throughout Indochina.[62] New Zealand shared with Australia many concerns about the future of the Cold War in the Asia-Pacific. Doidge noted that "it will be a cardinal objective of Soviet policy to bring Japan within the Communist orbit."[63] Others throughout New Zealand policymaking circles held similar assessments about the expansionist nature of the Communist powers and their ambition to seize territory throughout the Asia-Pacific.[64]

In the estimation of Australia and New Zealand, which reflected the ongoing influence of domino theory on strategic thinking, the likelihood of Communist expansion throughout Southeast Asia was growing ever more likely. The latest successes of the Viet Minh in inflicting heavy losses on the French forces fighting the Indochina War caused concern that Communist intentions were not restricted to Vietnam only. If Communist forces assumed control of Vietnam, they would have a secure base in which to launch their revolutionary ambitions into Cambodia, Laos, and Thailand. From here, revolution could spread to Malaya. The Menzies and Holland governments had committed to fight the Communist insurgency inside Malaya in part because of the fear that the country could function as a future Communist base to directly launch assaults against the Australian mainland. Obtaining sufficient security provisions therefore remained the central objective of policymakers in Canberra and Wellington.

Many antipodean policymakers saw Communist movements throughout the Asia-Pacific as a credible and growing threat to their own security interests.[65] The growing economic improvement of Japan and its reassertion as what one Australian report termed the "senior partner" in Asian diplomacy were also concerning. The antipodean powers recognized that the United States would want their support in the form of trade concessions to help Japan secure exports in Southeast Asia, which would certainly come at their expense.[66] A mixture of fears that surrounded a reassertion of Japanese militarism and the growth of Communist advances lay at the heart of Australian and New Zealand thinking about why British proposals remained worthy of consideration. Despite the promise of ANZUS, military planning between the United States, Australia, and New Zealand had since failed to achieve the desired levels of military cooperation.[67]

The Eisenhower administration's unwillingness to provide additional resources for the Asia-Pacific region complicated efforts to improve the security situation for the Menzies and Holland governments. Both powers recognized that it was pointless to discuss how to defend areas such as Malaya within the framework of ANZUS without Britain being a part of the discussions.[68] The United Kingdom was providing the vast majority of forces for quelling the Communist insurgency inside Malaya. British naval assets would also be required to support the Australian Royal Navy if the sea-lanes were to remain open in the event of any Communist takeover of power in Southeast Asia.[69] From Canberra and Wellington's perspective, it would be helpful to involve the United Kingdom in order to manage external security challenges effectively.

Nevertheless, Churchill's ideas about ANZUS and ANZAM had become steadily less attractive to both Australian and New Zealand policymakers. They appreciated that the United States did not want Britain in ANZUS for its own set of reasons, and overcoming this obstacle appeared insurmountable. As such, discussing the subject of British membership in ANZUS would only delay discussion on other matters. Moreover, British plans for Pacific security did not necessarily prioritize Australian interests. One Australian briefing memorandum from the DEA makes this concern clear: "The United Kingdom wants a voice in Pacific strategy appropriate to her interests. These interests include not only the defence of United Kingdom possessions but also the opportunity to influence American policy on major strategic issues." As the briefing starkly pointed out: "The United Kingdom tends to look at Pacific defence from a European point of view, her interests do not necessarily coincide with ours."[70]

New Zealand did not view British intentions to be quite as self-interested or manipulative as policymakers across the Tasman did. As far as Wellington perceived matters, it was essential to overcome the imbroglio over British membership in ANZUS to focus on the practical process of planning a credible defense for the broader Asia-Pacific region. Yet, as was well known in New Zealand circles, the United States remained opposed to such proposals: "One fact remains abundantly clear. The United States authorities have no present intention of establishing any agency, either on the political or military level, which would have overall responsibility for the regional defence of the Far East as NATO may be assumed to have in respect of Europe."[71] Without such a commitment, as the prime minister was warned, "ANZAM will be ineffective unless linked with United States for overall Pacific Defence."[72]

Differing interests concerning the promotion of security in the Asia-Pacific divided the United States, United Kingdom, Australia, and New Zealand despite a shared belief about the growing Communist menace throughout the Asia-Pacific and specifically in Southeast Asia. The United States had no enthusiasm for British plans to expand ANZUS or to establish a new Pacific security pact. Australia was less opposed to such ambitions and New Zealand remained sympathetic, but, largely because of U.S. resistance and the value they placed on ANZUS, both powers chose at this time not to promote British plans.

The British Commonwealth meeting of June 1953 saw these differing strategic assessments on how best to promote collective security come to a head. The briefing materials provided to Menzies by his staff reveal considerable apprehension about the meeting with Churchill due to continuing British exclusion from ANZUS.[73] Holland was keenly aware of the need to pacify British complaints.[74] Both the Australian and New Zealand governments had been right to worry about the outcome of these talks. As the U.S. ambassador to London informed Washington, there had been a "desultory and inconclusive private conversation on ANZUS" between Churchill and Menzies.[75] Newspaper reports went further, explaining that there was a clash between the two leaders. While Menzies would publicly describe such reporting as a "monstrous invention," the minutes of the meeting appear to corroborate this assessment of events.[76]

During this meeting with Menzies and Holland, Churchill took the opportunity to press his case about the current objectionable state of affairs.[77] Stressing that "very intimate relations . . . might be impaired in future if a solution were not found to the problem of planning Pacific strategy," he concluded that "in view of the difficulty of associating the United Kingdom with ANZUS, some wider form of Pacific pact should be considered."[78] It seems reasonable to conclude that Churchill's comments were suggestive of a threat to reconsider current British security commitments to Australia and New Zealand if a solution to the current impasse failed to emerge.

Menzies refused to accept Churchill's argument that the United Kingdom deserved membership in ANZUS. The suggestion of a new Pacific security also received little support. As Menzies explained, the idea was worthy of consideration but the matter needed more thought before Australian commitment would be given.[79] After further discussions, Menzies made it clear that he would not allow the question of British admission to disrupt ANZUS. Holland likewise endorsed Menzies's stance.[80] Churchill's diplomacy was evidently failing to achieve its ambitions. With U.S. opposition clear, both antipodean leaders concluded that for the time being the status quo was preferable to seeking ANZUS expansion and running the risk of losing the American commitment.

The *Melbourne Herald* captured the essence of the meeting when it declared that Menzies had taken a "firm stand" over the issue of British membership to ANZUS.[81] Press attention on this matter meant that the United Kingdom, Australia, and New Zealand could no longer so easily hide their obvious disagreement concerning the future of security cooperation in the Asia-Pacific. On returning to Australia, Menzies informed the press that "we understand and sympathize with the desire of Britain to be associated with ANZUS, but if America is not willing to extend the membership of ANZUS, there is nothing Australia . . . can do about it short of breaking up the treaty; and this we are not willing to do."[82] Such statements irritated Washington for they rightly believed Menzies was placing the blame for Britain's ANZUS exclusion entirely and publicly on the Eisenhower administration. New Zealand officials instead appear to have avoided discussing the matter in public or in any detail. Nevertheless, both antipodean powers received a warning from Washington that apportioning blame on the Eisenhower administration was "contrary to the tripartite understanding."[83]

Australian sympathies to the British cause were now wearing thin. Menzies made it clear to his colleagues that he would no longer allow ANZUS to be "disrupted" by the question of British admission. In a prepared speaking note, he explained that he felt like a "battered punching ball" because of British criticism, stressing that "if you [UK] want to destroy ANZUS you're going the right way about it."[84] His foreign minister, Richard Casey, had also become adamantly opposed to British admission. Casey resented the implication that the Australians required British "hand holding" in any alliance with the United States. Moreover, Churchill's ideas for a broader Pacific security pact could now endanger the existing U.S. security commitments to the Asia-Pacific. Eisenhower's New Look strategy meant the United States would be looking to limit any further security commitments. Reopening the subject of ANZUS membership could therefore precipitate the Eisenhower administration's reassessment of its entire commitment to Australian security.[85] Australian policymakers believed that the current political climate in Washington, which was becoming further embroiled in McCarthyism, would only encourage isolationist foreign policies.

Spender was particularly concerned with Churchill's proposals. In a lengthy note from Washington, he warned of the dangers:

> I specially want to stress, if we allow anything to interfere with ANZUS, whether on the political or military plane, we will lose the only means we have of any effective entry into USA political and military thinking at a high level and the intimacy which ANZUS unquestionably affords us. For the first time we have got a toe hold into the councils in USA which affect the world and its destiny at a high and acknowledged level through ANZUS. I cannot tell you how glad I am that you are resolved that we shall not relinquish it.[86]

Spender's comments echoed opinion inside Canberra's foreign policymaking elite, which believed that ANZUS's real importance was that it "provides our one means of access to American thinking on global war." Australia should therefore resist British proposals that could potentially disrupt this access.[87]

The opinion of the Australian defense establishment also cautioned against hasty agreement with the British government. While cooperation with the United States had not been as full or as wide as initially hoped in Australian circles, there were some recent signs suggesting that the U.S. now considered ANZUS to be a proper security pact. As a case in point, Washington offered to dispatch a delegation to Melbourne to begin discussions on strategic planning. Admiral Radford's promotion to chairman of the Joint Chiefs of Staff had also led to encouraging signs that the United States was now prepared to enter more comprehensive U.S.-Australian defense cooperation. Although the United States accepted that "there exists a sound basis for de facto" cooperation between ANZUS and ANZAM planning, it also signaled that it did not want ANZUS cooperation to become "married to ANZAM."[88] Swiftly improving strategic cooperation between the U.S. and Australia was conspicuous given recent British offers of improved alliance cooperation. Delaying agreement with the British government therefore served Australian interests by encouraging and improving U.S. cooperation.[89]

Canberra subsequently informed London in June 1953 that Australia had decided not to request that the United States allow British membership in ANZUS. Writing to Churchill, Menzies argued that "the ANZUS arrangement has political reality in New Zealand and the United States as well as in Australia. It is a political fact of the first magnitude. In any of these countries, moves which had the effect of destroying or even weakening this arrangement would be liable to serious misunderstanding."[90]

Familiar U.S. excuses had also taken root in the Southern Hemisphere by summer 1953. Australian policymakers suggested that British membership in ANZUS would create the impression that it would create a "white man's club" and would therefore damage relations between its members and other Asian powers.[91] This explanation was largely disingenuous as the decision to exclude the United Kingdom from ANZUS had more to do with U.S. pressure and Australia's changing interests. The emergence of concerns about racial justice was curious given that they had not previously played a major role in Australian security panning. Such justifications were nevertheless useful to temper domestic and international criticism for unpopular policy choices.

In contrast, the New Zealand government had not yet given up hope of securing British membership for ANZUS. Its minister in Washington, Leslie Munro, quietly raised the issue of British membership with the U.S. State Department in July 1953. The U.S. position, however, remained consistent.[92] U.S. reluctance was clear, but the State Department had hinted Washington could open talks with London about "joint planning under ANZAM-ANZUS on the defence of territories for which [the] United Kingdom were responsible."[93] As Munro noted, this would be a "desirable line of development."[94] Such optimism proved misplaced as Radford vetoed the opening of any talks with London about ANZUS-ANZAM defense discussions. For his part, Dulles believed that such talks were also unnecessary. Given the obvious lack of enthusiasm in Washington and Canberra for British membership in ANZUS, Wellington conceded that it would be better not to pursue the matter.[95] Much like their antipodean neighbor, New Zealand highly prized the ANZUS arrangement not least because it was the country's only avenue by which to obtain access to the United States' strategic thinking on the highest level.[96] This evidence tempers claims of the "ANZAC dilemma." Australia and New Zealand may have felt "the pull between old habits of thought and emotion and the necessities imposed by geography and the present state of world affairs," but their preferences were sufficiently clear to lessen the difficulty of any such choice.[97]

The absence of any real support from the other members of the treaty had once again undermined Churchill's ambition of obtaining ANZUS membership. The British prime minister, however, refused to accept defeat. Throughout the remainder of 1953, Churchill stepped up his diplomacy with the U.S. and Australia. His long-held commitment to British influence in the region, and an appreciation that ill health could soon remove him from office, drove Churchill's unwillingness to accept exclusion from ANZUS.[98]

Maintaining Exclusion

Antipodean rejection of Churchill's proposals was hugely frustrating for London but failed to strike a decisive blow against British ambitions. Having achieved little with Australia and New Zealand, Churchill again looked across the Atlantic to see if ANZUS membership for the United Kingdom was possible. The British ambassador to Washington Sir Roger Makins, who had replaced Oliver Franks earlier in the year, met with U.S. representatives in September 1953 to press the case for British inclusion in ANZUS. Membership, he learned, was no longer a possibility for the United Kingdom. The explanations offered in defense of this position focused on familiar fears of a "white man's club," which would offend Asian sensibilities. Establishing a broader Pacific security pact was also unpopular as such an organization would involve French participation and thereby threatened to bring the United States directly into France's Indochina war.[99]

As Dulles privately told the Australian government, expanding ANZUS into some broader Pacific security pact would only lead to a mess.[100] The Joint Chiefs of Staff were unequivocal in rejecting British membership in ANZUS. In their assessment, the British received a "free flow of information" on matters concerning ANZUS military planning so Britain's actual membership was not required. Churchill's continued demands for ANZUS membership therefore reflected "considerations pertaining to prestige" or "internal politics."[101] Although the assessments of the JCS had accurately identified some of the influences motivating British foreign policy, they downplayed or neglected many other pressing strategic concerns. For New Zealand's part, there was a clear sense that the United States was growing increasingly impatient with the continual pressing for British membership in ANZUS. As Wellington was informed, efforts to even raise the issue of opening discussion about U.S. contributions to ANZAM defense had been brushed aside.[102]

Explanations based on race, which still continued to obscure the pursuit of more pressing national interests, were empowered by the worsening position of France inside Indochina. As U.S. diplomats argued, extending ANZUS would be either a "racist" undertaking as it would be an exclusively "white man's pact" inside Asia or a discriminatory one as it would not afford French membership, to which they were surely entitled given their interests in the region. Moreover, if France secured membership in ANZUS, Dulles suggested that it would give the impression that ANZUS was a "colonial organization."[103] Consequently, the United States rebuffed Churchill's proposals for either British membership in ANZUS or a new Pacific security pact.[104]

In a further sign that the United States was determined to maintain ANZUS as an exclusive tripartite alliance, Dulles forcefully extinguished any lingering hopes that might exist in Canberra and certainly did exist in Wellington about supporting British membership in ANZUS. In a thinly veiled threat to any supporters of ANZUS expansion, the U.S. secretary of state made plain the consequences: "Efforts to enlarge ANZUS would result in its dissolution."[105] Although persuasion and compromise formed the bedrock of U.S. alliances during the Cold War, things were sometimes not so simple.[106] A communiqué issued at the end of the 1953 ANZUS Council meeting thus explicitly ruled out extending membership.[107] In the course of 1953, then, the antipodean powers had received veiled threats from both Britain and the United States concerning strategic abandonment. Even if such threats were unlikely to have been acted on, especially with the benefit of hindsight, they nevertheless underline the rough character of negotiations between Western powers at this time. Reinforcing Dulles's rough diplomacy with Australia and New Zealand, the U.S. cemented its preference for existing arrangements without formal defense ties.

The issue of British membership in ANZUS had now reached its bitter conclusion. As the *Melbourne Herald* exclaimed, "ANZUS Ministers Say 'No' to Britain."[108] The headline was accurate but obscured the fact that Dulles had insisted on British exclusion, just as he had during the original discussions in February 1951. Canberra and Wellington understood just how reluctant Washington was to allow British membership in ANZUS and finally bowed to its wishes on this matter.[109] Churchill's hopes that Eisenhower's ascension to the presidency would help the United Kingdom to gain access to ANZUS were evidently disappointed. Of the three members of ANZUS, only the New Zealand leadership remained hopeful that the United Kingdom could eventually join the organization. Holland, even after the latest round of talks with Dulles, suggested that Australia and New Zealand had to formulate a way of bringing the UK into ANZUS.[110] It was Canberra, however, that suggested a partial solution in the form of offering London the right to discuss the military aspects of ANZUS planning privately. Both Washington and Wellington "raised no objection" to this proposal.[111]

Nevertheless, the British could not be granted formal membership in ANZUS, nor could military planning between ANZUS or ANZAM or a combination of the Five Power Agency be merged.[112] By the end of the year, all three members of the ANZUS pact agreed to exclude the United Kingdom from the treaty. As the minutes of the ANZUS Council meeting of September 1953 read, "The Council affirmed its readiness to consider any measure which would strengthen the defense of the area. It unanimously concluded, however, that to attempt to enlarge its membership would not contribute materially to this end."[113]

This final decision on the question of ANZUS expansion dealt a considerable blow to Churchill's attempts to improve both Britain's position throughout the Asia-Pacific and levels of strategic and economic cooperation among the Western powers in Southeast Asia. The ANZUS members, however, had to handle their British ally carefully. While the "mother country" could no longer provide for all the security needs of Australia and New Zealand, entrenched security, economic, political, and cultural ties remained in place. On the political front, Britain's final omission from ANZUS sparked considerable protest inside the respective parliaments of Australia and New Zealand.[114] Public diplomacy therefore followed, with Casey making a deliberate point of issuing a statement that British exclusion from ANZUS did not mean Australia was "drifting away from the British Commonwealth."[115] Wellington decided to avoid a public response and preferred to complain privately that they and Australia had been "unfairly subjected" to criticism by London.[116]

Washington was also keen to prevent disagreement over ANZUS affecting other areas of strategic cooperation with London. The U.S.-UK relationship involved extensive collaboration between the two powers, which senior U.S. policymakers were keenly aware helped promote U.S. interests. As Radford put it, the U.S.-UK relationship was the "most important element in the defence of the free world."[117] Consequently, both Radford and Dulles requested that Canberra and Wellington inform London that all three members of ANZUS had unanimously agreed to exclude the United Kingdom. As Dulles further reminded his Australian and New Zealand colleagues, the entire security of the Western position would suffer from a serious chasm in U.S.-UK relations.[118]

It is important not to exaggerate the seriousness of the rift between the United States and United Kingdom over ANZUS. Both states recognized the need for continued strategic and economic cooperation in other parts of the world. Furthermore, the United States would soon welcome British support in the wider region. Owing to events in Indochina by the middle of the year, senior elements within the U.S. military had come to recognize the need for five-power planning, which would include the United Kingdom and France, for the defense of Southeast Asia. As such, Britain could now talk to the U.S. directly on the broader subject of security in the Asia-Pacific region and Southeast Asia in particular. Radford had not concluded, however, that military planning required any formal merging of ANZUS discussions with those taking place within the framework of ANZAM. Nor was Radford a convert to British membership to ANZUS. As Radford made clear to his antipodean opposite numbers earlier in the year, while "certain arrangements" had already been worked out at the military level between ANZUS and ANZAM, "no useful purpose would be served by establishing a formal relationship."[119]

London issued a restrained statement, expressing only its pity at exclusion.[120] British policymakers nevertheless believed that the United Kingdom's exclusion from ANZUS was wholly the fault of the United States. Understandably, Australian officials were keen to encourage the British to think in such ways. In contradiction to Dulles's suggestion that the United Kingdom not learn that their exclusion was due to the U.S., Canberra informed London otherwise. Australian officials even noted the stern diplomacy Dulles had deployed against them to retain the exclusive tripartite nature of the ANZUS Treaty: "Mr Dulles at one stage professed readiness, if Australia and New Zealand, really wished it, to let the United Kingdom into Anzus. But he made it clear that if that happened, it would therefore be the end of Anzus as a treaty having any value to the three parties."[121]

The antipodean powers made little mention of their own growing doubts about the consequences of British membership in ANZUS. Australia, having secured its security pact with the United States, was determined to hold on to it. Wellington remained more sympathetic to London's plight, and conscious of British resentment, but recognized the need to pursue its own interests first. The comment of one senior New Zealand security planner captured this ambition succinctly: "I feel that so long as the United Kingdom are excluded (it is most difficult to see a way for them to come in) their opposition and suspicion of the Council will continue. But that, I hope, will not deter us from working it and securing our own interests here in the Pacific."[122] Ultimately, policymakers in Canberra and Wellington looked to promote their own security interests even if doing so created unease and irritation in London. Yet both the Menzies and Holland governments skillfully sought to shift any possible recriminations toward the Eisenhower administration and away from them.

By the close of 1953, Churchill's expectations for obtaining British membership in ANZUS or establishing a new Pacific security treaty had radically diminished. As the *Daily Telegraph* correctly reported in the lead-up to the U.S.-UK Bermuda Conference in December, the British prime minister had decided not to push the case for membership of ANZUS with the U.S. president anymore. He also surrendered his Pacific security pact proposals. Churchill consequently left the subject alone during his discussions with Eisenhower. As he realized, the United States would not move on this subject, so it was counterproductive to aggravate relations when other important matters were open for discussion. Churchill was keen to obtain Eisenhower's support for a great power summit to negotiate permanent solutions to geopolitical differences and quietly shelved his pursuit of ANZUS.[123]

The ANZUS debacle had demonstrated the compartmentalization of the U.S.-UK relationship and the weakness of British power in relation to its superpower ally. Exclusion also mirrored global trends of comparative British decline and U.S. growth. In September, the United States finally reached agreement with Franco's Spain to allow U.S. bases on Spanish soil. In Greece, the United States was pushing the Greek government to replace the existing Royal Navy's mission with a U.S. one. Throughout the Middle East, British policymakers also believed that they were being pushed aside by the United States, even if such assumptions were questionable. When taken together it is unsurprising that commentators see this as a period of "Uncle Sam" superseding "John Bull" and of the United States ably assisting in Britain's global decline.[124]

The British Commonwealth's strategic unity was also under growing strain by late 1953. The British Chiefs of Staff had rightly concluded that Australia was never going to provide the desired level of military force to the Middle East in the event of a global war. As such, it was now preferable to secure an Australian commitment to Malaya.[125] At subsequent talks conducted by the military staffs of all three countries in Melbourne in October, there was agreement that once the British Commonwealth Division from Korea had withdrawn, Australia would base two infantry battalions with supporting air and naval assets in Singapore permanently. In the event of a major war, Australia would now deploy its main forces to Malaya and not to the Middle East. Although the minutes of the meeting suggested "a cordial united family," one of its members was exhibiting a far more independent attitude to global security.[126]

Canberra had become increasingly concerned with events in Southeast Asia, in particular France's precarious position in Indochina, which existed alongside ongoing tensions in Indonesia and Malaya. There were also ongoing doubts about U.S. security commitments in the region.[127] ANZUS had evidently failed to provide the desired level of access to U.S. military planning or to lead to the creation of joint staff talks. Nevertheless, the treaty provided a U.S. security guarantee, thereby presenting an alternative to the one supplied by the United Kingdom, which meant that Australia could be more flexible in the pursuit of its own security interests. In these circumstances, Australia now chose to prioritize its own regional security interests over those of the British Commonwealth.

Given these changed strategic realities, Australia would look to prioritize the defense of its near north. During the ANZAM Council meeting of September 1953, Australian officials proposed the establishment of a British Commonwealth Strategic Reserve in Malaya, later known as the British Commonwealth Far East Strategic Reserve (BCFESR). This reserve would draw on forces from Britain, Australia, and New Zealand, in an effort to deter potential Communist Chinese aggression. Briefing material in preparation for this meeting reveals that Australia was clearly pushing for this change in policy.[128] The Australians were worried that the United States would not be supportive of this policy shift. Prior to the ANZUS Council meeting, Australian officials had exhibited concerns that Dulles would push for them to increase commitments in the Middle East.[129] Yet there is limited evidence of any such reaction. As Australia announced the decision in an ANZAM Council meeting, the United States was not yet immediately aware of such proposals. Events in Indochina in the coming months, however, would help to override any concerns about this shift in strategic focus.

In the following months, the Australians entered detailed discussions with their New Zealand counterparts about reconsidering their efforts in the ANZAM region.[130] Subtly divergent policy preferences soon emerged. Although Wellington increasingly appreciated the dangers posed by Communism in Southeast Asia, and recognized shifting strategic circumstances in Europe, it urged Canberra to lessen the speed at which it was seeking to push through these major strategic planning adjustments. New Zealand policymakers remained wedded to the idea that the Middle East, and not Southeast Asia or the near north as argued in Australian circles, should be the priority for British Commonwealth defense planning for the time being.[131] Strategic thinking in Wellington mirrored Washington and London in prioritizing the resources and geographical position of the Middle East in the event of a global war with the Communist powers, and planning reflected this reality.[132] While New Zealand accepted that its air forces would be required in Malaya in the event of a global war, it remained committed to sending its infantry division to the Middle East.[133] Practical considerations also informed thinking in Wellington. Any planning for defending the broader ANZAM region would require the cooperation of London and Paris, both of which had considerable military resources in the area. Planning without their cooperation would therefore be ineffective, a point that New Zealand diplomats and military officers explained forthrightly to their Australian counterparts and was a point on which they seemed to agree.[134]

The decision by the Australian government to prioritize its strategic planning to the near north and Southeast Asia in particular was significant because it signaled the end of any pretense to a global British Commonwealth strategic defense policy. A key Commonwealth country was now prioritizing its own regional security to the detriment of any broader global plans. Furthermore, by shifting its security focus, Australia had managed to encourage the British government to look more closely at Southeast Asia and establish some sort of formal defense planning for the region. It is no coincidence that once the Australian government had confirmed its decision to prioritize the defense of Southeast Asia, the United Kingdom urged the United States to turn the current ad hoc discussions into "a political and military command structure along NATO lines for Southeast Asia."[135] By playing a greater and more formal role in Australia's local security issues, the United Kingdom could promote its own preferences within broader British Commonwealth defense planning.

Although London was now willing to suggest that a new defense organization should emerge along the lines of NATO, Washington remained adamantly opposed. U.S. policymakers still preferred bilateral security agreements, as evidenced by the U.S.–Republic of Korea defense treaty of October 1953.[136] Yet support for formal strategic cooperation would soon emerge as growing threats made the region more important than ever before. The military situation inside Southeast Asia had deteriorated for the French throughout the second half of the year, and Western fears of Communist intervention in Indochina were rising. The United States would soon look to other countries for support in its defense of the region. Such interest in Southeast Asia and the Asia-Pacific more broadly would finally provide an opportunity to establish a formal strategic alliance comprising the United States, the United Kingdom, Australia, and New Zealand.

CHAPTER 6

Divided Action

Throughout 1954, the United States began to consider seriously the creation of a wider strategic alliance in the Asia-Pacific that would include the United Kingdom, Australia, and New Zealand. Such a policy reversal reflected growing concerns about Communist expansion in Southeast Asia. Events in Indochina were especially alarming. As the Communist-backed Viet Minh appeared increasingly likely to seize power in Vietnam, the U.S. finally looked toward collective security responses to prevent a Communist advance into Southeast Asia. Although the French collapse at Dien Bien Phu in May 1954 catalyzed the decision-making process in Washington, serious discussions about some type of collective security arrangement for Indochina had begun months prior. Congress's preference for a multilateral solution, concerns about appearing to act as an imperial or racist power, and the rising cost of the Cold War meant that the United States preferred not to proceed alone.

The United States consequently looked abroad for support for collective action. Only a small number of states, however, could provide substantial military resources. Washington focused its attention on London, Canberra, and Wellington. Fundamental disagreements among all four states concerning Cold War strategy persisted throughout negotiations. Although welcoming the opportunity for closer cooperation in the realm of security planning, the United Kingdom, Australia, and New Zealand all resisted U.S. ideas about immediate and major military commitments in the region. Even the existence of ANZUS proved insufficient motivation for Canberra and Wellington to agree to support Washington's request for military support. The treaty instead appeared to have the opposite effect as antipodean officials feared the dilution or dissolution of existing trilateral strategic arrangements in favor of a wider alliance. All three British Commonwealth powers instead drove debate away from immediate military action toward longer-term alliance building.

Securing Indochina

During World War II, France had lost control of Indochina to Japan in 1941. There followed a war between Japanese forces and the Viet Minh, a nationalist guerrilla group led by Ho Chi Minh, that sought Vietnamese independence. As Japan came closer to defeat in World War II, the Allies had to decide Indochina's political future. France was determined to reclaim its fallen Asian empire. The British were prepared to support French ambitions largely because they feared trustee arrangements, whereby former colonial territories would come under United Nations' control, would be replicated throughout the British Empire. Churchill could hardly acquiesce to the dismantling of his French allies' empire while retaining the British Empire. British forces, along with assistance from Nationalist China, therefore ejected Japan from Indochina in the summer of 1945 and handed back authority to France. Immediate wrangling between the French and Viet Minh began, which soon descended into open conflict. By the end of the year, the Viet Minh were engaged in a guerilla war against French colonial rule in Indochina.[1]

The U.S. would have preferred placing the state under an international "trusteeship." Roosevelt remained highly suspicious of European colonial intentions in the Asia-Pacific and feared that French efforts to reclaim their fallen Asian empire would only exacerbate ongoing tensions in the region.[2] The president explained in 1944 that the United States would not accept either France or the United Kingdom reclaiming their lost Asian territory without first being notified of their intentions.[3] Nevertheless, the United States largely ignored French efforts inside Indochina. The U.S. was far more concerned about securing a postwar settlement in Europe.[4] As Roosevelt made clear, he did not want to get "mixed up" in questions about the future of Indochina.[5] Yet as Cold War tensions escalated and the containment of Soviet power became ever more important, France's fight against the Viet Minh assumed greater attention in U.S. policymaking circles. Washington no longer viewed France as fighting the forces of Asian nationalism; France was now facing a Communist-supported Viet Minh, which had revolutionary ambitions for the whole of Indochina.[6] This shift in U.S. opinion is illustrated by Dean Acheson, who in December 1945, even prior to the outbreak of full-scale war between the French and the Viet Minh, warned U.S. officials that a "Communist-dominated, Moscow-orientated Indochina" would be a direct threat against the interests of the United States. The U.S. should therefore do all it could to support "the non-Communist elements in Vietnam."[7] A desire for continued French support for U.S. security plans in Western Europe, coupled with the fear that Ho Chi Minh was a "dedicated Communist and Stalinist lackey," meant that the Truman administration steadily began to support French military efforts against the Viet Minh.[8]

U.S. policymakers were not alone in thinking that France was fighting the forces of international Communism inside Indochina. British, Australian, and New Zealand security analysts reached similar conclusions.[9] Events inside Indochina were of greatest concern to the antipodean governments. For the Australian security establishment, any success for the Viet Minh in Indochina was in reality a success for the Chinese Communist Party. In Australian eyes, the Viet Minh were proxies for Communist expansion throughout Southeast Asia. Success for the Viet Minh would only encourage the People's Republic of China to grow its influence across the rest of Indochina and into neighboring territories in Southeast Asia.[10] Such assessments were shared by policymakers on the other side of the Tasman Sea.[11]

While events in Indochina remained a concern, they existed on the periphery of antipodean thinking, which instead focused on the Middle East and wider Asia-Pacific throughout the 1940s and early 1950s. As the probability of Viet Minh success grew, however, so too did Australian and New Zealand worries about the broader ramifications for their own security. Only Australia felt that these events required the prioritization of regional security in the immediate future. As the Australian Joint Intelligence Committee warned in 1952, "In the absence of armed assistance from the Western Powers, there is a strong possibility that by 1957 the Vietminh with increasing Chinese assistance, will have forced the French to withdraw, and will be in effective control of the whole of Indo-China."[12] Australia therefore sought to encourage a more effective security organization for preventing a Communist takeover.[13] The seriousness and speed of events inside Indochina crystallized thinking in Canberra toward the prioritization of their own regional security, ahead of British Commonwealth interests focused on the Middle East and Western Europe.

U.S. involvement in Indochina has received extensive coverage elsewhere.[14] By the time Truman left office, the United States had become the principal source of financial and military assistance for the French fight against the Viet Minh. Such assistance was both considerable, having already provided in the region of $700 million, and growing.[15] The Eisenhower administration followed its predecessor's lead and steadily increased U.S. assistance for France and the region more generally. In January 1954, for instance, Eisenhower gave his approval for the creation of a "freedom fund," which was designed to improve the socioeconomic conditions of Southeast Asian states.[16] Mirroring the concerns of the previous administration, Eisenhower and his national security team were convinced that if the Viet Minh captured control of Vietnam, it would be a proxy victory for the PRC. As the president himself suggested in a public address on 7 April, allowing one Communist success would precipitate a "domino effect" throughout the region.[17]

Dulles put it more starkly when he claimed that "if Vietnam fell into hostile hands, and if the neighboring countries remained weak and divided, then the Communists could move on into all of Southeast Asia."[18] As the secretary of state noted in a public interview, his biggest concern was "what are we [the United States] to lose next?" Fighting the Viet Minh had assumed the mantle as the "free world's fight" against international Communism.[19] Losing even a portion of Indochina to Communist forces was unacceptable for the Eisenhower administration, as evidenced by the National Security Council's policy statement on Southeast Asia: "Communist dominations, by whatever means, of all of Southeast Asia would seriously endanger in the short term, and critically endanger in the longer term, United States security interests. . . . The loss of the struggle in Indochina, in addition to its impact in Southeast Asia and South Asia, would therefore have the most serious repercussions on U.S. and free world interests in Europe and elsewhere."[20] U.S. strategy, articulated in the clearest of terms by the National Security Council, was designed "to prevent the countries of Southeast Asia from passing into the Communist orbit; to persuade them that their best interest lies in greater cooperation and stronger affiliations with the rest of the free world."[21]

U.S. policy reflected a mixture of strategic and economic considerations. Losing the region to the Communist sphere of influence would lead to the loss of strategic raw materials, such as significant quantities of rubber, tin, and petroleum. As one National Security Council policy planning paper made clear in January 1954, "The loss of Southeast Asia would have serious economic consequences for many nations of the free world and conversely would add significant resources to the Soviet bloc. . . . Furthermore, this area has an important potential as a market for the industrialized countries of the free world."[22] The United States also sought greater industrial development and private investment in the region to ensure a gradual improvement in living conditions, which would in turn promote political stability and healthy participation in the world economy. The opening of regional markets and international trade more broadly was therefore a crucial component for success.[23] The U.S. believed that promoting the economic prosperity of Southeast Asia as a whole would assist in the struggle against Communism.[24]

On January 21, 1954, the National Security Council decided to establish a high-level committee to deal with the problems of Southeast Asia as a whole.[25] As the Joint Chiefs of Staff argued, the only thing that deterred Communist China from expanding into Southeast Asia was U.S. power.[26] U.S. policymakers looked at various avenues for continuing military action against any Viet Minh government that would come into being following the potential collapse of France in Indochina. John Foster Dulles had told the National Security Council on January 14 that "we could carry on effective guerrilla operations against this new Vietminh government as they had made for our side and against the legitimate governments of the Associated States in recent years." Allen Dulles, director of the Central Intelligence Agency, explained that "the CIA was already working on such plans." Clearly, then, U.S. policymakers were building military contingencies in the event of France's defeat in Indochina.[27]

The likelihood of French defeat had grown considerably in the opening months of 1954. Following successes in the latter half of the previous year, the French army had moved a significant portion of its forces to garrison Dien Bien Phu. Here, operations began to interrupt Viet Minh supply lines into neighboring Laos with a view to drawing the Viet Minh into a major confrontation. The Viet Minh, under the leadership of General Vo Nguyen Giap, surrounded and besieged the French garrison. It quickly became apparent that the French were on the verge of a crushing defeat.[28] Unbeknown to French military commanders, the Viet Minh had managed to bring heavy artillery pieces into range of the French garrison. On March 13, 1954, the Viet Minh opened fire and stunned the French, putting the airstrip at Dien Bien Phu out of commission and thereby hindering hopes for reinforcing the position. Viet Minh forces overran a fortified French Foreign Legion position later in the evening. The French, under the leadership of General Henri Navarre, now faced a prolonged siege. Policymakers in Washington assumed that French defeat at Dien Bien Phu would precipitate, or at the very least strongly encourage, a complete collapse of the French position throughout the entirety of Indochina and thus deliver a triumph for Communism as a whole and for the PRC in particular. The French foreign minister Georges

Bidault reinforced this point in conversation with Dulles by making it clear that without massive U.S. assistance in preventing a defeat at Dien Bien Phu, French public opinion would insist on full withdrawal from Indochina. Subsequently, if French forces fell, agreement at the proposed Geneva Conference—which would convene on April 26, 1954, to discuss outstanding issues between East and West concerning the Korean peninsula, the situation of Vietnam, and the possibility of restoring peace to Indochina—was likely to favor the Communist powers.[29]

The strong possibility of France's defeat led to the Eisenhower administration's reappraisal of its entire strategy in Southeast Asia. For the president, it was of "vital importance" to hold "the position" in Southeast Asia: "It was the neck of a bottle and it was essential to keep the cork in."[30] One critical problem, however, was obtaining sufficient public support for any necessary action given widespread ignorance of the challenge. As Eisenhower lamented, "Many American people thought that Saigon was something to eat."[31] By early 1954, Washington began to explore a range of options for helping to reverse the French situation that included the possibility of military intervention. As Dulles recorded, Eisenhower "agreed basically that we should not get involved in fighting in Indochina unless there were the political pre-conditions necessary for a successful outcome. He did not, however, wholly exclude the possibility of a single strike, if it were almost certain this would produce decisive results."[32]

Washington explored a range of options for bolstering the French position. After a series of discussions, U.S. policymakers decided to continue to provide logistical and financial support for the French army to encourage the French government to maintain its war effort against the Viet Minh. The issue of direct U.S. military intervention in the conflict would now become a serious question for discussion. The introduction of ground forces into Vietnam was something to which Eisenhower remained strongly opposed. His closest advisers largely agreed with this analysis.[33] Walter Bedell Smith, who served as Eisenhower's chief of staff during World War II and was now serving as deputy secretary of state, told Anthony Eden that the U.S. would only introduce ground forces into Vietnam "over [his] dead body."[34] Yet military support for France via air and naval assets remained viable options as the French position in Indochina deteriorated.[35]

Unilateral U.S. military action in Indochina was problematic for political reasons. As Eisenhower told his national security team with "great emphasis," there was "no possibility whatever of U.S. unilateral intervention in Indochina, and we had best face that fact. Even if we tried such a course, we would have to take it to Congress and fight for it like dogs, and with very little hope of success."[36] Congressional leaders made clear to the White House that their support for any military intervention was contingent on being able to "internationalize" the conflict.[37] There were also concerns about free riding by European allies in the sense that U.S. actions would support European interests without these states providing assistance. As Dulles admitted during one conversation, there was little chance of Congress endorsing the United States "going it alone" in order "to save the British Commonwealth" in Southeast Asia.[38]

These political considerations alone would have been sufficient to convince the president that he required international support for any actions he desired to undertake in Indochina. Fears of appearing as an imperialist, colonial, or racist power, however, further encouraged Eisenhower to look for alliance partners in the Asia-Pacific. The president had reached the conclusion that a purely Western intervention in Indochina was undesirable and any long-term solution to the challenges facing Indochina required the United States to build solidarity among a wide range of Western and Asian states, regardless of their actual military capabilities, in order to defend against Communism in the region.[39] During one session of the National Security Council, the U.S. vice president Richard Nixon gave an airing to such a viewpoint when he concluded that an exclusive Western intervention inside Indochina "would be almost as bad for the United States as would be unilateral U.S. intervention, since it would be interpreted by the Asian nations as sheer colonialism."[40]

Eisenhower and Dulles concurred with Nixon's assessment. The minutes of the meeting record that "the president strongly reaffirmed his anxiety over any arrangement which was confirmed to the five white nations and left out the Asian states."[41] Eisenhower and Dulles were both aware that if the United States undertook unilateral action inside Indochina it could damage long-term relationships with other Asian states, enflaming charges of racism leveled at the United States from the Communist powers and neutral states such as India.[42] Military action, within the framework of a broad alliance that consisted of both Western and Asian states, was therefore desirable in order to credibly refute such accusations.[43] As Eisenhower later told the press, it was a sine qua non that a Southeast Asian security alliance involved Asian membership.[44]

Yet Washington remained largely focused on securing support from Western powers; Asian support could follow thereafter, once the main contours of the security alliance had emerged. When Congress had declared it would only support U.S. involvement in Indochina if the conflict was "internationalized," this was interpreted by the Eisenhower administration as meaning they wanted British support, evidently prioritizing the material contribution that the United Kingdom could make toward any military effort. Accordingly, Dulles contacted the British ambassador Roger Makins and requested that both the U.S. and British government should "have talks" to establish what could be done about France's deteriorating position in Indochina.[45] As confirmed by the National Security Council in April 1954, U.S. policy would focus on "organizing a regional grouping" and then "gaining British support for U.S. objective in the Far East, in order to strengthen U.S. policies in the area."[46] Building an international alliance for the Asia-Pacific and especially for Southeast Asia was now a central goal of U.S. diplomacy. Antipodean involvement was preferable, but British support for this new organization and for U.S. policies throughout the Asia-Pacific was essential.[47]

Securing support for military action was not the same as sanctioning action. Eisenhower and Dulles remained undecided on whether U.S. military intervention was required. The U.S. secretary of defense Charles Wilson was much clearer in his thinking. The United States should "forget about Indochina" and focus its attention on securing the rest of Southeast Asia. This was an opinion shared by all the Joint Chiefs of Staff, barring its chairman, Admiral Radford, who, among all of Eisenhower's advisers, was the most determined to initiate military action. Yet the absence of allied support effectively ruled out U.S. intervention in any guise. The United States needed to acquire allies if the president was to initiate any military action inside Indochina.[48]

Collective Security

U.S. efforts to win international support began in earnest with Dulles delivering his "united action speech," officially titled "The Threat of a Red Asia," on March 29, 1954. He warned that "if Communist forces won uncontested control over Indochina or any substantial part thereof, they would surely resume the same pattern of aggression against other free peoples in the area. . . . The United States feels that that possibility should not be passively accepted but should be met by united action."[49] As Dulles had agreed with the president prior to delivering his speech, the language he used would clearly illustrate that the United States was not "appeasing" the People's Republic of China. Instead, it would serve as a strong statement that emphasized to the press the commitment of the United States to "deeds" and not just "words."[50] Eisenhower supported Dulles's efforts by emphasizing publicly the strategic importance of retaining Indochina in the Western camp. As the president told reporters, the loss of Indochina to Communism was "incalculable to the free world."[51]

Washington's attention turned toward London.[52] On liaising with British officials, Dulles found that there was limited enthusiasm for united action in Indochina. They believed that intervention was likely to precipitate a war against the PRC in a similar fashion to events during the Korean War. Having brokered a cease-fire only a year earlier with North Korea, there was little enthusiasm in London for another major crisis.[53] More alarming yet, the British believed that if any such war escalated, it would likely lead to Soviet intervention, which would escalate into a global conflagration and produce what Churchill feared the most: "an assault by hydrogen bombs" on the United Kingdom.[54] As the prime minister remarked a year earlier, he had "lived seventy-eight years without hearing of bloody places like Cambodia" and he therefore saw no reason to allow East-West disputes over such places to lead to global war.[55] In a secret planning paper, however, British intelligence had called Indochina the "front line of the Cold War in South-East Asia."[56] Yet this conclusion did not necessitate a military response for the British cabinet. The British believed that such action was futile, as a war against the PRC would escalate quickly to involve the Soviet Union. London's reaction to a New Zealand staff paper, which suggested that planning for a war solely against the PRC should begin, highlighted a clear reluctance to commit to military force.[57]

Although the British government was reluctant to support united action as currently proposed, it did welcome the opportunity to capitalize on U.S. proposals and pursue its interests in the region. As London informed Washington, it was open to creating an alliance of Asia-Pacific powers of a "more general and enduring nature," which contradicted Dulles's preference for a "temporary arrangement."[58] The British government saw these U.S. proposals for united action as a means of securing their long-term ambition of creating a broader alliance in the Asia-Pacific that included both British and U.S. participation and rectified their continuing exclusion from ANZUS and strategic planning in the region more generally. As Eden suggested, Dulles's proposals could "remove the anomaly of our exclusion from the ANZUS pact" and "contribute directly" to British interests.[59] As correspondence within the British government revealed: "Our object must, of course, be to profit by the historic decision which the United States appear to be taking to accept far-reaching commitments on the mainland of Asia."[60] Such statements highlight the strategic calculations of the British government. Even when considering the risks of military action inside Indochina, British policymakers were also concerned about obtaining ANZUS membership and longer-term interests in Southeast Asia.

The U.S. intensified its efforts to convince the United Kingdom to support united action. The president now wrote directly to the prime minister. Eisenhower urged Churchill to support his efforts and, in an effort to quell British apprehensions, insisted that he did not believe British or U.S. ground troops would be required for any military operations in Indochina. He instead proposed that a new security coalition would be formed that would clearly demonstrate to the Chinese Communists that supporting the Viet Minh would "inevitably lead to the growing power of the forces arrayed against them."[61] As Eisenhower argued, a physical deterrent would be sufficient to stave off disaster in Indochina for Western interests.

The Eisenhower administration also sought to exploit Britain's relationship with both Australia and New Zealand. Dulles called Percy Spender and Leslie Munro to his house to discuss the united action proposals, and it was here that he applied the diplomatic squeeze to his guests. He suggested that Australia and New Zealand should agree to "contribute forces" to a new organization that could possibly commit to fight Communist forces inside Indochina. As Dulles reasoned, it was in their own best interests to support such action because Communist success in Indochina would only "increase the direct threat to Australia, New Zealand, the Philippines, and the entire off-shore island chain."[62]

More assertive U.S. diplomacy toward the British government followed in early April as Washington looked to link London's support for united action with the continuation of U.S. security cooperation in other areas of the world. As the minute of one meeting between the British ambassador to the United States Roger Makins and U.S. officials read,

> If the UK and Australia and New Zealand, whose vital interests would be directly threatened if Indochina fell, were not enough concerned to do anything about it or join in any effective form of united action, there would be opposition on part of the US Congress and people to having the US pick up the burden on a unilateral basis. In other words, we would not be disposed to commit our forces to defend British and Commonwealth interests in Malaya, Australia and New Zealand when the British, Australians and New Zealanders simply sat on their hands. . . . This in turn could certainly have a most serious impact on the support we were contributing to our collective arrangements in areas other than Southeast Asia.[63]

Dulles subsequently informed the Australian foreign minister Richard Casey that if Britain, Australia, and New Zealand would not provide armed assistance in Indochina, then the United States could well "wash its hands of responsibility in South-East Asia."[64] The combination of direct threats to the protection of British Commonwealth interests, in conjunction with Dulles's earlier attempts to gain support from Australia and New Zealand, put immense stress on the British government to support united action.

The British cabinet debated the U.S. proposals. Eden believed that the size of the proposed alliance was problematic for it would cover too great a region for a security umbrella to prove effective. Moreover, without adequate resources, it would fail to provide a credible defense. Establishing an alliance with the specific task of preventing Communist success inside Indochina was also seen by Eden as a U.S. "warning" to the PRC and not as "a permanent security system" for Southeast Asia. If the Viet Minh managed to eject France from even a portion of Vietnam, the alliance would have "to withdraw ignominiously or to embark on warlike action against China."[65] Such a set of circumstances would risk escalation to a global conflict that Churchill and Eden's foreign policy sought to avoid.

Calculations about the United Kingdom's long-term relations with the British Commonwealth also drove the Churchill government to reject Dulles's proposal. Uppermost in British minds were the likely ramifications that establishing a new alliance would have with India and the other so-called Colombo powers, namely Burma, Indonesia, Ceylon, and Pakistan. Given India's growing socioeconomic power and its influence within the neutral bloc, Eden was keen to foster cooperation. As such, he was sympathetic to the neutralist outlook advanced by Jawaharlal Nehru and was determined that any security pact should not be overtly anti-Chinese for fear of jeopardizing the likelihood of Colombo power membership.[66] Dulles was close to the mark when he claimed that the "intense British desire to keep India within the Commonwealth gives Nehru close to a veto power over British Asian policies."[67] As Eden noted, with the Colombo powers in mind, any successful alliance in Southeast Asia required the "widest possible measure of Asian support."[68]

London was also unconvinced that a victory for the Viet Minh inside Indochina would lead to the disastrous consequences that Washington suggested. As the British Joint Intelligence Committee concluded, "The risk of a Communist invasion of Siam, should the Viet Minh secure part or whole of the Indo-Chinese frontier, would be slight." Instead, the real danger would be that Communist forces could infiltrate states with the objective of "fomenting trouble" among the various existing dissident groups.[69] Such trouble was seen as likely to spread to Malaya where the British were continuing to fight the Communist insurgency. Nevertheless, even in the event of increased Communist infiltration into Thailand, Malaya, or Burma, senior British policymakers and military officials remained reasonably confident that they would be able to resist Communist expansion adequately.[70] As Churchill made clear, "We think we can hold Malaya even if Indo-China falls."[71] Eisenhower himself accepted this conclusion. As he told his National Security Council, the British would attend to the defense of Malaya as a "routine matter," and in the event of a global war, Britain would "defend Malaya to the bitter end."[72] For London and Washington, these dominoes in Southeast Asia evidently posed different risks and would likely fall in different directions.

Personalities rather than just policies also help explain the attitude of the British government toward Dulles's united action proposals. As historians have demonstrated, the Eden-Dulles personality clash contributed to U.S.-UK differences.[73] Both Churchill and Eden had intensely disliked the appointment of Dulles as U.S. secretary of state. They believed that they were justified in their concerns, as Dulles had shown what they believed to be a lack of flexibility as it pertained to negotiations over the future of Germany and the Middle East. Dulles's efforts to push the United States and the NATO alliance to accept the doctrine of "massive retaliation" only confirmed their fears about U.S. foreign policy precipitating nuclear war. British policymakers concluded that Dulles was well intentioned but his mind-set led to policies that would precipitate a global war.[74] The choice of Radford to push the united action proposals hardly helped matters. The admiral was perhaps even more unpopular than Dulles in London for British policymakers believed that he was determined to pursue a war against the PRC at almost any cost. Radford had been urging the likes of Australia and New Zealand in the previous year to commit to his idea for military action against mainland China if the PRC initiated a "major assault" against Indochina.[75] With both Dulles and Radford pushing the proposals, it seemed as if united action was simply a euphemism for a war against the PRC.

British assessments were largely accurate; Radford believed that crushing the Viet Minh could very well precipitate a war with the PRC and in fact welcomed such a conflict.[76] The admiral argued that the United States had to "go after the seat of Communist power in the Far East, namely, China. If we did not do this . . . measures we took around the periphery of Indochina were of little avail."[77] Dulles in conversation with Eisenhower further explained that Radford and the JCS were of the opinion that any discussion of defending Indochina was simply pointless. The United States should strike the PRC and "in this connection atomic weapons should be used."[78] Eisenhower agreed that, in the event of an unprovoked full-scale assault by the PRC against Indochina, the United States would have to make sure that there would be "no half measures or frittering around. The Navy and Air Force should go in with full power, using new weapons, and strike at air bases and ports in mainland China."[79] Personalities may not have been decisive in convincing London not to support Washington's proposals but they certainly added weight to the growing resistance to united action. As Dulles himself recognized, Radford had been a poor choice of diplomat, as the British tended to interpret his assessments as being overly belligerent.[80]

Even though the British government may have wanted to establish a Pacific security pact, and were aware of U.S. pressure to cooperate, this did not mean they would grant support for U.S. military action inside Indochina. The British government ultimately concluded that united action was simply too risky to support. Despite U.S. pressure, it was desirable to postpone establishing any new alliance until after the Geneva talks had concluded. London had identified a valuable diplomatic opportunity to realize its own ambitions in the region but would need to wait for the right moment to achieve its objectives. Eden therefore focused only on obtaining an Indochina settlement at Geneva and would look to establish a new Pacific alliance thereafter.[81]

The prime minister gave clarity to British policy in a statement before the House of Commons on April 27, 1954, when he announced that the United Kingdom would give no undertakings on Southeast Asia until after the conclusion of the recently begun Geneva Conference.[82] These talks were set to begin in late April to discuss outstanding East-West differences in Korea and Indochina. As such, the British government undertook a major diplomatic effort to reach a political settlement at the Geneva Conference.[83] As Dulles rather sourly reported to the president, the British were "badly frightened" by the rumblings of a U.S.-PRC confrontation over Indochina and were determined to avoid actions that could help precipitate such an eventuality.[84]

The Geneva Conference

The Geneva Conference convened on April 26, 1954. Participants from East and West began discussions concerning the future of the Korean peninsula, the situation in Vietnam, and the possibility of peace in Indochina.[85] The end of the war in Korea in July 1953 had influenced Eden's decision to take a leading role in the forthcoming Geneva talks. The British foreign secretary was determined to avoid exacerbating tensions that might precipitate a global war and lead to "the destruction of Western Europe."[86] London's diplomatic ambitions at the conference consequently threatened to create a rift with Washington. Eden was prepared to negotiate a settlement to the war inside Indochina, which would probably involve the partition of Vietnam.

For the Eisenhower administration, such a solution was unacceptable. Partitioning Vietnam was in effect handing over control of a portion of that state to the Communists. Such an approach was tantamount to appeasement, rarely something of which a Western politician wishes to be accused, especially not a president that was approaching midterm elections. Eisenhower was heavily involved in this campaigning and was keen to avoid foreign policy matters damaging Republican election chances.[87] Domestic-political concerns aside, strategic calculations also informed U.S. thinking. By allowing the Viet Minh to control a portion of Vietnam, they would enjoy a safe haven from which to recuperate and launch their revolutionary ambitions across the rest of Indochina and Southeast Asia. As one internal U.S. planning paper suggested, "A compromise settlement on any of the bases now apparent would be tantamount to opening up Southeast Asia to Communist control."[88]

Eisenhower had written to Churchill earlier in April warning of the "possibility of the Communists driving a wedge between us," yet a U.S.-UK confrontation had now become unavoidable.[89] Dulles later subjected Eden to what the latter recorded as a "prolonged, and at moments somewhat heated, onslaught about [the British] attitude" at the Geneva Conference.[90] The secretary of state also implied in his conversation with Eden that a failure to support U.S. calls for united action would have ramifications for U.S.-UK cooperation in other areas of the world. As Dulles reported back to Washington, he had informed Eden that a "failure of [the] British to rally to our side would almost certainly produce consequences extending beyond that area."[91] Evidently, the U.S. secretary of state was seeking to leverage existing U.S. cooperation with the United Kingdom in other areas of the world to convince London to follow Washington's line in Indochina. Dulles's stern diplomacy had followed the lead set by the president, who had spelled out in clearer terms how such linkage would apply in practical terms.

Eisenhower believed that continued U.S. military assistance to British forces in Hong Kong in the event of a war with the PRC was directly dependent on cooperation in Indochina. As the president informed one his aides, "My argument to the British has been that if we all went in together into Indo China at the same time, that would be fine but if they don't go in with us, they don't expect us to help them defend Hong Kong. We must have collective security or we'll fall."[92] The Eisenhower administration was engaging in rough diplomacy with its British ally, much as it had with Australia and New Zealand in the previous year concerning the future of ANZUS. By threatening to reassess existing U.S.-UK cooperation throughout the Asia-Pacific, the president was hoping to exert the necessary pressure to convince the British government to support U.S. plans for Indochina.

Rough U.S. diplomacy failed to overcome the United Kingdom's concerns about united action. The British foreign secretary refused to alter his stance that military intervention inside Indochina should be avoided. Nor would Eden be convinced by Dulles to change his opinion that France would have to negotiate an end to its war inside Indochina, which would likely involve the partition of Vietnam. As Eden informed Washington, he was "not prepared to give any undertakings about United Kingdom military action in Indochina in advance of the results of Geneva."[93] Eden's position was emboldened by news received on May 7, 1954, that French forces had been defeated at Dien Bien Phu. French defeat severely weakened the diplomatic hand that the Western powers could play against their Communist rivals.

By May, Dulles was becoming increasingly concerned with British intentions during the negotiations. He suspected that the United Kingdom was looking to manipulate any U.S. commitment to the defense of Indochina as a means of shoring up Britain's numerous other Asian interests. By advancing the idea of partitioning Vietnam as part of a cease-fire inside Indochina, Dulles suspected that "cleverly, the British could be able to pass as the peacemakers and go between East and West, and would strengthen their ties with India and Malaysia, without any real expense by the UK."[94] Radford concurred, arguing that the British were attempting to "lay the groundwork for a set-up which would be much in their favor but not in ours."[95]

Yet U.S. diplomacy was by now having more impact on the British government's position on Indochina. Eden was concerned that U.S.-UK differences could spill over into other areas of the world and thereby cause long-term damage to British interests. Strategic cooperation was extremely close in the realms of intelligence analysis, nuclear relations, and military planning in Europe. Safeguarding such cooperation remained at the forefront of Eden's mind during these negotiations. Eden therefore hinted to Washington that British support for security planning for the broader Southeast Asian region was materializing. On May 5, while still adamantly opposed to military intervention, Eden suggested to Dulles that the British government would enter five-power staff discussions—that would consist of the United Kingdom, the U.S., France, Australia, and New Zealand—about the situation in Indochina and Southeast Asian security more broadly. As Washington recognized, this represented "a considerable compromise on [Britain's] part."[96]

Military discussions did not mean that somehow the British government was now committed to intervening militarily in Indochina. London viewed these talks as a way to temper transatlantic disagreements. Furthermore, talks were to act as a stalking horse for evaluating just what type of security cooperation Washington would be prepared to accept in the Asia-Pacific. For Eden, the problems in Southeast Asia were largely political. The Western powers suffered from a lack of legitimacy and struggled to garner sufficient indigenous support for maintaining their interests throughout the region. If the West could not win active support from the countries of Southeast Asia, then it should seek "benevolent neutrality" as military action would never actually secure Western interests in the long term. Winning support from Asian states was therefore imperative if any new security organization for Southeast Asia was to be successful. To secure such support, any collective grouping had to serve as a lasting defensive organization and "not a hastily contrived expedient to meet the present crisis."[97] Eden was confident that he could deliver such an organization as his discussions with representatives from Pakistan and Ceylon suggested that neither would oppose a Southeast Asian defense organization. As Eden predicted, if the United States supported his efforts at Geneva, then Indian support for the "negotiated settlement" for Indochina would also become more likely.[98]

While U.S. officials viewed a comprehensive organization as an admirable ambition, the top priority with the Geneva Conference now under way was to establish any Southeast Asian security arrangement as quickly as possible. A potential military intervention inside Indochina might also still be required to help improve France's current position. Military action had therefore still not been ruled out by the Eisenhower administration. As Dulles informed the National Security Council, managing to obtain both Indian and Pakistani membership in a new Asian security alliance would be a coup for the United States, but ultimately this would take too long to achieve.[99] In U.S. estimations, time was of the essence because, following France's surrender at Dien Bien Phu, the PRC was now deciding whether to "grab the entirety of Indochina or to continue to obtain it in a piecemeal fashion."[100] It was therefore imperative that a form of collective security now emerge in order to demonstrate the willingness of the West to defend its interests in Indochina. In turn, this grouping would help mollify the demands of the Communist bloc at the Geneva Conference and provide valuable diplomatic advantage in the negotiations. If the PRC did decide to "grab" the rest of Indochina, however, this new organization would leave the United States well placed to respond militarily.[101]

The task for Dulles, then, was to establish such an alliance. The chances of obtaining British support still looked remote. Yet Washington did not see the position of London as holding a veto over U.S. military intervention inside Indochina. Despite Congress's preference for British support, and the president's statement that without their cooperation military intervention was "impossible," Eisenhower laid out plans on April 4, 1954, that U.S. intervention was a possibility.[102] The deteriorating situation in Indochina appeared to have overcome serious doubts about military action in Indochina independent of the United Kingdom. Eisenhower's national security team thus tentatively agreed during the April 29 NSC meeting that the United States would look to form a new Southeast Asian alliance that could undertake military action inside Indochina without British participation. Nixon was the first to countenance such action. The vice president even argued that Australian support for intervention would be forthcoming without British participation. Considerable doubt existed as to whether Australia would commit to a new organization without British membership, but Nixon insisted that his "unnamed sources" suggested that they would.[103] Dulles thus telegrammed the U.S. delegation at the Geneva talks informing them that "it might not be indispensable that the UK participates at the outset" on any "internationalizing [of] the war."[104]

Antipodean Action

The president was willing to countenance the possibility of military action but remained extremely reticent about such an undertaking without the support of a broader alliance. Eisenhower remained unwilling to engage in military action unilaterally. Accordingly, the position of the other potential alliance members increased in importance. Washington now looked to the Southern Hemisphere.[105] The likelihood of receiving support from Canberra and Wellington for some sort of military intervention inside Indochina appeared strong given that both antipodean powers had grown steadily concerned about the growing menace posed by Communist forces in Southeast Asia.

Nevertheless, Menzies and Holland understood that Eisenhower was unwilling to offer the type of Southeast Asian security alliance that they wanted. Instead, Washington was requesting antipodean support for a rather ambiguously phrased united action. Canberra and Wellington were under no illusion as to what this proposal really meant: Australian and New Zealand support for military intervention in Indochina. Strong reservations swiftly emerged in both Canberra and Wellington. The timing of the U.S. proposals was especially difficult for Menzies as they came amid the campaigning for the forthcoming general election set for May 29, 1954. U.S. proposals for a new alliance, which could see Australia committing to a war inside Indochina, were unlikely to win votes. Postponing agreement on the U.S.

plans was therefore desirable for domestic political reasons alone. During the election, the issue of Communism had led to extremely bitter campaigning, with the opposition Labour Party suggesting that Menzies was exaggerating the Communist threat for electoral advantage. The Liberal Party nevertheless won the election, aided in part by revelations about Soviet espionage in Australia that divided the opposition.[106]

In the assessment of key policymakers in both Canberra and Wellington, the conclusion had been reached that the French were fighting a losing war inside Indochina and defeat was inevitable. Military action was now too late. Casey made his disquiet about agreeing to united action most clear. In his assessment, the United States was acting without due consideration, and it was now foolhardy to commit militarily to prevent the inevitable partition of Vietnam. More worrying was the total lack of regard that the United States seemed to be giving to the possibility that the PRC might respond militarily to any Western intervention inside Indochina.[107]

Dulles failed to quell such concerns when he discussed his united action proposals with his Australian and New Zealand counterparts at the Geneva Conference. The U.S. secretary of state told both Casey and Webb that while a war with the PRC would be a "dreadful thing," if the PRC directly intervened in Indochina, then "we had to be ready to fight at some point to preserve our fundamental values."[108] More alarming were U.S. plans that did not define precisely what conditions would precipitate this new united action coalition to intervene militarily inside Indochina. Nor did U.S. plans illuminate the overarching objective of intervention. In response, the Australian and New Zealand cabinet demanded that the United States provide them with clearer strategic direction if they were to agree to united action.[109] In the meantime, diplomacy was the preferred course of action. As both Canberra and Wellington agreed, the Geneva Conference should be given a "genuine opportunity to reach a settlement" prior to their committing to military solutions.[110]

Strategic calculations about Australia and New Zealand's position vis-à-vis the United States were also apparent in the thoughts of senior antipodean policymakers. U.S. plans seemed to suggest a new and hastily arranged alliance for the defense of Indochina and for Southeast Asia. For Canberra, it was undesirable to establish such an alliance without first evaluating how this new organization would affect existing arrangements. Similar sentiments existed in Wellington. Ultimately, both antipodean powers were concerned that a new Southeast Asian security alliance would supersede the ANZUS alliance. If membership of this new organization contained multiple states, it would lessen the importance of Australia and New Zealand within their tripartite alliance with the United States. Media reports in Britain even suggested that the Eisenhower administration was considering greatly expanding ANZUS as a way of tackling the crisis in Indochina. Such stories generated considerable apprehension and led to Canberra and Wellington requesting clarification on the matter from Washington.[111]

The Australian and New Zealand governments had jealously guarded their security pact with the United States, so proposals for a new alliance were always going to cause concern. Although Canberra and Wellington had previously sought the expansion of the treaty to include the United Kingdom, a wider pact involving many Asian-Pacific countries risked diluting Australia and New Zealand's relationship with the U.S. Moreover, as officials made known to their British counterparts, a treaty with Asian states could be "a very one-sided bargain" under which both powers would need to provide more assistance in spite of their own limited resources.[112]

None of this is to ignore the limitations of existing cooperation. Antipodean officials had already grown increasingly frustrated about the lack of military cooperation that had occurred after the signing of the ANZUS Treaty. As one senior New Zealand military officer noted in August 1953, the alliance would prove to be "not very effective" without improvements to the military cooperation between the ANZUS members.[113] The first military exercises conducted between the ANZUS pact members in June 1954 did little to change such assessments. So limited were these air exercises over New South Wales, it led Australian officials to question whether this U.S.-inspired Southeast Asian alliance meant that Washington was no longer interested in ANZUS.[114] Meanwhile, policymakers in New Zealand continued to worry that their influence within the treaty was becoming increasingly marginalized.[115]

Nevertheless, ANZUS, despite its limitations, provided direct discussions with U.S. policymakers and military officials. Steady progress in terms of joint strategic planning had been developing over the course of the previous three years. By March 1954, Radford had finally agreed to enter into formal discussions with Australian and New Zealand representatives about defining specific boundaries in the Asia-Pacific for the allocation of joint responsibilities between the three countries.[116] For antipodean policymakers, any new Southeast Asia arrangement should not interfere with the new consultative relationship established by ANZUS.

Both the Menzies and Holland governments therefore saw committing hastily to any new organization as unnecessarily risky in terms of the threat of war and the dilution of ANZUS. Canberra, in consultation with Wellington, consequently decided to delay Australian support for united action until it had established a firmer handle on U.S. and UK policy. The Australian cabinet would continue to discuss these issues at length.[117] Australian officials eventually hinted that support for united action would only be forthcoming if the United Kingdom also signed up. Later discussions then suggested that, regardless of London's position, Canberra would not support united action.[118]

Wellington was similarly reticent about responding too quickly and enthusiastically to Dulles's overtures for united action. In discussion with Menzies, Holland made clear his concern that New Zealand would be opposed to entering any new alliance that would automatically engage in military action inside Indochina. If military action inside Indochina was to be undertaken, then more thought was required before New Zealand would participate.[119] Yet New Zealand, much like Australia, was becoming more receptive to the idea of establishing a new alliance for Southeast Asia. In light of France's deteriorating position in Indochina, Wellington believed that a new approach might better serve its interests. As Holland noted at the time: "This is an important development, for it opens the possibility of a new intimacy of consultation between the United States and New Zealand which—provided the Americans have no ulterior motive—could be very useful, even though in present circumstances it is naturally likely to increase the pressure on us to make commitments in South East Asia."[120] Holland was certainly not opposed to the creation of a new Southeast Asian security alliance but he wanted to approach this proposal carefully and deliberately. He would not be rushed into giving his approval for a new organization that could lead New Zealand quickly into military action inside Indochina or would damage their longer-term strategic interests.

Much like Canberra, Wellington also harbored broader diplomatic concerns. In sum, the Holland government saw Dulles's latest proposals as a direct challenge to the exclusive relationships established with Washington via the ANZUS agreement. Dulles's suggestion for a broader Asian security alliance threatened to downgrade the importance of ANZUS and marginalize New Zealand within this new organization. New Zealand had always been the most reluctant of the three ANZUS powers to allow Asian membership of the alliance for a mixture of strategic and racial reasons. Strategically, Dulles's proposals now seemed to threaten to combine ANZUS and the U.S.-Philippine mutual assistance treaties. Philippine membership in ANZUS had been countenanced during the original ANZUS negotiations, but had been prevented, in part, by antipodean opposition. As New Zealand policymakers interpreted things, while they were the least influential power within ANZUS, they were at least in a tripartite alliance in which their opinion could be heard. In a broader alliance, New Zealand would likely see its position marginalized to the point whereby its voice was irrelevant. For New Zealand policymakers, then, the risk of losing the prize of ANZUS was simply unacceptable.[121]

Racial motivations also played a role in New Zealand thinking. Officials in Wellington made clear to their British counterparts "the low esteem in which they hold the administrations of many of the Asian countries." In contrast to NATO, the Asia-Pacific region included "different systems of government and ways of life and possess[es] no underlying common tradition or purpose." As British officials noted, such considerations carried a good deal more weight in New Zealand than was appreciated elsewhere. Formally associating with Asian countries with rapidly expanding populations might well put New Zealand "under great difficulty in maintaining the immigration restrictions by which she has so far managed to keep at arm's length a person of non-British, or at any rate, non-white, origin."[122]

The United Kingdom, Australia, and New Zealand were united in their response against U.S. calls for a new security alliance. ANZUS was clearly not a powerful enough inducement for Canberra and Wellington to acquiesce to Washington's wishes. The reverse actually seemed to be the case. ANZUS deterred both the Australian and New Zealand government from joining a new Asian security alliance precisely because leaders feared the dissolution of the existing strategic arrangements with the United States. Washington's earlier bilateral guarantee had therefore served to undermine its attempt to establish a broader multilateral solution. Even when the Eisenhower administration sought to punish Canberra and Wellington by refusing to hold an ANZUS Council meeting at Geneva, it still failed to encourage Menzies or Holland to support the U.S. proposals.[123] The lack of influence that the United States was able to exercise over its allies revealed the limitations of its own power but also its failure to foster adequate levels of strategic cooperation in the preceding decade.

In spite of these setbacks for U.S. diplomacy, by May 29, 1954, the United States and France had reached agreement on how U.S. military intervention inside Indochina could proceed. While Paris viewed the agreement as a useful diplomatic weapon in the talks with the Communist bloc, London saw it as demonstrative of U.S. determination to intervene militarily in Indochina and continued to resist such action.[124] Wellington and Canberra subsequently informed Washington that they would not support military intervention inside Indochina.[125] Whether this negative response from Australia and New Zealand was instrumental in convincing the president to rule out military intervention in Indochina by June 8 remains unclear.[126]

Antipodean resistance added strong voices to the growing chorus of opposition to united action outside the Eisenhower administration. In the absence of British participation, it may well have been decisive. Military action without support from these Western powers would have faced stern congressional opposition and contradicted earlier strategic objectives. Despite further efforts to win allied support for united action, the Eisenhower administration found its calls rejected from London, Canberra, and Wellington. The United States would need to compromise with its allies to secure its objectives in Southeast Asia.

CHAPTER 7

The Costs of Compromise

The likelihood of U.S.-led military intervention in Indochina had waned by the summer of 1954. The United States, United Kingdom, Australia, and New Zealand now sought to conclude the Geneva Conference on favorable terms with their adversaries and each other. To gather international support for U.S. plans, provide additional diplomatic advantage at the Geneva negotiations, and establish a visible deterrent to the Communist powers in Southeast Asia more broadly, the Eisenhower administration attempted to create a new security organization for the defense of the wider region. The pursuit of a collective security pact would produce serious divisions between all four powers. Progress toward the Manila Treaty or Southeast Asia Collective Defense Treaty (SEACDT), an agreement for collective defense in the region signed in September 1954, was often difficult as all four states sought to mold the final security organization in line with their own interests throughout the Asia-Pacific.

Compromises on all sides eventually produced agreement. After almost a decade since the end of World War II, the United States, United Kingdom, Australia, and New Zealand once again enjoyed a formal strategic alliance in the Asia-Pacific. The eventual creation of the Southeast Asia Treaty Organization (SEATO) in early 1955 complemented the short-term ambitions of all four Western powers in the region. Nevertheless, diplomatic bargaining preceding signature and ratification led to compromises that diluted the usefulness of the security alliance. The United States continued to limit commitments to joint planning after the implementation of the treaty. SEATO was therefore smaller, weaker, and less integrated than originally envisaged. The organization also lacked the necessary military and economic infrastructure to be effective, which helped encourage Australia and New Zealand to focus on regional rather than British Commonwealth interests, shifting focus away from the Middle East and Mediterranean and toward the "near north."

The Joint Study Group

As the prospect of U.S. military intervention in Vietnam faded in the absence of international support, the talks at Geneva pressed ahead. Discussion among leading Western powers about the possibility of establishing some form of new organization for Southeast Asian security moved swiftly forward. Five Power talks—involving the U.S., UK, France, Australia, and New Zealand—convened in Washington to discuss the nature of any potential security alliance and the type of assistance that could be provided to the Associated States of Indochina, namely Laos, Cambodia, and Vietnam. All expressed willingness to provide additional assistance in the economic and military realm, but there was no agreement as to what this would specifically involve.[1] As the U.S. summary of the discussions concluded, the "talks were amicable and polite but it seems questionable whether much constructive work was accomplished."[2]

There was little agreement concerning exactly which countries should participate in the proposed Southeast Asian security alliance or the extent of security cooperation.[3] London, Canberra, and Wellington were clear, however, that they preferred to retain the exclusive Five Power talks as the forum for resolving such questions so that they could maintain a significant degree of influence over proceedings. Privately, all three governments hoped that in time this forum would evolve into four-power talks following the French withdrawal from Indochina.[4] British diplomats made clear to their U.S. counterparts that London and Washington should arrive at any understanding in private and subsequent planning documents needed to remain among the two sides. Canberra and Wellington were absent from the discussions. The United Kingdom would instead inform and consult both antipodean powers on any agreements as they affected the Asia-Pacific region.[5] Australia and New Zealand both adopted a "wait-and-see" approach in the meantime, albeit reiterating their stance that no agreement should come at the expense of the ANZUS Treaty.[6]

The approach proposed by Britain was problematic for the United States. Both the Philippines and Thailand complained bitterly about their absence from the Five Power talks. As the Eisenhower administration had feared, excluding the Asian powers provided useful propaganda for the Soviet Union and PRC to use in their campaign to cast the United States as a racist power.[7] Thai diplomats were unimpressed. They described the talks as "another example of the archaic idea of the white man's burden."[8] The Philippine ambassador to Washington was also critical. He believed that this was a further example of the Western powers "drawing a color line in Asia."[9] Yet, in spite of such protestations, the U.S. continued to press ahead with the exclusive Five Power talks. The United Kingdom, and to a lesser extent the antipodean powers, provided valuable material support to the region and would help placate congressional demands that possible U.S. action in Indochina required international support. Washington could address complaints emanating from Thailand and the Philippines once the framework of the security alliance was in place. Racial considerations could complicate progress toward a new Southeast security organization, but as Washington recognized, Western powers were critical to the success of any new alliance.

Winning London's support for the new alliance was therefore an important element of Washington's plans. By June 21, 1954, it appeared that Eisenhower had won such support from Churchill. The British prime minister informed the president that his government would agree to establish a security alliance for Southeast Asia. The prime minister even went so far as to suggest that they should establish links between this new alliance and NATO.[10] This was a notable shift in British policy after months of resistance to U.S. efforts. As the likelihood of intervention had decreased, the British now felt increasingly confident that their support for a new security organization in Southeast Asia was not a prelude to military action in Indochina that could lead to a calamity akin to the Korean War.[11]

London had also grown steadily concerned that its continued opposition to Washington's plans would engender an irrecoverable rift in transatlantic relations. Such a situation could encourage the United States to form an alliance in the Asia-Pacific without the United Kingdom. Such a scenario would undermine the efforts of British policymakers to act as a calming influence over U.S. foreign policy and limit their influence in the region. Ultimately, the British government concluded that it was preferable to seek inclusion in a new security alliance in the Asia-Pacific, however imperfect it may be, rather than to accept exclusion. Anthony Eden chose to speak publicly about the possibility of a new security alliance for Southeast Asia. Talking before the House of Commons, the British foreign secretary announced that his government was supportive of U.S. plans for a new Southeast Asian security grouping and had entered discussions with the United States to work out the details. The actual form of this alliance was still to be agreed, but Churchill's forthcoming visit to Washington presented UK and U.S. leaders with an opportunity to thrash out the details.[12]

Churchill and Eden visited Washington in late June, for what the British prime minister believed to be his last official visit before retiring from politics. Despite ongoing U.S.-UK differences concerning Southeast Asia, the president and the prime minister agreed that a U.S.-UK Joint Study Group should convene to discuss how to establish a new security alliance in the region.[13] Disagreements, however, persisted. Churchill, following the advice proffered to him by his intelligence and defense advisers, insisted that any new Southeast Asian alliance should include Thailand, the Philippines, and potentially Burma. For the British, these areas were more important than Indochina and, more significant, were defensible; Indochina was already a lost cause.[14]

In contrast, Eisenhower wanted to extend the alliance to include "whatever can be salvaged" of Vietnam, Laos, and Cambodia. The president also sought British approval for a public communiqué, noting that the crossing of a designated geographical line by Communist forces in Southeast Asia would bring about retaliation from this new alliance.[15] As Eisenhower reasoned, if Communist forces crossed this line, it would legitimize any military action that would be undertaken in Southeast Asia and ensure international support for any subsequent military action.

This proposal met with immediate opposition from both Churchill and Eden. Demarcating a specific line, which if crossed would result in military action inside Indochina, never appealed to London due to the risks and diversions of resources involved. The British government was opposed to fighting a war in an area it deemed of secondary strategic importance. Indochina was simply not the place in which military power should be concentrated. It was a sideshow, which had the potential to misdirect Western efforts against Communism. With the United States seemingly willing to undertake far-reaching commitments on the mainland of Asia, the British worried that the Americans would squander this historic opportunity for cooperation. London was anxious that Washington would direct its efforts solely into Indochina to the neglect of other British interests.[16]

In the Southern Hemisphere, policymakers in Australia and New Zealand were closely monitoring the course of U.S.-UK diplomacy.[17] Canberra and Wellington sought to influence proceedings by informing Washington that their own support for a new security alliance was contingent on British

involvement. Such a move would encourage Washington to further pressure London into joining this new alliance and thereby secure a more effective Southeast Asian security pact, although never to the detriment of the
ANZUS Treaty. Moreover, if the United States failed to gain British acceptance, both antipodean powers had a legitimate basis for refusing to join
the alliance themselves, thereby preventing a major showdown with either
power and safeguarding Commonwealth solidarity.[18] The Menzies and Holland governments were therefore ensuring that Australia and New Zealand
would not be isolated from either their U.S. or British ally.

By the end of June, the chances of Washington achieving its ambition
of establishing a new Southeast Asian security organization prior to the
conclusion of the Geneva talks looked slim. London's enthusiasm had
waned following the disagreements that emerged in the talks at Washington. Australian and New Zealand support for the United States existed but
was contingent on British cooperation. Washington came to understand
that in order for any Southeast Asian security alliance to attract adequate
international support, agreement would have to follow the conclusion of
the Geneva talks. Negotiations had frustrated U.S. ambitions in the region
and proven corrosive to the establishment of any new security alliance for
Southeast Asia. As Eisenhower would later admit, Britain and the United
States had suffered an "antagonistic" relationship in the region driven by
competing strategic assessments of the Cold War: "The conclusion seems
inescapable that these differences come about because we do not agree on
the probable extent and the importance of further Communist expansion in
Asia . . . your own government seems to regard Communist aggression in Asia
as of little significance to the free world future."[19] Delay in this instance
represents an example of success for British postwar diplomacy in the Asia-
Pacific. By refusing to accede to U.S. demands, and benefiting from the
support of its Commonwealth partners, the British government had managed to ensure the failure of what it considered a problematic alliance in
Indochina.

During their earlier talks in Washington, Churchill and Eisenhower had
agreed that they would establish a joint study group, which comprised
political and military officials from both countries that would discuss common problems in Southeast Asia. This outcome represented a further success for the British government, which had now secured high-level bilateral
discussions with the United States. Six meetings of this joint study group
subsequently occurred between July 7 and July 17, during which both sides
discussed the nature of the proposed organization. The British repeatedly
stressed the need for greater economic and political commitments to the

region, whereas the U.S. desired a more military-based solution.[20] Differences persisted on this front and delayed progress. In addition, they discussed the issue of membership for this new Southeast Asian security alliance at length. The central question now revolved around which other countries should join the alliance. Following lengthy discussions, it was agreed that membership should be extended to Australia, New Zealand, France, the Philippines, Thailand, India, Pakistan, Ceylon, Indonesia, and Burma.[21]

Notable absentees from this alliance were apparent, including Japan, Nationalist China, and the Republic of Korea. This new security organization also excluded European powers such as Portugal and the Netherlands, which retained imperial holdings in the region. The limited membership of the organization reflected compromises based principally on the competing interests of the United States and the United Kingdom and to a lesser extent Australia and New Zealand. By encouraging the United States to compromise on the scope of its desired Southeast Asian security pact, the result was a far more limited and inherently weaker alliance than the Eisenhower administration had originally intended.[22]

The decision to exclude Japan is illustrative of such compromises. Despite Japan's central position within overall U.S. strategy for Asia-Pacific security and the country's growing industrial and economic power within the region, the United States conceded its exclusion.[23] U.S. officials consequently looked at avenues for incorporating Japanese economic muscle into the defense of Southeast Asia without formally tying it into a security pact.[24] To be sure, U.S. policymakers already harbored doubts about the diplomatic consequences of including Japan.[25] Its inclusion in a Southeast Asian security alliance could stir up resentment from Southeast Asian states that had not forgotten how the Japanese Empire had behaved during World War II. Yet it was British resistance, and more so that exercised by Australia and New Zealand, that ensured Japanese exclusion.[26]

The Australian government informed the U.S. that it would view Japanese membership as "deeply provocative" given the still recent horrors of World War II, which made it politically difficult for the Menzies government to enter a formal security alliance with Japan. Menzies was concerned by the likely domestic opposition that this agreement would generate for the prime minister.[27] Privately, officials in the Australian government informed their counterparts in New Zealand that Japanese membership of SEATO would be an "impossible" condition for them to accept.[28] This was an opinion shared by the Holland government. Subsequently, New Zealand informed Washington that they too would not enter a new alliance that included membership for Japan.[29]

Also significant were the strategic conclusions reached by Australia and New Zealand concerning the effect of Japanese membership on their standing within the proposed alliance. As both U.S. and British policymakers were well aware, Australia and New Zealand remained "anxious" that any new Southeast Asian security alliance had the potential to "submerge" ANZUS and downgrade their relationship with the United States.[30] An organization with fewer powerful members was, in the assessment of the antipodean powers, preferable to a much broader alliance, as it would allow each antipodean power to exert greater influence over alliance strategy.[31] As Canberra and Wellington emphasized in their communications with Washington, it was imperative that this new organization did not "weaken or supplant ANZUS."[32] When Dulles suggested that "he wanted to raise the question of the future of ANZUS in relation to SEATO," the secretary of state was immediately met with the response that "the firm opinion [of Australia and New Zealand is] that ANZUS should be preserved whatever other arrangements might be made."[33] As one New Zealand official noted later in the year, it was imperative to avoid the impression that ANZUS had been "swallowed up" by SEATO.[34] Such a stance was understandable given the importance that policymakers in Canberra and Wellington attached to ANZUS, not least as it was the only forum in which both antipodean powers could gain direct access to the strategic planning of Washington and thereby exact a level of influence over U.S. policy. The New Zealand Department for External Affairs believed the ANZUS Council was the only forum in which they could exert a degree of influence over "United States thinking on Far Eastern and other political problems."[35]

British officials argued that Japanese membership was unacceptable because of the likely negative reaction it would engender from other Asian states that still harbored wartime resentment toward Japan. Japanese membership simply risked alienating too many Asian states. Inclusion would therefore prove counterproductive. Self-interest also motivated London's thinking given that the British were concerned that Japanese membership threatened to weaken their own influence within any new organization.[36] British officials were already anxious about Japan's rising power in the region, especially its growing trade and commercial influence, a concern increasingly shared by Australian officials.[37]

Membership for Nationalist China and the Republic of Korea was similarly problematic for the British Commonwealth powers, especially as both states desired a Pacific security pact.[38] London, Canberra, and Wellington agreed that the PRC would interpret extending membership to either state as an overtly hostile act, which could encourage it to crush the Nationalist

Chinese government in Formosa. For all three states, it would be a grave mistake to establish an alliance that would see them drawn into such a war. Membership for both countries would also create an alliance that was too far-reaching geographically and would be underresourced, thereby placing greater burdens on the antipodean powers. As Richard Casey noted in his diary: "We do not want to see South Korea, Japan and Formosa in SEATO, because the addition of each of these countries would inevitably mean an extension of Australia's responsibilities and obligations, in that we might be obliged to come to their defence if they got into trouble."[39] New Zealand agreed that membership should be similarly defined and strictly limited.[40]

Dulles, desiring a swift resolution to the membership question, grudgingly accepted that Japan, Nationalist China, and the Republic of Korea could not be founder members of this new Asian alliance. Importantly, though, he managed to obtain agreement that the question of extending membership to the likes of Japan would be revisited in the future.[41] From the very origins of the new Asian security alliance, British, Australian, and New Zealand opinions had managed to shape agreement to reflect their own national interests. SEATO was not therefore merely a U.S. construct, but rather a compromise between leading Western powers in the region.

None of this is to suggest the U.S. failed to pursue its own interests in these talks. The Eisenhower administration was equally selective about which states should be involved in this new Asian security alliance. Strategic calculations largely influenced such decision making, but they were also informed by broader ideological and racial factors. The United States did not invite Portugal to join the new organization because of the fear that Communist propagandists would cast the United States as an imperial power upholding European colonialism. The same logic applied to the Netherlands' exclusion from the alliance.[42] Although membership for the United Kingdom would certainly encourage similar criticisms, British inclusion brought considerable material benefits, which outweighed such criticisms. Eisenhower nevertheless appreciated the importance of involving regional powers. The president appreciated that other Southeast Asian states, especially Burma, were making the argument that any security alliance had to include Southeast Asian participation, as it would otherwise give the impression that the region would be exchanging "one imperialism for another."[43]

Such perceptions mattered to a president who was deeply concerned that the proposed treaty for Southeast Asian security was not solely between "the five white nations and left out Asian states."[44] The fear of appearing to act in an imperial or racist fashion again influenced the course of U.S. foreign policy. As a National Security Council planning paper outlined, "the old taint of colonialism will offer new difficulties" in U.S. efforts to work closely with France in Indochina.[45] Eisenhower emphasized this point in communication with Churchill, telling him that for Americans, "colonies" was a "naughty word."[46] Consequently, the president told his National Security Council, "Small or not, such nations as Thailand at least provided the semblance of Asian participation" in a Southeast Asian security alliance.[47] This point was emphasized publicly as the president declared that "proper Asiatic nations" must be members of any new Pacific security pact.[48] In order to play down perceptions of imperialism or racism, U.S. officials also saw Indian membership as desirable, despite Jawaharlal Nehru's continuing intransigence toward much of U.S. foreign policy.[49] The president realized that Indian inclusion would provide the new alliance with major political capital and would dampen possible criticism that the United States was building a "white man's pact" inside Asia.

Establishing a new security organization that took account of all these divergent interests, especially concerning membership, would therefore be a complicated process that would necessitate considerable compromises on all parts. A "semblance of Asian participation" was a fitting choice of words. Many Asian states, including Burma and India, would never become members of SEATO. Ultimately, the participation of some Asian states was required less for practical military purposes than for a semblance of racial equality. The president was committed to secure Asian participation in some form, however superficial. Eisenhower concluded that if the United States was cast as a "racist power," it would undermine efforts to win indigenous support from the peoples of the Asia-Pacific. Dulles made a similar point to the British ambassador to Washington, Roger Makins, informing him that "the United States had weakened her leadership and her mission in the world by supporting or appearing to support British and French policies in the Middle East and North Africa, thus incurring the charge of being an imperialist power."[50] As Dulles had written publicly in 1950, "If the Communist parties in Western Europe feel that they can make political capital by charging the United States with intent to turn these countries [in the Asia-Pacific] into colonies, it is clear that we must be scrupulously careful in our relations with countries which, within the last five years, have in fact been colonial possessions of the West."[51]

London was aware of such sensitivities in Washington. Makins took pains to remind Eden that for U.S. policymaking elites it was imperative not to appear as an imperialist or racist power: "Opposition and dislike of colonialism is, as I have said, deeply imbedded in the American mind. Because of their association with us and with the French, they have swallowed their scruples, and on the whole have used their influence to support the colonial system at all events to the point of being called the arch-imperialist power."[52] The UK needed to remain sensitive to these concerns. As the ambassador warned, "If they take on fresh commitments without participation, or, alternatively, move back towards ideas of peripheral defence, which is the likely alternative, they will with some relief be able to indulge their natural feelings against colonialism. With the growing pains in most of our colonies and with the French difficulties in North Africa, this, on the basis of a resentful or frustrated America, is not an attractive prospect."[53]

Agreement at Geneva

As the discussions about a new Southeast Asian security alliance continued, the British foreign secretary pressed ahead with his diplomatic efforts at the Geneva conference. Eden's efforts at securing a diplomatic solution paid off. On July 21, all sides reached a settlement that brought a cease-fire to the war inside Indochina. Vietnam would divide into two separate zones along the seventeenth parallel with a demilitarized area on each side demarcating the partition. Ho Chi Minh's Viet Minh would govern the northern zone, and the originally French-supported government of Bao Dai, the chief of state of the state of Vietnam (South Vietnam), would govern the southern zone. Outside military intervention also ended with neither half of Vietnam permitted to join any military alliances. Viet Minh and French forces were to evacuate their positions and regroup in their respective zones. National elections would take place in 1956 under international supervision, thereby illustrating that the partition of Vietnam was an intentionally temporary arrangement. The agreement, as Eden admitted, was "not completely satisfactory" but "had stopped an eight year war and reduced international tension to a point of instant danger to world peace."[54] Given that many in the British government secretly believed that no agreement could be found in Indochina that would "adequately safeguard" Western interests, the Geneva settlement was simply making the best of a difficult situation.[55]

The Australian and New Zealand governments were generally pleased with the outcomes arrived at in Geneva. In Canberra's assessment, the French had mishandled the military situation in Indochina, and their inability to provide the Associated States of Indochina with any real political autonomy exacerbated current difficulties.[56] Casey noted that, given the circumstances, Eden had done about as well as could have been reasonably expected. Menzies subsequently issued a public statement that welcomed the agreement at Geneva.[57] Wellington would offer a similarly positive response.

As the minister for external affairs Clifton Webb announced before the New Zealand parliament, "The settlement was probably the best that could be expected in the circumstances."⁵⁸ Several developments had also come out of the temporary resolution of the Indochina crisis, which could potentially advance the long-term strategic ambitions of the antipodean powers. Principally this included the possibility of a security alliance for the Asia-Pacific that would involve British participation and exist in addition to ANZUS.⁵⁹

The Eisenhower administration did not share such positive appraisals. Some in the cabinet believed that the Geneva accords had at least managed to buy the state of Vietnam a brief respite from Communist attack and therefore helped protect the wider Asia-Pacific region. Nevertheless, as many in Washington interpreted events, Eden's diplomacy during the negotiations had continually cast the United States as the obstacle to finding a peaceful solution. Such diplomacy irritated the Eisenhower administration, not least because Eden ensured that if no agreement was reached, he would "place on [the] shoulders of [the] U.S.[,] responsibility for [the] failure of [the] Geneva Conference and [the] fall of [the] French Government."⁶⁰ In the assessment of Dulles's deputy Walter Bedell Smith, Eden's diplomacy had failed to prevent the advance of Communism throughout Southeast Asia. As Smith remarked skeptically, "Diplomacy is rarely able to gain at the conference table what cannot be gained or held on the battlefield."⁶¹ Dulles was furious, likening Eden's role at Geneva to that of Neville Chamberlain at Munich in 1938. Others, including the president, simply believed that Eden's efforts had merely legitimized Communist control of the northern half of Vietnam.⁶² One National Security Council planning document was damning in its verdict of Eden's Geneva diplomacy, concluding that "it completed a major forward stride for communism which may lead to the loss of Southeast Asia."⁶³ Given such reservations, the United States refused to officially recognize the agreements reached at Geneva.

U.S. policymakers believed it was inevitable that the Viet Minh would eventually seek to consume its southern neighbor. As one U.S. memorandum from September 1954 made clear: "We agree that the Viet Minh represent a Communist force aggressively opposed to the ideals and the interests of the free peoples of the Associated States and of France and the United States. We will firmly oppose the extension of influence or control of the Viet Minh movement and will work toward political, military and economic goals in Indochina which will strengthen the Associated States' Governments and which will enable them to maintain their independence."⁶⁴ U.S. officials had simplified the situation in Indochina by viewing events through a Cold War lens. Competition for political control inside Indochina touched on a more complex set of factors, including nationalism, decolonization, regionalism, and religion. Policymakers, however, often downplayed these complexities.[65] Resisting an apparently inevitable Communist attack became the administration's priority for Southeast Asia. As Canberra learned, the prevailing mood in Washington was that South Vietnam was "going down the drain" and that significant action was necessary.[66] Improving the stability of the government of South Vietnam via direct and covert means was now undertaken with greater urgency. Financial and military assistance continued, and a comprehensive U.S. covert intelligence operation designed to support Saigon now began.[67] A key element of this resistance package also involved reaching agreement with Britain, Australia, and New Zealand for a new Southeast Asian security alliance.

With the Geneva talks concluded, British support for establishing a new security organization for the Asia-Pacific, and Southeast Asia in particular, had grown considerably. Growing support also reflected the British government's confidence in achieving its broader economic and security ambitions in the Asia-Pacific. Senior officials would go on to suggest that a treaty could "provide an umbrella beneath which we can persuade the Americans to spend money" in the region, both in terms of military and economic investment.[68] Churchill went as far as to suggest in personal correspondence with Eisenhower that with the Geneva conference now settled, they should seek to establish a security pact with the "widest lines" of membership.[69] In an effort to construct an organization along British lines, Churchill wrote directly to Eisenhower, claiming that the time was ripe for "establishing a firm front against Communism in the Asia-Pacific sphere."[70] Securing U.S. commitment remained a key element of Churchill's approach to safeguarding British interests in the region. Eisenhower responded positively to Churchill's overture and U.S.-UK talks convened to discuss the nature of the new alliance. On August 14, the U.S. issued a statement that the nation and like-minded governments would pursue a "collective security arrangement" and meet on September 6 to discuss the idea. The governments of Australia, France, New Zealand, Pakistan, Philippines, Thailand, and the United Kingdom signaled their support soon after.[71]

Progress toward international cooperation nevertheless remained difficult. Some U.S. policymakers remained suspicious of British membership demands, specifically the inclusion of the Colombo powers, fearing an attempt to stack the organization with countries supportive of British objectives. As Charles Wilson, the U.S. secretary of defense, warned Dulles, "I feel the British are playing their relatively weak hand in Asia far more shrewdly than we are playing our strong one."[72] The United States rejected British ideas about voting machinery within SEATO, noting that in the future when membership expands, a group of "neutrals" or a British Commonwealth bloc could "exercise a controlling voice" within the new alliance.[73] As further evidence of such concerns, the U.S. swiftly rejected the Philippines' suggestion that SEATO should establish a council that would be able to authorize action if three-quarters of the membership voted in favor because Washington "would not have a controlling voice," which was "wholly unacceptable."[74] The Eisenhower administration was evidently sensitive to any agreement that could curtail its freedom of action. In a similar fashion to its handling of the ANZUS Treaty, the United States wished to cooperate with interested parties but would only do so in a manner of its choosing. Limited commitments remained central to Eisenhower's Cold War strategy, and he resisted any challenges to this objective.

In contrast to previous negotiations in the Asia-Pacific region, however, the U.S. had shown that it was willing to accommodate some British demands concerning membership. This altered stance reflected the difficulty of Washington's diplomatic position vis-à-vis London. If it refused to give in to any British demands, London would likely refuse to sign up to the new security organization for Southeast Asia, which meant that Australia and New Zealand would also likely do the same. International cooperation remained essential to placate Congress and to provide necessary material support against further Communist advances throughout the region.

During the talks, Washington stressed to London that the focus of the new organization had to be on Southeast Asia and resisted suggestions to broaden the organization's coverage. This undermined British efforts to have their Asian assets, particularly their interests in Hong Kong, protected by a new U.S. security umbrella. In return, however, London extracted a number of concessions from Washington. If the new organization focused on Southeast Asia, then its remit could not stretch to include Formosa, the security of which the British government remained unwilling to guarantee. In addition, the British remained opposed to the Associated States of Indochina gaining membership, as this would directly violate the terms of the Geneva Accords. Washington grudgingly acquiesced to London's wishes.[75]

The nature of U.S.-UK diplomacy was frustrating for the Eisenhower administration. The British government's insistence that the new organization be regionally focused and exclude membership of Nationalist China deeply irritated many U.S. policymakers.[76] The U.S. subsequently pursued a further bilateral alliance, creating the U.S.–Republic of China security treaty in December 1954.[77] The proposed SEACDT treaty, Dulles complained, "leaves us in a weak position," but he feared there was no alternative for we "can't afford to hand the other side complete victory in both quarters on a silver platter."[78] As such, any alliance was preferable to no alliance at all. Dulles admitted privately that the member states of this new security organization "are so weak and feeble, one wonders if it is good to have a treaty with them."[79] Competing national interests—as well as competing conceptions of Cold War strategy—had once again exerted a significant influence on both the nature and scope of this emerging security alliance.

Negotiations on a wide variety of issues continued throughout August and September 1954. Officials from each state debated the wording of the final treaty, the types of military cooperation to be undertaken, and the socioeconomic roles the new organization would assume. U.S. officials accepted that significant economic assistance was important for the stability of the region but were vague on the details of funding. The British did not dispute the merits of this idea yet looked to ensure that it would be Washington, and not London, that would provide the majority of this support.[80] Debate rumbled on regarding what would actually precipitate a military response. Dulles's inclusion of the phrase "Communist aggression" sparked considerable differences of opinion. Washington argued that this phrase was required to send a clear warning to the Soviet Union and PRC to deter further incursions into the state of Vietnam. London, Canberra, and Wellington argued that the term was simply too broad and had the potential for the new organization to be manipulated into military action. Following resistance from many other potential members of the treaty, Dulles eventually conceded that the phrase be struck from the final wording of the proposed treaty.[81] On September 6, all sides reached agreement over a draft version of the security treaty.[82] Each member—Australia, France, New Zealand, Pakistan, the Philippines, Thailand, the United Kingdom, and the United States—accepted these agreements would be ratified by their respective domestic authorities and the treaty obligations would enter into force in the New Year.

The British, Australian, and New Zealand governments had managed to secure a new defense pact on seemingly favorable terms. The ratification of SEATO represented the United States' first formal commitment to work with all three British Commonwealth powers for the collective defense of Southeast Asia. The resultant organization would enter into force on February 19, 1955. This agreement meant that eight independent states dotted around the world would work together to resist the threat of Communism in the region.[83] As John Lewis Gaddis contends, the creation of this Asian security alliance allowed the United States to construct a "geostrategic great wall" around both the Soviet Union and PRC.[84] It also had benefits for the antipodean powers, given that it would involve the participation of the United Kingdom and did not appear to supersede ANZUS. As W. David McIntyre explains, "The advantage of SEATO for the Tasman neighbors was that it involved them with the United States in a wider arrangement than ANZUS, and where the link with Britain was also retained."[85]

The signatories of the Manila Treaty nevertheless recognized the limitations of the agreement. The organization would have no unified command and no specifically allocated forces, thereby diluting its power and weakening its contribution to regional security.[86] The United States continued to resist pressure to station ground forces in Southeast Asia, instead preferring to rely on nuclear armaments. As one New Zealand official later noted, "It was clear that no practicable defence of South East Asia [was] possible without the use of nuclear weapons."[87] Economic, domestic-political, and strategic concerns convinced Washington that the deployment of U.S. ground troops to secure Southeast Asia was not in the best interests of the United States.[88] The United States also remained opposed to the establishment of any formalized body of advisers within SEATO that would discuss military planning, fearing that such a body would be too unwieldy to manage, too large to reach concrete military agreements, and too insecure to avoid information leaks.[89] The United Kingdom shared these concerns but felt that if military planning within SEATO was to proceed then it should occur on a four-power basis with the United States, Australia, and New Zealand.[90] Such an arrangement would provide the British government with a greater opportunity to influence proceedings away from public scrutiny.

Although SEATO's military shortcomings are well documented, its socioeconomic ambitions also fell short of initial expectations. In conversation with senior Australian policymakers, British officials made clear that they believed it was likely that Indochina would "be Communist within 18 months," and that they should direct their attention to building support for non-Communist political actors throughout the rest of Southeast Asia and improving the socioeconomic situation in the region.[91] As such, Casey and Munro had emphasized the need for the organization to concentrate on the "economic aspects" of regional security.[92] Nevertheless, the United States largely ignored antipodean preferences, and neither Australia nor New Zealand proved willing to push the matter. Although all signatories to SEACDT sought to improve levels of investment and trade more broadly, budgetary limitations, and domestic pressures made SEATO an inappropriate framework with which to assist economic development in the wider region. The Colombo Plan instead became the primary vehicle for an Asian economic aid program. The U.S. remained keen to avoid any suggestion that is was creating a Marshall Plan for Asia.[93] Formal commitments to any bolder economic organization therefore ceased from this point onward.[94]

Strategic Reassessments

The months between the completion of the Manila Treaty negotiations and the emergence of SEATO highlight the ongoing difficulties of strategic cooperation in the early Cold War. When Canberra and Wellington pushed Washington to reconvene military discussions within the ANZUS forum, the United States rejected the proposal. Exchanges within the U.S. government reveal that "in order to not offend Asians, it was preferable for the U.S. to wait until [the] Manila Pact organization was underway" before looking to engage in any further military discussions with non-Asian states.[95] As Eisenhower explained in early September, "any indication to our Asian partners that the white members of the Manila Pact are engaging in secret military planning under the Treaty, to the exclusion of the Asian members, would have the most profound political and psychological repercussions and might result in the disintegration of the Manila partnership."[96] It was at this point that the Eisenhower administration proposed that military planners for all eight powers should convene to discuss strategic planning.[97] Casey hinted in his diary that the creation of the organization, which included the participation of Asian states, was good for public relations reasons because it ensured that it "gets away from the resistance to Communism in Asia being regarded as a white man's preoccupation."[98]

Anxieties still existed in the United States over the threat posed to Southeast Asia from Communism, not least the ongoing violence precipitated by Viet Minh forces that threatened to undermine Bao Dai's control of South Vietnam.[99] When Dulles liaised with political leaders of Southeast Asian states in early 1955, he received the same message. In sum, better security provisions were necessary to prevent continued Communist infiltration and subversion.[100] Washington subsequently agreed that SEATO should begin military planning. A desire for progress, however, presented a challenge to equality in planning. Many officials in Washington and London believed that it might be more effective to convene an exclusive group—namely, four-power talks between the United States, the United Kingdom, Australia, and New Zealand—given that the major military and economic resources for SEATO's defense would come from only these members and that the necessary forums for security cooperation already existed.

Eden had previously recognized the predicament posed by these four-power talks, noting that "in practice the real planning would have to be done on a 4-power basis by ourselves, the Australians and New Zealanders with the Americans. But great caution will be needed if this is to be done without offence to the French and to the Asian parties to the Manila Treaty."[101] Yet private talks were a huge boon as they provided London, as well as Canberra and Wellington, with a private forum in which to discuss strategic planning in Southeast Asia. All three governments sought to exploit the SEATO agreement as a way in which to increase their access to U.S. thinking for the defense of the entire Asia-Pacific and for establishing formal channels for military planning.

Casey and Munro put this case to Dulles during talks at an ANZUS Council meeting in October 1954. They claimed that Australia and New Zealand did not desire to "leave everything to the United States," but in order for both countries to "pull [their] full weight" they would require "proper access to the United States mind on the planning side."[102] Casey even proposed that strategic planning should continue "under the counter" as ANZUS would "serve as a cover for what would in effect be SEATO strategic planning—its true purpose not being known—and that 'make believe' planning be undertaken bilaterally by the U.S. with each of the other four countries."[103] Munro ably supported such claims, suggesting that the three ANZUS powers and the United Kingdom already had established practices for sharing sensitive intelligence material so could press ahead with joint planning for the region in confidence of maintaining secrecy.[104]

Antipodean efforts proved ineffective. Dulles provided no response to suggestions of secret planning and rebuffed the idea that Canberra and Wellington needed additional access to U.S. military planning. The failure of the talks to generate substantial agreement, the ongoing instability of Indochina, and the increased defense obligations associated with the Manila Treaty encouraged the Australian prime minister that his earlier inclination to shift focus away from the defense of the Middle East had been correct.[105] When Australian military officials met with their British and New Zealand counterparts in October and November 1954, they informed them that Australia would now prioritize the defense of Southeast Asia.[106]

In contrast to the talks held in Melbourne in the previous year, in which Australia had only discussed prioritizing regional defense, these talks now confirmed a clear focus on Southeast Asia. These changed strategic circumstances also encouraged New Zealand to reconsider its strategic planning and policies. As Macmillan informed Churchill: "The Manila Treaty has been signed under which New Zealand has accepted increased defence obligations in South East Asia. In these new circumstances, the Chiefs of Staff consider that it would be only natural if the New Zealand government should consider that the right place for their land forces to be deployed in global war would be Southeast Asia rather than the Middle East."[107] Policymakers in London were disappointed by the strategic adjustment of the antipodean powers but appreciated that they could not provide adequate security assurances to Australia and New Zealand. As such, the United Kingdom reluctantly acceded to antipodean strategic realignment.[108] All that British officials and policymakers could do now was to criticize the decisions taken by Canberra and Wellington.[109]

In early 1955, Churchill, Menzies, and Holland agreed that Australia and New Zealand's primary aim in a general war would be the preservation of the security of Southeast Asia, focusing on rapid deployment to the Malayan area, and the creation of a strategic reserve in Malaya as a deterrent to Communist expansion.[110] Menzies subsequently informed Holland that "the Australian Government has accepted the principle that the main aim of Australia should be to assure the safety of South East Asia in a general war."[111] The Australian prime minster would formally announce his decision to participate in the British Commonwealth Far East Strategic Reserve (BCFESR) in April 1955.[112] Although Evatt and the Labour Party had criticized these plans, a public opinion poll in February earlier that year showed that a majority of Australians would support the deployment of Australian troops to help garrison Malaya.[113]

Recent events inside Indochina had encouraged Australian policymakers to take a more forthright approach to regional threats. Following a visit to Indochina, Casey warned Menzies in March that the situation was so precarious that Vietnam, Laos, and Cambodia could all "fall into communist hands" within the year.[114] Ultimately, Canberra's decision makers confirmed that they would have to focus their priorities on their near north if they were to safeguard their own security.[115] In addition, the Australian Treasury was keenly aware of, and increasingly concerned by, the level of commitment required by Australia to sustain any obligations to the Middle East and Mediterranean.[116]

In the same month, the New Zealand Department of External Affairs produced a long report titled "ANZAM Planning for the Defence of Malaya and South East Asia."[117] It noted that the defense of the ANZAM region was fundamentally linked to retaining control over Malaya in the event of a war: "The defence of the ANZAM Region depends on the security of Malaya, which initially hinges on the integrity of neighbouring countries for defence in depth. Conversely, Malaya is the keystone of the defence of adjacent countries, and provides a base for operations in war. Malaya also gives defence in depth to Australia and New Zealand, and is the key to air and sea communications in South East Asia. It is also a source of important raw materials."[118] As the report went on to argue, "Communist successes in Indochina have brought the threat much closer. Consequently, in war, the time available for external reinforcement of Malaya has been reduced. The threat to Malaya would increase were there any further deterioration of the situation in South East Asia."[119] The report endorsed Canberra's view that both antipodean powers should squarely focus their resources and strategic focus on defending the ANZAM region.

The prime minister endorsed this assessment and the New Zealand Defence Department ushered in the necessary changes to Wellington's strategic planning and policies. In March 1955, New Zealand plans now reflected that "in global war, all three New Zealand services *may be* committed to the defence of the Malayan area as well as other parts of the ANZAM region. In cold war, some naval and air forces will be based there as part of the strategic reserve and it is likely that the Army will also provide a force."[120] This pivot toward defending the ANZAM region was confirmed in April by the New Zealand Defence Department: "In the event of global war, and unless there is any major change in the strategic situation as now forecast, New Zealand land and air forces will be employed in the South East Asia region, *instead of in the Middle East*. Naval Forces and the maritime squadrons of the Air Force not required for local defence will be deployed elsewhere in the ANZAM region."[121] Although Malaya's strategic significance evidently drove New Zealand's security planning, so too did changes in strategic outlook more broadly. Many policymakers believed that the advent of thermonuclear weapons had made outright war less likely, but limited war outside of Europe now seemed possible, especially following the events of the Korean War.[122] In addition, New Zealand's commitment to Malaya reflected a still strong attachment to the United Kingdom and Holland's belief that cooperation would ensure assistance from the British in the event of a future emergency.[123]

New Zealand's strategic pivot away from the Middle East and Mediterranean toward the ANZAM region was now agreed. The urgency shown in Australian diplomacy in bringing about this change, however, had caused immense concern and irritation in the inner circle of the Holland government.[124] Canberra's enthusiasm risked making errors that could have been mitigated by more thorough planning, especially concerning the placement of strategic priorities. Furthermore, Australia's eagerness meant that it had sometimes failed to inform Wellington of the changes it was proposing to Washington. There was a clear sense that Canberra was sidelining Wellington from decisions that would have a critical effect on New Zealand's external policies.[125]

Nevertheless, policymakers in Wellington decided to follow Canberra's lead in large part because cooperation with Australia would promote New Zealand's own security interests. In the subsequent months, Wellington informed Canberra privately that it would bolster its military contingent in Malaya. These efforts would include the dispatch of the New Zealand Special Air Service and a public announcement of its decision to prioritize the defense of the ANZAM region, which would involve it withdrawing its air force from bases in the Mediterranean.[126] The New Zealand division intended for the Middle East would now go to Malaya, and existing air squadrons withdrew shortly afterward. This signaled a radical change in the defense relationship of Australia and New Zealand.[127] As Christopher Pugsley has noted, the defense of Southeast Asia would be the "central concern" of New Zealand's strategic policy for the next thirty-four years.[128] By the middle of 1955, the British government could no longer count on Australian and New Zealand contributions to help uphold its interest in the Middle East and Mediterranean.

The antipodean powers' prioritization of regional security alone does not fully account for the United Kingdom's eventual withdrawal from the Middle East. To be sure, broader strategic and economic circumstances, U.S. influence, and Arab national pressure all played a role.[129] Nevertheless, Britain's position in the region became increasingly untenable without the material and political support provided by Australia and New Zealand. London, as well as Washington, believed that the antipodean powers' commitment to deploying forces to the Middle East was vital if the British were to maintain their position there in the event of war. Strategic planners in both the United States and United Kingdom believed that Britain had to "hold the line" in the Middle East, and New Zealand's contribution would be important if this was to be achieved.[130] There were clear requirements for additional land forces in the Middle East, which the antipodean powers had traditionally fulfilled and which no other state was willing to provide. This strategic shift also marked the end of a coordinated British Commonwealth security planning system focused on the Middle East and the end of efforts to share the cost of imperial defense.[131]

Inner-Circle Planning

Almost from the advent of the SEATO alliance, planners in London, Canberra, and Wellington wished to establish what they called "inner circle" planning, namely four-power staff talks between the United States, United Kingdom, Australia, and New Zealand. U.S. plans to push forward with its military preparations inside Southeast Asia, such as building new runways in Thailand and equipping the South Vietnamese government with armaments, convinced planners in all three countries that they needed to know what U.S. plans were so that they could add realism to their own planning.[132] The Australian Defence Committee argued that "while ANZAM has most important functions, however, its work will be ineffectual unless it is linked with United States plans for the overall defence of the Pacific area."[133] Practical security considerations also influenced thinking. As the United Kingdom, Australia, and New Zealand all recognized, "the Non-Asian members of SEACDT are not willing to discuss Top SECRET plans for the defence of South East Asia with the Asian members" given that the latter were perceived to have insecure systems for transferring information throughout their bureaucracies.[134] Without the exchange of military information then, broader alliance preparations would always be hindered, perhaps fundamentally so.

Of the three Commonwealth powers, Australia took the lead in trying to establish "inner circle" planning.[135] Internal assessments for the Menzies government had indicated that there were already large gaps in the military resources required to uphold the defense of the ANZAM region in a time of war.[136] Inner-circle planning offered an opportunity to address these material and strategic concerns. Menzies had made this point clear in his communication with Holland in February 1955. The Australian secretary of the Department of Defense Frederick Shedden informed his New Zealand counterpart that Australian efforts to convince the Eisenhower administration to enter into these talks would begin soon.[137] Establishing formal agreements between the ANZAM members and the United States on what exactly their military response would be to certain eventualities was vital if credible security planning was to take place.[138]

Australian efforts to convince the United States of the need for inner-circle planning once again proved ineffective. The United States remained unwilling to commit additional and already scarce resources to the defense of Southeast Asia. The crisis of 1954 had passed, and the reduced likelihood of conflict in Vietnam had marginalized the military purpose of SEATO. Furthermore, the PRC had become a far more pressing concern, not least following the Taiwan Strait Crisis, whereby Mao began military operations against the ROC.[139] Radford himself believed that "this was a moment for a showdown with Communist China."[140] U.S. attention had begun to shift northward to China. As such, appeals from even the closest of allies for inner-circle planning with a view to committing additional resources to SEATO were never likely to succeed. Even when Casey assured Washington that this four-power planning could remain "completely secret," the Eisenhower administration remained reluctant to commit more fully to strategic planning.[141]

Casey had previously feared that the institutional opposition posed by the Pentagon to alliance planning for the defense of Southeast Asia would prove too high a hurdle to overcome.[142] As one report supplied by Casey to the Australian cabinet noted, "no spectacular results" had emerged from the recent meetings with the SEATO members regarding revisions to military planning and provisions.[143] Menzies was initially more confident that increased cooperation between the four powers would soon come to fruition, a confidence that reflected his recent talks with Eisenhower and Dulles in Washington. He was soon to be disappointed, however, when Canberra learned that Radford had vetoed the idea of four-power talks about Malayan defense.[144] As Radford informed Canberra, "It is most inappropriate to conduct consultations outside the framework of SEATO."[145]

Canberra and Wellington's hopes of a stronger United States commitment to Southeast Asian security, and hence antipodean security more broadly, were ultimately disappointed. As Australia and New Zealand complained in subsequent years, the United States' interest in supporting SEATO appeared fleeting and limited. The new security commitments promised by the alliance ultimately failed to alleviate antipodean security concerns much closer to home.[146] Australian and New Zealand ambitions to establish "an arrangement whereby the United States and the ANZAM partners can be associated in military planning in South East Asia" failed to materialize from the Radford talks in August 1955.[147]

All that Radford proposed was further discussions between all of the treaty members of SEATO, which the Menzies government deemed "unrealistic."[148] Australian defense planners received a disappointing response to their suggestion for further strategic planning for the region.[149] In the New Zealand estimation, Radford had responded coolly to the idea of four-power talks.[150] Events in Southeast Asia failed to convince Radford to change his long-standing objections to providing U.S. support for defending Malaya, which he considered a secondary concern.[151] As the chairman of the U.S. Joint Chiefs of Staff informed both Canberra and Wellington, "I feel defence of Malaya lies to [the] North and further that greatest threat to Malaya stems from internal subversion rather than from overt external aggression. Therefore I feel strongly that planning efforts most likely to result in successful defence of Malaya are those directed towards maintaining security and sovereignty of northern countries."[152]

Such a response was, in the view of one highly influential New Zealand official, most unsatisfactory.[153] When the Australian ambassador to

Washington, Percy Spender, pressed the case for an additional U.S. commitment to be made for Malayan defense in the framework of this new Southeast Asian security alliance, he again found little enthusiasm on the part of Radford.[154] While willing to dispatch a U.S. officer to Melbourne to meet with the ANZAM planners, Spender sensed that the chairman of the Joint Chiefs remained opposed to preparing for the defense of the ANZAM area. Radford remained wedded to the logic that defense of the ANZAM region would be served by ensuring security "further north," namely striking China in its homeland. As the chairman informed both the Australian and New Zealand governments, the United States did not possess "sufficient resources to be adequately strong in every potentially threatened area."[155] Radford did not speak for the president or his cabinet, to be sure, but he did oversee planning for SEATO, and thus his position on the matter was of considerable significance. Hard choices were required, but he believed that focusing resources on mainland China would best serve U.S., Australian, and New Zealand security.

Following talks with Dulles at the annual ANZUS Council meeting in September, it was evident that the U.S. secretary of state was not interested in entering detailed staff talks with Canberra and Wellington about Southeast Asia or the ANZAM area. As Casey noted of the meeting, Dulles never even opened his briefing material, which would have allowed him to discuss in detail the types of security planning that both Canberra and Wellington desired.[156] The Eisenhower administration's position was therefore frustrating and, more important, was perceived in Australian and New Zealand policymaking circles as undermining any hopes of improving antipodean security beyond existing agreements. As Wellington admitted, "As we know nothing of United States military plans for defence of the wider area it is only common prudence for us to prepare plans for the defence of the area for which we are responsible."[157]

SEATO had failed to deliver the type of security cooperation and planning between the four Western powers that policymakers in the British Commonwealth states had envisaged.[158] By October, policymakers in Canberra and Wellington noted that inner-circle planning was "non-existent at present."[159] Such planning was more important than ever as antipodean planners feared that the situation in Southeast Asia was becoming ever more dangerous. One New Zealand Staff Planning report in October 1955, for example, estimated that the position of South Vietnam remained precarious, and if this fell to Communist control, then the probability of Communist success throughout the rest of Indochina would significantly increase.[160] In these circumstances, the antipodean powers accepted that they would have to look beyond Malaya and eventually cooperate with wider SEATO planning, which they had initially considered to be of secondary importance.[161]

Washington's unwillingness to discuss its plans had a knock-on effect on London's willingness to make plans for defending Southeast Asia. As the British Joint Chiefs informed both Canberra and Wellington, "In absence of knowledge of any United States plans for counter action in the event of overt Communist aggression in South East Asia it would be unrealistic for Commonwealth countries alone to make plans for Allied military action."[162] Although SEATO had allowed the United States, the United Kingdom, Australia, and New Zealand to participate in abstract discussion concerning security in the Asia-Pacific, the absence of detailed planning limited any prospect of a coherent or united response to the Communist threat.

The United States seized on a familiar excuse to legitimize the limitations of four-power talks. Following the ANZUS Council meeting, the U.S. reported that it was "strongly opposed to anything which could be interpreted by the Asian members of the Pact as being a 'hard white core.'"[163] Such concerns had been encouraged by the first large-scale meeting of African and Asian states in Bandung in Indonesia earlier in the year, whereby representatives of twenty-nine states discussed the role of the Third World in the Cold War and openly opposed colonialism.[164] Although racial and imperial considerations did play a role in U.S. foreign policy, they existed alongside more pressing strategic concerns. Radford had already noted that the U.S. was unwilling to discuss top-secret plans with any Asia-Pacific members through the framework of SEATO, allegedly for fear of security leaks.[165] In addition, only two months earlier, Radford had explained that the United States could not undertake more serious security cooperation because it lacked the material resources necessary to make detailed planning credible.[166] The language of racial equality therefore once again served as a convenient explanation with which to downplay the pursuit of U.S. interests in the Asia-Pacific, much of which came at the expense of its allies. These events echoed the United States' earlier efforts to justify British exclusion from ANZUS. Revealingly, documents intended for exclusive use by the National Security Council candidly admitted that U.S. strategy to "block Communist expansion" would be "less influenced by European allies than in respect to Atlantic affairs."[167] The United States evidently preferred a more independent approach to the pursuit of security in the region. While SEATO had ostensibly brought the four Western powers together in the defense of the Asia-Pacific, strategic disunity persisted.

Conclusion

The United States, United Kingdom, Australia, and New Zealand had all cooperated closely in the Second World War. In the postwar period, they continued to enjoy close relations in many quarters and came to recognize the potential for future global conflict. All four states' interest in securing the Asia-Pacific grew steadily in response to the evolving Communist threat in the region. Formalized cooperation could have allowed policymakers in each country to prepare for these threats more effectively, helping them to share the burdens of containment in the region as well. Progress toward mutual security planning was nevertheless slow and difficult.

Scholars who focus on power politics to explain state behavior will find much in the archives to support their claims. All four states prioritized security in the main, pursued their own interests, and struggled to fully understand the intentions of their allies as well as their rivals.[1] Competing security assessments certainly explain much of the Western powers' disunity in the Asia-Pacific. These states shared many threats, to be sure, but they could also interpret them differently. For instance, domino theory increasingly informed strategic planning in Washington, London, Canberra, and Wellington in the postwar period. Yet policymakers in all four capitals often concluded that these dominoes could fall in different directions at different times.[2] As such, what alarmed one state could prove far less threatening to another, which complicated planning and undermined strategic cooperation.

The United States, United Kingdom, Australia, and New Zealand dealt with problems that arose in their strategic relations with each other largely through negotiation. Nevertheless, relations between these democratic states were not always smooth; rough diplomacy did sometimes occur.[3] Defection was never contemplated, but all four states made limited threats of abandonment to advance their interests. The United States threatened to withdraw from ANZUS, for instance, to squash antipodean calls for British membership in the treaty. During the negotiations preceding the ANZUS Treaty, the antipodean powers intimated that they were willing to reassess their commitments to the Middle East if a U.S. security guarantee was not forthcoming. The United Kingdom also employed similar threats to Australia and New Zealand in pursuit of membership in the same security pact.

However close these four powers might have been to one another, they remained separate, sovereign states with their own economic and military interests. The United States and the United Kingdom were reluctant to surrender scarce resources to the Asia-Pacific, which they considered to be of lesser strategic significance than Europe or the Middle East, up until the 1950s. The cost of collective security was merely one strand of each state's broader economic interests. The Cold War had divided the world into two economic blocs, but significant disagreements persisted among Western states in their own bloc.[4] Trade policies and broader financial considerations slowed progress toward formalized strategic cooperation. Tensions between the United States and the British Commonwealth states concerning the revival of Japan or its inclusion in any alliance, for instance, were more than merely the result of strategic differences about how best to effectively oppose Communism in the Asia-Pacific. Disagreements also reflected competing ideas about economic practices in the wider region, most notably the persistence of the imperial preference system between members of the British Commonwealth and the challenges to international trade posed by the revival of a significant competitor in the region.

Security and economic concerns were important but represent only two drivers of strategic disunity. The archives also offer some support for scholars' attempts to explain international politics with reference to domestic politics and social or cultural influences.[5] Doubts about public support, concerns about reelection, or respect for the norms of democratic behavior informed decision making in all four capitals. Leaders were sometimes reluctant to cooperate with one another when facing potentially unpopular outcomes. Perceptions about foreign peoples and national identities also influenced

U.S., British, Australian, and New Zealand actions in the Asia-Pacific as political scientists have claimed.[6] The international composition of ANZUS and SEATO, for instance, reflected more than just security or economic concerns. Nevertheless, domestic-political and ideational forces should be understood in conjunction with security and economic-based concerns. Leaders sometimes justified their decisions in disingenuous or misleading ways. Although political concerns or ideas about race and imperialism could certainly drive and deter foreign policies, governments sometimes used them to downplay or legitimize the pursuit of strategic or economic interests that were more difficult to justify to domestic and international audiences.

Archival research in four countries, focusing on policymaking over the course of a decade, helps refine and advance the work of historians and political scientists. The historiography has tended to overlook or downplay the significance of imperialism and race, international economics, and domino theories in complicating postwar diplomacy in the Asia-Pacific.[7] Scrutiny of relevant government and private papers also helps political scientists, and scholars of international relations in particular, by informing their theoretical and empirical claims. Detailed analysis of high-level decision-making casts light on the foreign policies of democratic states and the intricacies of international security cooperation.[8] A deeper appreciation of quadrilateral diplomacy helps us grasp the complex and shifting nature of strategic disunity in the early Cold War.

Complications befell the security agreements that emerged in the Asia-Pacific in the 1950s. ANZUS continued to function as a limited security alliance but failed to survive in its tripartite form following New Zealand's suspended membership in 1985. SEATO would face ongoing military and economic challenges and, following Communist success in Indochina, eventually dissolved in 1977. Focusing on the limitations of these security agreements, however, threatens to obscure their historical significance. Closer attention to ANZUS and SEATO helps cast light on key events in the early Cold War, ranging from the emergence of a lenient Japanese peace treaty through to the withdrawal of antipodean military commitments in the Middle East and Mediterranean. Agreements reached in this period also help explain the participation of Australia and New Zealand in the Vietnam War and Britain's absence from the conflict.[9] An analysis of ANZUS and SEATO highlights the complexity and difficulty of international cooperation. Security treaties do not always emerge naturally or efficiently in the face of shared and significant threats.

Notes

Introduction

1. Historians, political scientists, and policymakers have used a variety of terms to describe the region in question, including "the Orient," "the Pacific," and "the Far East." For the purposes of consistency and clarity, we refer to "the Asia-Pacific" region throughout this book, which includes East Asia, South Asia, Southeast Asia, and Oceania.

2. For a recent account of the United States' bilateral alliances with the Republic of Korea, the Republic of China, Japan, and Philippines, see Victor Cha, *Powerplay: The Origins of the American Alliance System in Asia* (Princeton, NJ: Princeton University Press, 2016).

3. The members of SEATO included Australia, France, New Zealand, Pakistan, Philippines, Thailand, United Kingdom, and the United States. On a "geostrategic great wall," see John Lewis Gaddis, *We Now Know: Rethinking Cold War History* (Oxford: Oxford University Press, 1997), 169.

4. ANZUS and SEATO cover two separate regions within the Asia-Pacific. ANZUS is concerned with an armed attack on the Pacific territories of any of the three signatories that ranged from the Aleutians in the North Pacific to the Chatham Islands in the Southeast Pacific and a multitude of islands in the central and West Pacific. In contrast, SEATO was restricted to Southeast Asia.

5. Quote within Minutes of ANZUS Meeting, 11 October 1954, in *Foreign Relations of the United States* (hereafter *FRUS*) *1952–54*, vol. 12, part 1, 940.

6. Department of State, Policy Statement: Australia, 21 April 1950, in *FRUS 1950*, vol. 6, 193.

7. The National Archives, Kew, United Kingdom (hereafter TNA): FO 371 / 111882, Tahourdin to Powell, 25 August 1954.

8. On shortcomings, see, for instance, P. E. Eckel, "SEATO: An Ailing Alliance," *World Affairs* 134.2 (1971): 97–114; Leszek Buszynski, "SEATO: Why It Survived until 1977 and Why It Was Abolished," *Journal of Southeast Asian Studies* 12.2 (1981): 287–96; Leszek Buszynski, *SEATO: The Failure of an Alliance Strategy* (Singapore: Singapore University Press, 1983); and Panagiotis Dimitrakis, *Failed Alliances of the Cold War: Britain's Strategy and Ambitions in Asia and the Middle East* (London: I. B. Tauris, 2011), 85–106. For a more positive appraisal, see Damien Fenton, *To Cage the Red Dragon: SEATO and the Defence of Southeast Asia, 1955–1965* (Singapore: Singapore University Press, 2012).

9. On the concept of abandonment—which can range from defection through to a failure to make good on explicit commitments—being unlikely in a bipolar system, see Glen Snyder, "The Security Dilemma in Alliance Politics," *World Politics* 36.4 (1984): 461–95, esp. 466–67, 483–84.

10. Marc Trachtenberg, *The Cold War and After: History, Theory, and the Logic of International Politics* (Princeton, NJ: Princeton University Press, 2012), 139; and Gaddis, *We Now Know*, 199–203, 288–89. Rough diplomacy between Western states would proceed throughout the Cold War. See, for instance, Gerald Hughes and Thomas Robb, "Henry Kissinger and the Diplomacy of Coercive Linkage in the 'Special Relationship' with Britain, 1969–77," *Diplomatic History* 37.4 (2013): 861–905.

11. TNA: PREM 11/404, H.C. to the prime minister, 6 October 1953.

12. Robert Ferrell, ed., *The Diary of James Hagerty* (Bloomington: Indiana University Press, 1983), 49, diary entry, 26 April 1954.

13. TNA: PREM 11/404, Pacific Defence: Minutes of a Meeting held at 10 Downing Street, 10 June 1953.

14. Notes of the Australian-New Zealand-United States talks in Canberra, 15–17 February 1951, in *Documents on New Zealand External Relations: The ANZUS Pact and the Treaty of Peace with Japan*, ed. Robin Kay (Wellington: V. R. Ward Government Printer, 1985), vol. 3, doc. 226, 593.

15. Memorandum of Discussion, 6 April 1954, in *FRUS 1952–54*, vol. 13, part 1, 1253–54 and 1254.

16. Memorandum of Discussion, 10 May 1954, in *FRUS 1952–54*, vol. 13, part 1, 468; and Memorandum of Conversation: Indochina, 3 April 1954, in record group (RG) 59 Lot64D199, box 18, National Archives II, College Park, Maryland (hereafter NAII).

17. United States Minutes of the Second Meeting of the Joint Study Group, 8 July 1954, in *FRUS 1952–54*, vol. 12, part 1, 611.

18. New Zealand National Archives: Te Rua Mahara o te Kāwanatanga, Wellington, New Zealand (hereafter NZNA): R23447332 ABFK 19754 W576758 34/5/2 part 2, Casey's message in From the Australian High Commissioner's Office, Wellington, 5 August 1954; and NZNA: R23447332 ABFK 19754 W576758 34/5/2 part 2, From the New Zealand Ambassador, Washington, to the Minister of External Affairs, Wellington, Tel. 295, 5 August 1954.

19. Presidential Press Conference, 7 April 1954, in *Public Papers of the Presidents: Dwight D. Eisenhower* (Washington, DC: Government Printing Office, 1960), 2:382–84.

20. TNA: CAB 158/17 JIC 54 (14) Final, Communist Threat to Siam: Report by the Joint Intelligence Committee, 4 February 1954; and TNA: CAB 158/17 JIC 54 (49) Final, The Political Situation in Malaya in event of certain eventualities, 5 July 1954. Southeast Asian countries also held different views of domino theory. On this point, see Ang Cheng Guan, "The Domino Theory Revisited: The Southeast Asia Perspective," *War & Society* 19.1 (2001): 109–30; and Ang Cheng Guan, "Southeast Asian Perceptions of the Domino Theory," in *Connecting Histories: Decolonization and the Cold War in Southeast Asia, 1945–1962*, ed. Christopher E. Goscha and Christian F. Ostermann, chap. 12 (Stanford, CA: Stanford University Press, 2009).

21. For claims about the earlier influence of domino theory on U.S. and British foreign policy, see Fredrik Logevall, *Embers of War: The Fall of an Empire and the Making of America's Vietnam* (New York: Random House, 2012), 223; and Wen-Qing Ngoei, "The Domino Logic of the Darkest Moment: The Fall of Singapore, the Atlantic Echo Chamber, and 'Chinese Penetration' in U.S. Cold War Policy toward Southeast Asia," *Journal of American-East Asian Relations* 21.3 (2014): 215–45.

22. TNA: CAB 158/7 JIC (49) 40 Final, Report by the Joint Intelligence Committee: The Implications of a Communist Success in China, 30 September 1949.

23. Report by the Staff Planners to the Military Representatives to the ANZUS Council, 25 November 1952, in *FRUS 1952–54*, vol. 12, part 1, 245.

1. National Interests

1. For good overviews on this cooperation see Roger Bell, *Unequal Allies: Australian-American Relations and the Pacific War* (Melbourne: Melbourne University Press, 1977); and Mark A. Stoler, *Allies and Adversaries: The Joint Chiefs, the Grand Alliance, and U.S. Strategy in World War II* (Chapel Hill: University of North Carolina Press, 2000).

2. Winston S. Churchill, *The Second World War*, vol. 3, *The Grand Alliance* (London: Reprint Society, 1950), 477.

3. Gerhard L. Weinberg, *A World at Arms: A Global History of World War II* (Cambridge: Cambridge University Press, 1994), 138–61.

4. David Reynolds, "1940: Fulcrum of the Twentieth Century?," *International Affairs* 66.2 (1990): 325–50.

5. Mark A. Stoler, *Allies in War: Britain and America against the Axis Powers, 1940–1945* (London: Hodder & Arnold, 2005), 74–93. Also see Ronald Spector, *Eagle against the Sun: The American War with Japan* (London: Cassell, 2001).

6. Paul Kennedy, *The Rise and Fall of the Great Powers: Economic Change and Military Conflict from 1500 to 2000* (London: Fontana, 1989), 455, 458.

7. As Bruce Cumings outlines, this was an important moment in U.S. history for it was now a world power able to exercise decisive influence in the two major oceans of the world. As Cumings argues: "America is the first world power to inhabit an immense land mass open at both ends to the world's two largest oceans—the Atlantic and the Pacific." See Bruce Cumings, *Dominion from Sea to Sea: Pacific Ascendancy and American Power* (New Haven, CT: Yale University Press, 2009), x.

8. David Reynolds, "Churchill, Roosevelt and the Wartime Anglo-American Alliance," chap. 3 in *From World War to Cold War: Churchill, Roosevelt and the International History of the 1940s* (Oxford: Oxford University Press, 2006), 50.

9. Alex Danchev and Daniel Todman, eds., *War Diaries 1939–1945: Field Marshal Lord Alanbrooke* (London: Weidenfeld & Nicolson, 2001), 706.

10. Weinberg, *World at Arms*, 871–75.

11. The classic work on how racist attitudes held by both U.S. and Japanese policymakers and soldiers contributed to the violence in the Pacific war is John W. Dower, *War without Mercy: Race and Power in the Pacific War* (New York: Pantheon, 1987).

12. Quote from C. L. Sulzberger, *A Long Row of Candles: Memoirs and Diaries 1934–54* (London: MacDonald, 1969), 15 October 1945, 262. See also William Roger Louis, *Imperialism at Bay: The United States and the Decolonization of the British Empire, 1941–1945* (Oxford: Oxford University Press, 1987); and Peter Clarke, *The Last Thousand Days of the British Empire: Churchill, Roosevelt, and the Birth of the Pax Americana* (London: Bloomsbury, 2009), 23–26.

13. Warren Kimball, *Forged in War: Roosevelt, Churchill, and the Second World War*, new ed. (Chicago: Ivan R. Dee, 2002), 197.

14. Louis, *Imperialism at Bay*, 7. The seminal study of U.S.-UK competition in the war against Japan remains Christopher Thorne, *Allies of a Kind: The United States, Britain, and the War against Japan, 1941–1945* (Oxford: Oxford University Press, 1978).

15. David Reynolds, *In Command of History: Churchill Fighting and Writing the Second World War* (London: Allen Lane, 2004), 43–44.

16. Harriman Memorandum of Conversations, 10 February 1945 in *FRUS: Conferences at Malta and Yalta, 1945* (Washington, DC: Government Printing Office, 1955), 894–96; and Agreement Regarding Entry of the Soviet Union into War against Japan, 11 February 1945, ibid., 984.

17. S. M. Plokhy, *Yalta: The Price of Peace* (London: Penguin, 2010), 332. See the map contained in Gordon Barrass, *The Great Cold War: A Journey through the Hall of Mirrors* (Stanford, CA: Stanford University Press, 2009), 28.

18. Chiefs of Staff Committee Minute 11/1946, 20 March 1946, in *Documents on Australian Foreign Policy, 1946, January–June*, vol. 9, doc. 134.

19. For two contrasting interpretations about FDR's approach at Yalta, see Wilson Miscamble, *From Roosevelt to Truman: Potsdam, Hiroshima, and the Cold War* (Cambridge: Cambridge University Press, 2007), 61–73; and Frank Costigliola, *Roosevelt's Lost Alliances: How Personal Politics Helped Start the Cold War* (Princeton, NJ: Princeton University Press, 2012), 232–50.

20. Christopher Baxter, *The Great Power Struggle in East Asia, 1944–50* (Basingstoke: Palgrave Macmillan, 2009), 36–37.

21. Winston S. Churchill, *The Second World War*, vol. 6, *Triumph and Tragedy* (London: Reprint Society, 1956), 320–21.

22. For a good account on Truman's actions at this time see Miscamble, *From Roosevelt to Truman*, 172–219. On the importance of atomic weaponry to Truman's thinking at the end of World War II see Campbell Craig and Sergey Radchenko, *The Atomic Bomb and the Origins of the Cold War* (New Haven, CT: Yale University Press, 2008), 62–89.

23. Marc Trachtenberg, *A Constructed Peace, The Making of a European Peace Settlement, 1945–63* (Princeton, NJ: Princeton University Press, 1999), 27–29.

24. J. Samuel Walker, *Prompt and Utter Destruction: Truman and the Use of Atomic Bombs against Japan* (Chapel Hill: University of North Carolina Press, 2004), 77–91; and Ward Wilson, "The Winning Weapon? Rethinking Nuclear Weapons in Light of Hiroshima," *International Security* 31.4 (2007): 162–79.

25. George Herring, *From Colony to Superpower: U.S. Foreign Relations since 1776* (Oxford: Oxford University Press, 2011), 594.

26. Julian Zelizer, *Arsenal of Democracy: The Politics of National Security—from World War II to the War on Terrorism* (New York: Basic Books, 2012), 57–58; and Herring, *From Colony to Superpower*, 650.

27. The literature on the United States' centrality to the international order after the Second World War is quite enormous. For an overview see Herring, *From Colony to Superpower*, 595–650.

28. Vladimir O. Pechatnov, "The Soviet Union and the World," in *The Cambridge History of the Cold War*, ed. Melvyn Leffler and Odd Arne Westad, vol. 1, *Origins* (Cambridge: Cambridge University Press, 2012).

29. Harry S. Truman, *Memoirs by Harry S. Truman: Year of Decision, 1945* (New York: Doubleday, 1955), 82; and Geoffrey Roberts, "Sexing Up the Cold War: New

Evidence on the Molotov-Truman Talks of April 1945," *Cold War History* 4.2 (2004): 117.

30. John Lewis Gaddis, *Strategies of Containment: A Critical Appraisal of Postwar American National Security Policy*, rev. ed. (Oxford: Oxford University Press, 2005), 2–52.

31. Ernest R. May, *"Lessons" of the Past: The Use and Misuse of History in American Foreign Policy* (New York: Oxford University Press, 1973), 33.

32. Melvyn P. Leffler, *A Preponderance of Power: National Security, the Truman Administration, and the Cold War* (Stanford, CA: Stanford University Press, 1992), 100–140.

33. Walter Millis, ed., *The Forrestal Diaries: The Inner History of the Cold War* (London: Cassell, 1952), 198–99.

34. Memorandum by the acting Department of State member (Matthews) to the State-War-Navy Coordinating Committee, 1 April 1946, in *FRUS 1946*, vol. 1, 1167–71; quote at 1170.

35. Peter Hahn, *Crisis and Crossfire: The United States and the Middle East since 1945* (Lincoln: Potomac Books, 2005), 5–9 and appendixes 1–3.

36. Williamson Murray and Allan R. Millett, *A War to Be Won: Fighting the Second World War* (Cambridge, MA: Harvard University Press, 2001), 196–233.

37. These included the Japanese-owned Volcano Islands and Marcus Island, French-owned outposts such as Nouméa, and the British-Franco island of Espiritu Santo. See Leffler, *Preponderance of Power*, 57.

38. Leffler, *Preponderance of Power*, 56. On U.S. military planning for the Asia-Pacific area for the postwar world see Michael Sherry, *Preparing for the Next War: American Plans for Postwar Defense, 1941–1945* (New Haven, CT: Yale University Press, 1977), 52–54; Stoler, *Allies and Adversaries*, 190–200; and "Examination of U.S. Requirements for Military Bases," in RG 218, CCS 360, 25 August 1945, NAII.

39. Memorandum to be forwarded by the State-War-Navy coordinating Committee to the Secretary of State, undated (circa July 1945), in File: Bases Foreign-Military, President's Secretary Files, box 150, Harry S. Truman Library, Independence, Missouri (hereafter HSTL).

40. Policy concerning Trusteeships: State-War-Navy Coordinating Committee, Note by the Secretaries, 24 June 1946, in File: Trusteeships, Pacific Islands, President's Secretary Files, box 121, HSTL. The JCS reiterated this stance in the weeks ahead. See Strategic Areas and Trusteeships in the Pacific, Note by the Secretaries, 2 July 1946, in File: Trusteeships, Pacific Islands, President's Secretary Files, box 121, HSTL.

41. Millis, *Forrestal Diaries*, 137; Memorandum by the Secretaries of State, War and Navy to President Truman, 18 April 1945, in *FRUS 1945*, vol. 1, 350–51; and Memorandum by the Secretary of State to the Under Secretary of State, 18 April 1945, in *FRUS 1945*, vol. 1, 350.

42. Memorandum for the President, 9 June 1945, in File: Australia, President's Secretary Files, box 150, HSTL.

43. McIntosh to Berendsen, 18 November 1946, in Ian McGibbon, ed., *Undiplomatic Dialogue: Letters between Carl Berendsen and Alister McIntosh* (Wellington: Auckland University Press, 1993), 109. See also P. G. A. Orders, *Britain, Australia, New Zealand and the Challenge of the United States, 1939–46: A Study in International History* (Basingstoke: Palgrave Macmillan, 2003), 116–18.

44. W. D. McIntyre, *Background to the Anzus Pact: Policy-Making, Strategy and Diplomacy, 1945–55* (Basingstoke: Palgrave Macmillan, 1994), 82–83.

45. Eggleston to Evatt, 25 January 1946, in *Documents on Australian Foreign Policy, 1946, January–June*, vol. 9, doc. 54.

46. National Archives of Australia, Canberra, Australia (hereafter NAA): A5954, 1800/10, Minutes of the Twelfth meeting of Prime Ministers at 10 Downing Street, 6 May 1944.

47. Testimony on the Pacific Islands Trusteeship Agreement, 7 July 1947, in Larry I. Bland, Mark A. Stoler, Sharon Ritenour Stevens, and Daniel D. Holt, eds., *The Papers of George Catlett Marshall: "The Whole World Hangs in the Balance," January 8, 1947–September 30, 1949* (Baltimore: Johns Hopkins University Press, 2012), 6:172.

48. A good example of how U.S. diplomacy had irritated opinion in the three British Commonwealth states can be found in NZNA: R17722423 ABHS 950 W5422 14 111 3/1 part 2, Pacific Island Bases: Memorandum for the Secretary of External Affairs, 24 December 1947.

49. The Ambassador in the United Kingdom (Winant) to the Secretary of State, 4 January 1945, in *FRUS 1945*, vol. 6, 1–3; and Memorandum of Conversation by Mr. John M. Leddy, 9 July 1945, ibid., 61–66.

50. Clarke, *Last Thousand Days*, 511–12. For a detailed account, see Richard N. Gardner, *Sterling-Dollar Diplomacy: The Origin and Prospects of Our International Economic Order* (London: McGraw, 1969), esp. 208–24.

51. Department of State, Policy Statement, 21 April 1950, in *FRUS 1950*, vol. 6, 189–90; and Orders, Challenge of the United States, 179–83.

52. Dean Acheson, *Present at the Creation: My Years in the State Department* (New York: W. W. Norton, 1969), 427.

53. On the occupation of Japan see, for instance, Eiji Takemae, *Inside GHQ: The Allied Occupation of Japan and Its Legacy* (New York: Continuum, 2002).

54. Japan had after all been identified by George Kennan as one of the key states that had to be kept out of the Soviet Union's orbit. See The Charge in the Soviet Union (Kennan) to the Secretary of State, 22 February 1946, National Security Archive, http://www2.gwu.edu/~nsarchiv/coldwar/documents/episode-1/kennan.htm.

55. Thomas H. Etzold, "The Far East in American Strategy, 1948–1951," in *Aspects of Sino-American Relations since 1784*, ed. Thomas Etzold (New York: Orchard Books, 1978), 110–16.

56. Thomas Etzold and John Lewis Gaddis, eds., *Containment: Documents on American Policy and Strategy, 1945–1950* (New York: Columbia University Press, 1978), 252–64.

57. Leffler, *Preponderance of Power*, 104–40.

58. See, for example, Draft Report by the National Security Council Staff: Measures required to achieve U.S. objectives with respect to the USSR, 30 March 1949, in *FRUS 1949*, vol. 1, 271–77.

59. The United States was steadily building military installations around the globe. See Report by the National Security Council: Airfield Construction in the United Kingdom and the Cairo-Suez Area, 15 April 1949, in *FRUS 1949*, vol. 1, 285; and Memorandum by the Executive Secretary of the National Security Council (Souers) to the Council, 11 May 1949, in *FRUS 1949*, vol. 1, 299–311.

60. For a good overview of how U.S. intelligence interpreted the threat posed by the Soviet Union in the Asia-Pacific region see Hal Friedman, "The 'Bear' in the Pacific? US Intelligence Perceptions of Soviet Strategic Power Projection in the Pacific Basin and East Asia, 1945–1947," *Intelligence and National Security* 12.4 (1997): 75–101. For an extended discussion see Hal Friedman, *Creating an American Lake: United States Imperialism and Strategic Security in the Pacific Basin, 1945–1947* (Oxford: Praeger, 2000), 17–36.

61. Nicholas Tarling, *Britain, Southeast Asia and the Onset of the Pacific War* (Cambridge: Cambridge University Press, 1996), 58–63.

62. Louis Morton, *Strategy and Command: The First Two Years* (Washington, DC: Office of the Chief of Military History, Department of the Army, 1962), 82–94. For a discussion on what a "Pacific first" approach would have entailed see Mark A. Stoler, "The 'Pacific-First' Alternative in American World War II Strategy," *International History Review* 2.3 (1980): 432–52.

63. Ashley Jackson, *The British Empire and the Second World War* (London: Continuum, 2006), 513–24.

64. Christopher Bayly and Tim Harper, *Forgotten Armies: The Fall of British Asia 1941–1945* (London: Allen Lane, 2004), esp. chaps. 2–4.

65. Weinberg, *World at Arms*, 872.

66. President Roosevelt's Press Conference Notes and Statement to the Press, 22–23 January 1943, in *FRUS: The Conferences at Washington, 1941–1942, and Casablanca, 1943*, 836–39. For the Casablanca conference and subsequent Anglo-U.S. diplomacy see Louis, *Imperialism at Bay*, 274–88.

67. TNA: PREM 3/160 Churchill to the Chiefs of Staff, 12 September 1944.

68. Nicholas Evan Sarantakes, "One Last Crusade: The British Pacific Fleet and Its Impact on the Anglo-American Alliance," *English Historical Review* 491 (2006): 429–66; and Christopher Baxter, "In Pursuit of a Pacific Strategy: British Planning for the Defeat of Japan, 1943–45," *Diplomacy and Statecraft* 15.2 (2004): 253–77.

69. Louis, *Imperialism at Bay*, 433.

70. Christopher Bayly and Tim Harper, *Forgotten Wars: Freedom and Revolution in Southeast Asia* (Cambridge, MA: Harvard University Press, 2007), 137–90.

71. Alec Cairncross and Barry Eichengreen, *Sterling in Decline* (New York: Wiley-Blackwell, 1983), xvii; and Paul Kennedy, *The Realities behind Diplomacy: Background Influences on British External Policy, 1865–1980* (London: Fontana, 1981), 317.

72. Alec Cairncross, *The British Economy since 1945: Economic Policy and Performance, 1945–90* (New York: Wiley-Blackwell, 1992), 47–48.

73. Truman, *Year of Decision*, 255; George Kennan, *Memoirs, 1925–1950* (Boston: Little, Brown, 1967), 267–70.

74. David Sanders, *Losing an Empire, Finding a Role: British Foreign Policy since 1945* (Basingstoke: Macmillan, 1990), 48; and David Reynolds, *Britannia Overruled: British Policy and World Power in the 20th Century* (London: Longman, 1991), 178–79.

75. Clarke, *Last Thousand Days*, xviii.

76. Robert Skidelsky, *John Maynard Keynes*, vol. 3, *Fighting for Freedom, 1937–1946* (London: Macmillan, 2000), 403–58; and Correlli Barnett, *Collapse of British Power* (repr., London: Faber & Faber, 2011), 592. On postwar Britain more generally, see Peter Hennessy, *Never Again: Britain 1945–1951* (London: Vintage, 2006).

77. Harriman made these comments to the U.S. secretary of the navy, James Forrestal. See diary entry, 22 July 1946, in Millis, *Forrestal Diaries*, 186.

78. Churchill, *Triumph and Tragedy*, 288–90, 319–21.

79. Curtis Keeble, *Britain, the Soviet Union and Russia* (New York: St. Martin's, 2000), xii.

80. Josef Foschepoth, "British Interest in the Division of Germany after the Second World War," Journal of Contemporary History 21.3 (1986): 391–92.

81. Robert Rhodes James, *Anthony Eden* (London: Papermac, 1987), 281.

82. TNA: CAB 121/400 COS (44) 485 (0) (PHP), War Cabinet, Chiefs of Staff Committee: Future Relations with France, 25 May 1944; and Danchev and Todman, *War Diaries 1939–1945*, 693–94, 697.

83. Jonathan Haslam, *Russia's Cold War: From the October Revolution to the Fall of the Wall* (New Haven, CT: Yale University Press, 2011), 1–2.

84. David Carlton, "Churchill and the Two 'Evil Empires,'" in *Winston Churchill in the Twenty-First Century*, ed. David Cannadine and Roland Quinault (Cambridge: Cambridge University Press, 2004), 176.

85. TNA: CAB 120/691, "Operation Unthinkable: Russia: Threat to Western Civilization," Memorandum by the Joint Planning Staff, 11 August 1945.

86. David Reynolds, *Summits: Six Meetings That Shaped the Twentieth Century* (New York: Basic Books, 2007), 145.

87. Keeble, *Britain, the Soviet Union and Russia*, xii.

88. Vernon Bogdanor, *The People and the Party System: The Referendum and Electoral Reform in British Politics* (Cambridge: Cambridge University Press, 1981), 35.

89. Clement Attlee to the President of the United States, 25 September 1945 in File: Attlee, Clement R, Miscellaneous, President's Secretary Files, box 149, HSTL.

90. Alan Bullock, *Ernest Bevin: Foreign Secretary, 1945–1951* (Oxford: Oxford University Press, 1985), 190–98. For more on this topic, see C. J. Bartlett, *The Long Retreat: A Short History of British Defence Policy* (London: Macmillan, 1972).

91. Anne Deighton, "Britain and the Cold War, 1945–1955," in Leffler and Westad, *Origins*, 118–22.

92. NAA: A6712 1, Minutes of the Meeting of Prime Minister, 15 May 1944.

93. Martin Folly, *Churchill, Whitehall and the Soviet Union, 1940–45* (Basingstoke: Palgrave Macmillan, 2000), 139.

94. On Attlee's long-held anti-Soviet leanings see C. R. Attlee, *As It Happened* (London: Heinemann, 1954), 91–92; and Kenneth Harris, *Attlee* (London: Weidenfeld & Nicolson, 1995), 156–57.

95. Balfour to Bevin, 9 August 1945, in *Documents of British Policy Overseas: Britain and America: Negotiation of the United States Loan, August–December 1945* (London: Her Majesty's Stationery Office, 1986), series 1, vol. 3, 17.

96. Baxter, *Great Power Struggle*, 30–31.

97. Bullock, *Ernest Bevin*, 198–201; James Byrnes, *Speaking Frankly* (New York: Harper, 1947), 53–60; Memorandum of Conversation by the United States Delegation, 19 December 1945, in *FRUS 1945*, vol. 2, 680–87; and United States Delegation Minutes, 20 December 1945, ibid., 692–99.

98. TNA: PREM 4/31, Churchill Minute, 10 January 1945. For the most damning critique of Churchill's premiership and the legacy bequeathed to the Attlee

government see John Charmley, *Churchill's Grand Alliance: The Anglo-American Special Relationship 1940–57* (London: Hodder & Stoughton, 1995), 537–47.

99. Cairncross, *British Economy since 1945*, 80–85.

100. Kennedy, *Realties behind Diplomacy*, 362–69. Bevin quote in Piers Brendon, *The Decline and Fall of the British Empire* (London: Vintage, 2008), 373. On "decline" as a debatable historical description, see Jim Tomlinson, "Inventing 'Decline': The Falling Behind of the British Economy in the Post-war Years," *Economic History Review* 49.4 (1996): 731–57.

101. Tarling, *Britain, Southeast Asia and the Onset of the Cold War*, 3–8.

102. Krishnan Srinivasan, *The Rise, Decline and Future of the British Commonwealth* (Basingstoke: Palgrave Macmillan, 2007), 5–42.

103. As expressed in Report by Defence Committee, 11 November 1948, in *Documents on Australian Foreign Policy, 1948–49: The Commonwealth, Asia and the Pacific*, vol. 14, doc. 104.

104. TNA: CAB 129/1, Memorandum by the Prime Minister, 1 September 1945.

105. Alex Danchev, "The Cold War 'Special Relationship' Revisited," *Diplomacy and Statecraft* 17.3 (2006), 579–95. See also Thomas K. Robb, *A Strained Partnership? US-UK Relations in the Era of Détente* (Manchester: Manchester University Press, 2013), 11–13.

106. Ritchie Ovendale, *Anglo-American Relations in the Twentieth Century* (Basingstoke: Macmillan, 1998), 66.

107. Marshall to Acheson, 7 April 1947, in Bland, Stoler, Stevens, and Holt, *Papers of George Catlett Marshall*, 6:91.

108. JIC 340/1, Estimate of British Post-War Capabilities and Intentions, 13 February 1946 in RG 218, Geographic File 1942–5, folder: CCS 000.1 Great Britain, box 82, NAII.

109. Clarke, *Last Thousand Days*, 477.

110. Karl Hack, *Defence and Decolonisation in Southeast Asia* (London: Curzon, 2001), 57.

111. This was a constant point of disagreement between U.S. and British officials. See, for instance, Memorandum on the Negotiations leading to the Anglo-American joint statement on commercial policy, 6 December 1945, in File: Britain, President's Secretary Files, box 150, HSTL; and the Secretary of State to the Embassy in the United Kingdom, 18 January 1947, in *FRUS 1947*, vol. 3, 1–3.

112. For overviews on Australia's war effort in the Pacific see Bruce Cumings, *Reluctant Nation: Australia and the Allied Defeat of Japan, 1942–45* (New York: Oxford University Press, 1992); and D. Horner, *High Command: Australia and Allied Strategy, 1939–1945* (Sydney: George Allen & Unwin, 1982).

113. For debates about "betrayal" and the significance of the Australian entry into the war against Japan in 1942 see Augustine Meaher IV, *The Road to Singapore: The Myth of British Betrayal* (Canberra: Australian Scholarly Publishing, 2010); Peter Dean, ed., *Australia 1942: In the Shadow of War* (Cambridge: Cambridge University Press, 2012); and David Day, *The Great Betrayal: Britain, Australia and the Onset of the Pacific War, 1939–42* (North Ryde: Angus & Robertson, 1988). For more on Curtin, see Bruce Cumings, *John Curtin: A Life* (Sydney: Harper Collins, 1999); and John Edwards, *Curtin's Gift: Reinterpreting Australia's Greatest Prime Minister* (Sydney: Allen & Unwin, 2005).

114. Peggy Warner, *The Coffin Boats: Japanese Midget Submarine Operations in the Second World War* (London: Leo Cooper, 1986), chap. 9. For the Churchill quote see Lord Moran, *Winston Churchill: The Struggle for Survival 1945–1965* (London: Constable, 1966), 21. On Churchill and Australia more broadly, see Graham Freudenberg, *Churchill and Australia* (Sydney: Macmillan Australia, 2008).

115. Weinberg, *World at Arms*, 320–21. This is not to suggest that Churchill was prepared to write Australia off as an acceptable loss: Roland Quinault, "Churchill and Australia: The Military Relationship 1899–1945," *War and Society* 6.1 (1988): 60.

116. John Curtin, "The Task Ahead," *Melbourne Herald*, 27 December 1941.

117. John McKerrow, *The American Occupation of Australia, 1941–45: A Marriage of Necessity* (Cambridge: Cambridge Scholars, 2013).

118. Orders, *Challenge of the United States*, 111–21.

119. NAA: A6712 1, Minutes of a Meeting held at 10 Downing Street, Meeting of Prime Ministers, 15 May 1944.

120. James Curran, *Curtin's Empire* (Cambridge: Cambridge University Press, 2011), 97–103.

121. TNA: PREM 8/8, From the Dominions Office to Canada, New Zealand et al., 29 August 1945. For more on Evatt, see Alan Renouf, *Let Justice Be Done: The Foreign Policy of Dr H. V. Evatt* (St. Lucia: Queensland University Press, 1983); and Peter Crockett, *Evatt: A Life* (Melbourne: Oxford University Press, 1993).

122. TNA: PREM 8/8, Letter from the Prime Minister [Chifley] to the Prime Minister [Attlee], undated [22 August 1945]. Newspaper opinion is surmised within TNA: PREM 8/8, From Australia to the Dominions Office, 25 August 1945.

123. TNA: PREM 8/8, Letter from the British Prime Minister to the Australian Prime Minister, 25 August 1945; and David Dilks, ed., *The Diaries of Sir Alexander Cadogan, 1938–1945* (London: Cassell, 1971), diary entry, 23 May 1945, 745.

124. British complaints and the conclusions to draw from Evatt's actions are discussed in TNA: PREM 8/8, From New Zealand to the Dominions Office, 31 August 1945.

125. Stephen Bell, *Ungoverning the Economy: The Political Economy of Australian Economic Policy* (Oxford: Oxford University Press, 1997), 69–72; and Rodney Maddock, "The Long Boom 1940–1970," in *The Australian Economy in the Long Run*, ed. Rodney Maddock and Ian W. McLean (Cambridge: Cambridge University Press, 1987).

126. Tim Rooth, "Imperial Self-Insufficiency Rediscovered: Britain and Australia 1945–51," *Australian Economic History Review* 39.1 (1999): 29–51; and John Singleton and Paul L. Robertson, *Economic Relations between Britain and Australasia 1945–1970* (Basingstoke: Palgrave, 2002), 1–25.

127. A point that Australian policymakers emphasized to Washington. For example, see Memorandum of Conversation with Sir Frederick Shedden, 20 April 1949, from Secretary of State Files, Dean Acheson Papers, HSTL.

128. David Lee, *The Political Economy of Australia's Postwar Foreign and Defence Policy* (Sydney: Allen & Unwin, 1995), 73, 107–8, 135.

129. David Lee, "Protecting the Sterling Area: The Chifley Government's Response to Multilateralism, 1945–9," *Australian Journal of Political Science* 25.2 (1990): 178–95; and Tim Rooth, "Australia, Canada, and the International Economy in the Era of Postwar Reconstruction, 1945–50," *Australian Economic History Review* 40.2 (2000): 127–52.

130. Alan Watt, *The Evolution of Australian Foreign Policy, 1938–1965* (Cambridge: Cambridge University Press, 1967), 301.

131. Chiefs of Staff Committee Minute 3/1947, 28 October 1947, in *Documents on Australian Foreign Policy, 1947*, vol. 12, doc. 161.

132. Chifley quoted in Council of Defence [1] Minute, 12 March 1947, in *Documents on Australian Foreign Policy, 1947*, vol. 12, doc. 163. See also Orders, *Challenge of the United States*, 157.

133. For terms of the ANZAC pact, see http://www.austlii.edu.au/au/other/dfat/treaties/1944/2.html.

134. As late as 1950, there was still no consensus as to the area to be covered by this agreement, but it was to include Australia, New Zealand, and Malaya. Broadly, the area to defend was considered to encompass the "Southwest Pacific zone." For the quote see NAA: A816 14/301/387, Procedure for future planning in relation to British Commonwealth Defence in the ANZAM Area, signed by F. A. McLaughlin, 15 September 1949.

135. NAA: A816 14/301/349, Machinery for Co-operation in British Commonwealth Defence, undated.

136. For detailed documentation on ANZAM planning see NAA: A5954, 1626/4, Strategic Planning in relation to Co-operation in British Commonwealth Defence, attached to Minute by Defence Committee at Meeting Held on Thursday, 8 June 1950; and NAA: A2031/147/1951, Strategic Concept for the Defence of ANZAM Region, 31 May 1951.

137. Ian McGibbon, *New Zealand and the Korean War*, vol. 1, *Politics and Diplomacy* (Oxford: Oxford University Press, 1993), 32.

138. As noted by the British government in TNA: FO 371/101242, The ANZAM Concept, undated.

139. Attlee to Chifley, 17 August 1947, in *Documents on Australian Foreign Policy, 1947*, vol. 12, doc. 180.

140. NAA: A5954 1800/10, Minutes of 18th Meeting at 10 Downing Street, 22 May 1946.

141. NAA: A5954 1800/10, Minutes of the 5th Meeting held at 10 Downing Street, Meeting of Prime Ministers, 26 April 1946. This was confirmed later: NAA: A816 14/301/349, From UKSLIA Melbourne to Ministry of Defence London, 20 May 1948.

142. Evatt to Chifley, 1 July 1946, from *Documents on Australian Foreign Policy: 1946, July–December*, vol. 10, doc 1.

143. Memorandum for the President, 8 May 1946 in File: Australia, President's Secretary Files, box 150, HSTL; and Memorandum for the President, 7 October 1947, in File: Australia, President's Secretary Files, box 150, HSTL.

144. Baxter, *Great Power Struggle*, 103.

145. David Day, *Chifley* (Sydney: HarperCollins, 2001), 432–34.

146. Chifley to Beasley, 18 February 1946, in *Documents on Australian Foreign Policy, 1946, January–June*, vol. 9, doc. 96.

147. Chifley to Evatt, 24 October 1947, in *Documents on Australian Foreign Policy, 1947*, vol. 12, doc. 225.

148. On tensions within the Australian government and from the opposition concerning reliance on the United Nations and the threat posed by the Soviet Union, see

David Lee, *Search for Security: The Political Economy of Australia's Postwar Foreign and Defence Policy* (Sydney: Allen & Unwin, 1995), 77, 81.

149. Renouf, *Let Justice Be Done*, 126–29; and Ashley Hogan, *Moving in Open Daylight: Doc Evatt, an Australian at the United Nations* (Sydney: Sydney University Press, 2008), 1–7.

150. Their positions were reported in TNA: FO 371/70189, J. P. G. Finch to Sir N. Charles, 22 January 1948; and ibid., Sir N. Charles to the Secretary of State, 24 January 1948.

151. Quote from TNA: FO 371/70189, Message from Mr Chifley to the Prime Minister in Telegram no. 8, Canberra to London, 22 January 1948.

152. Memorandum for the President, 2 May 1948, in File: Australia, President's Secretary Files, box 150, HSTL.

153. Quote in TNA: FO 371/70189, Message from Mr Chifley to the Prime Minister in Telegram no. 8, Canberra to London, 22 January 1948.

154. Biographical Sketch of Dr Evatt, attached to Memorandum for the President, 7 October 1947, File: Australia, President's Secretary Files, box 150, HSTL.

155. Christopher Waters, *The Empire Fractures: Anglo-Australian Conflict in the 1940s* (Melbourne: Australian Scholarly Publishing, 1995), 5–9.

156. Evatt quoted in TNA: FO 371/700189, The UK High Commissioner in the Commonwealth of Australia to London, 16 April 1948. See, for example, Chifley to Evatt, 16 October 1948 in *Documents on Australian Foreign Policy, 1948–49: The Commonwealth, Asia and the Pacific*, vol. 14, doc. 101.

157. Evatt to Minter, 24 January 1946, in *Documents on Australian Foreign Policy, 1946, January–June*, vol. 9, doc. 50.

158. Memorandum of Conversation with the Ambassador of Australia, Norman Makin, 21 September 1949, in Secretary of State Files, Acheson Papers, HSTL.

159. Australian Government to Addison, 25 February 1946, in *Documents on Australian Foreign Policy, 1946, January–June*, vol. 9, doc. 110; McFarlane to Melville, 1 February 1946, ibid., doc. 115; Evatt to Department of External Affairs, 11 June 1946, ibid., doc. 303; Evatt to Beasley and Hodgson, 13 January 1947, in *Documents on Australian Foreign Policy, 1947*, vol. 12, doc. 238; and NAA: A5954 1800/10, Minutes of First Meeting at 10 Downing Street: Meetings of Prime Ministers, 23 April 1946.

160. Jeffrey Richelson and Desmond Ball, *The Ties That Bind: Intelligence Cooperation between the UKUSA Countries* (London: Allen & Unwin, 1985).

161. Council of Defence [1] Minute, 12 March 1947, in *Documents on Australian Foreign Policy, 1947*, vol. 12, doc. 163.

162. Mention of this is made in Massey to Evatt, 5 February 1947, in *Documents on Australian Foreign Policy, 1947*, vol. 12, doc. 167.

163. On Anglo-Australian nuclear testing, see Lorna Arnold, *A Very Special Relationship: British Atomic Weapon Trials in Australia* (London: Her Majesty's Stationery Office, 1987).

164. Hollis to Shedden, 10 March 1947, in *Documents on Australian Foreign Policy, 1947*, vol. 12, doc. 169. See also report by the Joint Planning Committee, 20 February 1947, ibid., doc. 168; and Kevin to Burton, 9 May 1947, ibid., doc. 171.

165. Joint Intelligence Committee Appreciation 2/1948, 24 November 1948, in *Documents on Australian Foreign Policy, 1948: The Commonwealth, Asia and the Pacific*, vol. 14, doc. 122. The Australian Chiefs of Staff and JIC had both warned of the

Soviet Union's ambitions previously: Chiefs of Staff Committee Minute 11/1946, 20 March 1946, in *Documents on Australian Foreign Policy, 1946, January–June*, vol. 9, doc. 134; and Joint Intelligence Committee Appreciation 1/47, 27 March 1947, in *Documents on Australian Foreign Policy, 1947*, vol. 12, doc. 160.

166. Compare and contrast the Australian assessment in Joint Intelligence Committee Appreciation 2/1948, 24 November 1948, in *Documents on Australian Foreign Policy, 1948: The Commonwealth, Asia and the Pacific*, vol. 14, doc. 122, with the British JIC's appreciation in TNA: CAB 158/1 JIC (47) 1, Soviet Interests, Intentions and Capabilities, Report by the Joint Intelligence Sub-Committee, 6 August 1947.

167. For example, see David Lowe, *Menzies and the "Great World Struggle": Australia's Cold War 1948–1954* (Sydney: University of New South Wales Press, 1999); Waters, *Empire Fractures*; and Day, *Chifley*.

168. On this subject, see Nancy Taylor, *The Official History of New Zealand in the Second World War, 1939–1945: The Home Front* (Wellington: Historical Publications Branch, 1965), http://nzetc.victoria.ac.nz//tm/scholarly/tei-WH2-1Hom.html.

169. McIntyre, *Background to the Anzus Pact*, 3. See also Ian McGibbon, *The Oxford Companion to New Zealand Military History* (Auckland: Oxford University Press, 2000), 223. On the closeness of the bond between New Zealand and Britain in the war, see British diplomatic oral history programme, Churchill College Archives centre, interview by D. M. McBain with J. K. Hickman, First Secretary, Wellington, 1959–62 (1995), 6–7.

170. J. V. T. Baker, *The Official History of New Zealand in the Second World War 1939–1945: War Economy* (Wellington: Historical Publications Branch, 1965), 570, 573, http://nzetc.victoria.ac.nz/tm/scholarly/tei-WH2Econ.html. For more on economic policymaking in New Zealand, see Malcolm McKinnon, *Treasury: A History of the New Zealand Treasury, 1840–2000* (Auckland: Auckland University Press, 2003), 112–87; and Jim McAloon, *Judgements of All Kinds: Economic Policy-Making in New Zealand, 1945–1984* (Victoria: University of Wellington Press, 2013).

171. Baker, *War Economy*, 25, 526–27.

172. Keith Sinclair, *A History of New Zealand* (repr., London: Penguin, 2001), 354; and John Singleton, "New Zealand, Britain and the Survival of the Ottawa Agreement, 1945–77," *Australian Journal of Politics and History* 43.2 (1997): 168–82.

173. See a number of letters between Churchill and Curtin and Churchill and Fraser on this point in Winston S. Churchill, *The Second World War*, vol. 4, *The Hinge of Fate* (London: Reprint Society, 1953), 19–31.

174. On the theme of independence, see Malcolm McKinnon, *Independence and Foreign Policy: New Zealand in the World since 1935* (Auckland: Auckland University Press, 1993), esp. chap. 4.

175. The Minister of External Affairs to the Minister for External Affairs in Australia, 27 March 1947, in *ANZUS Pact*, vol. 3, *ANZUS Pact and the Treaty of Peace with Japan*, doc. 5, 12–13; and The First Secretary, New Zealand Legation, Washington, to the Secretary of External Affairs, 13 May 1947, in *ANZUS Pact*, doc. 26, 46–47.

176. McKinnon, *Independence and Foreign Policy*, 101; and McGibbon, *New Zealand and the Korean War*, 1:124–25.

177. Memorandum by the Department of External Affairs on the General Attitude to the Japanese Settlement, 11 August 1947, in *ANZUS Pact*, doc. 58, 94–95.

178. Ibid.

179. McGibbon, *New Zealand and the Korean War*, 1:16.

180. Roberto Rabel, *New Zealand and the Vietnam War: Politics and Diplomacy* (Auckland: Auckland University Press, 2005), 12–15; and Christopher Pugsley, *From Emergency to Confrontation: The New Zealand Armed Forces in Malaya and Borneo, 1949–1966* (Oxford: Oxford University Press, 2003), 22–25.

181. NZNA: R16700704 ACIE 8799 EA10 4/7, Pacific Pact: Prime Ministers Statement, 11 January 1949.

182. Ibid.

183. Ibid.

184. Ibid.

185. NZNA: R22228431 W2619 83 111 3/3/1, part 1, From the New Zealand High Commissioner, London, to Mr Shanahan, 8 July 1949.

186. McGibbon, *New Zealand and the Korean War*, 1:32–33.

187. For examples of New Zealand concerns, see The Minister of External Affairs to the Secretary of State for Commonwealth Relations, 15 July 1947, in *ANZUS Pact*, doc. 42, 68–69; The High Commissioner for Canada to the Secretary of External Affairs, 23 July 1947, in *ANZUS Pact*, doc. 49, 81–83; and The New Zealand Minister, Washington, to the Minister of External Affairs, 24 July 1947, in *ANZUS Pact*, doc. 50, 83–85.

188. McGibbon, *New Zealand and the Korean War*, 1:15.

189. Berendsen to McIntosh, 30 November 1944, in McGibbon, *Undiplomatic Dialogue*, 90.

190. NZNA: R17722423 ABHS 950 W5422 14 111 3/1 part 2, An Appreciation by the Joint Planning Committee: New Zealand's Strategic Interests in the Pacific and Far East, May 1947.

191. NZNA: R17722423 ABHS 950 W5422 14 111 3/1 part 2, Note for Mr Nash, 12 April 1946.

192. McGibbon, *New Zealand and the Korean War*, 1:21.

193. It was estimated that a four-to-six-year time frame would be required for New Zealand to provide significant qualitative and quantitative improvements to its armed services. See NZNA: R20821 AAFD 811 W2347 148, I CAB 223/3/1, Notes on Order of Battle, undated (April–May 1947).

194. McGibbon, *New Zealand and the Korean War*, 1:23.

195. Ibid., 28–31.

196. McKinnon, *Independence*, 112.

197. David R. Devereux, *The Formulation of British Defence Policy towards the Middle East* (Basingstoke: Palgrave Macmillan, 1990), 77–78.

198. Pugsley, *From Emergency to Confrontation*, 6–10.

199. McGibbon, *New Zealand and the Korean War*, 1:32.

200. Security concerns were the primary drivers of these tensions surrounding ANZAM. On fear of domination by Australia and even dislike of Australians as important motivating factors concerning intra-Dominion tensions, see McKinnon, *Independence*, 115–16.

201. McGibbon, *New Zealand the Korean War*, 1:33.

202. NZNA: R17722423 ABHS 950 W5422 14 111 3/1 part 2, From the Minister of External Affairs, Wellington to the Minister of External Affairs, Canberra, 7 August 1947.

203. The Secretary of External Affairs to the Official Secretary, Office of the High Commissioner for New Zealand, Canberra, 29 September 1949, *ANZUS Pact*, doc. 184, 506.

204. Orders, *Challenge of the United States*, 173; and McGibbon, *New Zealand and the Korean War*, 1:24–25.

205. Policy Statement of the Department of State: United States Relations with New Zealand, 24 September 1948, in *FRUS 1948*, vol. 6, 9.

206. NZNA: R22228431 W2619 83 111 3/3/1, part 1, Analysis of New Zealand's basic interests in the Pacific in relation to the proposed pact, Memorandum for the Prime Minister, 8 August 1949.

207. On the United States' prewar ambitions in the Asia-Pacific, see Michael Green, *By More Than Providence: Grand Strategy and American Power in the Asia Pacific since 1783* (New York: Columbia University Press, 2017), 155–87.

2. Crisis and Cooperation

1. Barrass, *Great Cold War*, 60–61.

2. On domino theory as the central organizing concept behind U.S. containment strategy, see Robert Jervis and Jack Snyder, eds., *Dominoes and Bandwagons: Strategic Beliefs and Great Power Competition in the Eurasian Rimland* (New York: Oxford University Press, 1991), 3. On U.S. and British concerns that Communist success in one country would produce similar outcomes in neighboring states, see Ngoei, "Domino Logic of the Darkest Moment," 230–31. On British concerns about the extent of Soviet designs, the spread of Communism, and the rise of nationalism see TNA: CAB 158/4 (Part 2) JIC 48 (48) 87 (0), Report by the Joint Intelligence Committee, 6 August 1948; and TNA: CAB 159/3 JIC (48) 22nd meeting, 12 March 1948.

3. John Prados, *Vietnam: The History of an Unwinnable War, 1945–1975* (Lawrence: University Press of Kansas, 2009), 20.

4. Tim Harper, *The End of Empire and the Making of Malaya* (Cambridge: Cambridge University Press, 1999), 152. Further discussion on this is provided in Phillip Deery, "Malaya, 1948: Britain's Asian Cold War?," *Journal of Cold War Studies* 9.1 (2007): 34–35.

5. Hack, *Defence and Decolonisation*, 143–46.

6. TNA: PREM 8/1406, Memorandum by the Colonial Office, April 1949. See also Rory Cormac, *Confronting the Colonies: British Intelligence and Counterinsurgency* (London: Hurst, 2013), 56–59.

7. David French, *Army, Empire, and Cold War: The British Army and Military Policy, 1945–1971* (Oxford: Oxford University Press, 2011), 32–33.

8. NAA: A816 14/301/307, Report by the Joint Planning Committee, 19 May 1950; and NAA: A5954, 1626/4, Minute by Defence Committee, 8 June 1950.

9. Chiefs of Staff Committee Minute 3/1947, 28 October 1947, in *Documents on Australian Foreign Policy, 1947*, vol. 12, doc. 161.

10. Follow the documentation in TNA: CO 537/6331. Also see TNA: PREM 8/1406, Situation in Malaya, 5 March 1949.

11. TNA: PREM 8/1406, Memorandum by the Secretary of State for the Colonies, 5 March 1949.

12. Pugsley, *From Emergency to Confrontation*, 10–22.

13. TNA: PREM 8/1406, 21st Conclusion, Malaya: Possibility of Australian assistance, 11 March 1949. On Australian military operations during the Malayan emergency see Peter Dennis and Jeffrey Grey, *Emergency and Confrontation: Australian Military Operations in Malaya and Borneo 1950–1966: The Official History of Australia's Involvement in Southeast Asian Conflicts 1948–1975* (London: Allen & Unwin, 1996).

14. On Malaya as an internal struggle, see Renouf, *Let Justice Be Done*, 271; and Dennis and Grey, *Emergency and Confrontation*, 5–21.

15. On U.S. thinking see Basic U.S. Security Resource Assumptions: Staff Paper, 1 June 1949 in FRUS 1949, vol. 1, 343.

16. Deery, "Malaya," 37–38; Barrass, *Great Cold War*, 64; and Richard H. Immerman, *John Foster Dulles: Piety, Pragmatism, and Power in U.S. Foreign Policy* (Wilmington, DE: S.R. Books, 1999), 88–89.

17. Noel Barber, *The War of Running Dogs: Malaya 1948–1960* (London: Cassell, 2004), 42–43. At the start of the Eisenhower administration, an overview on U.S. assistance to Britain in Malaya was undertaken that demonstrated the growth of U.S. involvement. Memorandum of Conversation, 4 February 1953 in RG 59 Lot 64D199 The Secretary and Under Secretary's Memoranda of Conversation, box 18, NAII.

18. A. W. Martin, *Robert Menzies: A Life*, vol. 2, *1944–1978* (Melbourne: Melbourne University Press, 1999), 86–97, 118–25, 138–51.

19. Lee, *Search for Security*, 107–9.

20. Dennis and Grey, *Emergency and Confrontation*, 22–44.

21. Ibid., 22.

22. TNA: DEFE 4/30 COS 50, 55th Meeting, Chief of Staff Minutes of a Meeting, 3 April 1950.

23. A total 1,073,154 votes were cast to contest eighty parliamentary seats. The incumbent Labour Party won 506,073 votes and thirty-four seats. The National Party won 556,805 votes and forty-six seats, so Sidney Holland became the new prime minister. See Clifford Norton, *New Zealand Parliamentary Election Results 1946–1987* (Wellington: Victoria University of Wellington, 1988), 181.

24. Ian McGibbon, "The Defence of New Zealand 1945–1957," *New Zealand in World Affairs*, vol. 1 (Wellington: New Zealand Institute of International Affairs, 1991), 156.

25. McIntyre, *Background to the Anzus Pact*, 142. On tensions between plans to deploy to the Middle East and the government's economizing policies in early 1950, see McKinnon, *Independence*, 115.

26. McIntyre, *Background to Anzus Pact*, 118.

27. TNA: PREM 8/1406, Situation in Malaya and Hong Kong: Memorandum by the Secretary of State for the Colonies, 13 March 1950; and David R. Devereux, "Britain, the Commonwealth and the Defence of the Middle East, 1948–56," *Journal of Contemporary History* 24.2 (1989): 332.

28. McKinnon, *Treasury*, 190, 193.

29. Pugsley, *From Emergency to Confrontation*, 6–7.

30. For instance, see Leffler, *Preponderance of Power*, 333–39; and Baxter, *Great Power Struggle*, 146–49.

31. Follow the discussion within the Australian cabinet here: NAA: CRS A4638/ XM1, Cabinet Minutes, 2 May 1950.

32. The major Australian discussions can be followed in NAA: CRS A4638/XM1, Cabinet Minutes, 2 May 1950. See also Lowe, *Menzies*, 199, n. 60.

33. McGibbon, *New Zealand and the Korean War*, 1:16.

34. NZNA: R22228431 W2619 83 111 3/3/1, part 1, Memorandum for the Prime Minister, 8 August 1949. As detailed in an earlier New Zealand cabinet meeting, the ambition of both New Zealand and Australia was to obtain "security both from Asiatic and Communist aggression." See NZNA: R22228431 W2619 83 111 3/3/1, part 1, Notes on Pacific Pact, 27 July 1949.

35. For an opposing assessment see Travis J. Hardy, "The Consanguinity of Ideas: Race and Anti-communism in the U.S.-Australian Relationship, 1933–1953" (PhD diss., University of Tennessee, 2010).

36. NZNA: R22228431 W2619 83 111 3/3/1, part 1, Memorandum for the Prime Minister, 8 August 1949.

37. Ibid.

38. On the course of the conflict, see Odd Arne Westad, *Decisive Encounters: The Chinese Civil War, 1946–1950* (Stanford, CA: Stanford University Press, 2003).

39. Russell Buhite, "'Major Interests': American Policy toward China, Taiwan, and Korea, 1945–1950," *Pacific Historical Review* 47.3 (1978): 425–51; Bland and Stoler, *Papers of George Marshall*, 6:34–44; and Simei Qing, *From Allies to Enemies: Visions of Modernity, Identity, and U.S.-China Diplomacy, 1945–1960* (Cambridge, MA: Harvard University Press, 2007), 3–56. Also see Memorandum from Mr Patterson attached to George Marshall to the President, 4 March 1947, in File: China, President's Secretary Files, box 151, HSTL.

40. For more on the relationship between the Soviet Union and China, see Dieter Heinzig, *The Soviet Union and Communist China 1945–1950: The Arduous Road to the Alliance* (London: M. E. Sharpe, 2003). On the logic of America's response to rising powers on its periphery, and the importance of perceived threats to regional balances, see Evan Braden Montgomery, *In the Hegemon's Shadow: Leading States and the Rise of Regional Powers* (Ithaca, NY: Cornell University Press, 2016).

41. Zelizer, *Arsenal of Democracy*, 92.

42. Report to the President, China and Korea, September 1947, 60 in File: China, President's Secretary Files, box 151, HSTL.

43. The Soviet Effort in China, Memorandum from the U.S. Naval Attaché in Nanking, China, 12 September 1947, in File: China, President's Secretary Files, box 152, HSTL.

44. See CMNAVWESPA to the Commander in Chief, Far East, 3 May 1948, in RG 218 Geographic File 1948–50, China, box 17, NAII.

45. Ernest R. May, "1947–48: When Marshall Kept the U.S. Out of War in China," *Journal of Military History* 66.4 (2002): 1003–6.

46. Sulzberger, *Long Row of Candles*, 6 February 1949, 385. U.S.-Chinese relations and the Marshall involvement can be followed in Larry I. Bland, Roger B. Jeans, and Mark F. Wilkinson, *George C. Marshall's Mediation Mission to China, December 1945–January 1947* (Lexington, VA: George Marshall Foundation, 1998).

47. For a good overview see Frank Dikotter, *The Tragedy of Liberation: A History of the Chinese Revolution 1945–1957* (London: Bloomsbury, 2013).

48. Jung Chang and Jon Halliday, *Mao: The Unknown Story* (London: Vintage, 2007), 426–33.

49. Zelizer, *Arsenal of Democracy*, 81–96.

50. John Foster Dulles, *War or Peace* (New York: Macmillan, 1950), 148.

51. Richard M. Fried, *Nightmare in Red: The McCarthy Era in Perspective* (Oxford: Oxford University Press, 1991), 147, 168.

52. Memorandum of Conversation with Senator William F. Knowland, Senator Alexander H. Smith and Mr. Jack K. McFall, 5 January 1950, in Secretary of State Files, Acheson Papers, HSTL. Also see Gayle B. Montgomery and James W. Johnson, *One Step from the White House: The Rise and Fall of Senator William F. Knowland* (Berkeley: University of California Press, 1998), 96–98.

53. Charles B. Deane to the President, 19 October 1949, in File: Far East, President's Secretary Files, box 155, HSTL. Similar arguments about the necessity of defending U.S. interests throughout the region were made by other senators and congressmen. See for instance Memorandum for the President from the Secretary of Defense, 15 December 1949, in File: Formosa, President's Secretary Files, box 155, HSTL. Intelligence reports provided to the president suggested that China would now become an agent of Soviet Communism. See JCS Intelligence report on the long-term prospects of Chinese Communism, 18 August 1949, in RG 218 Geographic File 1948–50: China, box 20, NAII.

54. Bruce R. Kuniholm, "U.S. Policy in the Near-East: The Triumphs and Tribulations of the Truman Administration," in *The Truman Presidency*, ed. Michael J. Lacey (Cambridge: Cambridge University Press, 1989), 306.

55. Staff Paper prepared for the National Security Resources Board and the National Security Council by an Interdepartmental Working Group: Basic U.S. Security Resources Assumptions, 1 June 1949, in *FRUS 1949*, vol. 1, 339.

56. Trachtenberg, *Constructed Peace*, 95–96.

57. Nancy Tucker, *Patterns in the Dust: Chinese-American Relations and the Recognition Controversy 1949–1950* (New York: Columbia University Press, 1983).

58. Memorandum from R. Love to Robert G. Barnes, 5 June 1950, in Secretary of State Files, Acheson Papers, HSTL.

59. Gaddis, *Strategies of Containment*, 82–90. On NSC-68 and its impact see Ernest May, ed., *American Cold War Strategy: Interpreting NSC 68* (Bedford: St. Martin's, 1993), 23–81; and Curt Cardwell, *NSC 68 and the Political Economy of the Early Cold War* (Cambridge: Cambridge University Press, 2012). NSC-68 can be read in full here: A Report to the President Pursuant to the President's Directive of 31 January 1950, 7 April 1950, in *FRUS 1950*, vol. 1, 235–92.

60. Leffler, *Preponderance of Power*, 355–60; and Ken Young, "Revisiting NSC 68," *Journal of Cold War Studies* 15.1 (2013): 3–33. On domestic factors influencing U.S. policy see Thomas Christensen, *Useful Adversaries: Grand Strategy, Domestic Mobilization, and Sino-American Conflict, 1947–1958* (Princeton, NJ: Princeton University Press, 1996).

61. For a good overview see Lanxin Xiang, *Recasting the Imperial Far East: Britain and America in China, 1945–1950* (London: M. E. Sharpe, 1995). For specific examples of U.S.-UK disagreement about how to handle the escalating Chinese Civil War see, for instance, Lovett to Secretary Marshall, 18 August 1947, in File: China, President's Secretary Files, box 151, HSTL.

62. Malcolm Murfett, *Hostage on the Yangtze: Britain, China, and the Amethyst Crisis of 1949* (Annapolis, MD: Naval Institute Press, 1991).

63. TNA: CAB 158/7 JIC (49) 40 Final, Report by the Joint Intelligence Committee: The Implications of a Communist Success in China, 30 September 1949.

64. McKinnon, *Independence*, 118.

65. Bevin quoted in Views of the British Government Respecting Hong Kong, 27 September 1949, in RG 218 Geographic File 1948–50, China, box 18, NAII.

66. On Hong Kong's importance see Catherine Schenk, *Hong Kong as an International Financial Centre: Emergence and Development, 1945–65* (London: Routledge, 2001).

67. For their part, the JCS believed that British estimations about defending Hong Kong were "over optimistic." See Report by the Joint Strategic Survey Committee to the Joint Chiefs of Staff, British views respecting Hong Kong, 30 September 1949, in RG 218 Geographic File 1948–50, China, box 18, NAII.

68. TNA: CAB 129/37, CP. (39) 214, Recognition of the Chinese Communist Government, Memorandum by Ernest Bevin, 24 October 1949; TNA: CAB 129/37, CP. (49) 248, Recognition of the Chinese Communist Government, Memorandum by Ernest Bevin, 12 December 1949; and TNA: CAB/128/16, CM. (49) 72nd Conclusions, 15 December 1949.

69. Chifley to Attlee, 30 May 1949, in *Documents on Australian Foreign Policy, 1948: The Commonwealth, Asia and the Pacific*, vol. 14, doc. 283; and Evatt to Bevin, 19 October 1949 ibid., doc. 273.

70. Ritchie Ovendale, "Britain and the Cold War in Asia," in *The Foreign Policy of the British Labour Government, 1945–1951*, ed. Ritchie Ovendale (Leicester: Leicester University Press, 1984), 130.

71. For the longer-term Australian and New Zealand ambition of securing British and U.S. security cooperation see The Official Secretary, Office of the High Commissioner for New Zealand, Canberra, to the Secretary of External Affairs, 27 October 1950, in *ANZUS Pact*, doc. 202, 549–50; Notes on Defence Aspects of the Japanese Peace Settlement, 31 January 1951, in *ANZUS Pact*, doc. 208, 558–63; and Minutes of a Meeting of the Chiefs of Staff Committee and Officers of the Department of External Affairs, 6 February 1951 in *ANZUS Pact*, doc. 209, 564–69.

72. Memorandum of Conversation by the Secretary of State, 26 July 1949, in *FRUS 1949*, vol. 1, 361–64; and Memorandum by the Assistant Secretary of State for Congressional Relations to the Secretary of State, 6 August 1949, ibid., 377–79.

73. Lawrence Kaplan, *NATO before the Korean War: April 1949–1950* (Kent, OH: Kent State University Press, 2013), 12–29.

74. Statement by the Secretary of State, 18 May 1949, in Press Conference File, 1949–53, January–June 1949, Acheson Papers, box 72, HSTL.

75. Note by the Secretaries of the State–Army–Navy–Air Force Coordinating Committee, 15 March 1949, in *FRUS 1949*, vol. 1, 257–59. On the efforts to establish this European security framework, see Trachtenberg, *Constructed Peace*, 86–91.

76. Record of the Meeting of the State-Defense Policy Review Group, 27 February 1950, in *FRUS 1950*, vol. 1, 170; and Forms and Scale of Soviet Attack against North America, Note by the Secretaries to the Joint Intelligence Committee, JIC 491/12, 28 June 1950, 6 in RG 218 Central Decimal File 1948–50, 092 (9-10-45) sec. 19–25, box 36, NAII. For the figures quoted, see Barrass, *Great Cold War*, 83.

77. President Truman to the Executive Secretary of the National Security Council, 1 July 1949 in *FRUS 1949*, vol. 1, 350–52; and Memorandum by the Chairman of

the Council of Economic Advisers to the National Security Council, 30 September 1949, ibid., 394–98.

78. Policy Paper Approved by the Foreign Assistance Correlation Committee, 7 February 1949 in *FRUS 1949*, vol. 1, 250–57; quote at 252.

79. Report by the SANACC Subcommittee for Rearmament: Military Aid Priorities, 18 August 1948 in *FRUS 1949*, vol. 1, 259–67. Australia's position is noted at 263. Contrast this with the assessment of the United Kingdom that was deemed vital as a "source of production and as an advanced base." Ibid., 265.

80. Memorandum by the Counselor (Charles Bohlen), 14 April 1949 in *FRUS 1949*, vol. 1, 277–78.

81. Memorandum by the Counselor (Kennan) to the Secretary of State, 6 January 1950, in *FRUS 1950*, vol. 1, 129.

82. Much has been written on Kennan and his influence on U.S. foreign policy. For the official biography see John Lewis Gaddis, *George F. Kennan: An American Life* (London: Penguin, 2011). Gaddis does not emphasis how ideas about race affected Kennan's foreign policy thinking. Frank Costigliola, the editor of the Kennan diaries, gives much greater emphasis to how cultural ideas influence policymaking. See Frank Costigliola, ed., *The Kennan Diaries* (New York: W. W. Norton, 2014); and Costigliola, "Is This George Kennan?," *New York Review of Books*, 8 December 2011.

83. Martin, *Menzies*, 86–97, 118–25, 138–51.

84. Plan SPEEDWAY is the codename given to the general plans for defending the Middle East, Near East, and North Africa against a Soviet assault. See TNA: DEFE 4/18 COS (48) 168th Meeting, Chiefs of Staff Committee: Minutes of Meeting held on 24 November 1948. For further discussion on U.S. war plans, see Steven T. Ross, *American War Plans 1945–1950* (London: Routledge, 1996), 25–52; 151–55.

85. TNA: DO 121/121 Record of a Meeting between Minister of Defence, Secretary of State and General Stewart, 8 June 1950. On British concern about a Pacific security pact see TNA: PREM 8/1148 Pacific Pact briefing memorandum, undated [June 1950].

86. The minutes can be followed in full here: TNA: CAB 133/78. The discussions that exclusively deal with economic cooperation can be followed here: TNA: CAB 133/79.

87. David Lowe, "Percy Spender and the Colombo Plan 1950," *Australian Journal of Politics & History* 40.2 (1994): 162–76; and McKinnon, *Independence*, 116.

88. Devereux, *Formulation of British Defence Policy*, 78–80.

89. TNA: CAB 133/78 Minutes of the Second Meeting, 9 January 1950.

90. Ibid.

91. TNA: CAB 21/1760 Commonwealth Relations Appreciation on Colombo Conference, attached to Jamin to Norman Brook, 22 February 1950.

92. TNA: CAB 133/78 Minutes of the First Meeting held in Senate House, Colombo, 9 January 1950.

93. The origins of the Korean War have received considerable attention; see William Stueck, *Rethinking the Korean War: A New Diplomatic and Strategic History* (Princeton, NJ: Princeton University Press, 2002).

94. The Secretary of State to the Embassy in Korea, 24 June 1950, in *FRUS 1950*, vol. 7, 126. Acheson was then further informed about the invasion by the future

secretary of state, Dean Rusk. See Dean Rusk, *As I Saw It* (New York: W. W. Norton, 1990), 162–63.

95. Harry S. Truman, *Memoirs of Harry S. Truman: 1946–52, Years of Trial and Hope* (Old Saybrook, CT: Konecky & Konecky, 1956), 332–33; and Richard E. Neustadt and Ernest R. May, *Thinking in Time: The Uses of History for Decision Makers* (New York: Free Press, 1986), 41, 89.

96. Memorandum of Teletype Conference, Prepared in the Department of the Army, 25 June 1950, in *FRUS 1950*, vol. 7, 136.

97. The Ambassador in the Soviet Union (Kirk) to the Secretary of State, 25 June 1950, in *FRUS 1950*, vol. 7, 139; and Intelligence Estimate prepared by the Estimates Group, Office of Intelligence Research, Department of State, 25 June 1950 in *FRUS 1950*, vol. 7, 148–54. The key documentation for revealing Soviet and Chinese acquiescence in the North Korean invasion is found in Cable from Roschin to Stalin relaying Mao's request for clarification on North Korea taking action against South Korea, 13 May 1950, from Wilson Center Digital Archive, http://digitalarchive.wilsoncenter.org/document/115977. For more on the Soviet and Chinese role, see Youngho Kim, "The Origins of the Korean War: Civil War or Stalin's Rollback?" *Diplomacy & Statecraft* 10.1 (1999): 186–214.

98. Merle Miller, ed., *Plain Speaking: Conversations with Harry S. Truman* (London: Victor Gollancz, 1974), 269–73.

99. Nathan F. Twining, *Neither Liberty nor Safety: A Hard Look at U.S. Military Policy and Strategy* (New York: Holt, Rinehart and Winston, 1966), 59.

100. Memorandum of Conversation by the Ambassador at large (Jessup), 25 June 1950, in *FRUS 1950*, vol. 7, 157–61; quote at 158.

101. Robert J. Donovan, *The Tumultuous Years: The Presidency of Harry S. Truman, 1949–53* (New York: W. W. Norton, 1982), 256.

102. On public opinion and the outbreak of the Korean War, see Steven Casey, *Selling the Korean War: Propaganda, Politics, and Public Opinion, 1950–1953* (Oxford: Oxford University Press, 2008), 19–31.

103. Andrew Preston, *Sword of the Spirit Shield of Faith: Religion in American War and Diplomacy* (New York: Random House, 2012), 479.

104. Miller, *Plain Speaking*, 273.

105. Memorandum of Conversation by the Ambassador at large (Jessup), 25 June 1950, in *FRUS 1950*, vol. 7, 157–61. Specific military reprisals are discussed at 158, 159.

106. Resolution UN 82 can be read in full here: Karel Wellens, *Resolutions and Statements of the United Nations Security Council (1946–1989)* (Leiden: Brill, 1990), 252.

107. Jebb's speech at the United Nations can be watched here: British Pathé, http://www.britishpathe.com/video/gladwyn-jebb-speaks-at-un-conference.

108. Gill Bennett, *Six Moments of Crisis: Inside British Foreign Policy* (Oxford: Oxford University Press, 2013), 11–17.

109. Malcolm Chalmers, *Paying for Defence: Military Spending and British Decline* (London: Pluto, 1985), 48–49.

110. Geoffrey Warner, "Anglo-American Relations and the Cold War in 1950," *Diplomacy and Statecraft* 22.1 (2011): 50.

111. Ibid., 51, 56.

112. TNA: CAB/128/17, CM. (50) 39th Conclusions, 27 June 1950.

113. Attlee actually voted against the Munich agreements in the House of Commons unlike the arch "anti-appeaser," Winston Churchill, who abstained from the vote. Nicklaus Thomas-Symonds, *Attlee: A Life in Politics* (London: I. B. Tauris, 2012), 86.

114. On the idea of the United Kingdom exercising decisive international influence through the United States see Kevin Ruane and James Ellison, "Managing the Americans: Anthony Eden, Harold Macmillan and the Pursuit of 'Power-by-Proxy' in the 1950s," *Contemporary British History* 18.3 (2004): 147–67, esp. 147–48.

115. On the cabinet discussions that took place see TNA: CAB 128/18 CM (50) 48 and 49th Conclusions, 20 and 24 July 1950; and TNA: CAB 195/8 Secretary of the Cabinet's notes of a Cabinet meeting, 25 July 1950. On the divisions within the British cabinet see Bennett, *Six Moments of Crisis*, 11–17. Oliver Franks quote from Hennessy, *Never Again*, 404. Shinwell quote is from Bennett, *Six Moments of Crisis*, 11.

116. See, for instance, Maddock, "Long Boom 1940–1970," 79–83; and Baker, *War Economy*, 570, 573. Major military spending by the United States would also help alleviate dollar shortages. On this point, see Lee, *Search for Security*, 135.

117. Martin, *Menzies*, 154.

118. McGibbon, *New Zealand and the Korean War*, 1:83.

119. Devereux, *Formulation of British Defence Policy*, 80.

120. Ian McGibbon, "The Impact of the Korean War on the Establishment of Diplomatic Relations between New Zealand and the Republic of Korea," *New Zealand Journal of Asian Studies* 15.2 (2013): 16.

121. Ian McGibbon, *New Zealand and the Korean War*, vol. 2, *Combat Operations* (Oxford: Oxford University Press, 1997), 9.

122. For New Zealand's contribution at the onset of the war, see ibid., 18–25.

123. Australia had agreed to dispatch an RAAF fighter squadron based in Japan and two naval vessels to the U.S. command in Korea. On 1 July 1950, HMAS *Bataan* and HMAS *Shoalhaven* left Japanese waters to deploy U.S. ground forces to Pusan. The following day, No. 77 Squadron, led by the wing commander Lou Spence, began ground support operations over Korea and in doing so became the first British Commonwealth and United Nations unit to see action in the Korean War. Robert O'Neill, *Australia in the Korean War, 1950–53* (Canberra: Australian Government Publishing Service, 1981), 47–52.

124. Ibid., 32, 47–56, 65–66.

125. See chapter 3 for further discussion.

126. TNA: PREM 11/1148, Minutes of a Meeting held at 10 Downing Street, 14 July 1950. The financial elements of these discussions are detailed in chapter 3.

127. Memorandum of Telephone Conversation with Secretary of Defense Louis Johnson, 13 July 1950, Secretary of State Files, Acheson Papers, HSTL; and Memorandum of Conversation, 29 July 1950, Secretary of State Files, Acheson Papers, HSTL.

128. Martin, *Menzies*, 156–59.

129. For an overview of the war, see Theodore Reed Fehrenbach, *This Kind of War: The Classic Korean War History—Fiftieth Anniversary Edition* (London: Brassey's, 2000).

130. Russell Stolfi, "A Critique of Pure Success: Incheon Revisited, Revised, and Contrasted," *Journal of Military History* 68.2 (2004): 505–25.

131. Draft Memorandum by Mr. John P. Davis of the Policy Planning Staff, 22 September 1950, in *FRUS 1950*, vol. 7, 753–55; Draft Memorandum, Planning Adviser, Bureau of Far Eastern Affairs, 22 September 1950, ibid., 756–59; and Minutes of the Ninth Meeting of the United States Delegation to the United Nations General Assembly, 28 September 1950, ibid., 799–806, 826.

132. Thomas Hennessey, *Britain's Korean War: Cold War Diplomacy, Strategy and Security, 1950–53* (Manchester: Manchester University Press, 2013), 108–31.

133. O'Neill, *Australia and the Korean War*, 65–66; and McGibbon, *New Zealand and the Korean War*, 81–85.

134. Australian, New Zealand, and U.S. discussion on Korean support and the possibility of a Pacific Security pact can be followed here: The Official Secretary, Office of the High Commissioner for New Zealand, Canberra, to the Secretary of External Affairs, 27 October 1950, in *ANZUS Pact*, doc. 202, 548–51.

135. The Deputy Under Secretary of State (Matthews) to the Special Assistant to the Secretary of Defense for Foreign Military Affairs and Assistance (Burns), 16 September 1950, in *FRUS 1950*, vol. 7, 731.

136. Fehrenbach, *This Kind of War*, 160–237.

137. For two contrasting accounts, see Geoffrey Perret, *Old Soldiers Never Die: The Life of Douglas MacArthur* (New York: Random House, 1996), 560–66; and William Manchester, *American Caesar: Douglas MacArthur, 1880–1964* (London: Hutchinson, 1979), 633–50. MacArthur's lengthy defense of his actions is contained in Douglas MacArthur, *Reminiscences* (New York: McGraw-Hill, 1964), 372–437.

138. Leffler, *Preponderance of Power*, 405. For discussion back in Washington about MacArthur's latest suggestions, see Minutes of the National Security Council, 28 November 1950, in Attlee Meeting, December 1950, President's Secretary Files, box 149, HSTL.

139. David McCullough, *Truman* (New York: Simon & Schuster, 1992), 825–26. Truman also communicated to Attlee that the United States had "no intention" of utilizing nuclear weapons in Korea except to prevent a "major military disaster." See TNA: PREM 8/ 1560, Record of Washington Talks, 4 December 1950.

140. Memorandum of Conversation, 5 December 1950, Secretary of State Files, Acheson Papers, HSTL.

141. P. Edwards and G. Pemberton, *Crises and Commitments: The Politics and Diplomacy of Australia's Involvement in Southeast Asian Conflicts, 1948–1965* (Sydney: Allen & Unwin, 1992), 109; and McGibbon, *New Zealand and the Korean War*, 2:182–85.

142. McIntosh to Berendsen, 15 December 1950, in McGibbon, *Undiplomatic Dialogue*, 252.

143. Alan R. Millett, *The War for Korea, 1950–1951: They Came from the North* (Lawrence: University Press of Kansas, 2010), 333–75.

144. Thomas Fleming, "The Man Who Saved Korea," in *The Cold War: A Military History*, ed. Robert Cowley (New York: Random House, 2005), 106.

145. In August 1950, Truman had been advised by the Joint Chiefs of Staff to quadruple the size of the U.S. Army from 247,000 to 1,081,000 troops. Truman's decision to increase the defense budget allowed for this rapid increase in the size of the army. See Memorandum for the President, 22 August 1950, in File: Joint Chiefs of Staff, President's Secretary's Files, box 107, HSTL.

146. Proclamation 2914: Proclaiming the Existence of a National Emergency, President Truman, 16 December, 1950, available at https://www.trumanlibrary. org/proclamations/index.php?pid=473&st=&st1= (accessed 11 April 2013). Truman's request for additional funding can be found in President's Special Message to Congress, 1 December 1950, in *Public Papers of the Presidents of the United States: Harry S. Truman, 1950* (Washington, DC: Government Printing Office, 1965), 728–31; and Proclaiming the Existence of a National Emergency, President Truman, 16 December, 1950, ibid., 746–47.

147. Acheson, *Present at the Creation*, 478–90.

148. Nicolson diary entry, 31 December 1950, in Stanley Olson, ed., *The Harold Nicolson Diaries* (London: Collins, 1980), 347. U.S. concerns as expressed by Congress and senior national security policymakers can be followed in Memorandum by the Assistant Secretary of State for Congressional Relations to the Under Secretary of State, 26 January 1950, in *FRUS 1950*, vol. 1, 140–41; Record of the Eighth Meeting of the Policy Planning Staff, 2 February 1950, ibid., 142–43; Memorandum of Conversation by the Secretary of State, 24 March 1950, ibid., 206–9; and National Intelligence Estimate, 15 November 1950, ibid., 414–16.

149. Meeting of the President with Congressional leaders in the Cabinet Room, 13 December 1950, in File: Attlee Meeting, December 1950, President's Secretary Files, box 149, HSTL.

150. Millett, *War for Korea*, 376–416.

151. See, for instance, NAA, A4940, C228, Percy Spender Report to Cabinet, Pacific Defence Pact: Forthcoming Exploratory Talks with Mr John Foster Dulles, 15 February 1951; Memorandum by Messrs. John H. Ferguson and Robert W. Tufts of the Policy Planning Staff, 19 January 1951, in *FRUS 1951*, vol. 1, 37–40; Paper prepared by the Deputy Director of the Policy Planning Staff, 8 February 1951, ibid., 44–48; and Study by the Joint Chiefs of Staff, 15 January 1951, ibid., 62–75.

152. Bruce Kuklick, *Blind Oracles: Intellectuals and War from Kennan to Kissinger* (Princeton, NJ: Princeton University Press, 2006), 43–48; quote at 45. Kennan quoted in Memorandum by the Counselor (Kennan) to the Secretary of State, 6 January 1950, in *FRUS 1950*, vol. 1, 138. On Nitze at this time see David Milne, *Worldmaking: The Art and Science of American Diplomacy* (New York: Farrar, Straus & Giroux, 2015), 281–84.

153. Memorandum by the Chief of Naval Operations for the Joint Chiefs of Staff, 23 July 1950, in RG 218 Geographic Files, Far East, box 22, NAII.

154. Memorandum by the Secretary of State to the Executive Secretary of the National Security Council, 26 October 1950, in *FRUS 1950*, vol. 1, 402.

155. Memorandum by the Chairman of the National Security Resources Board (Symington) to the President, undated (circa January 1951), in *FRUS 1951*, vol. 1, 21–33.

3. A Negotiated Alliance

1. Study Prepared by the Director of the Policy Planning Staff (Nitze), 8 February 1950, in *FRUS 1950*, vol. 1, 147.

2. Report by the National Security Council on the Position of the United States with Respect to Indochina, 27 February 1950, in Neil Sheehan, *The Pentagon Papers: The Secret History of the Vietnam War* (New York: Bantam Books, 1971), 361.

3. For such planning see James Bonbright to the Secretary of State, 22 March 1950, in RG 218 Geographic File 1948–50: China, box 20, NAII; and Vietnam and the implementation of the United States Economic and Military Assistance program, undated (March 1950), in RG 218 Geographic File 1948–50: China, box 20, NAII.

4. For a detailed account of negotiations, elements of which feature below, see Thomas K. Robb and David James Gill, "The ANZUS Treaty during the Cold War: A Reinterpretation of US Diplomacy in the Southwest Pacific," *Journal of Cold War Studies* 17.4 (2015): 109–57. See also Neville Meaney, "Look Back in Fear: Percy Spender, the Japanese Peace Treaty, and the ANZUS Pact," *Japan Forum* 15.3 (2003): 399–410.

5. Spender quoted in The Official Secretary, Office of the High Commissioner for New Zealand, Canberra, to the Secretary of External Affairs, 27 October 1950, in *ANZUS Pact*, doc. 202, 549–50. Also see The Assistant Secretary, Chiefs of Staff Committee, to the Secretary of External Affairs, 28 April 1950, in *ANZUS Pact*, doc. 19, 536–45; and The Minister of External Affairs to the New Zealand Ambassador, Washington, 9 May 1950, in *ANZUS Pact*, doc. 200, 545–47.

6. Martin, *Menzies*, 96–97. Menzies's speech is reported in full here: TNA: PREM 11/1121, Lecture by Mr Menzies, 12 July 1950.

7. TNA: PREM 8/1148 Pacific Pact Briefing Memorandum, undated [June 1950].

8. The Official Secretary, Office of the High Commissioner for New Zealand, Canberra, to the Secretary of External Affairs, 27 October 1950, in *ANZUS Pact*, doc. 202, 549–50.

9. During the British Commonwealth defense ministers meeting of June 1951, Menzies would commit to sending two divisions within a year of the outbreak of war. Australia would also station fighter jets on bases in Malta. See Lee, *Search for Security*, 120; and Chris Clark, "What about New Zealand? The Problematic History," in *ANZAC Dirty Dozen: 12 Myths of Australian Military History*, ed. Craig Stockings (Sydney: University of New South Wales Press, 2012), 64–65. Until 1954, New Zealand guaranteed one infantry division and five RNZAF squadrons for the defense of Egypt, Suez, and the Persian Gulf. On this point, see James Waite, "Contesting 'the Right of Decision': New Zealand, the Commonwealth, and the New Look," *Diplomatic History* 30.5 (2006): 901.

10. Hack, *Defence and Decolonisation*, 79; and Lowe, *Menzies*, 76–80.

11. TNA: PREM 11/1148, Minutes of a Meeting held at 10 Downing Street, 14 July 1950.

12. Planning for the dispatch of forces to the Middle East began soon after Menzies assumed office. See NAA: A816 14/301/387, Note of Defence Committee Agendum No. 32/1950, Military Assistant Secretary, 30 May 1950.

13. TNA: PREM 11/1148, Minutes of a Meeting held at 10 Downing Street, 14 July 1950. For Menzies's reflection on this meeting, see Robert Menzies, *Afternoon Light: Some Memories of Men and Events* (London: Penguin, 1970), 141–42.

14. Catherine R. Schenk, *The Decline of Sterling: Managing the Retreat of an International Currency* (Cambridge: Cambridge University Press, 2010), 37.

15. Lee, *Search for Security*, 107–9, 135–36.

16. Rooth, "Imperial Self-Insufficiency," 29–51.

17. For the Menzies talks and Australian motivations see Cablegram from Spender to Menzies, 21 July 1950, in *Documents on Australian Foreign Policy: The 1951 ANZUS*

Treaty, vol. 17, doc. 11; Cablegram from Menzies to Spender, 22 July 1950, ibid., doc. 12; Cablegram from Spender to Menzies and Australian Delegation, United Nations, 26 July 1950, ibid., doc. 13; Cablegram from Menzies to Fadden, 3 August 1950, ibid., doc. 14; and Cablegram from Embassy in Washington to Spender, 3 August 1950, ibid., doc. 15. For the U.S. briefing material on the Menzies visit and the expectations from it, see Background Memoranda prepared in the Department of State, 24 July 1950, in RG 59 743.13/7, box 2450, NAII; Memorandum by the Assistant Secretary of State for European Affairs, Perkins, to the Secretary of State, 27 July 1950, in RG 59 743.13/7, box 2750, NAII; and Report prepared by the Department of State on the visit of Menzies, undated in RG59 743.138, box 750, NAII. For U.S. surprise that Menzies never raised the possibility of a security pact, see The Secretary of State to the Embassy in Australia, 3 August 1950, in FRUS 1950, vol. 6, 206–7.

18. Address of the Prime Minister of Australia to the House of Representatives of the United States Congress, 1 August 1950, in TNA: DO 35/3871010. U.S. concerns about both Australia's and New Zealand's commitment to the war can be found here: Memorandum by the Chief of Staff, U.S. Army for the Joint Chiefs of Staff: Problems to be discussed with the Australian Prime Minister, 24 August 1950, RG 218 Geographic File 1948–50 Australia, box 10, NAII.

19. Memorandum of Conversation, 28 July 1950, Acheson Papers, HSTL; and Memorandum of Conversation, 31 July 1950, ibid.

20. Cablegram from Menzies to Fadden, 3 August 1950, in *Documents on Australian Foreign Policy: The 1951 ANZUS Treaty*, vol. 17, doc. 14.

21. Martin, *Menzies*, 169–72. A good overview on Menzies planning can be found in David Lee, "The National Security Planning and Defence Preparations of the Menzies Government, 1950–1953," *War and Society* 10.2 (1992): 119–38.

22. TNA: PREM 8/1121, Note of a Conversation between the Prime Minister and Mr Spender, 4 September 1950.

23. Talk between Percy Spender and Dean Acheson, 18 September 1950, in RG 59 53D444, NAII.

24. Record of a Discussion with Mr John Foster Dulles 14 October 1950, contained in The Deputy Secretary of External Affairs to the Prime Minister, 27 October 1950, in *ANZUS Pact*, doc. 140, 409.

25. Leffler, *Preponderance of Power*, 391–93.

26. Report by the Joint Chiefs of Staff, Strategic Evaluation of United States Security Needs in Japan, 9 June 1949, in *FRUS 1949*, vol. 2, part 2, 774–77; quote at 777.

27. Memorandum for the Secretary of Defense, 18 May 1948, in File: Japan, President's Secretary Files, box 159, HSTL.

28. Report by the Joint Strategic Plans Committee to the Joint Chiefs of Staff on the impact of current Far Eastern Developments, 14 September 1949, in RG 218 Geographic File 1948–50, China, box 18, NAII.

29. Report by the Joint Chiefs of Staff, Strategic Evaluation of United States Security Needs in Japan, 9 June 1949, in *FRUS 1949*, vol. 2, part 2, 774.

30. Roger Dingman, "Strategic Planning and the Policy Process: American Plans for War in East Asia, 1945–1950," *U.S. Naval War College Review* 32.6 (1979): 4–21. For the JCS's specific concerns expressed in the text, see *FRUS 1949*, vol. 7, part 2, 774–77; and Memorandum of Conversation, 24 April 1950, Secretary of State Files, Acheson Papers, HSTL.

31. Robert Beisner, *Dean Acheson: A Life* (Oxford: Oxford University Press, 2006), 470–71. Even once the terms of the peace treaty had been secured, Acheson continued to emphasize to the president how important ratification was. As Acheson claimed, without the successful implementation of the peace treaty, it could not be assumed that a "satisfactory status quo" inside Japan could be maintained. See Memorandum for the President by Dean Acheson, 28 June 1951, in File: Japanese Peace Treaty, President's Secretary Files, box 159, HSTL.

32. Keith D. McFarland and David L. Roll, *Louis Johnson and the Arming of America: The Roosevelt and Truman Years* (Bloomington: Indiana University Press, 2005), 268–71; and Memorandum of Conversation, 24 April 1950, Secretary of State Files, Acheson Papers, HSTL.

33. MacArthur to the Defence Department in Washington D.C., 28 December 1950, in RG 218 Geographic File 1948–50, box 35, NAII.

34. Michael Schaller, *The American Occupation of Japan: The Origins of the Cold War in Asia* (Oxford: Oxford University Press, 1985), 142–69; Perret, *Old Soldiers*, 535; and Intelligence Estimate, Office of Intelligence and Research, 25 June 1950, in *FRUS 1950*, vol. 7, 151.

35. Howard Schonberger, "The Japan Lobby in American Diplomacy, 1947–1952," *Pacific Historical Review* 46.3 (1977): 327–59.

36. The final treaty saw this implemented with Japan having to pay no reparations to the victims of its aggression. Japan would, however, bilaterally agree with a number of states in the following decades to pay financial compensation. See Barrass, *Great Cold War*, 70.

37. Intelligence Estimate, Office of Intelligence and Research, 25 June 1950, in *FRUS 1950*, vol. 7, 151.

38. Membership included the Soviet Union, United Kingdom, United States, China, France, Netherlands, Canada, Australia, New Zealand, India, and the Philippine Commonwealth. On the commission itself, see Samuel S. Stratton, "The Far Eastern Commission," *International Organization* 2.1 (1948): 1–18.

39. Baxter, *Great Power Struggle*, 102.

40. Ibid., 169.

41. TNA: FO 371/93016, Bill Denning to the Foreign Office, 5 February 1951.

42. Peter Lowe, *Contending with Nationalism and Communism: British Policy towards Southeast Asia, 1945–65* (Basingstoke: Palgrave, 2009), 34–36.

43. The Ambassador in the United Kingdom to the Secretary of State, 4 June 1951, in *FRUS 1951*, vol. 6, part 1, 1105–6; and The Ambassador in the United Kingdom to the Secretary of State, 8 June 1951, ibid., 1109–10.

44. Cairncross, *British Economy*, 49, 79–80, 99–104. For an example of British complaints, see TNA: FO 371/76208, William Strang to Ernest Bevin, 27 February 1949.

45. Visit of Prime Minister Yoshida: South and Southeast Asian Economic Cooperation, 5 November 1954, in MCO74, folder 8, box 1, John Foster Dulles Papers, Mudd Manuscript Library, Princeton University, New Jersey (hereafter JFDP).

46. Extract from Minutes of the Commonwealth Meeting on Foreign Affairs, 11 January 1950, in *ANZUS Pact*, doc. 109, 297–309; quote at 299.

47. Talk between Percy Spender and Dean Acheson, 18 September 1950, in RG 59 53D444, NAII; The Acting High Commissioner for the United Kingdom, Wellington, to the Minister of External Affairs, 8 August 1949, in *ANZUS Pact*, doc. 96, 271; The

First Secretary, New Zealand, Washington, to the Secretary of External Affairs, 14 September 1949, in *ANZUS Pact*, doc. 102, 282; and The Deputy Secretary of External Affairs to the Official Secretary, Office of the High Commissioner for New Zealand, London, 18 April 1950, in *ANZUS Pact*, doc. 118, 340–48.

48. The British Commonwealth Conference, 26 August–2 September 1947 in *ANZUS Pact*, doc. 66, 174–94. See especially 177–79.

49. See the following: The Minister for External Affairs in Australia to the Prime Minister, 24 August 1947, in *ANZUS Pact*, doc. 61, 127–45; quote at 127.

50. Memorandum by the Department of External Affairs on the General Attitude to the Japanese Settlement, 11 August 1947, in *ANZUS Pact*, doc. 58, 95.

51. Memorandum of Conversation by the Secretary of State, 28 July 1950, RG 59 743.13/8-750, NAII; Memorandum of Conversation by the Secretary of State, 31 July 1950, RG 59 743.13/8-750, NAII; and The Secretary of State to the Embassy in Australia, 3 August 1950, in *FRUS 1950*, vol. 6, part 1, 204–7.

52. Record of a Discussion with Mr John Foster Dulles, 14 October 1950, contained in The Deputy Secretary of External Affairs to the Prime Minister, 27 October 1950, in *ANZUS Pact*, doc. 140, 409.

53. The Ambassador in the United Kingdom to the Secretary of State, 4 June 1951, in *FRUS 1951*, vol. 6, part 1, 1105–6; and The Ambassador in the United Kingdom to the Secretary of State, 8 June 1951, ibid., 1109–10.

54. Memorandum of Conversation, 4 February 1950, Secretary of State Files, Acheson Papers, HSTL.

55. The Secretary of State to the Secretary of Defense, 24 November 1950, in *FRUS 1950*, vol. 6, part 1, 225.

56. On connections between overseas security commitments and allies' economic policies during the Cold War, see Hubert Zimmermann, *Money and Security: Troops, Monetary Policy, and West Germany's Relations with the United States and Britain, 1950–1971* (Cambridge: Cambridge University Press, 2002), 103, 107, 140, 227; and Francis J. Gavin, *Gold, Dollars, and Power: The Politics of International Monetary Relations, 1958–1971* (Chapel Hill: University of North Carolina Press, 2007), 33–35, 64–67.

57. Department of State Policy Statement, 21 April 1950, in *FRUS 1950*, vol. 6, part 1, 189–90. Certainly this was the impression given by both Australian and New Zealand officials. See The New Zealand Ambassador, Washington, to the Minister of External Affairs, 25 April 1950, in *ANZUS Pact*, doc. 120, 350–52; and The Acting High Commissioner for New Zealand, London, to the Minister of External Affairs, 15 May 1950 in *ANZUS Pact*, doc. 125, 358.

58. Memorandum of Conversation by the Deputy to the Consultant (Allison), 18 January 1951, in *FRUS 1951*, vol. 6, part 1, 804.

59. Memorandum by the Secretary of State of a Meeting at the White House between the President and General Eisenhower, 18 November 1952, in *FRUS 1952–54*, vol. 1, part 1, 22–29.

60. On Eisenhower's concerns see Zelizer, *Arsenal of Democracy*, 124–36.

61. Memorandum of Conversation, 9 January 1951, Secretary of State Files, Acheson Papers, HSTL. This was a consistent position in New Zealand arguments about a Pacific security pact. For instance, Prime Minister Fraser noted in August 1949 that a Pacific security pact that did not include the "big powers" would "end

in nothing." See NZNA: R22228431 W2619 83 111 3/3/1, part 1, Memorandum, 5 August 1949.

62. Dulles and Dean Rusk, who was undersecretary of state for Far Eastern affairs at this stage of his career, were both advocates of a more comprehensive Asia-Pacific security pact. The Joint Chiefs of Staff were also coming around to the idea that the U.S. should enter into limited security pacts throughout Asia-Pacific. See Thomas Schoenbaum, *Waging Peace and War: Dean Rusk in the Truman, Kennedy, and Johnson Years* (London: Harper Collins, 1988), 226–29.

63. The Minister of External Affairs to the New Zealand Ambassador, Washington, 22 December 1950, in *ANZUS Pact*, doc. 143, 416–17; and The Counsellor, New Zealand Embassy, Washington, to the Secretary of External Affairs, 5 January 1951, in *ANZUS Pact*, doc. 146, 424–25.

64. Memorandum from R. Love to Robert G. Barnes, 5 June 1950, Secretary of State Files, Acheson Papers, HSTL.

65. For examples of this quid pro quo in U.S. thinking see Draft Letter to Mr Dulles [from Dean Acheson], attached in The Secretary of State to the Secretary of Defense (Marshall), 9 January 1951, in *FRUS 1951*, vol. 6, part 1, 789; Memorandum by Mr Robert A. Fearey of the Office of Northeast Asian Affairs, undated [January 1951], in *FRUS 1951*, vol. 6, 815; and Memorandum by the Consultant to the Secretary, 12 April 1951, in *FRUS 1951*, vol. 6, part 1, 976. Dean Rusk would make this linkage between an antipodean security alliance and Australia and New Zealand's agreement for a nonpunitive Japanese peace treaty publicly known. See J. G. Starke, *The ANZUS Treaty Alliance* (Melbourne: Melbourne University Press, 1965), 34. For examples of continuing trade and commercial disputes between Canberra, London, and Wellington with Washington see Memorandum of Conversation, 31 March 1950, Secretary of State Files, Acheson Papers, HSTL.

66. The New Zealand Ambassador, Washington, to the Minister of External Affairs, 19 January 1951, in *ANZUS Pact*, doc. 149, 438–39.

67. From the prime minister to Doidge in The New Zealand Ambassador, Washington, to the High Commissioner for New Zealand, Canberra, 9 February 1951, in *ANZUS Pact*, doc. 220, 585; and Memorandum of Conversation with Delegation from New Zealand, Elbert Mathews, and G. Hayden Raynor, 6 February 1951, Secretary of State Files, Memoranda of Conversations File, 1949–1953, File: February 1951, box 68, Acheson Papers, HSTL.

68. Memorandum of Conversation with Delegation from New Zealand, Elbert Mathews, and G. Hayden Raynor, 6 February 1951, Secretary of State Files, Memoranda of Conversations File, 1949–1953, File: February 1951, box 68, Acheson Papers, HSTL.

69. Devereux, *Formulation of British Defence Policy*, 88.

70. Memorandum of Conversation with Delegation from New Zealand, Elbert Mathews, and G. Hayden Raynor, 6 February 1951, Secretary of State Files, Acheson Papers, HSTL.

71. Ibid.

72. NAA: A4940, C228 Percy Spender Report to Cabinet, Pacific Defence Pact: Forthcoming Exploratory Talks with Mr John Foster Dulles, 15 February 1951.

73. Draft Letter to Mr Dulles [from Dean Acheson] attached in The Secretary of State to the Secretary of Defense (Marshall), 9 January 1951, in *FRUS 1951*, vol. 6,

part 1, 789. See also Hal Brands, *What Good Is Grand Strategy? Power and Purpose in American Statecraft from Harry S. Truman to George W. Bush* (Ithaca, NY: Cornell University Press, 2014), 52–53.

74. Notes of the Australian–New Zealand–United States Talks in Canberra, 15–17 February 1951, in *ANZUS PACT*, doc. 226, 593.

75. Ibid., 594.

76. Ibid., 601.

77. Notes of the Australian-New Zealand-United States Talks in Canberra, 15–17 February 1951, in *ANZUS PACT*, doc. 226, 597–98. Dulles's reluctance in creating the ANZUS Treaty therefore contrasts with claims of "pactomania" by his critics. On this point, see Matthew Jones, "A 'Segregated' Asia? Race, the Bandung Conference, and Pan-Asianist Fears in American Thought and Policy, 1954–1955," *Diplomatic History* 29.5 (2005): 851.

78. Notes of the Australian–New Zealand–United States Talks in Canberra, 15–17 February 1951, in *ANZUS PACT*, doc. 226, 598.

79. The ANZUS Treaty in full can be accessed here: ANZUS Treaty Text, Australian Politics, http://australianpolitics.com/topics/foreign-policy/anzus-treaty-text.

80. Nor was ANZUS a panacea for relations between the antipodean powers. Australia and New Zealand continued to disagree on a number of key strategic issues: Andrew Kelly, "Discordant Allies: Trans-Tasman Relations in the Aftermath of the ANZUS Treaty, 1951–1955," *Journal of Australian Studies* 41.1 (2017): 83, 95. On the wider objective of alliance building, see, for instance, Paul W. Schroder, "Alliances, 1815–1945: Weapons of Power and Tools of Management," in *Systems, Stability and Statecraft: Essays on the International History of Modern Europe*, ed. David Wetzel, Robert Jervis, and Jack S. Levy (Basingstoke: Palgrave Macmillan, 2004), 196, 202; and Cha, *Powerplay*, 19–20.

81. Minutes of a Meeting of the Chiefs of Staff Committee and Officers of the Department of External Affairs, 6 February 1951, in *ANZUS Pact*, doc. 209, 567.

82. Though it was accepted that the Soviet Union did not pose a "direct threat" to New Zealand. See ibid., 544.

83. The Minister of External Affairs to the New Zealand Ambassador, Washington, 9 May 1950, in *ANZUS Pact*, doc. 200, 546.

84. McGibbon, *New Zealand and the Korean War*, 1:287.

85. NZNA: R23447528 ABFK 19754 W5767 91 42 1/1 part 1, Minute by the Defence Committee, 8 February 1951.

86. See, for example, The New Zealand Commissioner, Washington, to the Minister of External Affairs, 1 June 1951, in *ANZUS Pact*, doc. 266, 723.

87. Memorandum of Conversation, 8 February 1951, in *FRUS 1951*, vol. 1, 149.

88. As reported to the New Zealand prime minister: The New Zealand Permanent Representative to the United Nations, to the Prime Minister, 18 March 1952, in *ANZUS Pact*, doc. 305, 779. On the reluctance of the chiefs, see NSC48/5, United States Objectives, Policies and Courses of Action in Asia, 17 May 1951, in *FRUS 1951*, vol. 6, part 1, 31–63.

89. Notes of the Australian-New Zealand-United States Talks in Canberra, 15–17 February 1951, in *ANZUS Pact*, doc. 226, 593. Spender also desired direct cooperation with NATO. See David Lowe, *Australia between Empires: The Life of Percy Spender* (London: Chatto & Windus, 2010), 125.

90. NZNA: R17722424 ABHS 950 W5422 14 111/3/5 part 5, Ambassador to Minister, 1 June 1951; ibid., Minutes of a Meeting between Spender, McNicol, Corner, Dulles, and Totara in Washington within Washington to Wellington, 1 June 1951; and ibid., Pacific Security Pact: Background of Negotiations, Note by Department of External Affairs, 23 May 1951.

91. For the draft version of the ANZUS Treaty see Security Treaty with Australia and New Zealand, Memorandum for the President from Dean Acheson, 10 July 1951, in File: Australia, President's Secretary Files, HSTL.

92. Lowe, *Australia between Empires*, 124–25.

93. The New Zealand Ambassador, Washington, to the Minister of External Affairs, 14 March 1950, in *ANZUS Pact*, doc. 198, 522–36; quotes at 523, 524.

94. Report by the Joint Planning Committee: The Defence of the Pacific-Strategic Background and Examination of the Military Requirements for a Pacific Defence Pact: The Assistant Secretary, Chiefs of Staff Committee to the Secretary of External Affairs, 28 April 1950, in *ANZUS Pact*, 538. For a broader discussion on New Zealand elite attitudes toward the Soviet Union, see A. C. Wilson, *New Zealand and the Soviet Union, 1950–1991: A Brittle Relationship* (Wellington: Victoria University Press, 2004).

95. NZNA: R20821655 AAFD 811 W2347 148 I CAB 233/6/1, Proposed Pacific Pact to Accompany a Japanese Peace Treaty, JPC (51) 3, Note by the Secretary, 7 February 1951.

96. Lowe, *Menzies*, 26; and Department of State, Policy Statement, 21 April 1950, in *FRUS 1950*, vol. 6, part 1, 189–90. On U.S. efforts to bring down the system of imperial preference during and after World War II, and British resistance, see Louis, *Imperialism at Bay*, 42; and Richard Toye, "The Attlee Government, the Imperial Preference System and the Creation of the Gatt," *English Historical Review* 118.478 (2003): 912–39.

97. Department of State, Policy Statement: Australia, 21 April 1950, in *FRUS 1950*, vol. 6, part 1, 193.

98. Ibid.

99. Notes of a Cabinet Discussion, 22 March 1951, in *ANZUS Pact*, doc. 240, 673.

100. Leffler, *Preponderance of Power*, 14.

101. Notes of the Australian-New Zealand-United States Talks in Canberra, 15–17 February 1951, in *ANZUS Pact*, doc. 226, 609. On the obvious discomfort that Philippine membership created in Australian and New Zealand policy-making circles, see The Minister of External Affairs to the New Zealand Ambassador, Washington, 21 February 1951, in *ANZUS Pact*, doc. 230, 624; and Notes on Discussions held in the Department of External Affairs, 19 March 1951, in *ANZUS Pact*, doc. 237, 662–63.

102. Meg Gurry, "Leadership and Bilateral Relations: Menzies and Nehru, Australia and India, 1949–1964," *Pacific Affairs* 65.4 (1992–93): 510–26.

103. Report by the Joint Planning Committee, 28 April 1950, in *ANZUS Pact*, doc. 199, 538–43.

104. Background Papers for the Australia–New Zealand–United States (ANZUS) Council Preparations, 24 July 1952, Secretary of State Files, Acheson papers, HSTL.

105. NZNA: R23447528 ABFK 19754 W5767 91 42 1/1 part 1, For Doidge from Spender, 16 April 1951.

106. Notes of Discussions held in the Department of External Affairs, 19 March 1951, in *ANZUS Pact*, doc. 237, 663.

107. For a more detailed discussion of the Japanese peace treaty, see Matthew Jones, *After Hiroshima: The United States, Race and Nuclear Weapons in Asia, 1945–1965* (Cambridge: Cambridge University Press, 2010), 117–30.

108. See British complaints about Japanese economic revival to Washington here: Memorandum of Conversation, 7 March 1950, Secretary of State Files, Acheson Papers, HSTL.

109. A point Dulles emphasized in his talks: Notes of the Australian-New Zealand-United States Talks in Canberra, 15–17 February 1951, in *ANZUS Pact*, doc. 226, 602.

110. NZNA: R17722632 ABHS 950 W5422 32 111 3/3/9 part 1, Japanese Peace Treaty and Pacific Security Pact, 1 April 1951.

111. McIntosh to Berendsen, 16 March 1951, in McGibbon, *Undiplomatic Dialogue*, 255.

112. Rusk quoted in NZNA: R23447528 ABFK 19754 W5767 91 42 1/1 part 1, From the New Zealand Ambassador, Washington to the Minister of External Affairs, Wellington, Tel 123, 13 April 1951. The British ambassador, Oliver Franks, had told both Spender and Berendsen that the British government preferred a tripartite agreement and for the Philippines to be provided a security arrangement with Washington "in another way." See NZNA: R23447528 ABFK 19754 W5767 91 42 1/1 part 1, From the New Zealand Ambassador, Washington to the Minister of External Affairs, Wellington, Tel. 106, 6 April 1951.

113. For Dulles's expression that British exclusion from an Asia-Pacific alliance prevented a broader alliance being created, see Notes of the Australian–New Zealand–United States Talks in Canberra, 15–17 February 1951, in *ANZUS Pact*, doc. 226, 602. For British complaints, see The Assistant Secretary, Chiefs of Staff Committee to the Secretary of External Affairs, 28 April 1950, in *ANZUS Pact*, doc. 199, 537; Editorial Note of Meeting held on 29 January 1951, in *FRUS 1951*, vol. 6, part 1, 826; and Memorandum by Allison of a Conversation on the Japanese Peace Settlement between Franks and Graves of the British Embassy with Dulles, Babcock and Allison, 12 January 1951, in RG 59 694.001/1-1251, NAII.

114. Mention of British opposition to Filipino membership is referenced here: Summary of a Meeting of Commonwealth Defence Ministers, London, June 1951, in NZNA: R17722424 ABHS 950 W5422 14 111/3/5 part 5; and Note from Department of External Affairs, 30 May 1951, in NZNA: R17722424 ABHS 950 W5422 14 111/3/5 part 5.

115. See the following paper that articulates UK strategic thinking: *Documents on British Policy Overseas*, 2nd series, vol. 4, *Korea 1950–51* (London: Her Majesty's Stationery Office, 1991), 411–31.

116. Position paper prepared in the Department of State: The Military Role of Australia and New Zealand, 29 December 1951, in *FRUS 1952–1954*, vol. 12, part 1, 1–3.

117. Memorandum by Secretary of State for Commonwealth Relations, 2 October 1950, box 1/9, Patrick Gordon Walker Papers, Churchill Archive, Cambridge University, United Kingdom (hereafter GNWR).

118. The High Commissioner for the United Kingdom to the Acting Secretary of External Affairs, 2 February 1951, in *ANZUS Pact*, doc. 210, 570.

119. Martin, *Menzies*, 168.

120. Notes of the Australian-New Zealand-United States Talks in Canberra, 15–17 February 1951, in *ANZUS Pact*, doc. 226, 604; NAA: A4940, C228, Percy Spender Report to Cabinet, 15 February 1951; for Holland from Menzies within The Minister for External Affairs in Australia to the Minister of External Affairs, 16 March 1951, in *ANZUS Pact*, doc. 236, 660–61; and Spender to Dulles, 8 March 1951, in MS 4875, file 5, box 1, Percy Spender Papers, National Library of Australia, Canberra, Australia (hereafter PSP).

121. Notes on conversations between Dulles, Spender, and Doidge, 16 and 17 February 1951, in RG 59 54D 423, NAII; Spender to Dulles, 8 March 1951, MS 4875 box 1, file 5, PSP.

122. NZNA: R17722424 ABHS 950 W5422 14 111/3/5, Note from Department of External Affairs, 30 May 1951.

123. NZNA: R722424 ABHS 950 W5422 14 111/3/5, Note by Doidge, 10 May 1951.

124. Memorandum by Satterthwaite to Thompson, 8 February 1950, in *FRUS 1950*, vol. 1, 144.

125. TNA: CAB 129/44 CP(51)64, Pacific Defence, 27 February 1951.

126. On the broader point, see Ronald Hyam, *Britain's Declining Empire: The Road to Decolonisation, 1918–1968* (Cambridge: Cambridge University Press, 2007), 162–67. For a specific example, see U.S.-UK discussion on present world situation, 20–24 July 1950 in File: Joint Chiefs of Staff, President's Secretary's Files, box 107, HSTL.

127. Editorial Note of Meeting held on 29 January 1951, in *FRUS 1951*, vol. 6, part 1, 826.

128. Editorial Note, 8 May 1951, in *FRUS 1951*, vol. 6, part 1, 1040.

129. NZNA: R17722424 ABHS 950 W5422 14 111/3/5, Casey to Doidge, 30 June 1951.

130. On the importance the British attached to Asia-Pacific affairs in general for maintaining this ambition of appearing as a "world power," see Christopher Baxter, "The Foreign Office and Post-war Planning for East Asia, 1944–45," *Contemporary British History* 21.2 (2007): 149–72.

131. For example, TNA: DO 35/2927 Gascoigne to Foreign Office, 7 February 1951; The High Commissioner for the United Kingdom to the Acting Secretary of External Affairs, 2 February 1951, in *ANZUS Pact*, doc. 210, 570; and The High Commissioner for New Zealand, Canberra, to the Minister of External Affairs, 5 February 1951, in *ANZUS Pact*, doc. 212, 572.

132. Such reports are in NZNA: R17722424 ABHS 950 W5422 14 111/3/5 part 5, Memorandum for Australian Embassy, Washington, 17 May 1951.

133. NZNA: R17722424 ABHS 950 W5422 14 111/3/5 part 5, Canberra to Wellington, 26 June 1951.

134. Quoted in *Evening Post* extract, 10 July 1951, in NZNA: R17722424 ABHS 950 W5422 14 111/3/5 part 5.

135. Schenk, *Decline of Sterling*, 122–23. For broader overviews on these developments, see Singleton and Robertson, *Economic Relations between Britain and Australasia*; and Noriko Yokoi, *Japan's Postwar Economic Recovery and Anglo-Japanese Relations, 1948–62* (London: Routledge, 2003).

136. John Williams, "ANZUS: A Blow to Britain's Self-Esteem," *Review of International Studies* 13.4 (1987): 243–63; and Steve Marsh, "Anglo-American Relations 1950–1: Three Strikes for British Prestige," *Diplomacy and Statecraft* 23.2 (2012): 304–30.

4. Selective Membership

1. On Britain's improving economic position, see Roger Middleton, *The British Economy since 1945* (Basingstoke: Macmillan, 2000), 71–74, 86–87.

2. Lanxin Xiang, "The Recognition Controversy: Anglo-American Relations in China, 1949," *Journal of Contemporary History* 27.2 (1992): 337.

3. Michael Hopkins, *Oliver Franks and the Truman Administration: Anglo-American Relations, 1948–1952* (London: Routledge, 2002), 145.

4. McGibbon, "Defence of New Zealand," 163–64.

5. Beisner, *Dean Acheson*, 502; and Roger Buckley, *U.S.-Japan Alliance Diplomacy, 1945–1990* (Cambridge: Cambridge University Press, 1992), 12–43. On U.S.-Indian difficulties see Robert J. McMahon, *Cold War on the Periphery: The United States, India, and Pakistan* (New York: Columbia University Press, 1994), 82–84; Paul McGarr, *The Cold War in South Asia: Britain, the United States and the Indian Subcontinent, 1945–1965* (Cambridge: Cambridge University Press, 2013), 31–33.

6. Preston, *Sword of the Spirit*, 454–55; and Thomas Borstelmann, *The Cold War and the Color Line: American Race Relations in the Global Arena* (Cambridge, MA: Harvard University Press, 2001), 41.

7. Memorandum of Conversation by the Special Assistant to the Consultant (Allison), 12 January 1951, in *FRUS 1951*, vol. 6, part 1, 794; and Dulles Memorandum for Rusk, 22 October 1951, ibid., 1381–82.

8. Memorandum of Conversation, 10 March 1950, Secretary of State Files, Acheson Papers, HSTL.

9. Memorandum of Conversation, 9 January 1951, Secretary of State Files, Acheson Papers, HSTL.

10. Mentioned in NZNA: R17722424 ABHS 950 W5422 14 111/3/5 part 5, Memorandum for Secretary of External Affairs, 23 April 1951.

11. Ben Limb, "The Pacific Pact: Looking Forward or Backward?," *Foreign Affairs* 29.4 (1951): 539–49.

12. Memorandum of Conversation, 9 January 1951, Secretary of State Files, Acheson Papers, HSTL.

13. Beisner, *Dean Acheson*, 637–40.

14. Memorandum by the Regional Planning Adviser (Ogburn) to the Assistant Secretary of State for Far Eastern Affairs (Allison), 21 January 1953, in *FRUS 1952–1954*, vol. 12, part 1, 260.

15. The Minister of External Affairs to the High Commissioner for the United Kingdom, 12 March 1951, in *ANZUS Pact*, doc. 234, 657. For further discussion on this, see Srdjan Vuceti, *The Anglosphere: A Genealogy of a Racialized Identity in International Relations* (Stanford, CA: Stanford University Press, 2012), 61–62.

16. Background Papers for the Australia–New Zealand–United States (ANZUS) Council Preparations, 24 July 1952, Secretary of State Files, Acheson Papers, HSTL.

17. Gwenda Tavan, *The Long, Slow Death of White Australia* (London: Scribe, 2005); and Neville Meaney, "The End of 'White Australia' and Australia's Changing Perceptions of Asia, 1945–1990," *Australian Journal of International Affairs* 49.20 (1995): 171–89.

18. Zelizer, *Arsenal of Democracy*, 126–34.

19. Cardwell, *NSC 68*, 218–22.

20. Memorandum for the President, January 1952, in File: Churchill, Winston: Truman Talks, President's Secretary's Files, box 100, HSTL. On the broader idea that U.S. and British resources had to prioritize other areas, see Memorandum on the Substance of Discussions at a Department of State–Joint Chiefs of Staff Meeting, 16 January 1952, in *FRUS 1952–1954*, vol. 12, part 1, 22–34; Memorandum by the Director of the Policy Planning Staff (Nitze), 5 March 1952, in *FRUS 1952–1954*, vol. 12, part 1, 68; and Memorandum on the Substance of Discussions at a Department of State–Joint Chiefs Staff Meeting, 5 March 1952, in *FRUS 1952–1954*, vol. 12, part 1, 55–68.

21. Negotiating Paper: European Integration, Memorandum for the President, 30 December 1951, in File: Churchill, Winston: Truman Meetings 100–2, President's Secretary's Files, box 100, HSTL. For similar views see, for instance, Report by the NSC, 14 February 1950, in File: Report: Effect of British Decline, National Security Council File, box 13, HSTL.

22. Negotiating Paper: Malaya, 2 January 1952, in File: Churchill, Winston: Truman Talks, Papers prepared by the Far East Division, President's Secretary's Files, box 100, HSTL.

23. Memorandum for the Secretary of Defense, 17 April 1951, in *FRUS 1951*, vol. 6, part 1, 992; and Memorandum by the Joint Chiefs of Staff to the Secretary of Defense (Lovett), 28 December 1951, in *FRUS 1952–1954*, vol. 12, part 1, 4–7.

24. Cablegram from External Affairs Office, 13 March 1951, in *Documents on Australian Foreign Policy, the 1951 ANZUS Treaty*, vol. 17, doc. 60.

25. Memorandum of meeting, 2 April 1951, Secretary of State Files, Acheson Papers, HSTL.

26. Rhiannon Vickers, *The Labour Party and the World: Evolution of Labour's Foreign Policy, 1900–51* (Manchester: Manchester University Press, 2004), 159–91.

27. Churchill quoted in Clarke, *Last Thousand Days*, 464.

28. For a good example of how "emotion" impacted Churchill's foreign policy and helped contribute to the outbreak of the Cold War, see Costigliola, *Roosevelt's Lost Alliances*, 88–89, 359–69.

29. Lord Moran, *Winston Churchill*, 228.

30. Louis, *Imperialism at Bay*, 14.

31. Clarke, *Last Thousand Days*, 5.

32. On Churchill emphasizing the importance of the Middle East and Western Europe, see Klaus Larres, *Churchill's Cold War: The Politics of Personal Diplomacy* (New Haven, CT: Yale University Press, 2001), 156–64.

33. Churchill to the Foreign Secretary, 16 November 1951, FO 800/780, M/53/51, the Papers of Sir Anthony Eden, Cadbury Research Library, Birmingham University, United Kingdom (hereafter Avon Papers).

34. Churchill to the President, 29 June 1952, in File: Churchill, Winston: Chronological, President's Secretary's Files, box 99, HSTL.

35. Larres, *Churchill's Cold War*, 156–60.

36. Soon after retaking office, Churchill suggested to Washington that London, Paris, and Washington needed to enter into discussions on how to defend Southeast Asia. For mention of this, see Negotiating Paper: Defense of Southeast Asia, 2 January 1952, in File: Churchill, Winston: Truman Meeting, 100–3, President's Secretary's Files, box 100, HSTL.

37. An example of Churchill's concerns about the United States can be found in Churchill to the Foreign Secretary, 16 November 1951, FO 800/780, M/53/51, Avon Papers.

38. D. R. Thorpe, *Eden: The Life and Times of Anthony Eden, First Earl of Avon, 1897–1977* (London: Chatto & Windus, 2003), 363; and R. A. Butler, *The Art of the Possible* (London: Hamilton, 1983), 223.

39. Chalmers, *Paying for Defence*, 54–56; and Cairncross, *British Economy*, 90–104.

40. Rooth, "Australia, Canada, and the International Economy," 127–33.

41. Richard Aldrich, *GCHQ: The Uncensored Story of Britain's Most Secret Intelligence Agency* (London: Harper, 2010), 89–90.

42. Acheson, *Present at the Creation*, 595.

43. Paper prepared by Deputy Director of the Policy Planning Staff, 8 February 1951, in *FRUS 1951*, vol. 1, 45.

44. Truman, *Memoirs: Years of Trial and Hope*, 259; John W. Young, *Winston Churchill's Last Campaign: Britain and the Cold War 1951–1955* (Oxford: Clarendon, 1996); and Larres, *Churchill's Cold War*, 167–70. The minutes of the meetings can be followed in Meeting of the President with Prime Minister Churchill, 7 January 1952, 11.00 a.m. in File: Churchill, Winston: Chronological, President's Secretary's Files, box 99, HSTL; Meeting of the President with Prime Minister Churchill, 7 January 1952, 5.00 p.m. in File: Meeting of the President with Prime Minister Churchill, National Security Council File, box 13, HSTL; Meeting of the President with Prime Minister Churchill, 7 January 1952, 8.00 p.m. in File: Meeting of the President with Prime Minister Churchill, National Security Council File, box 13, HSTL; and Meeting of the President with Prime Minister Churchill, 18 January 1952, in File: Churchill, Winston: Chronological, President's Secretary's Files, box 99, HSTL.

45. Steering Group briefing memorandum, 5 January 1952, in File: Churchill, Winston: Truman Meetings, President's Secretary's Files, box 100, HSTL.

46. Memorandum of Dinner Meeting between President Harry S. Truman and Prime Minister Winston Churchill, 6 January 1952, Secretary of State Files, Acheson Papers, HSTL.

47. Memorandum of Dinner Meeting between President Harry S. Truman and Prime Minister Winston Churchill, 6 January 1952, Secretary of State Files, Acheson Papers, HSTL. For the briefing material the president received and how it emphasized the need to reject Churchill's plans, see Negotiating Paper: Defense of Southeast Asia, 2 January 1952, in File: Churchill, Winston: Truman Meeting, 100–3, President's Secretary's Files, box 100, HSTL; and Negotiating Paper: A Pacific Security Pact, 2 January 1952, in File: Churchill Winston: Truman Meeting, 100–3, President's Secretary's Files, box 100, HSTL.

48. MS.Macmillan.dec.c.14, 27 September 1952, Harold Macmillan Papers, Bodleian Library, Oxford University.

49. For an indication that policymakers in Canberra and Wellington wanted to incorporate ANZUS and ANZAM planning, see, for instance, NZNA: R18872701 ACIE 8798 EA1 99 156 2/4/1, part 1, From the Minister of External Affairs, Wellington, to the New Zealand Ambassador, Washington, Tel. No. 133, 22 May 1952; and NZNA: R18872701 ACIE 8798 EA1 99 156 2/4/1, part 1, Notes of a Discussion with Australian Officials: Tripartite Security Treaty, 5 May 1952.

50. Larres, *Churchill's Cold War*, 218.

51. NAA: A 1631/3, Report of Joint Planning Committee, 3 April 1952.

52. The Prime Minister to the New Zealand Ambassador, Washington, 15 April 1952, in *ANZUS Pact*, doc. 309, 785.

53. For the longer-term ambition of securing British and U.S. security cooperation, see The Official Secretary, Office of the High Commissioner for New Zealand, Canberra, to the Secretary of External Affairs, 27 October 1950, in *ANZUS Pact*, doc. 202, 549–50; Notes on Defence Aspects of the Japanese Peace Settlement, 31 January 1951, in *ANZUS Pact*, doc. 208, 558–63; and Minutes of a Meeting of the Chiefs of Staff Committee and Officers of the Department of External Affairs, 6 February 1951, in *ANZUS Pact*, doc. 209, 564–69.

54. Menzies's position is detailed throughout NAA: A5954, 1424/3, Memorandum of Australian Government's Observations of United Kingdom Chiefs of Staff Memorandum COS (52) 685, attached to Prime Minister to High Commissioner, 27 March 1953.

55. For detailed documentation on ANZAM planning, see NAA: A5954, 1626/4, Strategic Planning in relation to Co-operation in British Commonwealth Defence, attached to Minute by Defence Committee at Meeting Held on Thursday, 8 June 1950; and NAA: A2031/147/1951 Strategic Concept for the Defence of ANZAM Region, 31 May 1951. For Australian thinking that it was essential to avoid replicating planning within ANZAM and ANZUS, see NAA: A5954, 1424/3, Memorandum of Australian Government's Observations of United Kingdom Chiefs of Staff Memorandum COS (52) 685, attached to Prime Minister to High Commissioner, 27 March 1953; and NAA: A5954 1420/2, Special Comments on Attached Paper on Machinery for Australian-United States Defence Co-operation, by Sir Frederick Shedden, 15 August 1952. For Australian opinion that ANZUS was complicating defense planning within the ANZAM context, see NAA: A1631/3, Report of Joint Planning Committee, 3 April 1952.

56. NAA: A2031/147/1951 Strategic Concept for the Defence of ANZAM Region, 31 May 1951.

57. NAA: A10299, A15, Spender to Casey, 18 March 1952, attached to B. Townsend to Mr Loveday, 9 July 1952; and The New Zealand Permanent Representative to the United Nations, New York, to the Minister of External Affairs, 17 March 1952, in *ANZUS Pact*, doc. 303, 776–77.

58. NZNA: R18872701 ACIE 8798 EA1 99 156 2/4/1, part 1, Minister of External Affairs Canberra [Casey] to the Minister of External Affairs, Wellington, Tel. No. 54, 19 June 1952; and NZNA R18872701 ACIE 8798 EA1 99 156 2/4/1, part 1, From the Minister of External Affairs, Wellington, to the New Zealand Ambassador, Washington, Tel. No. 133, 22 May 1952.

59. Memorandum of Conversation, 20 May 1952, Secretary of State Files, Acheson Papers, HSTL.

60. Memorandum of Conversation by the Secretary of State, 20 June 1952, in *FRUS 1952–1954*, vol. 12, part 1, 117–18; and Memorandum of Conversation, 20 June 1952, Secretary of State Files, Acheson Papers, HSTL.

61. Menzies, *Afternoon Light*, 140–41; and Memorandum of Conversation by the Secretary of State, 20 June 1952, in *FRUS 1952–1954*, vol. 12, part 1, 118–19.

62. Memorandum of Conversation, 20 May 1952, Secretary of State Files, Acheson Papers, HSTL.

63. Ibid.

64. The Acting Secretary of State to the Embassy in Australia, 24 May 1952, in *FRUS 1952–1954*, vol. 12, part 1, 93.

65. Follow the documentation in NAA: A816 58/301/454.

66. There were other tensions. Menzies's government had imposed import restrictions on a number of products, which had done considerable damage to British manufacturers. Representatives from the Federation of British Industries and from the Lancashire Cotton Mills lobbied Menzies to change Australia's tariff policies during his visit to England. See Martin, *Menzies*, 206–7.

67. See the discussion between Oliver Franks and Acheson: Memorandum of Conversation, 6 June 1952, Secretary of State Files, Acheson Papers, HSTL.

68. Negotiating Paper: The Military Role of Australia and New Zealand, 29 December 1951, in File: Churchill, Winston: Truman Talks, Papers provided by the Far East Division, President's Secretary's Files, box 100, HSTL.

69. NZNA: R17722424 ABHS 950 W5422 14 111/3/5, part 5, Summary of a Meeting of Commonwealth Defence Ministers, London, June 1951.

70. Devereux, *Formulation of British Defence Policy*, 92; and Lowe, *Menzies*, 152.

71. United States Minute of Bipartite Foreign Ministers Meeting with the United Kingdom, 26 May 1952, in *FRUS 1952–1954*, vol. 12, part 1, 96–97; and Memorandum of Conversation, 17 June 1952, Secretary of State Files, Acheson Papers, HSTL.

72. TNA: CAB/129/53 C(52) 202, Memorandum by Anthony Eden to Cabinet, 18 June 1952.

73. NZNA: R17722504 ABHS 950 W5422 33 111/3/3/15, part 1, London to Wellington, 11 June 1952.

74. NZNA: R17722504 ABHS 950 W5422 33 111/3/3/15, part 1, Minutes of Anzus Council Meeting, 13 August 1952.

75. Quote in NAA: A5954 1419/18, Personal for the Prime Minister and the Minister of Defence from Casey, 4 August 1952. Further breakdown of the talks on 5 August are provided in NAA: A5954 1419/18, Personal for the Prime Minister and the Minister of Defence from Casey, 5 August 1952; U.S. Minutes of First ANZUS Council, First Session, 4 August 1952, *FRUS 1952–1954*, vol. 12, part 1, 172–78, 194–201, 242–56.

76. Memorandum of Conversation, 15 April 1952, Secretary of State Files, Acheson Papers, HSTL; Memorandum of Conversation, 19 June 1952, Secretary of State Files, Acheson Papers, HSTL; and Memorandum of Conversation, 20 May 1952, Secretary of State Files, Acheson Papers, HSTL.

77. NZNA: R17722504 ABHS 950 W5422/33/111, ANZUS Council Meeting, Honolulu, August 1952: Report to the Cabinet.

78. The Secretary of State to the Secretary of Defense, 4 April 1952, in *FRUS 1952–1954*, vol. 12, part 1, 75; and Memorandum on the Substance of Discussions, 23 April 1952, in *FRUS 1952–1954*, vol. 12, part 1, 80–85.

79. Reported in NAA: A5954 1419/18 Personal for the Prime Minister and the Minister of Defence from Casey, 4 August 1952. On January 21, 1952, almost a year after ANZUS was agreed, General Omar Bradley, chairman of the JCS, appeared before the Foreign Relations Committee of the Senate to testify on the Japanese

peace treaty and the other treaties relating to security in the Pacific. Asked for Australia's and New Zealand's views concerning their security "as growing out of the present provisions of the treaty," he responded: "I do not know their views because I have not talked to them." See *Congressional Record*—Senate, March 20, 1952.

80. Munro met with Acheson and he pitched the idea that ANZUS should have a military chief stationed in Washington. For the record of the discussion, see Memorandum of Conversation, 19 June 1952, Secretary of State Files, Acheson Papers, HSTL.

81. For the quote, see NZNA: R22228450 ACIE 8798 W2691 84 111 3/3/30, part 1, From the Minister of External Affairs, Wellington, to the High Commissioner for New Zealand, London, Tel. 1311, 29 November 1952. For further internal analysis of the talks, see NAA: A5954 1419/18, For the Prime Minister and the Minister of Defence from Casey, 7 August 1952. Also see his full explanation about the nature of the talks with Acheson and Admiral Radford here: NAA: A5954 1419/18, For the Prime Minister and the Minister of Defence from Casey, 5 August 1952.

82. NZNA: ABHS W5422 950, box 33, Minute of Webb's report on the ANZUS Council of August 1952.

83. NZNA: ABHS W5422 950, box 33, Minute of Webb's report on the ANZUS Council of August 1952.

84. NZNA: R17722504 ABHS 950 W5422/33/111, ANZUS Council Meeting, Honolulu, August 1952: Report to the Cabinet.

85. NAA: A5954 1419/18, For the Prime Minister and the Minister of Defence from Casey, 7 August 1952.

86. As reported in NAA: A5954 1419/18, For the Prime Minister and the Minister of Defence from Casey, 7 August 1952; and NZNA: ABHS W5422950, box 33, Minute of Webb's report on the ANZUS Council of August 1952.

87. Acheson News Conference Speech, 12 August 1952, Department of State, *Bulletin.*

88. Casey gave the misleading public statement at the end of the conference that the existing ANZUS "machinery" would prove "sufficient and effective." No mention was made of the fact that both he and the New Zealand delegation had pressed for increased levels of cooperation during the discussions. See NZNA: R17722504 ABHS 950 W5422/33/111, Statement by the Right Hon. R. G. Casey, 10 August 1952.

89. TNA: FO 371/101239, From Washington to the Foreign Office, Tel. 906, 2 September 1952; and TNA: PREM 11/403, From Washington to Foreign Office, Tel. 906, 5 September 1952.

90. Casey explained the situation in some detail to Anthony Eden. See NAA: A5954 1419/18, For Eden from Casey, 7 August 1952.

91. TNA: FO 371 101239 WSC [Churchill] to the Foreign Secretary [Eden], 30 August 1952.

92. NZNA: R18872701 ACIE 8798 EA1 99 156 2/4/1, part 1, From the High Commission for New Zealand, London, to the Minister of External Affairs, Tel. No. 1050, 30 September 1952.

93. Ibid.

94. Salisbury quoted in TNA: PREM 11/403 Salisbury to the Prime Minister, 2 October 1952. Also see TNA: PREM 11/403 Lord Salisbury to Anthony Eden, 25 September 1952.

95. McGrigor quoted in NAA: A10299, A15, The High Commissioner to Australia to Richard Casey, 13 February 1953.

96. TNA: FO 371/101239, Minute on the ANZUS Council, 14 August 1952.

97. Clark, "What about New Zealand?," 64–65.

98. NAA: A5954, 1631/3, NAA, Report of Joint Planning Committee at Meeting Held on Thursday, 3 April 1952.

99. For evidence of U.S. suggestions that Australia and New Zealand should focus on regional security, see NZNA: R18872701 ACIE 8798 EA1 99 156 2/4/1, part 1, From the Minister of External Affairs, Wellington, to the New Zealand Ambassador, Washington, Tel. No. 133, 22 May 1952. NZNA: R17722505 ABHS 950 W5422/33/1111/3/3/15, part 2, First Meeting of the Military Representatives to the ANZUS Council, 22–25 September 1953, Paper: Recognition of the status of the ANZAM region as a possible theatre of war: Paper prepared by Australian Military Representative.

100. Report by the Joint Strategic Survey Committee to the Joint Chiefs of Staff on the problems to be discussed with the Australian Prime Minister, 28 July 1950, in RG 218 Geographic File 1948–50 Australia, box 10, NAII.

101. Logevall, *Embers of War*, 291–92.

102. NAA: A5954 1420/2, Special Comments by Sir Frederick Shedden, 15 August 1952; NAA: A5954 1420/2, Machinery for Australia-United States defence Co-operation, 15 August 1952; and Report by the Staff Planners, 25 November 1952, in *FRUS 1952–1954*, vol. 12, part 1, 242–56.

103. Lee, *Search for Security*, 120–21; and NAA, CRS, A1209/23, 57/5055, Minutes of meeting held in Cabinet room, 7 May 1952. The Australian commitment included one division available for the deployment to the Middle East at the outbreak of war. An additional two divisions would be made available for deployment within nine months of the outbreak of war. The RAAF squadron would become immediately available for service in the Middle East theater, but the decision to actually utilize this airpower would occur only after war had commenced.

104. NZNA: R17722504 ABHS 950 W5422/33/111, Report to the Cabinet, August 1952.

105. NAA: A10299, A15, Casey to Lord Beaverbrook, 16 December 1952.

106. NAA: A10299, A15, House of Representatives (Australia) Questions without Notice, 8 October 1952.

107. NZNA: R17722505 ABHS 950 W5422/33/1111/3/3/15, part 2, Clifton Webb to R. Heydon, 14 December 1953; and McKinnon, *Independence*, 11, 123.

108. NAA: A5461 1/4/2A, part 2, Casey to Eden, 29 September 1952.

109. NZNA: R20821655 AAFD 811 W2347 148 I CAB 233/6/1, Note of a discussion in Cabinet, 30 September 1952.

110. NZNA: R20821655 AAFD 811 W2347 148 I CAB 233/6/1, Note for the File: ANZUS, 13 October 1952.

111. Ibid.

112. McGibbon, *New Zealand and the Korean War*, 1:32.

113. TNA: FO 371/101242 ANZUS Minute, 19 November 1952.

114. Ibid.

115. NAA: A5954, 1424/3, Minutes of a Meeting, 12 December 1952.

116. Memorandum of Conversation, 20 June 1952, Secretary of State Files, Acheson Papers, HSTL; and Memorandum of Conversation, 11 November 1952, ibid.

117. NZNA: R18872701 ACIE 8798 EA1 99 156 2/4/1, part 1, From the High Commission for New Zealand, London, to the Minister of External Affairs, Tel. No. 1050, 30 September 1952.

118. NAA: A5461 1/4/2A, part 2, From High Commissioners Office in London to Department of External Affairs, Canberra, 8 October 1952; and Message from Sidney Holland to Canberra in NAA: A5461 1/4/2A, part 2, The New Zealand Ambassador in Washington to Canberra, 8 October 1952.

119. Memorandum by the United States Member of the Five-Power Ad Hoc Committee on Southeast Asia (Davies) to the Joint Chiefs of Staff, 5 February 1952, in *FRUS 1952–1954*, vol. 12, part 1, 36–39.

120. Review of the Current World Situation and ability of the forces being maintained to meet U.S. commitments, undated, File: Joint Chiefs of Staff, President's Secretary's Files, box 107, HSTL.

121. See Acheson's comments here: Memorandum of Conversation, 28 May 1951, Secretary of State Files, Acheson Papers, HSTL.

122. Note of a Tripartite Military Conversation on Southeast Asia by the Secretary (Lalor) and Deputy Secretary (Carns) of the Joint Chiefs of Staff, 11 January 1952, in *FRUS 1952–1954*, vol. 12, part 1, 8–22. Also see Report to the National Security Council by the Executive Secretary: United States Objectives and Courses of Action with Respect to Communist Aggression in Southeast Asia, 13 February 1952, in *FRUS 1952–1954*, vol. 12, part 1, 51.

123. Memorandum of Conversation by the Director of Policy Planning Staff (Nitze), 12 May 1952, in *FRUS 1952–1954*, vol. 12, part 1, 87–92.

124. TNA: PREM 11/403, J. W. Morrison to D. B. Pitblado, 21 November 1952.

125. TNA: PREM 11/404 COS (52) 684, Chiefs of Staff Committee: Future of ANZAM, 17 December 1952.

126. TNA: PREM 11/403, Norman Brook to the Prime Minister, 26 September 1952.

127. NAA: A5461 1/4/2A, part 2, From the Australian Embassy in Washington, D.C., to the Department of External Affairs, Canberra, 10 October 1952; and NZNA: R20821655 AAFD 811 W2347 148 I CAB 233/6/1, Note for the File: ANZUS, 13 October 1952.

128. TNA: PREM 11/403, Norman Brook to the Prime Minister, 26 September 1952; and TNA: PREM 11/403, Salisbury to the Prime Minister, 2 October 1952.

5. An Unwelcome Ally

1. NAA: A5954, 1424/3, Memorandum of Australian Government's Observations of United Kingdom Chiefs of Staff Memorandum COS (52) 685, attached to Prime Minister to High Commissioner, 27 March 1953.

2. NAA: A5954, 1424/3, Minutes of a Meeting held at No. 10 Downing Street, 12 December 1952.

3. Cairncross, *British Economy*, 104–5; and David James Gill, *Britain and the Bomb: Nuclear Diplomacy, 1964–70* (Stanford, CA: Stanford University Press, 2014), 11–50.

4. Churchill to Eden, 8 May 1953, Churchill Papers.

5. NAA: A5954, 1424/3, Minutes of a Meeting held at No. 10 Downing Street, 12 December 1952.

6. Ibid.

7. NZNA: R18872701 ACIE 8798 EA1 99 156 2/4/1, part 1, From the Minister of External Affairs, Wellington, to the New Zealand Ambassador, Washington, Tel. No. 9, 16 January 1953.

8. Joseph Newman, "Britain to Press Bid for Voice in Pacific Defense," *New York Herald Tribune*, 15 December 1952.

9. As reported in "U.S.-British Rift on ANZUS Defense Pact Soothed," *Christian Science Monitor*, 15 December 1952.

10. NZNA: R18872701 ACIE 8798 EA1 99 156 2/4/1, part 1, From the Minister of External Affairs, Wellington, to the New Zealand Ambassador, Washington, Tel. No. 9, 16 January 1953.

11. On the campaign, see John Robert Greene, *I Like Ike: The Presidential Election of 1952* (Lawrence: University Press of Kansas, 2017), 129–66. On Eisenhower and the war in Korea, see Robert A. Divine, *Foreign Policy and U.S. Presidential Elections, 1952–1960* (New York: New Viewpoints, 1974), esp. 45, 134.

12. Larres, *Churchill's Cold War*, 152–53.

13. "British Win Support on Voice in ANZUS," *Washington Post*, 14 December 1952. Other newspapers reported similar versions of this position. See "British Push Role in Pacific Defense," *New York Times*, 14 December 1952.

14. Larres, *Churchill's Cold War*, 182–85.

15. Kevin Ruane, "The Origins of the Eden-Dulles Antagonism: The Yoshida Letter and the Cold War in East Asia, 1951–1952," *Contemporary British History* 25.1 (2011): 141–56.

16. On the importance of religion in postwar U.S. politics and on the Eisenhower administration in particular, see Eric Foner, *The Story of American Freedom* (New York: W. W. Norton, 1998), 267–69; and Preston, *Sword of the Spirit*, 384–409. On Dulles, see Bevan Sewell, "Pragmatism, Religion, and John Foster Dulles's Embrace of Christian Internationalism in the 1930s," *Diplomatic History* 41.4 (2017): 799–823.

17. Dulles's talk about rolling back the Soviet Union was mainly for rhetorical purposes to gain domestic support. For a thorough analysis see László Borhi, "Rollback, Liberation, Containment, or Inaction? U.S. Policy and Eastern Europe in the 1950s," *Journal of Cold War Studies* 1.3 (1999): 67–110.

18. David Dutton, *Anthony Eden: A Life and Reputation* (London: Hodder, 1997), 144.

19. Thorpe, *Eden*, 381–83; John Colville, *The Fringes of Power: Downing Street Diaries*, vol. 2, *1941–April 1955* (London: Hodder & Stoughton, 1985), 321; Nicolson diary entry, 5 November 1952, in Olson, *Harold Nicolson Diaries*, 356; and Evelyn Shuckburgh, *Descent to Suez: Diaries, 1951–56* (New York: W. W. Norton, 1987), 23, 163–64.

20. Mr. John Foster Dulles, the Consultant to the Secretary, to the Supreme Commander for Allied Powers, 18 March 1951, in *FRUS 1951*, vol. 6, part 1, 931.

21. TNA: PREM 11/403, From New York to the Foreign Office, 6 January 1953; and Roger Makins to Anthony Eden, 9 January 1953, AP 20/16/23, Avon Papers.

22. Roger Makins to Anthony Eden, 4 March 1953, in FO 800/759, Con/53/33, Avon Papers.

23. Memorandum presented by the Prime Minister of the United Kingdom to President-Elect Eisenhower, January 1953, in *FRUS 1952–1954*, vol. 12, part 1, 256–57.

24. Memorandum by the Director of the Executive Secretariat, 8 January 1953, in *FRUS 1952–1954*, vol. 12, part 1, 258.

25. Dulles report on the Churchill Talks, 8 January 1953, in RG 59 Lot 64D199, box 18, NAII.

26. Ibid.

27. Memorandum by the Director of the Executive Secretariat, 8 January 1953, in *FRUS 1952–1954*, vol. 12, part 1, 259; and Memorandum of Conversation, 12 March 1953, in RG 59 Lot64D199, box 18, NAII.

28. NAA: A5954, 1424/3, From the Ambassador in Washington to the Department of External Affairs, 2 February 1953; and NZNA: R23447332 ABFK 19754 W576758 34/5/2, part 2, From the High Commissioner for New Zealand, Canberra, to the Minster of External Affairs, Wellington. Tel. 56, 12 March 1953.

29. NAA: A5954, 1424/3, From the Ambassador in Washington to the Department of External Affairs, 2 February 1953; NAA: A5954, 1424,1, For the Minister from Watt, 21 February, 1953; and NAA: A5954, 1424,1, For Spender from Casey, 12 February 1953.

30. NAA: A10299, A15, Spender to Menzies, 29 May 1953.

31. NZNA: R18872701 ACIE 8798 EA1 99 156 2/4/1, part 1, Australian Views on ANZUS, 14 May 1953.

32. The agreement is named after Radford and Admiral Collins. For mention of this, see NAA: A816/14/301/658 ANZAM planning and the defence of Malaya and Southeast Asia, March 1955.

33. Memorandum on the Substance of Discussions at a Department of State–Joint Chiefs of Staff Meeting, 20 February 1953, in *FRUS 1952–1954*, vol. 12, part 1, 276.

34. For example, see NAA: A5954, 1424/3, From the Ambassador in Washington to the Department of External Affairs, 2 February 1953; and NAA: A5954, 1680/2, A. McBride to the Prime Minister, 11 May 1953.

35. NAA: A 5954, 1424/3, L.P. Bourke to Sir Frederick Shedden, 27 March 1953; and NAA: A 5954, 1424/3, Sir Frederick Shedden to J. Plimsell, 21 March 1953. For New Zealand concerns see NZNA: R23447332 ABFK 19754 W576758 34/5/2, part 2, From the High Commissioner for New Zealand, Canberra, to the Minister of External Affairs, Wellington. Tel. 59, 17 March 1953; and ibid., From the Minister of External Affairs, Wellington, to the High Commissioner for New Zealand, Canberra, Tel. 55, 9 March 1953.

36. NAA: A 5954, 1424/3, The Future of ANZAM: Notes for Defence Committee, 22 April 1953.

37. Position Paper Prepared for the Secretary of State, 4 March 1953, in *FRUS 1952–1954*, vol. 12, part 1, 279.

38. Ibid.

39. NAA: A5954, 1424/3, The Secretary [Shedden] to Air Vice Marshall Walters, 2 April 1953; and ibid., Defence Committee Agendum: The Future of ANZAM,

7 April 1953. On efforts to defer the decision and the lengths to which the Australian government went to achieve this, see NAA: A5954, 1424/3, Sir Frederick Shedden to Air Vice Marshall G. Harcourt-Smith, 20 March 1953; and NAA: A5954, 1424/3, Sir Frederick Shedden to J. Plimsell, 21 March 1953. On the decision to separate ANZAM and ANZUS discussions, see NAA: A5954, 1680/2, Visit by a United Kingdom Chief of Staff and Planning Team, 20 June 1953.

40. For an indication of the types of concerns in Australian circles, see, for example, NAA: A5954, 1445/1, Joint Intelligence Committee (Melbourne), Appreciation NO. 6/1952: Probable Form and Scale of Attack within the ANZAM Region, April 1952; and NAA: A1838, TS687/1, part 3, NAA: New Zealand Attitude on Deployment of Forces, 22 September 1953.

41. NAA: A1838, TS687/1, part 3, Memorandum by Minister for External Affairs and Defence, 6 March 1953.

42. NAA: A5954, 1424/3, Memorandum of Australian Government's Observations of United Kingdom Chiefs of Staff Memorandum COS (52) 685, attached to Prime Minister to High Commissioner, 27 March 1953.

43. NZNA: R18872701 ACIE 8798 EA1 99 156 2/4/1, part 1, Extract from COS (53): South East Asia Staff Agency Preliminary Meeting, 24 February 1953.

44. NAA: A5954, 1424/3, From Secretary External Affairs to Secretary Defence Committee, 11 February 1953.

45. NAA: A5954, 1424/3, Memorandum of Australian Government's Observations of United Kingdom Chiefs of Staff Memorandum COS (52) 685, attached to Prime Minister to High Commissioner, 27 March 1953; and NAA: A5954, 1424/3, Future of ANZAM, Notes for Defence Committee Agendum, 22 April 1953.

46. NZNA: R18872701 ACIE 8798 EA1 99 156 2/4/1, part 1, Australian Views on ANZUS, 14 May 1953.

47. Menzies letter for Holland is contained in NZNA: R18872701 ACIE 8798 EA1 99 156 2/4/1, part 1, Robert Menzies to Sir Stephen Holmes, 27 March 1953.

48. NZNA: R18872701 ACIE 8798 EA1 99 156 2/4/1, part 1, Memorandum of Australian Government's Observations on United Kingdom Chiefs of Staff Memorandum, 30 March 1953.

49. NZNA: R17722505 ABHS 950 W5422/33/1111/3/3/15, part 2, For the Minister: ANZUS Council Meeting, 26 August 1953.

50. Robert R. Bowie and Richard H. Immerman, *Waging Peace: How Eisenhower Shaped an Enduring Cold War Strategy* (Oxford: Oxford University Press, 1997), 178–201.

51. Kennedy, *Rise and Fall of the Great Powers*, 495.

52. Emmet John Hughes, *The Ordeal of Power: A Political Memoir of the Eisenhower Years* (London: Macmillan, 1963), 72–73.

53. Hughes, *Ordeal of Power*, 140–44; Dwight D. Eisenhower, *Mandate for Change, 1953–1956: The White House Years* (New York: Doubleday, 1963), 171–72; and Jim Newton, *Eisenhower: The White House Years* (New York: Doubleday, 2011), 84–91.

54. Brands, *What Good Is Grand Strategy?*, 17–58.

55. Memorandum by the Director of the Executive Secretariat, 8 January 1953, in *FRUS 1952–1954*, vol. 12, part 1, 259.

56. Memorandum by the Regional Planning Adviser (Ogburn) to the Assistant Secretary of State for Far Eastern Affairs (Allison), 21 January 1953, in *FRUS 1952–1954*, vol. 12, part 1, 260.

57. Memorandum by the Assistant Secretary of State for Far Eastern Affairs to the Secretary of State, 29 January 1953, in *FRUS 1952–1954*, vol. 12, part 1, 263–65.

58. The Acting Secretary of State to the Secretary of Defense, 21 August 1953, in *FRUS 1952–1954*, vol. 12, part 1, 335.

59. On the Five Power talks, see Memorandum by the Assistant Secretary of State for Far Eastern Affairs (Robertson) to the Deputy Under Secretary of State (Matthews), 13 May 1953, in *FRUS 1952–1954*, vol. 12, part 1, 313–14; and Report by the Staff Planners to the Military Representatives of the Five Powers on the Conference held June 15 to July 1 1953, in *FRUS 1952–1954*, vol. 12, part 1, 319–28.

60. NAA: A5954, 1424/3, From the Australia Embassy Washington [Watt] to the Minister, 23 February 1953.

61. NAA: A816, 11/301/867, Brief for Australian Prime Minister, Department of External Affairs: Review of Soviet Policy, May 1953.

62. Ibid.

63. NZNA: R17722632 ABHS 950 W5422 32 111 3/3/9, part 1, Extract from Brief of Meeting: Tripartite Security Treaty: Japan, 28 July 1952.

64. The New Zealand Ambassador, Washington, to the Minister of External Affairs, 14 March 1950, in *ANZUS Pact*, doc. 198, 522–36. For Berendsen's own account, see Hugh Templeton, ed., *Mr Ambassador: Memoirs of Sir Carl Berendsen* (Wellington: Victoria University Press, 2008), 19, 213–14, 220.

65. See the conclusions reached by the Australian, New Zealand, and U.S. staff planners at the November 1952 ANZUS Council meeting, where the "domino theory" was clearly informing strategic thinking: Report by the Staff Planners to the Military Representatives to the ANZUS Council, 25 November 1952, in *FRUS 1952–1954*, vol. 12, part 1, 242–56.

66. NZNA: R17722505 ABHS 950 W5422/33/1111/3/3/15, part 2, For the Minister: ANZUS Council Meeting, 26 August 1953.

67. NAA: A5954, 1680/2, P.A. McBride to the Prime Minister, 11 May 1953; and NAA: A816, 11/301/867, Brief for Australian Prime Minister May 1953 from the Department of External Affairs.

68. Hack, *Defence and Decolonisation*, 79–82.

69. NAA: A816, 11/301/867, Brief for Australian Prime Minister: Item 7: ANZAM, ANZUS and Related Matters, June 1953; and NZNA: R18872701 ACIE 8798 EA1 99 156 2/4/1, part 1, Summary of ANZAM, ANZUS and Five Power Staff Agency, ANZUS Council Second Meeting, 10 September 1953.

70. NAA: A816, 11/301/867, Brief for the Australian Prime Minister from the Department of External Affairs, ANZUS, ANZAM and related matters, May 1953.

71. NZNA: R22228450 ACIE 8798 W2691 84 111 3/3/30, part 1, Memorandum for the Secretary of External Affairs, 1 May 1953.

72. NZNA: R18872701 ACIE 8798 EA1 99 156 2/4/1, part 1, Summary of ANZAM, ANZUS and Five Power Staff Agency, 10 September 1953.

73. NAA: A816, 11/301/867, Brief for the Australian Prime Minister, Meeting of Prime Ministers, 1953.

74. NZNA: R22228450 ACIE 8798 W2691 84 111 3/3/30, part 1, Memorandum for the Secretary of External Affairs, 1 May 1953.

75. The Ambassador in the United Kingdom to the Department of State, 16 June 1953, in *FRUS 1952–1954*, vol. 12, part 1, 318.

76. *Daily Mirror*, 12 June 1953. For Menzies denials, see NAA: A5954, 1424, 1, From Australian High Commissioner's Office to the Acting Prime Minister, 13 June 1953.

77. TNA: PREM 11/404 Pacific Defence: Minutes of a Meeting held at 10 Downing Street, 10 June 1953.

78. Ibid.

79. Ibid.

80. Ibid.

81. Trevor Smith, "Firm Stand on ANZUS," *Melbourne Herald*, 12 June 1953.

82. Ibid.

83. Memorandum of Telephone Conversation by the Director of the Office of British Commonwealth and Northern European Relations (Raynor), 24 July 1953, in *FRUS 1952–1954*, vol. 12, part 1, 330; and NZNA: R17722505 ABHS 950 W5422/33/1111/3/3/15, part 2, From the New Zealand Ambassador, Washington, to the Minister of External Affairs, Wellington, Tel. No 256, 28 July 1953.

84. NAA: A10299, A14, Speaking note for Robert Menzies, undated.

85. TNA: CAB 133/135, Minutes of the First Meeting held at 10 Downing Street, 3 June 1953.

86. NAA: A10299, A15, Spender to Menzies, 29 May 1953.

87. NAA: A816, 11/301/867, Brief for Australian Prime Minister by the Department of External Affairs, May 1953.

88. Memorandum by the Deputy Director of the Office of British Commonwealth and Northern European Affairs to the Deputy Under Secretary of State, 29 May 1953, in *FRUS 1952–1954*, vol. 12, part 1, 317; and NAA: A5954, 1424,1, For Watt from Moodie, 22 May 1953.

89. NAA: A5954, 1424,1, For Sir Frederick Shedden from Pollard, 5 June 1953; and NAA: A5954, 1424,1, Interview with Mr Byrd, Counsellor to the United States Embassy, 4 June 1953.

90. TNA: PREM 11/404, Sir Robert Menzies to Winston Churchill, 25 June 1953.

91. Ibid.

92. NZNA: R17722505 ABHS 950 W5422/33/1111/3/3/15, part 2, From the New Zealand Ambassador, Washington, to the Minister of External Affairs, Wellington, Tel. No. 226, 14 July 1953.

93. Ibid.

94. Ibid.

95. Ibid.

96. NZNA: R18872701 ACIE 8798 EA1 99 156 2/4/1, part 1, Summary of ANZAM, ANZUS and Five Power Staff Agency, 10 September 1953.

97. F. L. W. Wood, "The Anzac Dilemma," *International Affairs* 29.2 (1953): 184–92.

98. Roy Jenkins, *Churchill: A Biography* (London: Macmillan, 2001), 847, 861–68.

99. TNA: PREM 11/404, Foreign Office to Washington, 5 September 1953.

100. NAA: A10299, A14, To the Prime Minister from Richard Casey, 14 September 1953.

101. Memorandum by the Joint Chiefs of Staff to the Secretary of Defense, 8 September 1953, in *FRUS 1952–1954*, vol. 12, part 1, 343.

102. NZNA: R18872701 ACIE 8798 EA1 99 156 2/4/1, part 1, Summary of ANZAM, ANZUS and Five Power Staff Agency, 10 September 1953; and NZNA:

R18872701 ACIE 8798 EA1 99 156 2/4/1, part 1, From the Ambassador in Washington to the Minister of External Affairs, Wellington, Tel. No. 264, 1 August 1953.

103. Memorandum by the Secretary of State to the Assistant Secretary of State for European Affairs (Merchant) and the Counselor of the Department of State (MacArthur), 8 September 1953, in *FRUS 1952–1954*, vol. 12, part 1, 340.

104. TNA: PREM 11/404 Foreign Office to Washington, 5 September 1953.

105. Dulles is quoted in NAA: A10299, A14, To the Prime Minister from Richard Casey, 10 September 1953; and in NZNA: R17722505 ABHS 950 W5422/33/1111/3/3/15, part 2, Second Meeting of the ANZUS Council, 8 October 1953. The communiqué issued at the end of the second ANZUS Council made no mention of this statement by Dulles. This is available here: Communiqué on Second meeting of the Council of ANZUS, 10 September 1953, Department of State, *Bulletin*. The minutes of the ANZUS Council can be read here: United States Minutes of the Second Meeting of the ANZUS Council: First Session, 9 September 1953, in *FRUS 1952–1954*, vol. 12, part 1, 340–42; and United States Minutes of the Second Meeting of the ANZUS Council: Fourth Session, 10 September 1953, ibid., 344–51.

106. Trachtenberg, *Cold War and After*, 139.

107. TNA: PREM 11/404, British Embassy to Lord Salisbury, 15 September 1953.

108. "ANZUS Ministers Say No to Britain," *Melbourne Herald*, 11 September 1953.

109. See the following report, which makes this clear: NZNA: R17722505 ABHS 950 W5422/33/1111/3/3/15, part 2, The New Zealand Ambassador in Washington to the Minister of External Affairs, Wellington, Tel. No. 334, 10 September 1953.

110. NAA: A1828, TS687/1, part 3, New Zealand Attitude on Deployment of Forces, 22 September 1953.

111. NZNA: R17722505 ABHS 950 W5422/33/1111/3/3/15, part 2, Memorandum for the Secretary of External Affairs, 8 October 1953.

112. Radford was clear on this point. See NZNA: R17722505 ABHS 950 W5422/33/1111/3/3/15, part 2, Memorandum for the Secretary of External Affairs, Ambassador's interview with Admiral Radford, 2 September 1953.

113. NZNA: R17722505 ABHS 950 W5422/33/1111/3/3/15, part 2, Memorandum for the Secretary of External Affairs, 8 October 1953.

114. "M.H.R. Wants ANZUS Liaison with Britain," *Argus*, 16 September 1953.

115. "ANZUS Isn't Empire Breach," *Argus*, 20 October 1953.

116. NZNA: R17722505 ABHS 950 W5422/33/1111/3/3/15, part 2, Webb to Heydon, 14 December 1953.

117. NZNA: R17722505 ABHS 950 W5422/33/1111/3/3/15, part 2, Agreed Record of Proceedings, 9 September 1953.

118. NAA: A10299, A14, To the Prime Minister from Richard Casey; and United States Minutes of the Second Meeting of the ANZUS Council: Fourth Session, 10 September 1953, in *FRUS 1952–1954*, vol. 12, part 1, 350.

119. NZNA: R17722505 ABHS 950 W5422/33/1111/3/3/15, part 2, From the New Zealand Ambassador, Washington, the Minister of External Affairs, Wellington, Tel. No. 256, 28 July 1953.

120. "Pity UK's Not in ANZUS—Lord Swindon," *Argus*, 17 October 1953.

121. TNA: PREM 11/404, H.C. to the Prime Minister, 6 October 1953.

122. NZNA: R22228450 ACIE 8798 W2691 84 111 3/3/30, part 1, Foss Shanahan to Mr MacDonald, 10 September 1953.

123. "Wider ANZUS Role Planned," *Daily Telegraph*, 4 December 1953. The minutes of the Bermuda summit can be read here: TNA: FO 371/125138.

124. Donald Cameron Watt, *Succeeding John Bull: America in Britain's Place 1900–1975* (repr., Cambridge: Cambridge University Press, 2008), 111–43.

125. Lee, *Search for Security*, 123.

126. TNA, DEFE 11/97 COS (53) 130th meeting, 17 November 1953.

127. Lee, *Search for Security*, 123.

128. McGibbon, "Defence of New Zealand," 167; Matthew Jones, "The Radford Bombshell: Anglo-Australian-U.S. Relations: Nuclear Weapons and the Defence of South East Asia, 1954–57," *Journal of Strategic Studies* 27.4 (2004): 638; and NAA: A1209 1957/4652, British Commonwealth Defence Discussions, September 1953.

129. NZNA: R17722505 ABHS 950 W5422/33/1111/3/3/15, part 2, For the Minister: ANZUS Council Meeting, 26 August 1953.

130. On the Australian side, follow the material contained in NAA: A5954 1453/5. For New Zealand documentation, consult the following: NZNA R18872701 ACIE 8798 EA1 99 156 2/4/1, part 1, Memorandum for the Prime Minister's Department, Canberra, 2 December 1953; and NZNA: R17722505 ABHS 950 W5422/33/1111/3/3/15, part 2, Minute by the Defence Committee, 18 March 1954.

131. This was a point that Wellington had made clear on a number of occasions earlier in the year. NZNA: R17722505 ABHS 950 W5422/33/1111/3/3/15, part 2, Jack Shepard to Mr Shanahan, 12 August 1953; and NZNA: R17722505 ABHS 950 W5422/33/1111/3/3/15, part 2, Extract from Current Events Report, From Canberra to Wellington, 16 September 1953.

132. NZNA: R17722505 ABHS 950 W5422/33/1111/3/3/15, part 2, For the Minister: ANZUS Council Meeting, 26 August 1953.

133. McGibbon, "Defence of New Zealand," 167.

134. NZNA: R17722505 ABHS 950 W5422/33/1111/3/3/15, part 2, Extract from Current Events Report, From Canberra to Wellington, 16 September 1953.

135. The Ambassador in the United Kingdom to the Department of State, 8 December 1953, in *FRUS 1952–1954*, vol. 12, part 1, 357.

136. On the motivations for bilateral cooperation, see Victor D. Cha, "Powerplay Origins of the U.S. Alliance System in Asia," *International Security* 34.3 (2009–10): 174–76.

6. Divided Action

1. Prados, *Vietnam*, 14; and Richard Aldrich, *Intelligence and the War against Japan: Britain, America and the Politics of Secret Service* (Cambridge: Cambridge University Press, 2000), 4–9.

2. Memorandum for the President: Indochina, 2 November 1944, in President Subject Files, File: Indochina, FDR Library; and Franklin Roosevelt to Donovan, 17 November 1944, in President Subject Files, File: Indochina, FDR Library, Hyde Park, New York (hereafter FDR Library).

3. FDR to the Under-Secretary of State, 3 November 1944, in President Subject Files, File: Indochina, FDR Library.

4. Stephen E. Ambrose and Douglas Brinkley, *Rise to Globalism: American Foreign Policy since 1938*, 7th rev. ed. (London: Penguin 1993), 43.

5. Memorandum for the Secretary of State from Franklin Roosevelt, 1 January 1945, in President Subject Files, File: Indochina, FDR Library.

6. On the evolving situation, see Logevall, *Embers of War*, 98–120.

7. Ronald Eckford Mill Irving, *The First Indochina War* (London: Croom Helm, 1975), 99.

8. Beisner, *Dean Acheson*, 267–73; quote at 268.

9. Paul Ham, *Vietnam: The Australian War* (Sydney: HarperCollins, 2007), 42–49.

10. NAA: A1838, TS687/1, part 3, Memorandum by Minister for External Affairs and Defence, 6 March 1953.

11. NZNA: R23447332 ABFK 19754 W576758 34/5/2, part 2, For Doidge from the Prime Minister in From the Minister of External Affairs, Wellington, to the High Commissioner for New Zealand, London, Tel. No. 373, 24 April 1953.

12. NAA: A5954, 1445/1, Joint Intelligence Committee (Melbourne), Appreciation No. 6/1952, April 1952.

13. Peter Edwards, *Australia and the Vietnam War* (Sydney: University of New South Wales Press, 2014), 41–45.

14. It would be superfluous to cite all the relevant literature on the United States' growing involvement in the Vietnam War. For an excellent recent overview, see Logevall, *Embers of War*.

15. George C. Herring, *America's Longest War: The United States and Vietnam, 1950–1975* (New York: McGraw-Hill, 2002), 23–27.

16. Memorandum, 8 January 1954, in File: National Security Council, Jan through June 1954, RG 59 Lot 55D480, Records of the Bureau of Far Eastern Affairs, box 11, NAII.

17. The President's News Conference, 7 April 1954, in *Public Papers of the President of the United States: Dwight D. Eisenhower, 1954* (Washington, DC: Government Printing Office, 1960), 2:382–84.

18. Radio and Television Address to the Nation by the Secretary of State, 7 May 1954, in *FRUS 1952–1954*, vol. 16, 721.

19. The Dulles quote is from a 1952 interview on the Longines Wittnauer panel. The interview can be watched here: "John Foster Dulles Interview: U.S. Secretary of State under Dwight D. Eisenhower (1952)," *Longines Chronoscope*, Film Archive, YouTube, http://www.youtube.com/watch?v=7EJZdikc6OA (accessed 11 August 2013).

20. Statement of Policy of National Security Council on United States objectives and courses of action with respect to Southeast Asia, enclosed, 16 January 1954, in *FRUS 1952–1954*, vol. 12, part 1, 368. This document was known as NSC 5405 and is referenced in other documents accordingly.

21. Ibid.

22. Ibid.; Record of Third Plenary Session of Far East Regional Conference of the Foreign Operations Administration, 23 February 1954, in *FRUS 1952–1954*, vol. 12, part 1, 386; and National Security Council Meeting, 12 August 1954, ibid., 724.

23. For a classic political economy explanation of U.S. involvement in Indochina, see Gabriel Kolko, *Anatomy of a War: Vietnam, the United States, and the Modern Historical Experience* (New York: Free Press, 1985).

24. Record of the Third Plenary Session of the Far East Regional Conference of the Foreign Operations Administration, 23 February 1954, in *FRUS 1952–1954*, vol. 12, part 1, 389–93.

25. Memorandum of Discussion at 181st meeting of National Security Council, 21 January 1954, in *FRUS 1952–1954*, vol. 12, part 1, 381. See also the discussion in March 1954, where the president outlined how the United States could assist the Associated States of Indochina: Editorial Note, ibid., 399.

26. Prados, *Vietnam*, 31.

27. Memorandum of Discussion at the 180th Meeting of the National Security Council, 14 January 1954, in *FRUS 1952–1954*, vol. 12, part 1, 364.

28. For a recent overview, see Ted Morgan, *Valley of Death: The Tragedy at Dien Bien Phu That Led America into the Vietnam War* (New York: Random House, 2010).

29. Memorandum of Conversation, 26 April 1954, in *FRUS 1952–54*, vol. 13, part 2, 1386–88.

30. Record of Conversation, 11 August 1953, MS Sherfield 527, Washington Special Correspondence, Sherfield Papers, Bodleian Library, Oxford.

31. Ibid.

32. Memorandum of Conversation, 24 March 1954, in RG 59 Lot64D199, box 18, NAII. On Eisenhower's attitude to military involvement, see James Arnold, *The First Domino: Eisenhower, the Military and America's Intervention in Vietnam* (New York: William Morrow, 1991).

33. Memorandum of Discussion, 18 March 1954, in *FRUS 1952–1954*, vol. 13, part 1, 1132–33; and Memorandum of Conversation, 19 March 1954, ibid., 1133–34.

34. TNA: DEFE 11/228 Eden to the Foreign office, Tel. 137, 4 May 1954.

35. On 20 March 1954, Radford met with the president for one and a half hours and pressed the case that the French required immediate U.S. military assistance. Ferrell, *Diary of James C. Hagerty*, diary entry, 20 March 1954, 32. Two days later, Radford again met with the president and Dulles and argued that "the French were in a dangerous position and needed more B-26 bombers." See Hagerty Diary, 22 March 1954, in *FRUS 1952–1954*, vol. 13, part 1, 1140.

36. Memorandum of Discussion, 6 April 1954, in *FRUS 1952–1954*, vol. 13, part 1, 1253–54; and ibid., 1254. Yet interestingly, the British ambassador in Washington informed Eden later that year that "I believe the President could get the reluctant but resolute support of the majority of both parties in Congress for whatever steps he declared to be vital to resist the spread of Communism." See Roger Makins to Anthony Eden, 21 May 1954, MS Sherfield 527, Washington Special Correspondence, Sherfield Papers.

37. Memorandum of Discussion, 10 May 1954, in *FRUS 1952–1954*, vol. 13, part 1, 468. Even with an international coalition, some senators still expressed concerns about the "main problem," of raising an effective "native army in Indochina": *Congressional Record—Senate*, April 14, 1954, p. 5120.

38. Memorandum of Conversation: Indochina, 3 April 1954, in RG 59 Lot64D199, box 18, NAII.

39. These points were all put forward in Eisenhower to Churchill, 29 February 1954, box 6/3C, Churchill Papers; and Memorandum of Conversation, 5 May 1954, in *FRUS 1952–1954*, vol. 12, part 1, 446–48.

40. Memorandum of Discussion, 6 May 1954, in *FRUS 1952–1954*, vol. 12, part 1, 455.

41. Ibid.

42. For a fuller account of U.S. and British relations with India, see McGarr, *Cold War in South Asia*.

43. Memorandum of Conversation by Robert Cutler, Special Assistant to the President for National Security Affairs, 5 May 1954, in *FRUS 1952–1954*, vol. 12, part 1, 446–48.

44. Editorial Note, 19 May 1954, ibid., 492.

45. Memorandum of Conversation, Consultation with the British regarding the position of France, 27 March 1954, in RG 59 Lot64D199, box 18, NAII.

46. Memorandum of Discussion, 6 April 1954, in *FRUS 1952–1954*, vol. 12, part 1, 1264. For further discussion as to how to go about achieving these ambitions, see Memorandum for Mr. Lay, 15 July 1954, in NSC Series, Policy Papers Subseries, box 9, NSC5404 Mainland SE Asia (2), Dwight D. Eisenhower Presidential Library, Abilene, Kansas (hereafter DDEPL).

47. Memorandum of a Conversation with the president, 24 March 1954, in *FRUS 1952–54*, vol. 13, part 1, 1150; Memorandum of Discussion, 190th meeting of the National Security Council, in *FRUS 1952–54*, vol. 13, part 1, 1163–68.

48. Wilson's and Radford's assessments are in Memorandum of Conversation by Robert Cutler, Special Assistant to the President for National Security Affairs, 5 May 1954, in *FRUS 1952–1954*, vol. 12, part 1, 446–48.

49. "The Threat of a Red Asia," *Bulletin*, 29 March 1954, in *FRUS 1952–1954*, vol. 12, part 1, 400.

50. Memorandum of Conversation with the President, 24 March 1954, in RG 59 Lot64D199, box 18, NAII.

51. President's News Conference, 7 April 1954, in *Public Papers of the President of the United States: Dwight D. Eisenhower, 1954*, doc. 73, 383.

52. Tellingly, Dulles had given Makins prior notice of his united action speech. Memorandum of Conversation, 27 March 1954, in RG 59 Lot64D199, box 18, NAII.

53. None of this should have come as any great surprise given that Allen Dulles had informed the NSC early in the year that the United Kingdom was opposed to any sort of military escalation in Indochina for fear of direct Chinese intervention. See Memorandum for Executive Secretary from Allen Dulles, undated, in Office of the Special Assistant for National Security Affairs, NSC Series, Policy Papers Subseries, box 10, NSC 5416, DDEPL.

54. Alistair Horne, *Macmillan, 1894–1956*, vol. 1 (London: Macmillan, 1988), 346. Eden shared similar concerns. See Anthony Eden to the Prime Minister, 2 March 1954, FO 800/766, DEF/54/80/4, Avon Papers.

55. Diary entry, 28 April 1953, in Moran, *Winston Churchill*, 428.

56. TNA: CAB 131/12, 17 June 1952.

57. TNA: CAB 158/17 JIC 54 (29) Final, Threat to the New Zealand Area, Report by the Joint Intelligence Committee, 7 April 1954.

58. The British position is explained in Memorandum of Conversation, 16 April 1954, in *FRUS 1952–1954*, vol. 12, part 1, 427. Dulles's preference for a temporary arrangement is stated in Memorandum of Conversation, 27 March 1954, in RG 59 Lot64D199, The Secretary and Under Secretary's Memoranda of Conversation, box 18, NAII.

59. TNA: CAB 128/27, CC(54), 26th meeting of the Cabinet, 7 April 1954.

60. Rumbold to Makins, 26 May 1954, in Washington Special Correspondence, Sherfield Papers.

61. Message from the President to the Prime Minister, in The Secretary of State to the Embassy in the United Kingdom, 4 April 1954, in *FRUS 1952–1954*, vol. 13, part 1, 1240.

62. Memorandum of Conversation by the Deputy Assistant Secretary of State for European Affairs (Bonbright), 4 April 1954, in *FRUS 1952–1954*, vol. 13, part 1, 1231.

63. Memorandum by the Counselor (MacArthur) to the Secretary of State, 5 April 1954, in *FRUS 1952–1954*, vol. 13, part 1, 1244–45. A similar line of argument had been employed three days earlier: Memorandum of Conversation, 2 April 1954, in RG 59 Lot64D199, box 18, NAII.

64. Diary entry, 23 April 1954, in R. Casey, *Australian Foreign Minister: The Diaries of R. G. Casey, 1951–60* (London: Harper Collins, 1972), 137.

65. TNA: CAB 128/27, CC(54), 26th meeting of the Cabinet, 7 April 1954.

66. Eden's thinking is outlined in TNA: PREM 11/651, Foreign Secretary to the Prime Minister, 7 July 1954.

67. Memorandum to the President, 16 May 1954, White House Memoranda Series, box 1, JFDP.

68. TNA: DEFE 11/228, Geneva delegation to Foreign Office, Tel. 87, 1 May 1954. See also Anthony Eden, *Full Circle: The Memoirs of Sir Anthony Eden* (London: Cassell, 1960), 140–41.

69. TNA: CAB 158/17 JIC 54 (14), Final, Communist Threat to Siam: Report by the Joint Intelligence Committee, 4 February 1954.

70. TNA: CAB 158/17 JIC 54 (49), Final, The Political Situation in Malaya in event of certain eventualities, 5 July 1954.

71. Moran, *Winston Churchill*, 543.

72. Memorandum of Discussion at the 180th Meeting of the National Security Council, 14 January 1954, in *FRUS 1952–1954*, vol. 12, part 1, 363.

73. See, for example, Logevall, *Embers of War*, 481–509 (a chapter titled "Eden vs Dulles); and Thorpe, *Eden*, 401–10.

74. Trachtenberg, *Constructed Peace*, 125–45.

75. NZNA R17722505 ABHS 950 W5422/33/1111/3/3/15, part 2, Memorandum for the Secretary of External Affairs, Ambassador's interview with Admiral Radford, 2 September 1953.

76. Jones, *After Hiroshima*, 206–8.

77. Editorial Note, Radford conversation with John Foster Dulles and Allen Dulles, 14 May 1954, in *FRUS 1952–1954*, vol. 12, part 1, 485.

78. Memorandum of Conversation with the President, 25 May 1954, in *FRUS 1952–1954*, vol. 12, part 1, 512.

79. Conference in the President's Office, 2 June 1954, in *FRUS 1952–1954*, vol. 12, part 1, 531.

80. Memorandum of Conversation by Robert Cutler, Special Assistant to the President for National Security Affairs, 5 May 1954, in *FRUS 1952–1954*, vol. 12, part 1, 446.

81. On British deliberations, see TNA: PREM 11/645 C.C. (54), 31st Conclusions, 3 May 1954; TNA: CAB 128/27, CC(54), 26th meeting of the Cabinet, 7 April 1954; TNA: FO 371/112049, Policy towards Indo-China, 31 March 1954; TNA: CAB

129/67, C(54) 134, Minutes of the Cabinet, 7 April 1954; and TNA: CAB 129/68, C(54)177, Minutes of the Cabinet, 24 May 1954.

82. McIntyre, *Background to the Anzus Pact*, 379.

83. Kevin Ruane, "SEATO, MEDO, and the Baghdad Pact: Anthony Eden, British Foreign Policy and the Collective Defense of Southeast Asia and the Middle East, 1952–1955," *Diplomacy & Statecraft* 16.1 (2005): 175–76.

84. Logevall, *Embers of War*, 552.

85. There is a vast literature on the Geneva Conference of 1954. For a good insider account, see James Cable, *The Geneva Conference of 1954 on Indochina* (Basingstoke: Palgrave, 1986); and Eden, *Full Circle*, 107–45. On U.S. policy see, for instance, Richard H. Immerman, "The United States and the Geneva Conference of 1954: A New Look," *Diplomatic History* 14.1 (1990): 43–66; and Logevall, *Embers of War*, 549–76. For a good analysis on the British role, see Geoffrey Warner, "The Settlement of the Indochina War," in *The Foreign Policy of Churchill's Peacetime Administration, 1951–1955*, ed. John Young (Leicester: Leicester University Press, 1988).

86. Hennessey, *Britain's Korean War*, 277, 283.

87. Zelizer, *Arsenal of Democracy*, 126–29. For an example of how historical "mistakes" in the first half of the twentieth century were influencing Dulles's thinking, see Dulles to the Ambassador in Paris, 5 January 1954, in MCO74, box 11, JFDP.

88. Memorandum by Edmund A. Guillion to the Director of Staff (Bowie), 9 March 1954, in *FRUS 1952–1954*, vol. 16, 442.

89. The President to the Prime Minister, 5 April 1954, in CHUR, 6/3B, Churchill Papers.

90. TNA: PREM 11/645, From the Geneva Conference to the Foreign Office, Tel. 110, 2 May 1954. Dulles's account of the talks is here: The Secretary of State to the Department of State, 30 April 1954, in *FRUS 1952–1954*, vol. 12, part 1, 437.

91. The Secretary of State to the Department of State, 2 May 1954, in *FRUS 1952–1954*, vol. 12, part 1, 443.

92. Ferrell, *Diary of James C. Hagerty*, 49.

93. The Under Secretary of State to the Department of State, 5 May 1954, in *FRUS 1952–1954*, vol. 12, part 1, 450.

94. Memorandum of Conversation, 28 May 1954, in *FRUS 1952–1954*, vol. 12, part 1, 521–26.

95. Memorandum of Discussion, 6 May 1954, ibid., 455.

96. The Under Secretary of State to the Department of State, 5 May 1954, in *FRUS 1952–1954*, vol. 12, part 1, 450.

97. As Eden made clear in a memorandum he handed to Dulles. Dulles reported this here: Secretary of State to the Department of State, 30 April 1954, in *FRUS 1952–1954*, vol. 12, part 1, 437.

98. Eden quoted in Secretary of State to the Department of State, 30 April 1954, in *FRUS 1952–1954*, vol. 12, part 1, 437–38.

99. Minutes of the National Security Council, 20 May 1954, in *FRUS 1952–1954*, vol. 12, part 1, 497.

100. Ibid.

101. Ibid.

102. Editorial Note, in *FRUS 1952–54*, vol. 13, part 1, 1236. See also Sherman Adams, *Firsthand Report: The Story of the Eisenhower Administration* (New York:

Harper, 1961), 121–23. Dulles quote in The Secretary of State to the Embassy in France, 5 April 1954, in *FRUS 1952–1954*, vol. 13, part 1, 1242.

103. Minutes of a National Security Council Meeting, 29 April 1954, in *FRUS 1952–1954*, vol. 13, part 2, 1431–35.

104. The Secretary of State to the United States Delegation, 8 May 1954, in *FRUS 1952–1954*, vol. 16, 729.

105. Memorandum of Conversation by Robert Cutler, Special Assistant to the President for National Security Affairs, 5 May 1954, in *FRUS 1952–1954*, vol. 12, part 1, 448. On the relationship between Australia, New Zealand, and the United States in this period, see Henry W. Brands Jr., "From ANZUS to SEATO: United States Strategic Policy towards Australia and New Zealand, 1952–1954," *International History Review* 9.2 (1987): 268–69.

106. Martin, *Menzies*, 227–63, 266.

107. Edwards and Pemberton, *Crises and Commitments*, 140; Lowe, *Menzies*, 160; Casey, *Australian Foreign Minister*, 178–79; and Nông Văn Dân, *Churchill, Eden and Indo-China, 1951–1955* (London: Anthem, 2011), 76.

108. Memorandum of Conversation by the Adviser to the United States Delegation at the Geneva Conference, 2 May 1954, in *FRUS 1952–1954*, vol. 12, part 1, 441.

109. Lowe, *Menzies*, 162–63.

110. NAA: A10299/D8, Casey to the Australian Cabinet, undated.

111. Memorandum of Conversation by the Director of the Office of British Commonwealth and Northern European Affairs, 31 March 1954, in *FRUS 1952–1954*, vol. 12, part 1, 399–401. See also NZNA: R23447332 ABFK 19754 W576758 34/5/2, part 2, From the Minister of External Affairs to the New Zealand Ambassador, Washington, Wellington, Tel. 110, 4 May 1954.

112. Editorial Note, Memorandum of Conversation, 31 March 1954, in *FRUS 1952–1954*, vol. 12, part 1, 400.

113. NZNA: R17722518 ABHS 950 W5422 36/111/3/316, part 1, Leeter for Major-General W. G. Gentry, 31 August 1953.

114. NAA: A462(TS), 439/1/39, part 1, Record of Cabinet Meeting, 6 April 1954; Menzies to R. Heymanson, 15 July 1954, MS. 4936/1/15/132, Menzies Papers.

115. NZNA: R23447332 ABFK 19754 W576758 34/5/2, part 2, From the New Zealand Ambassador, Washington, to the Minister of External Affairs, Wellington, Tel. 245, 30 June 1954; and NZNA: R23447332 ABFK 19754 W576758 34/5/2, part 2, From the Minister of External Affairs to the New Zealand Ambassador, Washington, Tel. 168, 26 June 1954.

116. Note by the Secretaries to the Holder of JCS 2151/8, 12 March 1954, in RG 218 Geographic Files, 1954–56, box 11, NAII.

117. NAA: A462(TS), 439/1/39, part 1, Record of Cabinet Meeting, 6 April 1954.

118. Martin, *Menzies*, 266–68; and David Goldsworthy, *Losing the Blanket: Australia and the End of Britain's Empire* (Melbourne: Melbourne University Publishing, 2002), 19.

119. New Zealand concerns are expressed throughout NZNA: R23447332 ABFK 19754 W576758 34/5/2, part 2, For Doidge from the Prime Minister in From the Minister of External Affairs, Wellington, to the High Commissioner for New Zealand, London, Tel. No. 373, 24 April 1954; NZNA: R23447332 ABFK 19754 W576758 34/5/2, part 2, and For Webb from the Prime Minister in From the Minister of

External Relations, Wellington, to the New Zealand Delegation, Geneva Conference, Tel. No. 9, 4 May 1954.

120. NZNA: R23447332 ABFK 19754 W576758 34/5/2, part 2, From the High Commissioner for New Zealand, London, to the Minister of External Affairs, Wellington, Tel. 374, 22 April 1954.

121. NZNA: R23447332 ABFK 19754 W576758 34/5/2, part 2, From the Minister of External Affairs to the New Zealand Ambassador, Washington, Wellington, Tel. 110, 4 May 1954.

122. As reported by the British High Commissioner to New Zealand in TNA: DO 35/6073, 3984, Office of High Commissioner in New Zealand, 3 May 1954. Racial factors in determining New Zealand's foreign policy are discussed at length in TNA: FO 371/111867, High Commissioner to Commonwealth Relations Office, 3 July 1954; and Menzies to R. Heymanson, 15 July 1954, MS. 4936/1/15/132, Menzies Papers.

123. Memorandum by the Deputy Assistant Secretary of State for European Affairs to the Acting Secretary of State, 30 April 1954, in *FRUS 1952–1954*, vol. 12, part 1, 434–35.

124. TNA: FO 371/112089, Geneva (Eden) to Foreign Office, 30 May 1954; ibid., Eden to Foreign Office, 1 June 1954; and ibid., Eden to Foreign Office, 30 May 1954.

125. Memorandum of Conversation, 4 June 1954, in *FRUS 1952–1954*, vol. 12, part 1, 537–39; and Memorandum of Conversation, 4 June 1954, in *FRUS 1952–1954*, vol. 12, part 1, 540–44.

126. Hiroyuki Umetsu, "Australia's Response to the Indochina Crisis of 1954 amidst the Anglo-American Confrontation," *Australian Journal of Politics and History* 52.3 (2006): 406–14; and Gregory J. Pemberton, "Australia, the United States, and the Indochina Crisis of 1954," *Diplomatic History* 13.1 (1989): 45.

7. The Costs of Compromise

1. Report of Five Power Military Conference, 11 June 1954, in *FRUS 1952–1954*, vol. 12, part 1, 560–63.

2. Ruth Bacon to Mr. Dumbright, 30 July 1954, in File: Joint Study Group, RG 59 Lot55D480 Records of the Bureau of Far Eastern Affairs, box 11, NAII.

3. Report of Five Power Military Conference, 11 June 1954, in *FRUS 1952–1954*, vol. 12, part 1, 560–63.

4. As noted in TNA: DEFE 11/228, Report of the Five Power Military Conference of June 1954.

5. See, for instance, Joint U.S.-UK Study Group, 16 July 1954, 2, in File: Joint Study Group, RG 59 Lot55D480, Records of the Bureau of Far Eastern Affairs, box 11, NAII.

6. NZNA: R23447332 ABFK 19754 W576758 34/5/2, part 2, From the Minister of External Affairs to the New Zealand Ambassador, Washington, Tel. 168, 26 June 1954.

7. Memorandum of Conversation by the Officer in Charge of Thai and Malayan Affairs, 27 May 1954, in *FRUS 1952–1954*, vol. 12, part 1, 519–21; and The Secretary of State to the Embassy in the United Kingdom, 4 June 1954, in *FRUS 1952–1954*, vol. 12, part 1, 547–48.

8. Jones, "'Segregated' Asia?," 849.

9. Ibid.

10. Churchill to Eisenhower, 21 June 1954, in Peter G. Boyle, ed., *The Churchill-Eisenhower Correspondence, 1953–1955* (Chapel Hill: University of North Carolina Press, 1990), 147–49.

11. Churchill to Eisenhower, 21 June 1954, in *FRUS 1952–1954*, vol. 12, part 1, 570.

12. Eden in House of Commons debate, 23 June 1954, *Hansard*, series 5, vol. 529, columns 428–550.

13. Editorial Note, in *FRUS 1952–1954*, vol. 13, part 2, 1751; and The Secretary of State to the Embassy in France, 29 June 1954, ibid., 1757–58.

14. For British suggestions that Thailand and Malaya should really be the focus of Western efforts see, for example, TNA: PREM 11/645 Lord Salisbury to the Ministry of Defence, 30 April 1954; TNA: CAB 158/17 JIC 54 (14) Final, Communist Threat to Siam: Report by the Joint Intelligence Committee, 4 February 1954; and TNA: CAB 158/17 JIC 54 (15) Final, The effect on other countries of Siam going Communist, Report by the Joint Intelligence Committee, 11 March 1954.

15. Position paper prepared for the Churchill-Eden visit, 24 June 1954, in *FRUS 1952–1954*, vol. 12, part 1, 573–74; United States Memorandum of Bilateral Conversation with the United Kingdom, 26 June 1954, in *FRUS 1952–1954*, vol. 12, part 1, 576–80; and Agreed Minute of the Governments of the United Kingdom and United States, 27 June 1954, in *FRUS 1952–1954*, vol. 12, part 1, 580–81.

16. British concerns are expressed clearly in TNA: DEFE 11/228, Lord Swinton to the Minister, undated [circa 11 June 1954]; and Rumbold to Makins, 26 May 1954, in Washington Special Correspondence, Sherfield Papers.

17. On Australian thinking, see NAA: A462(TS), 439/1/39, part 1, Record of Cabinet Meeting, 6 April 1954; and Menzies to Heymanson, 15 July 1954, MS. 4936/1/15/132, Menzies Papers.

18. Casey stressed this point to Eden at the Geneva talks: From Geneva Conference [Eden] to Foreign Office, 17 May 1954, FO 800/757, Co/54/3, Avon Papers. For more on Australian and New Zealand motivations and concerns, see NAA: A462(TS), 439/1/39, part 1, Record of Cabinet Meeting, 6 April 1954; and NZNA: R23447332 ABFK 19754 W576758 34/5/2, part 2, From the High Commissioner for New Zealand, London, to the Minister of External Affairs, Wellington, Tel. 374, 22 April 1954.

19. Eisenhower to Churchill, 29 March 1955, in CHUR, 6/3B, Churchill Papers.

20. Report of Joint US-UK study group, South East Asia, 17 July 1954, in *FRUS 1952–1954*, vol. 12, part 1, 610–12.

21. Working Paper prepared for the United States–United Kingdom Joint Study Group by the Minister at the British Embassy, 7 July 1954, in *FRUS 1952–1954*, vol. 12, part 1, 605–9; United States Minutes of the Second Meeting of the Joint Study Group, 8 July 1954, in *FRUS 1952–1954*, vol. 12, part 1, 610–12.

22. For similar claims, see Roger Dingman, "John Foster Dulles and the Creation of the South-east Asia Treaty Organization in 1954," *International History Review* 11.3 (1989): 462; and Brands, "From ANZUS to SEATO," 268–69.

23. The following report supplied to Eisenhower at the onset of his presidency makes this point abundantly clear: United States Objectives and Courses of Action with Respect to Japan attached to The Under Secretary of State to the President,

19 February 1953, in NSC Series, Policy Papers Subseries, box 3, NSC 125—Policy Toward Japan (4), DDEPL.

24. See, for instance, Walter Robinson to John Allison, 6 December 1954, in RG 59 Lot 55D480, File: Correspondence [A], Records of the Bureau of Far Eastern Affairs, box 1, NAII.

25. For evidence that the United States was interested in the proposition, see Dulles to the Embassy in Tokyo and Saigon, 17 August 1954, from MC074, folder 22, box 4, JFDP.

26. The importance that U.S. policymakers attached to Japan maintaining their anti-Communist stance in the region is made clear in Visit of Prime Minster Yoshida: Japanese Defense Measures, 4 November 1954, in MC074, folder 7, box 1, JFDP.

27. United States Minutes of the Second Meeting of the Joint Study Group, 8 July 1954, in *FRUS 1952–1954*, vol. 12, part 1, 611.

28. NZNA: R23447332 ABFK 19754 W576758 34/5/2, part 2, Casey's message in From the Australian High Commissioner's Office, Wellington, 5 August 1954.

29. NZNA: R23447332 ABFK 19754 W576758 34/5/2, part 2, From the New Zealand Ambassador, Washington, to the Minister of External Affairs, Wellington, Tel. 295, 5 August 1954.

30. United States Minutes of the Second Meeting of the Joint Study Group, 8 July 1954, in *FRUS 1952–1954*, vol. 12, part 1, 611.

31. Lowe, *Menzies*, 172–74; and McIntyre, *Background to Anzus Pact*, 381–82. For Australian concerns, see NAA: A462(TS), 439/1/39, part 1, Record of Cabinet Meeting, 6 April 1954.

32. NZNA: R23447332 ABFK 19754 W576758 34/5/2, part 2, From the New Zealand Ambassador, Washington, to the Minister of External Affairs, Wellington, Tel. 246, 30 June 1954.

33. Ibid.

34. NZNA: R17722534 ABHS 950 W5422 14 111/3/3/1, part 9, Minutes of the Prime Ministers' Conference, London, January 1955.

35. NZNA: R17722505 ABHS 950 W5422/33/1111/3/3/15, part 2, Jack Shepard to Mr Shanahan, 12 August 1953.

36. United States Minutes of the Second Meeting of the Joint Study Group, 8 July 1954, in *FRUS 1952–1954*, vol. 12, part 1, 610–12.

37. Waugh to Secretary of State, 8 March 1954, in *FRUS 1952–54*, vol. 7, part 1, 171–74.

38. Views of Chinese Government on Pacific Pact and Sino-American Security Treaty, 10 March 1954, in MCO74, folder 7, box 1, JFDP.

39. Casey, *Australian Foreign Minister*, 17 August 1954, 176.

40. NZNA: R23447332 ABFK 19754 W576758 34/5/2, part 2, From the New Zealand Ambassador, Washington, to the Minister of External Affairs, Wellington, Tel. 306, 10 August 1954.

41. As hinted at here: Visit of Prime Minister Yoshida: Collective Security Arrangements and the Manila Pact, 5 November 1954 in MCo74, folder 7, box 1, JFDP.

42. Memorandum of Discussion, 6 May 1954, in *FRUS 1952–1954*, vol. 12, part 1, 454.

43. Memorandum of Conversation by the Officer in Charge of Burma Affairs, 10 May 1954, in *FRUS 1952–1954*, vol. 12, part 1, 471.

44. Memorandum of Discussion, 6 May 1954, in *FRUS 1952–1954*, vol. 12, part 1, 454.

45. Progress report on NSC5405, 30 July 1954, in NSC Staff Papers, OCB Central File Series, box 79, OCB 091 Southeast Asia File 2 (1), DDEPL.

46. Eisenhower to Churchill, 18 February 1955, in Boyle, *Churchill-Eisenhower Correspondence,* 198.

47. Memorandum of Discussion at the 195th Meeting of the National Security Council, 6 May 1954, in *FRUS 1952–1954*, vol. 12, part 1, 456.

48. President's News Conference, 19 May 1954, in *Public Papers of the President: Dwight D. Eisenhower, 1954*, doc. 115, 497.

49. McMahon, *Cold War on the Periphery*, 154–88.

50. Makins to Eden, 18 June 1954, in MS Sherfield 527, Washington Special Correspondence, Sherfield Papers.

51. Dulles, *War or Peace*, 229.

52. Makins to Eden, 21 May 1954, in MS Sherfield 527, Washington Special Correspondence, Sherfield Papers.

53. Ibid.

54. TNA: FO 371/11208, Eden to the Foreign Office, Tel. 1017, 21 July 1954.

55. TNA: CAB 158/17 JIC 54 (26), Final, The Future of the War in Indo China, Report by the Joint Intelligence Committee, 26 March 1954.

56. Eden to the Foreign Office, 12 June 1954, FO 800/761, Co/54/65, Avon Papers.

57. Statement by Prime Minister Menzies, 21 July 1954, in File: Joint Study Group, RG 59 Lot55D480, Records of the Bureau of Far Eastern Affairs, box 11, NAII.

58. Rabel, *New Zealand and the Vietnam War*, 30.

59. Lowe, *Menzies*, 172–78.

60. Pierre Mendès France, the prime minister of France, had publicly declared that if agreement on Indochina could not be settled by 28 June 1954, he would resign his office. See The Head of the United States Delegation (Smith) to the Secretary of State, 18 July 1954, in *FRUS 1952–1954*, vol. 16, 1429.

61. Herring, *America's Longest War*, 41.

62. Memorandum of Conversation by Robert Cutler, Special Assistant to the President for National Security Affairs, 28 May 1954, in *FRUS 1952–1954*, vol. 12, part 1, 526.

63. Progress report on NSC5405, 30 July 1954, in NSC Staff Papers, OCB Central File Series, box 79, OCB 091 Southeast Asia File 2 (1), DDEPL.

64. U.S. working draft minute on the situation in Indochina, contained in Kenneth T. Young to the Embassy in Saigon, Paris et al., 28 September 1954, in MC074, folder 22, box 4, JFDP.

65. Jessica M. Chapman, *Cauldron of Resistance: Ngo Dinh Diem, the United States, and 1950s Southern Vietnam* (Ithaca, NY: Cornell University Press, 2013), 3, 62–70; Mark Philip Bradley, "Making Sense of the French War: The Postcolonial Movement and the First Vietnam War: 1945–1954," in *The First Vietnam War: Colonial Conflict and Cold War Crisis*, ed. Mark Atwood Lawrence and Fredrik Logevall (Cambridge, MA: Harvard University Press, 2007), 39; and D. L. Anderson, *Trapped by Success: The Eisenhower Administration and Vietnam, 1953–1961* (New York: Columbia University Press, 1991), 121–26.

66. Quoted in NAA: A10299/D8, Percy Spender to the Minister, 25 October 1954.

67. On the intelligence operations, see Allen Dulles to J. Lawton Collins, 22 February 1955, in J. Lawton Collins Papers, box 27, Cooley James (1), DDEPL. On the financial and military assistance, see Progress Report on NSC 5405, 14 July 1954, in NSC Staff Papers, OCB Central Files Series, box 79, OCB 091.4 Southeast Asia (File #1) (9), DDEPL.

68. TNA: FO 371/111882, Tahourdin to Powell, 25 August 1954.

69. The prime minister, recovering a previously shelved idea, also suggested that they should now proceed to "bring . . . Great Britain in for the first time to ANZUS." The president, however, did not provide a detailed response. Churchill to Eisenhower, 9 July 1954, in Boyle, *Churchill-Eisenhower Correspondence,* 160.

70. Prime Minister to President, 21 June 1954, in *FRUS 1952–1954,* vol. 12, part 1, 569.

71. Editorial Note in *FRUS 1952–1954,* vol. 12, part 1, 735; Ambassador in Pakistan to Department of State, 4 August 1954, ibid., 704–5; Minutes of a Meeting held in the State Department, 5 August 1954, ibid., 705–8.

72. Secretary of Defense (Wilson) to the Secretary of State (Dulles), 17 August 1954, in *FRUS 1952–1954,* vol. 12, part 1, 737.

73. Ibid.

74. Acting Secretary of State to the Embassy in the Philippines, 28 August 1954, in *FRUS 1952–1954,* vol. 12, part 1, 805.

75. Minutes, 24 August 1954, in *FRUS 1952–1954,* vol. 12, part 1, 787–89.

76. See the following letter from William Harllee Bordeaux, the general secretary of the American Council of Christian Churches, to William Sebald, in which he suggested British actions toward Nationalist China and the PRC were tantamount to "appeasement." Bordeaux urged Sebald to encourage Dulles to take a much firmer line with the British government. Bordeaux and Dulles were personal acquaintances from Dulles's time as a head of the American Council of Christian Churches organization. For the letter, see Wm. Harllee Bordeaux to William Sebald, 2 December 1954, in File: Correspondence [B], RG 59 Lot 55D480, Records of the Bureau of Far Eastern Affairs, box 1, NAII.

77. On the motivations for bilateral cooperation, see Cha, "Powerplay Origins," 161.

78. Memorandum, 30 August 1954, in *FRUS 1952–1954,* vol. 12, part 1, 820–22.

79. Editorial note in *FRUS 1952–1954,* vol. 12, part 1, 823.

80. John Allison to Walter Robinson, undated, in File: Correspondence [A], RG 59 Lot 55D480, Records of the Bureau of Far Eastern Affairs, box 1, NAII.

81. Memorandum, 1 September 1954, in *FRUS 1952–1954,* vol. 12, part 1, 827–28; Verbatim Proceedings, 7 September 1954, ibid., 862–84; Verbatim Proceedings, 7 September 1954, ibid., 884–96.

82. The Southeast Asia Treaty agreement also contained a separate protocol setting out a treaty area that included Cambodia, Laos, and the "free areas" of Vietnam: Editorial Note in *FRUS 1952–1954,* vol. 12, part 1, 898; and Secretary of State to the Department of State, 8 September 1954, ibid., 897–98.

83. The members of SEATO included Australia, France, New Zealand, Pakistan, Philippines, Thailand, the United Kingdom, and the United States.

84. Gaddis, *We Now Know,* 169. See also Gary R. Hess, "The American Search for Stability in Southeast Asia: The SEATO Structure of Containment," in *The Great*

Powers in East Asia, 1953–1960, ed. Warren Cohen and Akira Iriye (New York: Columbia University Press, 1990).

85. McIntyre, *Background to the Anzus Pact,* 393–94.

86. George A. Modelski, *SEATO: Six Studies* (Melbourne: Australian National University, 1962), 38–39.

87. NZNA: R3447334 ABFK 18754 W5767 59 34/5/3, part 2, ANZUS and SEATO Military Planners' Meetings, 31 October 1955.

88. Jones, *After Hiroshima,* 289–317.

89. Minutes, 15 December 1954, in *FRUS 1952–1954,* vol. 12, part 1, 1044–46.

90. TNA: FO 371/111879, Washington to the Foreign Office, 14 August 1954.

91. NAA: A1209 1957/4060, Notes of Discussion between Australian Ministers and Mr Malcolm MacDonald, 17 November 1954.

92. NZNA: R23447332 ABFK 19754 W576758 34/5/2, part 2, Anzus meeting, Washington, 11 October 1954.

93. United States Minutes of a Manila Pact Working Group, 28 December 1954, in *FRUS 1952–1954,* vol. 12, part 1, 1075–78; Memorandum found in the Department of State Files: Memorandum from the Treasury to the NSC, 6 December 1954, ibid., 1026–28; Memorandum by the Assistant Secretary of State for Far Eastern Affairs to the Secretary of State, 25 October 1954, ibid., 953–55; and Editorial Note, ibid., 926–27.

94. Memorandum of Discussion at the 214th Meeting of the National Security Council, 12 September 1954, in *FRUS 1952–1954,* vol. 12, part 1, 903–8.

95. Memorandum, 18 October 1954, in *FRUS 1952–1954,* vol. 12, part 1, 951.

96. Memorandum, 5 September 1954, in *FRUS 1952–1954,* vol. 12, part 1, 848.

97. David McKnight, "Western Intelligence and SEATO's War on Subversion, 1956–63," *Intelligence and National Security* 20.2 (2005): 288–303.

98. Casey, *Australian Foreign Minister,* 4 August 1955, 212.

99. Prados, *Vietnam,* 42–43.

100. See, for instance, Memorandum of Conversation with Prime Minister Sasorith, 27 February 1955, in File: Secy Mem of Con, January–Feb 1955, in RG 59 Lot 64D19, The Secretary's and Undersecretary's Memoranda of Conversations, box 3, NAII; and Memorandum of Conversation with Defense Secretary Phouma, 27 February 1955 in File: Secy Mem of Con, January–Feb 1955, ibid.

101. TNA: PREM 11/647 John Colville Note, 4 October 1954.

102. NZNA: R23447332 ABFK 19754 W576758 34/5/2, part 2, Anzus meeting, 11 October 1954.

103. Minutes of ANZUS Meeting, 11 October 1954, in *FRUS 1952–1954,* vol. 12, part 1, 939–46; TNA: PREM 11/647, Richard Casey to the Prime Minister, 16 September 1954; NAA A5954/1667/49, South-East Asia–Australian Policy, 5 August 1954; and ibid., Menzies Statement to the House of Representatives, 5 August 1954.

104. NZNA: R23447332 ABFK 19754 W576758 34/5/2, part 2, Anzus meeting, 11 October 1954.

105. On Australia's increased defense obligations, see Watt, *Evolution of Australian Foreign Policy,* 155–58.

106. NAA: A1209 1957/4652, British Commonwealth Defence Discussions, September 1953. Material on this can be followed in NAA: A5954 1453/5. See especially Defence Committee Agendum, 8 November 1954; and ANZAM Arrangements–Query of the New Zealand Chiefs of Staff, 4 October 1954.

107. TNA: DEFE 13/58, The Deployment of New Zealand Land Forces in War, Harold Macmillan to the Prime Minister, 12 November 1954.

108. TNA, DEFE 13/58, Macmillan to the Prime Minister, 12 November 1954.

109. NAA: A5954/1461/3, For the Minister from the Secretary, 30 September 1955.

110. Edwards and Pemberton, *Crises and Commitments*, 167; and McGibbon, "Defence of New Zealand," 169.

111. NZNA: R18872701 ACIE 8798 EA1 99 156 2/4/1, part 1, Memorandum by the Australian Prime Minister, 9 February 1955.

112. Anthony MacDougall, *Australians at War* (Victoria: Five Mile, 2002), 326.

113. Edwards and Pemberton, *Crises and Commitments*, 162.

114. NAA: A10299/S9, Memorandum for Menzies from Casey, 9 March 1955. A similarly gloomy prognosis on the situation in Vietnam was provided at the end of the month by the Southeast Asian section of the Ministry of External Affairs. See NAA: A10299/S9, Situation in Vietnam, 30 March 1955.

115. NAA: 5954/1560/1, Paper by the Joint Planning Committee, 6 January 1955; and NAA: 5954/1560/1, Report by the Defence Committee, December 1954.

116. NAA: A10299/S9, Plimsoll to the Minister, 17 February 1955.

117. NZNA: R18872701 ACIE 8798 EA1 99 156 2/4/1, part 1, Memorandum by the Department of External Affairs, 29 March 1955.

118. Ibid.

119. Ibid.

120. NZNA: R18872701 ACIE 8798 EA1 99 156 2/4/1, part 1, Joint Planning Committee, JPC (55) 11, 11 March 1955.

121. Authors' italics. NZNA: R18872701 ACIE 8798 EA1 99 156 2/4/1, part 1, Memorandum for the Minister of Defence: Defence Policy CM (55) 16, 15 April 1955.

122. Ian McGibbon, "The Defence Dimension," in *Southeast Asia and New Zealand: A History of Regional and Bilateral Relations*, ed. Anthony L. Smith (Wellington: Victoria University Press, 2005), 13–15.

123. McGibbon, "Defence of New Zealand," 169.

124. NAA: A816/14/301/658, Memorandum for the Secretary, 15 July 1955. For more on strategic disagreements between Australia and New Zealand after ANZUS, see Kelly, "Discordant Allies," 86–92.

125. New Zealand concerns are all detailed in NZNA: R18872701 ACIE 8798 EA1 99 156 2/4/1, part 1, Memorandum for Mr McIntosh, 24 August 1955; and NZNA: R18872701 ACIE 8798 EA1 99 156 2/4/1, part 1, Memorandum: ANZAM Planning for the Defence of Malaya, Chief of Staff Committee, (55) 7, 23 March 1955.

126. On the decision to deploy the New Zealand SAS, see NAA: A816/14/301/658, AUSTDef Wellington to Defence Melbourne, 24 February 1955. For the thinking behind the broader shift in New Zealand's strategic focus, see NZNA: R3447334 ABFK 18754 W5767 59 34/5/3, part 2, Staff Planning Meeting—Pearl Harbour 1955: Future Trends in South East Asia, October 1955.

127. Devereux, *Formulation of British Defence Policy*, 93–94.

128. Pugsley, *From Emergency to Confrontation*, 10.

129. Wm. Roger Louis, *The British Empire in the Middle East, 1945–1951: Arab Nationalism, the United States, and Postwar Imperialism* (repr., Oxford: Oxford University Press, 1996), 737–45; Keith Kyle, *Suez: Britain's End of Empire in the Middle East*

(London: I. B. Tauris, 2003); Salim Yaqub, *Containing Arab Nationalism: The Eisenhower Doctrine and the Middle East* (Chapel Hill: University of North Carolina Press, 2004), 83–84, 103. On the Middle East and antipodean withdrawal, albeit with limited reference to ANZUS or SEATO, see Devereux, *Formulation of British Defence Policy*, 92–94. For other studies of antipodean policy in the Middle East, which underplay the importance of ANZUS and SEATO, see Malcolm Templeton, *Ties of Blood and Empire: New Zealand's Involvement in Middle East Defence and the Suez Crisis* (Auckland: Auckland University Press, 1994); and French, *Army, Empire, and Cold War*, 82–108.

130. McIntyre, *Background to the Anzus Pact*, 118.

131. TNA: DEFE 13/58 Macmillan to the Prime Minister, 12 November 1954. With the withdrawal of both Australia and New Zealand, British policymakers now looked to South Africa and African states more broadly to fill the void in the Middle East. (Some nine battalions were desired from "West Africa," and twelve battalions from "East Africa.") By November 1954, the vast bulk of British reinforcements for the Middle East in wartime were expected to come from Africa. However, by the end of 1955 it was apparent that South Africa itself was unlikely to provide any significant material assistance for Middle East defense. See Devereux, "Britain, the Commonwealth and the Defence of the Middle East 1948–56," 340–41.

132. NZNA: R18872701 ACIE 8798 EA1 99 156 2/4/1, part 1, Memorandum for Mr McIntosh: The Radford Reply on ANZAM, 24 August 1955.

133. NZNA: R18872701 ACIE 8798 EA1 99 156 2/4/1, part 1, Chiefs of Staff Committee, Joint Intelligence Committee, JIC (55) 2 T of R, 18 January 1955.

134. NZNA: R18872701 ACIE 8798 EA1 99 156 2/4/1, part 1, Memorandum for Mr McIntosh: The Radford Reply on ANZAM, 24 August 1955.

135. At the heart of both Canberra and Wellington's policy toward emphasizing security in the ANZAM region was the need to obtain detailed plans from Washington as to what they would do in the event of a number of possible contingencies occurring in the Asia-Pacific more broadly. For instance, what would the plan be if Vietnam became Communist? If Thailand became Communist? If the PRC invaded Indochina? The need to know what the United States was thinking was a central part of the New Zealand decision to focus upon the ANZAM region. See NZNA: R18872701 ACIE 8798 EA1 99 156 2/4/1, part 1, Memorandum by the Department of External Affairs, 29 March 1955.

136. See the projections contained in NAA: 5954/1560/1, Report by the Defence Committee, December 1954, 8, 12, 15, 16; and NAA: A10299/D8, Sir Philip McBride to Air Marshall McCauley, 2 December 1954.

137. NZNA: R18872701 ACIE 8798 EA1 99 156 2/4/1, part 1, Frederick Shedden to A. D. McIntosh, 21 February 1955.

138. NZNA: R18872701 ACIE 8798 EA1 99 156 2/4/1, part 1, Memorandum by the Australian Prime Minister, 9 February 1955.

139. On this episode, see Gordon H. Chang and He Di, "The Absence of War in the U.S.-China Confrontation over Quemoy and Matsu in 1954–1955: Contingency, Luck, Deterrence," *American Historical Review* 98.5 (1993): 1500–1524.

140. Jones, *After Hiroshima*, 265–69, quote on 267.

141. NAA: A10299/S9, Richard Casey Memorandum for the Cabinet, 16 March 1955.

142. Casey, *Australian Foreign Minister*, 25 September 1954, 188.

143. NAA: 10299/S9, Report by R. G. Casey, 17 March 1955.

144. NZNA: R18872701 ACIE 8798 EA1 99 156 2/4/1, part 1, From the High Commissioner for NZ, Canberra, to the Minister of External Affairs, Wellington, Tel. No. 131, 31 March 1955; and NZNA: R18872701 ACIE 8798 EA1 99 156 2/4/1, part 1, Robert Menzies to the High Commissioner, 31 March 1955.

145. NAA: A 5954/69, 1459/2, The Secretary to Admiral Harries, 31 August 1955.

146. NAA: A 5954/69, 1459/2, Minute by Defence Committee, 30 August 1955.

147. NZNA: R23447332 ABFK 19754 W576758 34/5/2, part 2, Meeting with the Minister of Defence, 12 August 1955.

148. NAA: A 5954/69, 1459/2, Cabinet Minute, Decision No. 602 (DPC), 17 August 1955.

149. NAA: A 5954/69, 1459/2, Australian Joint Service Staff to Sir Frederick Shedden, 19 August 1955.

150. NZNA: R18872701 ACIE 8798 EA1 99 156 2/4/1, part 1, Memorandum for Mr McIntosh, 24 August 1955.

151. Radford's letter is contained in NZNA: R18872701 ACIE 8798 EA1 99 156 2/4/1, part 1, Text of Canberra Telegram No. 788 to Commonwealth Relations Office, 11 August 1955.

152. NZNA: R18872701 ACIE 8798 EA1 99 156 2/4/1, part 1, Text of Canberra Telegram No. 788 to Commonwealth Relations Office, 11 August 1955.

153. NZNA: R18872701 ACIE 8798 EA1 99 156 2/4/1, part 1, From the High Commissioner in the United Kingdom to A. D. McIntosh, 29 August 1955.

154. Ibid.

155. Mention of this is made in NZNA: R3447334 ABFK 18754 W5767 59 34/5/3, part 2, Minute of Defence Committee, 22 September 1955. For the quote, see NZNA: R3447334 ABFK 18754 W5767 59 34/5/3, part 2, Defence Observations on Mr Casey's Cablegram No. 1028, 14 September 1955. Leslie Munro reported on a meeting he attended with Admiral Stump (U.S. commander of the Pacific Fleet) and the Australian chief of the navy, Admiral Wells. During this discussion, Admiral Stump suggested that the ANZUS powers should meet prior to a SEATO planning meeting that was set for November 1955. Stump further suggested that if the PRC moved on Southeast Asia, the United States would "bomb them including their cities and blockade their coast." NZNA: R3447334 ABFK 18754 W5767 59 34/5/3, part 2, From the New Zealand Ambassador, Washington, to the Minister of External Affairs, Wellington, Tel. 421, 24 September 1955.

156. Casey, *Australian Foreign Minister*, 24 September 1955, 218.

157. NZNA: R18872701 ACIE 8798 EA1 99 156 2/4/1, part 1, From the High Commissioner in the United Kingdom to A. D. McIntosh, 29 August 1955.

158. Such optimism is displayed in NAA: A1838, TS687/7/3, Records of Talks with General Sir Charles Loewen, 18 January 1955; NAA: A1838, TS687/7/3, McKnight to Brown, 17 February 1955; and NAA: A10299/S9, Casey Memorandum for the Cabinet, 16 March 1955.

159. NZNA: R3447334 ABFK 18754 W5767 59 34/5/3, part 2, ANZUS Military Planning, 26 October 1955.

160. NZNA: R3447334 ABFK 18754 W5767 59 34/5/3, part 2, Staff Planning Meeting—Pearl Harbour 1955: Future Trends in South East Asia, October 1955.

161. McGibbon, "Defence Dimension," 18.

162. NZNA: R18872701 ACIE 8798 EA1 99 156 2/4/1, part 1, From the High Commissioner in the United Kingdom to A. D. McIntosh, 29 August 1955.

163. NZNA: R3447334 ABFK 18754 W5767 59 34/5/3, part 2, For New Zealand Eyes Only, undated [circa November 1955].

164. Jones, *After Hiroshima*, 247, 276–79. On the challenge of the emerging non-aligned movement, see Robert J. McMahon, *The Limits of Empire: The United States and Southeast Asia since World War II* (New York: Columbia University Press, 1999), 69–70; and Christopher Waters, "After Decolonization: Australia and the Emergence of the Non-aligned Movement in Asia, 1954–55," *Diplomacy & Statecraft* 12.2 (2001): 153–74.

165. NZNA: R18872701 ACIE 8798 EA1 99 156 2/4/1, part 1, Memorandum for Mr McIntosh: The Radford Reply on ANZAM, 24 August 1955.

166. NZNA: R3447334 ABFK 18754 W5767 59 34/5/3, part 2, Defence Observations on Mr Casey's Cablegram No. 1028, 14 September 1955.

167. Memorandum for the OCB Working Group, NSC 5405, 21 September 1954, in NSC Staff Papers, OCB Central File Series, box 25, OCB 091 Burma File 1 (1), DDEPL.

Conclusion

1. The seminal works on structural realism are Kenneth Waltz, *Theory of International Politics* (New York: McGraw-Hill, 1979); and John Mearsheimer, *The Tragedy of Great Power Politics* (New York: W. W. Norton, 2001). On the logic of why states ally to balance against threats rather than against power alone, see Stephen M. Walt, *The Origins of Alliances* (Ithaca, NY: Cornell University Press, 1987), 5. For a neorealist account of why great powers such as the United States might doubt the value of alliances, see Joseph M. Parent and Sebastian Rosato, "Balancing in Neorealism," *International Security* 40.2 (2015): 51–86.

2. On the limitations of domino theory, see Jerome Slater, "Dominos in Central America: Will They Fall? Does It Matter?," *International Security* 12.2 (1987): 130. On the variety of domino beliefs, see Guan, "Domino Theory Revisited."

3. Trachtenberg, *Cold War and After*, 139; and Gaddis, *We Now Know*, 201.

4. Joanne Gowa, *Allies, Adversaries, and International Trade* (Princeton, NJ: Princeton University Press, 1995), 5, 120.

5. See, for instance, Peter B. Evans, Harold K. Jacobson, and Robert D. Putnam, eds., *Double-Edged Diplomacy: International Bargaining and Domestic Politics* (Berkeley: University of California Press, 1993); and Alexander Wendt, *Social Theory of International Politics* (Cambridge: Cambridge University Press, 1999).

6. For examples of such work focused on the Asia-Pacific region, see Christopher Hemmer and Peter J. Katzenstein, "Why Is There No NATO in Asia? Collective Identity, Regionalism, and the Origins of Multilateralism," *International Organization* 56.3 (2002): 575–607; and Jarrod Hayes, *Constructing National Security: U.S. Relations with India and China* (Cambridge: Cambridge University Press, 2015).

7. See, for instance, Ritchie Ovendale, *The English-Speaking Alliance: Britain, the United States, the Dominions and the Cold War, 1945–51* (London: Allen & Unwin, 1985); David Lee, "Australia, the British Commonwealth and the United States, 1950–53," *Journal of Commonwealth and Imperial History* 20.3 (1992): 445–59; Lee, *Search for*

Security; Brands, "From ANZUS to SEATO"; McIntyre, *Background to the Anzus Pact*; Lowe, *Menzies*, 76–83; and Dingman, "John Foster Dulles."

8. On the importance of careful historical research, and historiographical context more broadly, see Ian Lustick, "History, Historiography, and Political Science: Multiple Historical Records and the Problem of Selection Bias," *American Political Science Review* 90.3 (1996): 605–18.

9. Dennis Cuddy, "The American Role in Australian Involvement in the Vietnam War," *Australian Journal of Politics and History* 28.3 (1982): 340–53; and Rabel, *New Zealand and the Vietnam War*.

BIBLIOGRAPHY

National Archives and Libraries

National Archives, Canberra, Australia
National Archives II, College Park, Maryland, United States of America
Public Records Office, Kew, Britain
Te Rua Mahara o te Kāwanatanga, National Archives, Wellington, New Zealand

Private Papers

Bodleian Library, Oxford
    Macmillan, Harold. Private Papers.
    Sherfield, Lord. Private Papers.
Cadbury Library, University of Birmingham
    Avon, Lord. Private Papers.
Churchill College Archives, Cambridge
    Amery, Julian. Private Papers.
    Bevin, Ernest. Private Papers.
    Churchill, Winston. Private Papers.
    Gordon Walker, Patrick. Private Papers.
    Selwyn-Lloyd, John. Private Papers.
Eisenhower Presidential Library, Abilene, Kansas
    Collins, J. Lawton. Papers.
    National Security Council Series.
    National Security Council Staff Papers.
    White House Memoranda Series.
Mudd Library, Princeton University, Princeton, New Jersey
    Dulles, John Foster. Private Papers.
National Library of Australia, Canberra
    Menzies, Robert. Private Papers.
    Spender, Percy. Private Papers.
Roosevelt Library, Hyde Park, New York
    President Subject Files.
Truman Presidential Library, Independence, Missouri
    Acheson, Dean. Private Papers.
    Elsey, George. Private Papers.
    President's Secretary Files.

Published Documents

Congressional Record.
Documents on British Policy Overseas:

Britain and America: Negotiation of the United States Loan, August–December 1945.
Korea 1950–51, 2nd series, vol. 4.
Documents on Australian Foreign Policy:
  Volume 9, January–June 1946.
  Volume 10, July–December 1946.
  Volume 12, 1947, Australia and the Post War World.
  Volume 14, 1948–1949, Post War World: The Commonwealth, Asia and the Pacific.
  Volume 16, 1948–1949, Post War World: Beyond the Region.
  The ANZUS Treaty, 1951.
Documents on New Zealand External Relations:
  Volume 3, ANZUS Pact and the Treaty of Peace with Japan.
Foreign Relations of the United States:
  The Conferences at Washington, 1941–1942, and Casablanca, 1943.
  Conferences at Malta and Yalta, 1945.
  1945, Volume 1: General: The United Nations.
  1946, Volume 1: General.
  1948, Volume 5, part 2, The Near East, South Asia, and Africa.
  1949, Volume 1, National Security Affairs, Foreign Economic Policy.
  1950, Volume 1: National Security Affairs; Foreign Economic Policy.
  1950, Volume 6, East Asia and the Pacific.
  1950, Volume 7, Korea.
  1951, Volume 1: National Security Affairs; Foreign Economic Policy.
  1951, Volume 6, part 1, Asia and the Pacific.
  1951, Volume 6, part 2, Asia and the Pacific.
  1951, Volume 7, part 1, Korea and China.
  1952–54, Volume 7, part 1, General: Economic and Political Matters.
  1952–54, Volume 12, part 1, East Asia and the Pacific.
  1952–54, Volume 12, part 2, East Asia and the Pacific.
  1952–54, Volume 13, part 1, Indochina.
  1952–54, Volume 13, part 2, Indochina.
  1952–54, Volume 16, The Geneva Conference.
Hansard.
Public Papers of the Presidents:
  Harry S. Truman
  Dwight D. Eisenhower

Newspapers

Argus
Christian Science Monitor
Daily Mail
Daily Mirror
Financial Times
Melbourne Herald
New York Herald Tribune
New York Times
Sydney Morning Herald
Washington Post
Wellington Evening Post

Diaries and Memoirs

Acheson, Dean. *Present at the Creation: My Years in the State Department*. New York: W. W. Norton, 1969.

Adams, Sherman. *Firsthand Report: The Story of the Eisenhower Administration*. New York: Harper, 1961.

Attlee, C. R. *As It Happened*. London: Heinemann, 1954.

Bland, Larry I., Mark A. Stoler, Sharon Ritenour Stevens, and Daniel D. Holt, eds. *The Papers of George Catlett Marshall: "The Whole World Hangs in the Balance," January 8, 1947–September 30, 1949*. Baltimore: Johns Hopkins University Press, 2012.

Butler, R. A. *The Art of the Possible*. London: Hamilton, 1983.

Byrnes, James. *Speaking Frankly*. New York: Harper, 1947.

Casey, R. *Australian Foreign Minister: The Diaries of R. G. Casey, 1951–60*. London: Harper Collins, 1972.

Churchill, Winston S. *The Second World War*. Vol. 3, *The Grand Alliance*. London: Reprint Society, 1950.

——. *The Second World War*. Vol. 4, *The Hinge of Fate*. London: Reprint Society, 1953.

——. *The Second World War*. Vol. 6, *Triumph and Tragedy*. London: Reprint Society, 1956.

Colville, John. *The Fringes of Power: Downing Street Diaries*. Vol. 2, *1941–April 1955*. London: Hodder & Stoughton, 1985.

Costigliola, Frank, ed. *The Kennan Diaries*. New York: W. W. Norton, 2014.

Danchev, Alex, and Daniel Todman, eds. *War Diaries 1939–1945: Field Marshal Lord Alanbrooke*. London: Weidenfeld & Nicolson, 2001.

Dilks, David, ed. *The Diaries of Sir Alexander Cadogan, 1938–1945*. London: Cassell, 1971.

Eden, Anthony. *Full Circle: The Memoirs of Sir Anthony Eden*. London: Cassell, 1960.

Eisenhower, Dwight D. *Mandate for Change, 1953–1956: The White House Years*. New York: Doubleday, 1963.

Ferrell, Robert, ed. *The Diary of James C. Hagerty*. Bloomington: Indiana University Press, 1983.

Kennan, George. *Memoirs, 1925–1950*. Boston: Little, Brown, 1967.

MacArthur, Douglas. *Reminiscences*. New York: McGraw-Hill, 1964.

McGibbon, Ian, ed. *Undiplomatic Dialogue: Letters between Carl Berendsen and Alister McIntosh*. Wellington: Auckland University Press, 1993.

Menzies, R. *Afternoon Light: Some Memories of Men and Events*. London: Penguin, 1970.

Millis, Walter, ed. *The Forrestal Diaries: The Inner History of the Cold War*. London: Cassell, 1952.

Olson, Stanley, ed. *The Harold Nicolson Diaries*. London: Collins, 1980.

Rusk, Dean. *As I Saw It*. New York: W. W. Norton, 1990.

Shuckburgh, Evelyn. *Descent to Suez: Diaries, 1951–56*. New York: W. W. Norton, 1987.

Spender, Percy. *Politics and a Man*. London: Collins, 1972.

Sulzberger, C. L. *A Long Row of Candles: Memoirs and Diaries 1934–54*. London: MacDonald, 1969.

Truman, H. *Memoirs by Harry S. Truman: Year of Decisions, 1945*. New York: Doubleday, 1955.

——. *Memoirs of Harry S. Truman: Years of Trial and Hope, 1946–52*. Old Saybrook, CT: Konecky & Konecky, 1956.

Secondary Sources

Books

Aldrich, Richard. *GCHQ: The Uncensored Story of Britain's Most Secret Intelligence Agency*. London: Harper, 2010.

——. *Intelligence and the War against Japan: Britain, America and the Politics of Secret Service*. Cambridge: Cambridge University Press, 2000.

Ambrose, Stephen E., and Douglas Brinkley. *Rise to Globalism: American Foreign Policy since 1938*. 7th rev. ed. London: Penguin, 1993.

Anderson, D. L. *Trapped by Success: The Eisenhower Administration and Vietnam, 1953–1961*. New York: Columbia University Press, 1991.

Arnold, J. R. *The First Domino: Eisenhower, the Military and America's Intervention in Vietnam*. New York: William Morrow, 1991.

Arnold, Lorna. *A Very Special Relationship: British Atomic Weapon Trials in Australia*. London: Her Majesty's Stationery Office, 1987.

Baker, J. V. T. *The Official History of New Zealand in the Second World War 1939–1945: War Economy*. Wellington: Historical Publications Branch, 1965. http://nzetc.victoria.ac.nz/tm/scholarly/tei-WH2Econ.html.

Barber, Noel. *The War of Running Dogs: Malaya 1948–1960*. London: Cassell, 2004.

Barnett, Correlli. *Collapse of British Power*. Reprint, London: Faber & Faber, 2011.

Barrass, Gordon. *The Great Cold War: A Journey through the Hall of Mirrors*. Stanford, CA: Stanford University Press, 2009.

Bartlett, C. J. *The Long Retreat: A Short History of British Defence Policy*. London: Macmillan, 1972.

Baxter, Christopher. *The Great Power Struggle in East Asia 1944–50*. Basingstoke: Palgrave Macmillan, 2009.

Bayly, Christopher, and Tim Harper. *Forgotten Armies: The Fall of British Asia 1941–1945*. London: Allen Lane, 2004.

——. *Forgotten Wars: Freedom and Revolution in Southeast Asia*. Cambridge, MA: Harvard University Press, 2007.

Beisner, Robert. *Dean Acheson: A Life*. Oxford: Oxford University Press, 2006.

Bell, Roger. *Unequal Allies: Australian-American Relations and the Pacific War*. Melbourne: Melbourne University Press, 1977.

Bell, Stephen. *Ungoverning the Economy: The Political Economy of Australian Economic Policy*. Oxford: Oxford University Press, 1997.

Bennett, Gill. *Six Moments of Crisis: Inside British Foreign Policy*. Oxford: Oxford University Press, 2013.

Bland, Larry I., Roger B. Jeans, and Mark F. Wilkinson. *George C. Marshall's Mediation Mission to China, December 1945–January 1947*. Lexington, VA: George Marshall Foundation, 1998.

Bogdanor, Vernon. *The People and the Party System: The Referendum and Electoral Reform in British Politics*. Cambridge: Cambridge University Press, 1981.

Borstelmann, Thomas. *The Cold War and the Color Line: American Race Relations in the Global Arena*. Cambridge, MA: Harvard University Press, 2001.

Bowie, Robert R., and Richard H. Immerman. *Waging Peace: How Eisenhower Shaped an Enduring Cold War Strategy*. Oxford: Oxford University Press, 1997.

Boyle, Peter G., ed. *The Churchill-Eisenhower Correspondence, 1953–1955*. Chapel Hill: University of North Carolina Press, 1990.

Brands, Hal. *What Good Is Grand Strategy? Power and Purpose in American Statecraft from Harry S. Truman to George W. Bush*. Ithaca, NY: Cornell University Press, 2014.

Brendon, Piers. *The Decline and Fall of the British Empire*. London: Vintage, 2008.

Buckley, Roger. *U.S.-Japan Alliance Diplomacy, 1945–1990*. Cambridge: Cambridge University Press, 1992.

Bullock, Alan. *Ernest Bevin: Foreign Secretary, 1945–1951*. Oxford: Oxford University Press, 1985.

Buszynski, Leszek. *SEATO: The Failure of an Alliance Strategy*. Singapore: Singapore University Press, 1983.

Cable, James. *The Geneva Conference of 1954 on Indochina*. Basingstoke: Palgrave, 1986.

Cairncross, Alec. *The British Economy since 1945: Economic Policy and Performance, 1945–90*. New York: Wiley-Blackwell, 1992.

Cairncross, Alec, and Barry Eichengreen. *Sterling in Decline*. New York: Wiley-Blackwell, 1983.

Cardwell, Curt. *NSC 68 and the Political Economy of the Early Cold War*. Cambridge: Cambridge University Press, 2012.

Casey, Steven. *Selling the Korean War: Propaganda, Politics, and Public Opinion, 1950–1953*. Oxford: Oxford University Press, 2008.

Cha, Victor. *Powerplay: The Origins of the American Alliance System in Asia*. Princeton, NJ: Princeton University Press, 2016.

Chalmers, Malcolm. *Paying for Defence: Military Spending and British Decline*. London: Pluto, 1985.

Chang, Jung, and Jon Halliday. *Mao: The Unknown Story*. London: Vintage, 2007.

Chapman, Jessica M. *Cauldron of Resistance: Ngo Dinh Diem, the United States, and 1950s Southern Vietnam*. Ithaca, NY: Cornell University Press, 2013.

Charmley, John. *Churchill's Grand Alliance: The Anglo-American Special Relationship 1940–57*. London: Hodder & Stoughton, 1995.

Christensen, Thomas. *Useful Adversaries: Grand Strategy, Domestic Mobilization, and Sino-American Conflict, 1947–1958*. Princeton, NJ: Princeton University Press, 1996.

Clarke, Peter. *The Last Thousand Days of the British Empire: Churchill, Roosevelt, and the Birth of the Pax Americana*. London: Bloomsbury, 2009.

Cormac, Rory. *Confronting the Colonies: British Intelligence and Counterinsurgency*. London: Hurst, 2013.

Costigliola, Frank. *Roosevelt's Lost Alliances: How Personal Politics Helped Start the Cold War*. Princeton, NJ: Princeton University Press, 2012.

Craig, Campbell, and Sergey Radchenko. *The Atomic Bomb and the Origins of the Cold War*. New Haven, CT: Yale University Press, 2008.

Crockett, Peter. *Evatt: A Life*. Melbourne: Oxford University Press, 1993.

Cumings, Bruce. *Dominion from Sea to Sea: Pacific Ascendancy and American Power*. New Haven, CT: Yale University Press, 2009.

——. *John Curtin: A Life*. Sydney: HarperCollins, 1999.

——. *Reluctant Nation: Australia and the Allied Defeat of Japan, 1942–45*. New York: Oxford University Press, 1992.

Curran, James. *Curtin's Empire*. Cambridge: Cambridge University Press, 2011.

Dân, Nông Văn. *Churchill, Eden and Indo-China, 1951–1955*. London: Anthem, 2011.

Day, David. *Chifley*. Sydney: HarperCollins, 2001.

——. *The Great Betrayal: Britain, Australia and the Onset of the Pacific War, 1939–42*. North Ryde: Angus & Robertson, 1988.

Dean, Peter, ed. *Australia 1942: In the Shadow of War*. Cambridge: Cambridge University Press, 2012.

Dennis, Peter, and Jeffrey Grey. *Emergency and Confrontation: Australian Military Operations in Malaya and Borneo 1950–1966: The Official History of Australia's Involvement in Southeast Asian Conflicts 1948–1975*. London: Allen & Unwin, 1996.

Devereux, David R. *The Formulation of British Defence Policy towards the Middle East*. Basingstoke: Palgrave Macmillan, 1990.

Dikotter, Frank. *The Tragedy of Liberation: A History of the Chinese Revolution 1945–1957*. London: Bloomsbury, 2013.

Dimitrakis, Panagiotis. *Failed Alliances of the Cold War: Britain's Strategy and Ambitions in Asia and the Middle East*. London: I. B. Tauris, 2011.

Divine, Robert A. *Foreign Policy and U.S. Presidential Elections, 1952–1960*. New York: New Viewpoints, 1974.

Donovan, Robert J. *The Tumultuous Years: The Presidency of Harry S. Truman, 1949–53*. New York: W. W. Norton, 1982.

Dower, John W. *War without Mercy: Race and Power in the Pacific War*. New York: Pantheon, 1987.

Dulles, John Foster. *War or Peace*. New York: Macmillan, 1950.

Dutton, David. *Anthony Eden: A Life and Reputation*. London: Hodder, 1997.

Edwards, John. *Curtin's Gift: Reinterpreting Australia's Greatest Prime Minister*. Sydney: Allen & Unwin, 2005.

Edwards, Peter. *Australia and the Vietnam War*. Sydney: University of New South Wales Press, 2014.

Edwards, P., and G. Pemberton. *Crises and Commitments: The Politics and Diplomacy of Australia's Involvement in Southeast Asian Conflicts, 1948–1965*. Sydney: Allen & Unwin, 1992.

Etzold, Thomas, and John Lewis Gaddis, eds. *Containment: Documents on American Policy and Strategy, 1945–1950*. New York: Columbia University Press, 1978.

Evans, Peter B., Harold K. Jacobson, and Robert D. Putnam, eds. *Double-Edged Diplomacy: International Bargaining and Domestic Politics*. Berkeley: University of California Press, 1993.

Fehrenbach, Theodore Reed. *This Kind of War: The Classic Korean War History—Fiftieth Anniversary Edition*. London: Brassey's, 2000.

Fenton, Damien. *To Cage the Red Dragon: SEATO and the Defence of Southeast Asia, 1955–1965*. Singapore: Singapore University Press, 2012.

Folly, Martin. *Churchill, Whitehall and the Soviet Union, 1940–45*. Basingstoke: Palgrave Macmillan, 2000.

Foner, Eric. *The Story of American Freedom*. New York: W. W. Norton, 1998.

French, David. *Army, Empire, and Cold War: The British Army and Military Policy, 1945–1971*. Oxford: Oxford University Press, 2011.

Freudenberg, Graham. *Churchill and Australia*. Sydney: Macmillan Australia, 2008.

Fried, Richard M. *Nightmare in Red: The McCarthy Era in Perspective*. Oxford: Oxford University Press, 1991.

Friedman, Hal. *Creating an American Lake: United States Imperialism and Strategic Security in the Pacific Basin, 1945–1947*. Oxford: Praeger, 2000.

Gaddis, John Lewis. *George F. Kennan: An American Life*. London: Penguin, 2011.

——. *Strategies of Containment: A Critical Appraisal of American National Security Policy during the Cold War*. Rev. ed. New York: Oxford University Press, 2005.

——. *We Now Know: Rethinking Cold War History*. Oxford: Oxford University Press, 1997.

Gardner, Richard N. *Sterling-Dollar Diplomacy: The Origin and Prospects of Our International Economic Order*. London: McGraw, 1969.

Gavin, Francis J. *Gold, Dollars, and Power: The Politics of International Monetary Relations, 1958–1971*. Chapel Hill: University of North Carolina Press, 2007.

Gill, David James. *Britain and the Bomb: Nuclear Diplomacy, 1964–70*. Stanford, CA: Stanford University Press, 2014.

Goldsworthy, David. *Losing the Blanket: Australia and the End of Britain's Empire*. Melbourne: Melbourne University Publishing, 2002.

Gowa, Joanne. *Allies, Adversaries, and International Trade*. Princeton, NJ: Princeton University Press, 1995.

Green, Michael. *By More Than Providence: Grand Strategy and American Power in the Asia Pacific since 1783*. New York: Columbia University Press, 2017.

Greene, John Robert. *I Like Ike: The Presidential Election of 1952*. Lawrence: University Press of Kansas, 2017.

Hack, Karl. *Defence and Decolonisation in Southeast Asia*. London: Curzon, 2001.

Hahn, Peter. *Crisis and Crossfire: The United States and the Middle East since 1945*. Lincoln, NE: Potomac Books, 2005.

Ham, Paul. *Vietnam: The Australian War*. Sydney: HarperCollins, 2007.

Harper, Tim. *The End of Empire and the Making of Malaya*. Cambridge: Cambridge University Press, 1999.

Harris, Kenneth. *Attlee*. London: Weidenfeld & Nicolson, 1995.

Haslam, Jonathan. *Russia's Cold War: From the October Revolution to the Fall of the Wall*. New Haven, CT: Yale University Press, 2011.

Hayes, Jarrod. *Constructing National Security: U.S. Relations with India and China*. Cambridge: Cambridge University Press, 2015.

Heinzig, Dieter. *The Soviet Union and Communist China 1945–1950: The Arduous Road to the Alliance*. London: M. E. Sharpe, 2003.

Hennessey, Thomas. *Britain's Korean War: Cold War Diplomacy, Strategy and Security, 1950–53*. Manchester: Manchester University Press, 2013.

Hennessy, Peter. *Never Again: Britain 1945–1951*. London: Vintage, 2006.

Herring, George C. *America's Longest War: The United States and Vietnam, 1950–1975*. New York: McGraw-Hill, 2002.

——. *From Colony to Superpower: U.S. Foreign Relations since 1776*. Oxford: Oxford University Press, 2011.

Hogan, Ashley. *Moving in Open Daylight: Doc Evatt, an Australian at the United Nations*. Sydney: Sydney University Press, 2008.

Hopkins, Michael. *Oliver Franks and the Truman Administration: Anglo-American Relations, 1948–1952*. London: Routledge, 2002.

Horne, Alistair. *Macmillan 1894–1956*. Vol. 1. London: Macmillan, 1988.

Horner, D. *High Command: Australia and Allied Strategy, 1939–1945*. Sydney: George Allen & Unwin, 1982.

Hughes, Emmet John. *The Ordeal of Power: A Political Memoir of the Eisenhower Years*. London: Macmillan, 1963.

Hyam, Ronald. *Britain's Declining Empire: The Road to Decolonisation, 1918–1968*. Cambridge: Cambridge University Press, 2007.

Immerman, Richard H. *John Foster Dulles: Piety, Pragmatism, and Power in U.S. Foreign Policy*. Wilmington, DE: S. R. Books, 1999.

Irving, Ronald Eckford Mill. *The First Indochina War*. London: Croom Helm, 1975.

Jackson, Ashley. *The British Empire and the Second World War*. London: Continuum, 2006.

James, Robert Rhodes. *Anthony Eden*. London: Papermac, 1987.

Jenkins, Roy. *Churchill: A Biography*. London: Macmillan, 2001.

Jervis, Robert, and Jack Snyder, eds. *Dominoes and Bandwagons: Strategic Beliefs and Great Power Competition in the Eurasian Rimland*. New York: Oxford University Press, 1991.

Jones, M. *After Hiroshima: The United States, Race and Nuclear Weapons in Asia, 1945–1965*. Cambridge: Cambridge University Press, 2010.

Kaplan, Lawrence. *NATO before the Korean War: April 1949–1950*. Kent, OH: Kent State University Press, 2013.

Keeble, Curtis. *Britain, the Soviet Union and Russia*. New York: St. Martin's, 2000.

Kennedy, Paul. *The Realities behind Diplomacy: Background Influences on British External Policy, 1865–1980*. London: Fontana, 1981.

——. *The Rise and Fall of the Great Powers: Economic Change and Military Conflict from 1500 to 2000*. London: Fontana, 1989.

Kimball, Warren. *Forged in War: Roosevelt, Churchill, and the Second World War*. New edition. Chicago: Ivan R. Dee, 2002.

Kolko, Gabriel. *Anatomy of a War: Vietnam, the United States, and the Modern Historical Experience*. New York: Free Press, 1985.

Kuklick, Bruce. *Blind Oracles: Intellectuals and War from Kennan to Kissinger*. Princeton, NJ: Princeton University Press, 2006.

Kyle, Keith. *Suez: Britain's End of Empire in the Middle East*. London: I. B. Tauris, 2003.

Larres, Klaus. *Churchill's Cold War: The Politics of Personal Diplomacy*. New Haven, CT: Yale University Press, 2001.

Lee, David. *Search for Security: The Political Economy of Australia's Postwar Foreign and Defence Policy*. Sydney: Allen & Unwin, 1995.

Leffler, Melvyn P. *A Preponderance of Power: National Security, the Truman Administration, and the Cold War*. Stanford, CA: Stanford University Press, 1992.

Logevall, Fredrik. *Embers of War: The Fall of an Empire and the Making of America's Vietnam*. New York: Random House, 2012.

Louis, Wm. Roger. *The British Empire in the Middle East, 1945–1951: Arab Nationalism, the United States, and Postwar Imperialism*. Reprint, Oxford: Oxford University Press, 1996.

——. *Imperialism at Bay: The United States and the Decolonization of the British Empire, 1941–1945*. Oxford: Oxford University Press, 1987.

Lowe, David. *Australia between Empires: The Life of Percy Spender*. London: Chatto & Windus, 2010.

———. *Menzies and the "Great World Struggle": Australia's Cold War 1948–1954*. Sydney: University of New South Wales Press, 1999.

Lowe, Peter. *Contending with Nationalism and Communism: British Policy towards Southeast Asia, 1945–65*. Basingstoke: Palgrave, 2009.

MacDougall, Anthony. *Australians at War*. Victoria: Five Mile, 2002.

Manchester, William. *American Caesar: Douglas MacArthur 1880–1964*. London: Hutchinson, 1979.

Martin, A. W. *Robert Menzies: A Life*. Vol. 2, *1944–1978*. Melbourne: Melbourne University Press, 1999.

May, Ernest R., ed. *American Cold War Strategy: Interpreting NSC 68*. Bedford: St. Martin's, 1993.

———. *"Lessons" of the Past: The Use and Misuse of History in American Foreign Policy*. New York: Oxford University Press, 1973.

McAloon, Jim. *Judgements of All Kinds: Economic Policy-Making in New Zealand, 1945–1984*. Victoria: University of Wellington Press, 2013.

McCullough, David. *Truman*. New York: Simon & Schuster, 1992.

McFarland, Keith D., and David L. Roll. *Louis Johnson and the Arming of America: The Roosevelt and Truman Years*. Bloomington: Indiana University Press, 2005.

McGarr, Paul. *The Cold War in South Asia: Britain, the United States and the Indian Subcontinent, 1945–1965*. Cambridge: Cambridge University Press, 2013.

McGibbon, Ian. *New Zealand and the Korean War*. Vol. 1, *Politics and Diplomacy*. Oxford: Oxford University Press, 1993.

———. *New Zealand and the Korean War*. Vol. 2, *Combat Operations*. Oxford: Oxford University Press, 1997.

———. *The Oxford Companion to New Zealand Military History*. Auckland: Oxford University Press, 2000.

McIntyre, W. D. *Background to the Anzus Pact: Policy-Making, Strategy and Diplomacy, 1945–55*. Basingstoke: Palgrave Macmillan, 1994.

McKerrow, John. *The American Occupation of Australia, 1941–45: A Marriage of Necessity*. Cambridge: Cambridge Scholars, 2013.

McKinnon, Malcolm. *Independence and Foreign Policy: New Zealand in the World since 1935*. Auckland: Auckland University Press, 1993.

———. *Treasury: A History of the New Zealand Treasury, 1840 2000*. Auckland: Auckland University Press, 2003.

McMahon, Robert J. *Cold War on the Periphery: The United States, India, and Pakistan*. New York: Columbia University Press, 1994.

———. *The Limits of Empire: The United States and Southeast Asia since World War II*. New York: Columbia University Press, 1999.

Meaher, Augustine, IV. *The Road to Singapore: The Myth of British Betrayal*. Canberra: Australian Scholarly Publishing, 2010.

Mearsheimer, John. *The Tragedy of Great Power Politics*. New York: W. W. Norton, 2001.

Middleton, Roger. *The British Economy since 1945*. Basingstoke: Macmillan, 2000.

Miller, Merle, ed. *Plain Speaking: Conversations with Harry S. Truman*. London: Victor Gollancz, 1974.

Millett, Alan R. *The War for Korea, 1950–1951: They Came from the North*. Lawrence: University Press of Kansas, 2010.

Milne, David. *Worldmaking: The Art and Science of American Diplomacy.* New York: Farrar, Straus & Giroux, 2015.

Miscamble, Wilson. *From Roosevelt to Truman: Potsdam, Hiroshima, and the Cold War.* Cambridge: Cambridge University Press, 2007.

Modelski, George A. *SEATO: Six Studies.* Melbourne: Australian National University, 1962.

Montgomery, Evan Braden. *In the Hegemon's Shadow: Leading States and the Rise of Regional Powers.* Ithaca, NY: Cornell University Press, 2016.

Montgomery, Gayle B., and James W. Johnson. *One Step from the White House: The Rise and Fall of Senator William F. Knowland.* Berkeley: University of California Press, 1998.

Moran, Lord. *Winston Churchill: The Struggle for Survival 1945–1965.* London: Constable, 1966.

Morgan, Ted. *Valley of Death: The Tragedy at Dien Bien Phu That Led America into the Vietnam War.* New York: Random House, 2010.

Morton, Louis. *Strategy and Command: The First Two Years.* Washington, DC: Office of the Chief of Military History, Department of the Army, 1962.

Murfett, Malcolm. *Hostage on the Yangtze: Britain, China, and the Amethyst Crisis of 1949.* Annapolis, MD: Naval Institute Press, 1991.

Murray, Williamson, and Allan R. Millett. *A War to Be Won: Fighting the Second World War.* Cambridge, MA: Harvard University Press, 2001.

Neustadt, Richard E., and Ernest R. May. *Thinking in Time: The Uses of History for Decision Makers.* New York: Free Press, 1986.

Newton, Jim. *Eisenhower: The White House Years.* New York: Doubleday, 2011.

Norton, Clifford. *New Zealand Parliamentary Election Results 1946–1987.* Wellington: Victoria University of Wellington, 1988.

O'Neill, Robert. *Australia in the Korean War, 1950–53.* Canberra: Australian Government Publishing Service, 1981.

Orders, P. G. A. *Britain, Australia, New Zealand and the Challenge of the United States, 1939–46: A Study in International History.* Basingstoke: Palgrave Macmillan, 2003.

Ovendale, Ritchie. *Anglo-American Relations in the Twentieth Century.* Basingstoke: Macmillan, 1998.

——. *The English-Speaking Alliance: Britain, the United States, the Dominions and the Cold War, 1945–51.* London: Allen & Unwin, 1985.

Perret, Geoffrey. *Old Soldiers Never Die: The Life of Douglas MacArthur.* New York: Random House, 1996.

Plokhy, S. M. *Yalta: The Price of Peace.* London: Penguin, 2010.

Prados, John. *Vietnam: The History of an Unwinnable War, 1945–1975.* Lawrence: University Press of Kansas, 2009.

Preston, Andrew. *Sword of the Spirit Shield of Faith: Religion in American War and Diplomacy.* New York: Random House, 2012.

Pugsley, Christopher. *From Emergency to Confrontation: The New Zealand Armed Forces in Malaya and Borneo, 1949–1966.* Oxford: Oxford University Press, 2003.

Qing, Simei. *From Allies to Enemies: Visions of Modernity, Identity, and U.S.-China Diplomacy, 1945–1960.* Cambridge, MA: Harvard University Press, 2007.

Rabel, Roberto. *New Zealand and the Vietnam War: Politics and Diplomacy.* Auckland: Auckland University Press, 2005.

Renouf, Alan. *Let Justice Be Done: The Foreign Policy of Dr H. V. Evatt*. St. Lucia: University of Queensland Press, 1983.

Reynolds, David. *Britannia Overruled: British Policy and World Power in the 20th Century*. London: Longman, 1991.

——. *In Command of History: Churchill Fighting and Writing the Second World War*. London: Allen Lane, 2004.

——. *Summits: Six Meetings That Shaped the Twentieth Century*. New York: Basic Books, 2007.

Richelson, Jeffrey, and Desmond Ball. *The Ties That Bind: Intelligence Cooperation between the UKUSA Countries*. London: Allen & Unwin, 1985.

Robb, Thomas K. *A Strained Partnership? US-UK Relations in the Era of Détente*. Manchester: Manchester University Press, 2013.

Ross, Steven T. *American War Plans 1945–1950*. London: Routledge, 1996.

Sanders, David. *Losing an Empire, Finding a Role: British Foreign Policy since 1945*. Basingstoke: Macmillan, 1990.

Schaller, Michael. *The American Occupation of Japan: The Origins of the Cold War in Asia*. Oxford: Oxford University Press, 1985.

Schenk, Catherine R. *The Decline of Sterling: Managing the Retreat of an International Currency*. Cambridge: Cambridge University Press, 2010.

——. *Hong Kong as an International Financial Centre: Emergence and Development, 1945–65*. London: Routledge, 2001.

Schoenbaum, Thomas. *Waging Peace and War: Dean Rusk in the Truman, Kennedy, and Johnson Years*. London: Harper Collins, 1988.

Sheehan, Neil. *The Pentagon Papers: The Secret History of the Vietnam War*. New York: Bantam Books, 1971.

Sherry, Michael. *Preparing for the Next War: American Plans for Postwar Defense, 1941–1945*. New Haven, CT: Yale University Press, 1977.

Sinclair, Keith. *A History of New Zealand*. Reprint, London: Penguin, 2001.

Singleton, John, and Paul L. Robertson. *Economic Relations between Britain and Australasia 1945–1970*. Basingstoke: Palgrave, 2002.

Skidelsky, Robert. *John Maynard Keynes*. Vol. 3, *Fighting for Freedom, 1937–1946*. London: Macmillan, 2000.

Spector, Ronald. *Eagle against the Sun: The American War with Japan*. London: Cassell, 2001.

Srinivasan, Krishnan. *The Rise, Decline and Future of the British Commonwealth*. Basingstoke: Palgrave Macmillan, 2007.

Starke, J. G. *The ANZUS Treaty Alliance*. Melbourne: Melbourne University Press, 1965.

Stoler, Mark A. *Allies and Adversaries: The Joint Chiefs, the Grand Alliance, and U.S. Strategy in World War II*. Chapel Hill: University of North Carolina Press, 2000.

——. *Allies in War: Britain and America against the Axis Powers, 1940–1945*. London: Hodder & Arnold, 2005.

Stueck, William. *Rethinking the Korean War: A New Diplomatic and Strategic History*. Princeton, NJ: Princeton University Press, 2002.

Takemae, Eiji. *Inside GHQ: The Allied Occupation of Japan and Its Legacy*. New York: Continuum, 2002.

Tarling, Nicholas. *Britain, Southeast Asia and the Onset of the Pacific War*. Cambridge: Cambridge University Press, 1996.

Tavan, Gwenda. *The Long, Slow Death of White Australia*. London: Scribe, 2005.

Taylor, Nancy. *The Official History of New Zealand in the Second World War 1939–1945: The Home Front*. Wellington: Historical Publications Branch, 1965. http://nzetc.victoria.ac.nz//tm/scholarly/tei-WH2-1Hom.html.

Templeton, Hugh, ed. *Mr Ambassador: Memoirs of Sir Carl Berendsen*. Wellington: Victoria University Press, 2008.

Templeton, Malcolm. *Ties of Blood and Empire: New Zealand's Involvement in Middle East Defence and the Suez Crisis*. Auckland: Auckland University Press, 1994.

Thomas-Symonds, Nicklaus. *Attlee: A Life in Politics*. London: I. B. Tauris, 2012.

Thorne, Christopher. *Allies of a Kind: The United States, Britain, and the War against Japan, 1941–1945*. Oxford: Oxford University Press, 1978.

Thorpe, D. R. *Eden: The Life and Times of Anthony Eden, First Earl of Avon, 1897–1977*. London: Chatto & Windus, 2003.

Trachtenberg, Marc. *The Cold War and After: History, Theory, and the Logic of International Politics*. Princeton, NJ: Princeton University Press, 2012.

——. *A Constructed Peace, The Making of a European Peace Settlement, 1945–63*. Princeton, NJ: Princeton University Press, 1999.

Tucker, Nancy. *Patterns in the Dust: Chinese-American Relations and the Recognition Controversy 1949–1950*. New York: Columbia University Press, 1983.

Twining, Nathan F. *Neither Liberty nor Safety: A Hard Look at U.S. Military Policy and Strategy*. New York: Holt, Rinehart and Winston, 1966.

Vickers, Rhiannon. *The Labour Party and the World: Evolution of Labour's Foreign Policy, 1900–51*. Manchester: Manchester University Press, 2004.

Vuceti, Srdjan. *The Anglosphere: A Genealogy of a Racialized Identity in International Relations*. Stanford, CA: Stanford University Press, 2012.

Walker, J. Samuel. *Prompt and Utter Destruction: Truman and the Use of Atomic Bombs against Japan*. Chapel Hill: University of North Carolina Press, 2004.

Walt, Stephen M. *The Origins of Alliances*. Ithaca, NY: Cornell University Press, 1987.

Waltz, Kenneth. *Theory of International Politics*. New York: McGraw-Hill, 1979.

Warner, Peggy. *The Coffin Boats: Japanese Midget Submarine Operations in the Second World War*. London: Leo Cooper, 1986.

Waters, Christopher. *The Empire Fractures: Anglo-Australian Conflict in the 1940s*. Melbourne: Australian Scholarly Publishing, 1995.

Watt, Alan. *The Evolution of Australian Foreign Policy, 1938–1965*. Cambridge: Cambridge University Press, 1967.

Watt, Donald Cameron. *Succeeding John Bull: America in Britain's Place 1900–1975*. Reprint, Cambridge: Cambridge University Press, 2008.

Weinberg, Gerhard L. *A World at Arms: A Global History of World War II*. Cambridge: Cambridge University Press, 1994.

Wellens, Karel. *Resolutions and Statements of the United Nations Security Council (1946–1989)*. Leiden: Brill, 1990.

Wendt, Alexander. *Social Theory of International Politics*. Cambridge: Cambridge University Press, 1999.

Westad, Odd Arne. *Decisive Encounters: The Chinese Civil War, 1946–1950*. Stanford, CA: Stanford University Press, 2003.

Wilson, A. C. *New Zealand and the Soviet Union, 1950–1991: A Brittle Relationship*. Wellington: Victoria University Press, 2004.

Xiang, Lanxin. *Recasting the Imperial Far East: Britain and America in China, 1945–1950.* London: M. E. Sharpe, 1995.

Yaqub, Salim. *Containing Arab Nationalism: The Eisenhower Doctrine and the Middle East.* Chapel Hill: University of North Carolina Press, 2004.

Yokoi, Noriko. *Japan's Postwar Economic Recovery and Anglo-Japanese Relations, 1948–62.* London: Routledge, 2003.

Young, John W. *Winston Churchill's Last Campaign: Britain and the Cold War 1951–1955.* Oxford: Clarendon, 1996.

Zelizer, Julian. *Arsenal of Democracy: The Politics of National Security; From World War II to the War on Terrorism.* New York: Basic Books, 2012.

Zimmermann, Hubert. *Money and Security: Troops, Monetary Policy, and West Germany's Relations with the United States and Britain, 1950–1971.* Cambridge: Cambridge University Press, 2002.

Articles, Chapters, and Theses

Baxter, Christopher. "The Foreign Office and Post-war Planning for East Asia, 1944–45." *Contemporary British History* 21.2 (2007): 149–72.

——. "In Pursuit of a Pacific Strategy: British Planning for the Defeat of Japan, 1943–45." *Diplomacy and Statecraft* 15.2 (2004): 253–77.

Borhi, László. "Rollback, Liberation, Containment, or Inaction? U.S. Policy and Eastern Europe in the 1950s." *Journal of Cold War Studies* 1.3 (1999): 67–110.

Bradley, Mark Philip. "Making Sense of the French War: The Postcolonial Movement and the First Vietnam War: 1945–1954." In *The First Vietnam War: Colonial Conflict and Cold War Crisis,* edited by Mark Atwood Lawrence and Fredrik Logevall, 16–40. Cambridge, MA: Harvard University Press, 2007.

Brands, Henry W., Jr. "From ANZUS to SEATO: United States Strategic Policy towards Australia and New Zealand, 1952–1954." *International History Review* 9.2 (1987): 250–70.

Buhite, Russell D. "'Major Interests': American Policy toward China, Taiwan, and Korea, 1945–1950." *Pacific Historical Review* 47.3 (1978): 425–51.

Buszynski, Leszek. "SEATO: Why It Survived until 1977 and Why It Was Abolished." *Journal of Southeast Asian Studies* 12.2 (1981): 287–96.

Carlton, David. "Churchill and the Two 'Evil Empires.'" In *Winston Churchill in the Twenty-First Century,* edited by David Cannadine and Roland Quinault, 93–116. Cambridge: Cambridge University Press, 2004.

Cha, Victor D. "Powerplay Origins of the U.S. Alliance System in Asia." *International Security* 34.3 (2009–10): 158–96.

Chang, Gordon H., and He Di. "The Absence of War in the U.S.-China Confrontation over Quemoy and Matsu in 1954–1955: Contingency, Luck, Deterrence." *American Historical Review* 98.5 (1993): 1500–24.

Clark, Chris. "What about New Zealand? The Problematic History." In *ANZAC's Dirty Dozen: 12 Myths of Australian Military History,* edited by Craig Stockings, 51–72. Sydney: University of New South Wales Press, 2012.

Costigliola, Frank. "Is This George Kennan?" *New York Review of Books.* 8 December 2011.

Cuddy, Dennis. "The American Role in Australian Involvement in the Vietnam War." *Australian Journal of Politics and History* 28.3 (1982): 340–53.

Danchev, Alex. "The Cold War 'Special Relationship' Revisited." *Diplomacy and State-craft* 17.3 (2006): 579–95.

Deery, Phillip. "Malaya, 1948: Britain's Asian Cold War?" *Journal of Cold War Studies* 9.1 (2007): 29–54.

Deighton, Anne. "Britain and the Cold War, 1945–1955." In *The Cambridge History of the Cold War*, edited by Melvyn P. Leffler and Odd Arne Westad, vol. 1, *Origins*, 112–32. Cambridge: Cambridge University Press, 2010.

Devereux, David R. "Britain, the Commonwealth and the Defence of the Middle East, 1948–56." *Journal of Contemporary History* 24.2 (1989): 327–45.

Dingman, Roger. "John Foster Dulles and the Creation of the South-east Asia Treaty Organization in 1954." *International History Review* 11.3 (1989): 457–77.

——. "Strategic Planning and the Policy Process: American Plans for War in East Asia, 1945–1950." *U.S. Naval War College Review* 32.6 (1979): 4–21.

Eckel, P. E. "SEATO: An Ailing Alliance." *World Affairs* 134.2 (1971): 97–114.

Etzold, Thomas H. "The Far East in American Strategy, 1948–1951." In *Aspects of Sino-American Relations since 1784*, edited by Thomas Etzold, 102–26. New York: Orchard Books, 1978.

Fleming, Thomas. "The Man Who Saved Korea." In *The Cold War: A Military History*, edited by Robert Cowley, 104–119. New York: Random House, 2005.

Foschepoth, Josef. "British Interest in the Division of Germany after the Second World War." Journal of Contemporary History 21.3 (1986): 391–411.

Friedman, Hal. "The 'Bear' in the Pacific? U.S. Intelligence Perceptions of Soviet Strategic Power Projection in the Pacific Basin and East Asia, 1945–1947." *Intelligence and National Security* 12.4 (1997): 75–101.

Guan, Ang Cheng. "The Domino Theory Revisited: The Southeast Asia Perspective." *War & Society* 19.1 (2001): 109–30.

——. "Southeast Asian Perceptions of the Domino Theory." In *Connecting Histories: Decolonization and the Cold War in Southeast Asia, 1945–1962*, edited by Christopher E. Goscha and Christian F. Ostermann, chap. 12. Stanford, CA: Stanford University Press, 2009.

Gurry, Meg. "Leadership and Bilateral Relations: Menzies and Nehru, Australia and India, 1949–1964." *Pacific Affairs* 65.4 (1992–93): 510–26.

Hardy, Travis J. "The Consanguinity of Ideas: Race and Anti-communism in the U.S.-Australian Relationship, 1933–1953." PhD diss., University of Tennessee, 2010.

Hemmer, Christopher, and Peter J. Katzenstein. "Why Is There No NATO in Asia? Collective Identity, Regionalism, and the Origins of Multilateralism." *International Organization* 56.3 (2002): 575–607.

Hess, Gary R. "The American Search for Stability in Southeast Asia: The SEATO Structure of Containment." In *The Great Powers in East Asia, 1953–1960*, edited by Warren Cohen and Akira Iriye, 272–95. New York: Columbia University Press, 1990.

Hughes, Gerald, and Thomas Robb. "Henry Kissinger and the Diplomacy of Coercive Linkage in the 'Special Relationship' with Britain, 1969–77." *Diplomatic History* 37.4 (2013): 861–905.

Immerman, Richard H. "The United States and the Geneva Conference of 1954: A New Look." *Diplomatic History* 14.1 (1990): 43–66.

Jones, Matthew. "The Radford Bombshell: Anglo-Australian–U.S. Relations, Nuclear Weapons and the Defence of South East Asia, 1954–57." *Journal of Strategic Studies* 27.4 (2004): 636–62.

——. "A 'Segregated' Asia? Race, the Bandung Conference, and Pan-Asianist Fears in American Thought and Policy, 1954–1955." *Diplomatic History* 29.5 (2005): 841–68.

Kelly, Andrew. "Discordant Allies: Trans-Tasman Relations in the Aftermath of the ANZUS Treaty, 1951–1955." *Journal of Australian Studies* 41.1 (2017): 81–95.

Kim, Youngho. "The Origins of the Korean War: Civil War or Stalin's Rollback?" *Diplomacy & Statecraft* 10.1 (1999): 186–214.

Kuniholm, Bruce R. "U.S. Policy in the Near-East: The Triumphs and Tribulations of the Truman Administration." In *The Truman Presidency*, edited by Michael J. Lacey, 299–338. Cambridge: Cambridge University Press, 1989.

Lee, David. "Australia, the British Commonwealth and the United States, 1950–53." *Journal of Commonwealth and Imperial History* 20.3 (1992): 445–59.

——. "The National Security Planning and Defence Preparations of the Menzies Government, 1950–1953." *War and Society* 10.2 (1992): 119–38.

——. "Protecting the Sterling Area: The Chifley Government's Response to Multi-lateralism, 1945–9." *Australian Journal of Political Science* 25.2 (1990): 178–95.

Limb, Ben. "The Pacific Pact: Looking Forward or Backward?" *Foreign Affairs* 29.4 (1951): 539–49.

Lowe, David. "Percy Spender and the Colombo Plan, 1950." *Australian Journal of Politics & History* 40.2 (1994): 162–76.

Lustick, Ian. "History, Historiography, and Political Science: Multiple Historical Records and the Problem of Selection Bias." *American Political Science Review* 90 (1996): 605–18.

Maddock, Rodney. "The Long Boom 1940–1970." In *The Australian Economy in the Long Run*, edited by Rodney Maddock and Ian W. McLean, 79–105. Cambridge: Cambridge University Press, 1987.

Marsh, Steve. "Anglo-American Relations 1950–1: Three Strikes for British Prestige." *Diplomacy and Statecraft* 23.2 (2012): 304–30.

May, Ernest R. "1947–48: When Marshall Kept the U.S. Out of War in China." *Journal of Military History* 66.4 (2002): 1001–10.

McGibbon, Ian. "The Defence Dimension." In *Southeast Asia and New Zealand: A History of Regional and Bilateral Relations*, edited by Anthony L. Smith, 7–31. Wellington: New Zealand Institute of International Affairs and Victoria University Press, 2005.

——. "The Defence of New Zealand 1945–1957." In *New Zealand in World Affairs*, 1:145–76. Wellington: New Zealand Institute of International Affairs, 1991.

——. "The Impact of the Korean War on the Establishment of Diplomatic Relations between New Zealand and the Republic of Korea." *New Zealand Journal of Asian Studies* 15.2 (2013): 15–23.

McIntosh, Alister D. "The Origins of the Department of External Affairs and the Formulation of an Independent Foreign Policy." In *New Zealand in World Affairs*, by Alister D. McIntosh, 9–35. Wellington: New Zealand Institute of International Affairs, 1977.

McKnight, David. "Western Intelligence and SEATO's War on Subversion, 1956–63." *Intelligence and National Security* 20.2 (2005): 288–303.

Meaney, Neville. "The End of 'White Australia' and Australia's Changing Perceptions of Asia, 1945–1990." *Australian Journal of International Affairs* 49.20 (1995): 171–89.

——. "Look Back in Fear: Percy Spender, the Japanese Peace Treaty, and the ANZUS Pact." *Japan Forum* 15.3 (2003): 399–410.

Ngoei, Wen-Qing. "The Domino Logic of the Darkest Moment: The Fall of Singapore, the Atlantic Echo Chamber, and 'Chinese Penetration' in U.S. Cold War Policy toward Southeast Asia." *Journal of American-East Asian Relations* 21.3 (2014): 215–45.

Ovendale, Ritchie. "Britain and the Cold War in Asia." In *The Foreign Policy of the British Labour Government, 1945–1951*, edited by Ritchie Ovendale, chap. 5. Leicester: Leicester University Press, 1984.

Parent, Joseph M., and Sebastian Rosato. "Balancing in Neorealism." *International Security* 40.2 (2015): 51–86.

Pechatnov, Vladimir O. "The Soviet Union and the World." In *The Cambridge History of the Cold War*, edited by Melvyn Leffler and Odd Arne Westad, vol. 1, *Origins*, 90–111. Cambridge: Cambridge University Press, 2012.

Pemberton, Gregory J. "Australia, the United States, and the Indochina Crisis of 1954." *Diplomatic History* 13.1 (1989): 45–66.

Quinault, R. "Churchill and Australia: The Military Relationship 1899–1945." *War and Society* 6.1 (1988): 41–64.

Reynolds, David. "Churchill, Roosevelt and the Wartime Anglo-American Alliance." In *From World War to Cold War: Churchill, Roosevelt and the International History of the 1940s*, chap. 3. Oxford: Oxford University Press, 2006.

——. "1940: Fulcrum of the Twentieth Century?" *International Affairs* 66.2 (1990): 325–50.

Robb, Thomas K., and David James Gill. "The ANZUS Treaty during the Cold War: A Reinterpretation of U.S. Diplomacy in the Southwest Pacific." *Journal of Cold War Studies* 17.4 (2015): 109–57.

Roberts, Geoffrey. "Sexing Up the Cold War: New Evidence on the Molotov-Truman Talks of April 1945." *Cold War History* 4.2 (2004): 105–25.

Rooth, Tim. "Australia, Canada, and the International Economy in the Era of Postwar Reconstruction, 1945–50." *Australian Economic History Review* 40.2 (2000): 127–52.

——. "Imperial Self-Insufficiency Rediscovered: Britain and Australia 1945–51." *Australian Economic History Review* 39.1 (1999): 29–51.

Ruane, Kevin. "The Origins of the Eden-Dulles Antagonism: The Yoshida Letter and the Cold War in East Asia, 1951–1952." *Contemporary British History* 25.1 (2011): 141–56.

——. "SEATO, MEDO, and the Baghdad Pact: Anthony Eden, British Foreign Policy and the Collective Defense of Southeast Asia and the Middle East, 1952–1955." *Diplomacy & Statecraft* 16.1 (2005): 169–99.

Ruane, Kevin, and James Ellison. "Managing the Americans: Anthony Eden, Harold Macmillan and the Pursuit of 'Power-by-Proxy' in the 1950s." *Contemporary British History* 18.3 (2004): 147–67.

Sarantakes, Nicholas Evan. "One Last Crusade: The British Pacific Fleet and Its Impact on the Anglo-American Alliance." *English Historical Review* 491 (2006): 429–66.

Schonberger, Howard. "The Japan Lobby in American Diplomacy, 1947–1952." *Pacific Historical Review* 46.3 (1977): 327–59.

Schroder, Paul W. "Alliances, 1815–1945: Weapons of Power and Tools of Management." In *Systems, Stability and Statecraft: Essays on the International History of Modern Europe*, edited by David Wetzel, Robert Jervis, and Jack S. Levy, 195–222. Basingstoke: Palgrave Macmillan, 2004.

Sewell, Bevan. "Pragmatism, Religion, and John Foster Dulles's Embrace of Christian Internationalism in the 1930s." *Diplomatic History* 41.4 (2017): 799–823

Singleton, John. "New Zealand, Britain and the Survival of the Ottawa Agreement, 1945–77." *Australian Journal of Politics and History* 43.2 (1997): 168–82.

Slater, Jerome. "Dominos in Central America: Will They Fall? Does It Matter?" *International Security* 12.2 (1987): 105–34.

Snyder, Glen. "The Security Dilemma in Alliance Politics." *World Politics* 36.4 (1984): 461–95.

Stoler, Mark A. "The 'Pacific-First' Alternative in American World War II Strategy." *International History Review* 2.3 (1980): 432–52.

Stolfi, Russell. "A Critique of Pure Success: Incheon Revisited, Revised, and Contrasted." *Journal of Military History* 68.2 (2004): 505–25.

Stratton, Samuel S. "The Far Eastern Commission." *International Organization* 2.1 (1948): 1–18.

Tomlinson, Jim. "Inventing 'Decline': The Falling Behind of the British Economy in the Post-war Years." *Economic History Review* 49.4 (1996): 731–57.

Toye, Richard. "The Attlee Government, the Imperial Preference System and the Creation of the Gatt." *English Historical Review* 118.478 (2003): 912–39.

Umetsu, Hiroyuki. "Australia's Response to the Indochina Crisis of 1954 amidst the Anglo-American Confrontation." *Australian Journal of Politics and History* 52.3 (2006): 406–14.

Waite, James. "Contesting 'the Right of Decision': New Zealand, the Commonwealth, and the New Look." *Diplomatic History* 30.5 (2006): 893–917.

Warner, Geoffrey. "Anglo-American Relations and the Cold War in 1950." *Diplomacy and Statecraft* 22.1 (2011): 44–60.

——. "The Settlement of the Indochina War." In *The Foreign Policy of Churchill's Peacetime Administration, 1951–1955*, edited by John Young, 233–60. Leicester: Leicester University Press, 1988.

Waters, Christopher. "After Decolonization: Australia and the Emergence of the Non-aligned Movement in Asia, 1954–55." *Diplomacy & Statecraft* 12.2 (2001): 153–74.

Williams, John. "ANZUS: A Blow to Britain's Self-Esteem." *Review of International Studies* 13.4 (1987): 243–63.

Wilson, Ward. "The Winning Weapon? Rethinking Nuclear Weapons in Light of Hiroshima." *International Security* 31.4 (2007): 162–79.

Wood, F. L. W. "The Anzac Dilemma." *International Affairs* 29.2 (1953): 184–92.

Xiang, Lanxin. "The Recognition Controversy: Anglo-American Relations in China, 1949." *Journal of Contemporary History* 27.2 (1992): 319–43.

Young, Ken. "Revisiting NSC 68." *Journal of Cold War Studies* 15.1 (2013): 3–33.

Index

Acheson, Dean, 18, 48, 49, 50, 51, 69, 70, 71, 74, 89, 92, 95, 97, 136
and ANZUS, 77, 81, 95, 98, 100, 101, 102, 108
and Korean War, 55, 56, 60, 63, 64
Aden, 24
ANZAM. *See* Australia, New Zealand, and Malaya area Agreement
ANZUS. *See* Australia, New Zealand, United States Treaty
ANZUS Council meetings, 7, 94, 100, 101, 102, 105, 128, 132, 154, 162, 172, 178, 179
Attlee, Clement, 22, 23, 24, 25, 31, 33, 36, 50, 57, 58, 61, 62, 63, 67, 70, 84, 87, 88, 91, 92, 94, 190n94, 190n98, 204n113, 205n139
Australia
and economic development of, 3, 31, 68, 69, 98
and fear of Japan, 32, 46, 62, 73, 74, 75
and importance of ANZUS, 80, 85, 98, 101, 125, 151, 152
and political culture, 44, 69, 150, 151
and SEATO, 4, 6, 7, 161, 162, 163, 170, 172, 177
and Second World War, 25–33, 42, 84, 161
and sterling bloc, 27, 68
Australian Chiefs of Staff, 13, 28, 42
Australia, New Zealand, and Malaya area Agreement (ANZAM), 28, 38, 42, 84, 96, 97, 103, 106, 111, 112, 115, 116, 117, 122, 123, 125, 127, 128, 132, 173, 174, 175, 176, 177, 178
Australia, New Zealand, United States Treaty (ANZUS), 4, 5, 66, 119–124, 142, 146, 151, 152, 153, 154, 158, 160, 166, 168, 170, 181, 182, 183n4
and British exclusion from, 91–97, 102–108, 11, 112, 127–133, 179
and creation of, 78–82
and membership debate, 2, 80, 82–86, 88–91, 98, 99, 100, 101, 115–118, 125, 151, 152

Australian Security Intelligence Organisation, 32

Bandung Conference (1955), 179
Bao Dai, 165, 171
Beaverbrook, Lord, 105
Berendsen, Carl, 17, 63, 70, 79, 80
Bevin, Ernest, 22, 23, 24, 50, 54, 58, 61, 67
Borneo, 42
Bradley, Omar, 56
British Empire, 10, 12, 17, 18, 20, 22, 23, 25, 28, 92, 93, 112, 135
Burma, 7, 8, 33, 50, 104, 144, 159, 161, 163, 164
Butler, Robin Austin, 94
Byrnes, James, 15

Cambodia, 121, 142, 157, 159, 173, 241n82
Canada, 27, 30, 31, 38, 54, 76, 92, 209n38
Casey, Richard, 100, 101, 105, 106, 124, 129, 143, 151, 163, 165, 170, 171, 172, 173, 176, 177, 178
Central Intelligence Agency (CIA), 14, 138
Ceylon, 53, 144, 149, 161
Chamberlain, Neville, 22, 166
Chifley, Benedict, 26, 27, 30, 32, 43, 50, 67, 68, 80
Churchill, Winston, 5, 23, 25, 26, 85, 92, 99, 100, 103, 105, 111, 123, 126, 130, 145, 159, 160, 164, 167, 172, 173, 217n28, 217n32, 217n36, 218n37
and ANZUS, 94–97, 111–118
and Cold War, 93, 131, 142, 144
and Second World War, 10, 12, 13, 19, 20, 21, 22, 135, 204n113
Collins, Admiral Sir John, 115
Colombo Conference (1950), 53, 54, 55
Colombo Plan, 54, 55, 170
Commonwealth Far East Strategic Reserve, 43
Cripps, Stafford, 57, 68
Curtin, John, 25, 26, 32

Deane, Charles, 49
Democratic People's Republic of Korea, 55, 56, 57, 58, 61, 62, 63, 142, 203n97

Department of Defense (U.S.), 91, 101
Department of External Affairs (Australia), 81, 116
Department of External Affairs (New Zealand), 35, 74, 173
Dien Bien Phu, 134, 138, 139, 148, 149
Doidge, Frederick, 6, 63, 78, 79, 81, 83, 121
Domino theory, 7, 8, 41, 42, 45, 50, 59, 121, 137, 145, 180, 182, 184n20, 197n2, 227n65, 246n2
Dulles, Allen, 138, 233n53
Dulles, John Foster, 5, 6, 8, 48, 74, 75, 78, 81, 84, 88, 89, 90, 113, 114, 119, 120, 126, 127, 128, 129, 137, 138–140, 145, 148, 150, 151, 162, 164, 167, 168, 171, 177, 178
    and Geneva Conference, 146–150
    and negotiating ANZUS treaty, 78–82
    and united action, 140–143

Eden, Anthony, 21, 22, 85, 100, 103, 105, 106, 113, 114, 139, 142, 144, 145, 146, 158, 159, 164, 171
    and Geneva Conference, 146–150, 165–167
Eisenhower, Dwight, 5, 6, 7, 11, 76, 109, 113, 114, 119, 124, 137, 139, 140–143, 145, 147, 150, 158, 159, 160, 163, 166, 167, 168, 171, 177
Evatt, H. V., 17, 26, 27, 28, 29, 30, 31, 32, 50, 173

Ferguson, Homer, 76
Forde, Francis, 16, 26
Formosa, 48, 121, 163, 168
Forrestal, James, 15
France, 8, 11, 30, 41, 65, 67, 89, 90, 91, 100, 101, 103, 104, 105, 107, 110, 111, 115, 118, 119, 121, 127, 129, 131, 133, 134, 135, 136, 137, 138, 139, 141, 144, 148, 151, 153, 154, 157, 161, 164, 165, 166, 167, 169, 172, 183n3, 187n37, 209n38, 232n35, 240n60, 241n83
Franks, Oliver, 58, 92, 127, 214n112
Fraser, Peter, 27, 30, 35, 37, 38, 43, 74, 210n61

Gordon-Walker, Patrick, 83, 84
Graham, Billy, 56
Great Britain. *See* United Kingdom
Green, Theodore, 76

Ho Chi Minh, 135, 136, 165
Holland, Sidney, 5, 7, 37, 45, 46, 52, 58, 59, 63, 77, 80, 85, 95, 96, 102, 105, 106, 107, 111, 112, 118, 124, 128, 130, 150, 153, 160, 173, 174, 176
Hong Kong, 5, 20, 25, 42, 50, 51, 53, 58, 119, 147, 168, 201n67
Humphrey, George, 118

Imperialism, 2, 3, 12, 15, 32, 82, 87, 88, 90, 163, 164, 182
    and U.S. concerns with, 52, 66, 108, 120, 164
India, 7, 11, 19, 25, 42, 50, 52, 53, 54, 88, 92, 111, 140, 144, 148, 149, 161, 164
Indochina, 3, 4, 5, 6, 7, 8, 9, 20, 33, 41, 65, 89, 91, 101, 104, 105, 107, 110, 119, 121, 127, 129, 131, 132, 133, 134, 135–140, 145, 147, 150, 152, 157, 165, 170, 173, 182
Indonesia, 8, 90, 98, 131, 144, 161, 179
International trade, 3, 4, 9, 17, 18, 20, 23, 24, 25, 27, 28, 34, 37, 50, 68, 73, 81, 85, 118, 121, 138, 162, 170, 181, 211n65, 213n96

Japan, 3, 6, 12, 19, 39, 44, 45, 47, 53, 56, 59, 90, 103, 107, 121, 161, 162, 163, 181
    and antipodean fear of, 32, 35, 36, 46, 62, 70, 73, 74, 75, 78, 118
    and economic power, 4, 17, 18, 79, 81, 121
    and the Second World War, 10, 14, 16, 20, 25, 35, 42, 55, 135
    and strategic importance of, 13, 18, 65, 71, 85, 114, 188n54
Japanese Peace Treaty, 9, 32, 35, 62, 66, 82, 88, 89, 113, 114, 182
    and the creation, 70–78
Johnson, Louis, 60, 71
Joint Intelligence Committee (Australia), 136
Joint Intelligence Committee (UK), 41, 42, 50, 85, 144

Kay, Cyril, 117
Kennan, George, 52, 64, 188n54, 202n82
Knowland, William, 48, 56
Korean War, 55, 58, 60, 65, 70, 71, 72, 94, 142, 158, 174
    and Australian military involvement, 58, 60
    and British military involvement, 57–58
    and New Zealand military involvement, 59, 60
    and United States military involvement, 55–58, 61

Laos, 121, 138, 157, 159, 173, 241n82
Lend-lease, 20
Limb, Ben, 89
London Economic Conference, 112

MacArthur, General Douglas, 11, 18, 56, 61, 62, 64, 71, 72, 73, 114

Macmillan, Harold, 95, 172

Makins, Sir Roger, 127, 141, 143, 164, 233n52

Malaya, 28, 38, 41, 42, 84, 96, 97, 103, 106, 111, 112, 115, 116, 117, 122, 123, 125, 127, 128, 132, 173, 174, 175, 176, 177, 178

Malayan Emergency, 42, 45, 46
   and Australia, 43, 44
   and Britain, 46, 47
   and New Zealand, 45
   and United States, 43, 44

Malta, 24, 100, 103, 207n9

Manchuria, 45, 55, 56

Marshall, George, 17, 48, 75

Marshall Plan, 31, 76, 171

McCarthy, Joseph, 48, 125

Menzies, Robert, 5, 44, 52, 53, 58, 59, 60, 66–69, 80, 83, 95, 96, 97–99, 104, 106, 111, 112, 115, 116, 117, 118, 121, 123–125, 130, 150, 151, 153, 161, 173, 176, 177, 207n9

Middle East
   and African contribution toward defense of, 244n131
   and Australian military planning for, 44, 67, 68, 80, 83, 104, 110, 131, 136, 172, 173, 181
   and British military planning for, 41, 53, 84, 85, 92, 119
   and New Zealand military planning for, 38, 43, 45, 54, 59, 77, 80, 83, 100, 136, 174, 175, 181
   and strategic importance of, 24
   and U.S. military planning for, 45, 83, 119, 131

Military Intelligence Service, Section 5 (MI5), 32

Morrison, Herbert, 84

Munro, Leslie, 101, 126, 143, 170, 172, 221n80

National Security Council, 65, 137, 138, 140, 141, 145, 149, 163, 164, 166, 179

NATO. *See* North Atlantic Treaty Organization

Navarre, Henri, 138

Nehru, Jawaharlal, 52, 144, 164

Netherlands, 30, 67, 90, 161, 163, 209n38

New Zealand
   and economic development of, 3, 31, 68, 69, 98
   and fear of Japan, 32, 46, 62, 73, 74, 75

   and importance of ANZUS, 80, 85, 98, 101, 125, 151, 152
   and political culture, 44, 69, 150, 151
   and SEATO, 4, 6, 7, 161, 162, 163, 170, 172, 177
   and Second World War, 25–33, 42, 84, 161
   and sterling bloc, 27, 68

Nitze, Paul, 64, 65

Nixon, Richard, 140, 150

North Atlantic Treaty Organization (NATO), 31, 41, 43, 51, 53, 54, 64, 78, 79, 93, 97, 98, 99, 123, 133, 145, 154, 158, 170

Nuclear weapons, 11, 14, 15, 22, 40, 49, 62, 63, 93, 111, 113, 114, 119, 145, 148, 170, 174, 186n22, 194n163, 205n139

Pacific pact, 5, 36, 39, 46, 81, 123

Pakistan, 111, 144, 149, 161, 167, 169, 183n1, 241n83

Pearl Harbor, 10, 11, 42, 55, 78, 81, 82, 88, 90, 98, 100, 103, 111, 143, 158, 159, 161, 167, 168, 169

People's Republic of China (PRC), 1, 2, 7, 45, 47, 48, 49, 55, 62, 63, 73, 107, 121, 137, 138, 142, 144, 145, 147, 149, 151, 158, 241n241
   and Hong Kong, 50, 51, 147
   and Korean War, 55, 62, 63
   and Malayan Emergency, 41, 42
   and strategic importance, 2, 47, 48, 49, 71, 72, 84, 107, 114, 136, 137, 138, 141, 142, 144, 145, 146, 147, 149, 151, 162, 169, 176, 178

Philippines, 8, 12, 25, 47, 75

Portugal, 90, 103, 161, 163

Potsdam Conference, 14, 22, 27

Public opinion, 49, 56, 139, 173

Race, 2, 3, 9, 12, 35, 46, 52, 66, 75, 81, 87–91, 106, 108, 110, 111, 114, 120, 126, 127, 134, 140, 153, 154, 158, 163, 164, 171, 179, 182, 185n11, 202n82, 237n122
   and influence on Australian foreign policymaking, 46, 81, 171
   and influence on British foreign policymaking, 90, 108, 110, 114, 153
   and influence on New Zealand foreign policymaking, 35, 46, 81, 153, 154
   and influence on U.S. foreign policymaking, 12, 52, 75, 108, 120, 140, 164

Religion, 56, 167, 224n16
   and influence on U.S. foreign policymaking, 71, 113

Republic of Korea, 55, 56, 57, 58, 59, 89, 163
Ridgeway, Matthew, 64
Romulo, Carlos, 89
Roosevelt, Franklin, 11, 12, 13, 21, 135
Rough Diplomacy, 4, 6, 78, 123, 128, 130,
    147, 148, 181, 183n9, 184n10
    and Australia utilizing, 78
    and Britain utilizing, 128
    and New Zealand utilizing, 78
    and U.S. utilizing, 5, 127, 128, 147
Royal Australian Air Force (RAAF), 44,
    204n123, 222n103
Royal Australian Navy, 122
Royal Navy, 50, 131
Rusk, Dean, 82, 203n94

SEACDT. *See* Southeast Asia Collective
    Defense Treaty
SEATO. *See* South East Asia Treaty
    Organization
Sebald, William, 241n76
Shedden, Frederick, 176
Shinwell, Emmanuel, 58
Singapore, 7, 19, 20, 24, 25, 34, 41, 43, 44, 50,
    53, 90, 111, 131
Smith, Alexander, 48
Smith, Walter Bedell, 139, 166
South Africa, 38, 244n131
Southeast Asia Collective Defense Treaty, 2,
    156, 168, 170, 176
Southeast Asia Treaty Organization, 9, 156,
    169, 170, 171, 176, 179, 182
    and Australia, 7, 161, 162, 163, 172, 177
    and Britain, 4, 168, 170, 172
    and international membership of, 3, 6,
        163, 164, 171, 182, 183n3
    and New Zealand, 161, 162, 170, 172, 177
    and United States, 4, 157, 168, 171, 178
Soviet Union, 1, 2, 13, 14, 15, 18, 19, 21, 22,
    28, 29, 30, 31, 33, 37, 41, 42, 44, 45, 47,
    49, 53, 54, 55, 57, 58, 62, 64, 71, 72, 79,
    80, 83, 85, 88, 93, 114, 119, 120, 142,
    158, 169
Spender, Percy 6, 8, 53, 54, 55, 62, 67, 69, 70,
    74, 78, 79, 81, 98, 100, 115, 125, 143, 178
Stalin, Joseph, 13, 15, 21, 22, 33, 47, 48, 55,
    121

Taiwan Strait Crisis, 176
Thailand (Siam), 7, 41, 50, 144
Truman, Harry, 8, 14, 20, 21, 22, 48, 55, 56,
    61, 62, 63, 65, 69, 76, 77, 95, 99, 101,
    118, 137, 186n22

United Action, 8, 141–149, 151–155, 233n52
United Kingdom
    and ANZUS, 91–97, 102–108, 111–118,
        127–133, 179
    and concerns with Asian-Pacific strategy,
        13, 41, 85
    and domestic politics, 22, 85, 87, 88, 94, 112
    and economic weakness, 11, 13, 20, 23, 24,
        57, 58, 67, 82, 85, 87, 91, 94, 175
    and Geneva Conference, 146–150,
        165–167
    and grand strategy, 58
    and Middle East, 11, 19, 24, 45, 53, 54, 59,
        84, 91, 92, 111, 131, 174, 175, 181
    and People's Republic of China, 50, 51,
        61, 73, 88
    and Second World War, 19–25
    and united action, 141–149, 151–155
United Nations, 13, 14, 16, 17, 30, 35, 37, 57,
    58, 60, 61, 63, 135
United States of America, 12, 52, 55–58, 61,
    71, 75, 108, 113, 120, 140, 164
    and ANZUS, 78, 80, 81, 88, 90, 91, 127, 128
    and domestic anti-communism, 48, 49, 147
    and grand strategy, 50, 85, 119, 124
    and imperialism, 15, 52, 66, 87, 88, 108,
        120, 163, 164
    and Japan, 70–76
    and People's Republic of China, 41, 47,
        48, 49, 55, 56, 62, 73, 107, 121, 137, 138,
        145, 147, 149, 169, 176, 241n76
    and racism, 66, 88, 89, 140, 164
    and SEATO, 4, 157, 168, 171, 178
    and Second World War, 10–19
    and Soviet Union, 56, 71, 72, 85, 107, 113,
        119, 135
    and trusteeships, 12, 13, 16, 17, 30, 135
    and united action, 141–149, 151–155
U.S.–Republic of Korea defense treaty, 133

Viet Minh, 7, 41, 121, 135, 136, 137, 138, 139,
    143, 144, 145, 147, 165, 166, 171

Watt, Alan, 81, 116
Webb, Clifton, 81, 100, 101, 102, 105, 151,
    166
Wilson, Charles, 141, 167
World Bank, 14, 98

Yalta Conference, 12, 13, 15, 19, 21, 27

Ze-dong, Mao, 7, 45, 47, 48, 49, 50, 51, 70,
    72, 88, 176, 203n97